FALLACIOUS ECONOMICUS

Economic Fallacies

FALLACIOUS ECONOMICUS

Economic Fallacies

Correct Thinking
for
America and Americans

by
Theodore Muzio

New York
2017

Dedicated to the Memory of My Parents

Rose and Salvatore Muzio

ACKNOWLEDGEMENTS

Thanks belong to Prof. Carlo Muzio of St. John's University, New York, for his counsel and encouragement in the completion of this work.

Thanks to Dean Kathleen Vouté MacDonald of St. John's University, New York, for her confidence and encouragement in the initiation of this work.

Finally, this book would not have been possible without the support, encouragement and technical expertise of my editor and good friend, Anthony M. Bly of Evergreen Books. Tony also designed the front and back covers.

ISBN-13: 978-1534991941
ISBN-10: 1534991948

INTRODUCTION – PLEASE READ!

Bye, Bye, American Pie

America is in decline. The idea may be hard to accept, but get used to it: the U.S. is in decline ... economic decline. Some say cultural decline, as well. Measure decline globally, *relative* to its closest national rival, (still Red) China. Measure it at the personal level, in *absolute* terms of the typical American's actual and projected **standard of living.** Each metric tells of decline. Even worse, this decline is not a one year fluke or a temporary phenomenon. It has been a persistent (secular) trend for at least thirty years. Moreover, there is no sign of reversal. Worse yet, the decline comes "by our own hand."

The decline is the result of mistakenly adopting a bundle of **destructive,** fallacy ridden **national economic policies,** called **Globalism.** Hence, the rationale for this book.

Debt trifecta fuels the engine. Although enjoying very modest annual growth (scarcely 2%?), the U.S. economic engine is, in effect, sputtering, running on "fumes," a.k.a., DEBT. It is about to be overtaken by overly ambitious protégé (still Red) China. Meanwhile, at the street level, dark clouds have drifted over the current and future expected standard of living of most Americans. Income and wealth inequality is worsening. Each year the shrinking American middle class grows more fearful as it suffers a progressively smaller percent of the total income, a smaller piece of the economic "pie." Job, medical and retirement *insecurity* are pervasive. Is American decline really in doubt? Full impact of the decline has been disguised by the use of a **Trifecta of debt!**

1) Household debt. Household debt stands at almost twice the GDP. We, as **individuals** (especially lower income folks), have become overly reliant on borrowed money. Credit card use, home mortgage and car loans dominate. Student loans are a thorn in the side of young graduates. Borrowings enable us to live beyond our stagnating real incomes. **Two deficits** tell the rest of the story of a **nation** living beyond its means. Read all about it:

2) Trade deficit: a trade deficit occurs when imports exceed exports. We are habitually enjoying imported goods we are not paying for with earnings from current exports and foreign investments. In effect, we are borrowing goods from overseas. Imports not paid for with current exports are "paid for" with IOUs. A U.S. dollar is, in effect, a blank IOU to turn over whatever dollars buy in the U.S. Moreover, our trading partners seem to prefer cashing in those IOUs for U.S. assets (past goods) such as properties, corporations, and financial institutions rather than our current goods.

3) Federal Budget deficit: The story is not much better on the home front. We are enjoying government benefits (government spending) paid for - not with taxes – but with borrowed U.S. dollars. In a very convenient twist, a large chunk of the trade deficit dollars are recycled, i.e., loaned back to the U.S., helping finance the budget deficit. In fact, roughly two-thirds of the borrowed dollars come from countries with which we have a trade deficit. This habitual practice helps finance the *Federal budget deficit* every year but creates greater dependency on foreign lenders to help us meet our government commitments.

Over the years a **massive Federal debt** has emerged from accumulating those annual deficits. As a result, there is a huge Federal debt, about equal to one year's GDP ($20T). **Up to now the debt has been managed without entering a crisis. But, will this arrangement survive? Can the U.S. decline continue to be masked?**

In sum, thanks to the **debt Trifecta**, we have been burning the candle at both ends! We are enjoying goods beyond the ability of our current income to buy.

Although budget deficits and trade deficits add to our welfare *at the moment*, these are not viable strategies for long run prosperity. Those deficits come with future obligations to repay. **We cannot continue to live beyond our means!**

At some point, the music stops. **Excessive borrowing in pursuit of prosperity cannot go on forever. It is not a long run viable strategy. Indeed, it could be a ruinous path as overseas creditors continue to buy command and control of the U.S. economy.** In effect, we are in a hole, and if we keep digging – deeper and deeper – we will not be able to extricate ourselves without the most drastic, destructive measures. Our creditors will reduce or eliminate their lending. We may no longer borrow goods from trading partners. Taxes will rise and smother the economy. The fumes will dissipate and economic well-being will collapse.

The hard news is that wrong-headed government policies of the past fifty years – especially **Globalism** – must be assigned most of the blame for America's **growth stagnation** and relative decline.

Globalism is the full scale adoption and promotion of Globalization as national policy. Yes, Globalism instigated lop-sided so-called "free trade" deals, the open borders disaster and the manufacturing Diaspora. American leaders were misguided or disregarded the negative impact of Globalism on the national economy, national security and the standard of living of ordinary folks. One world government and redistribution of income and wealth on a worldwide scale are the aims of Globalism. The guiding philosophy behind Globalism is **Globalthink, where U.S. policy makers are more concerned with Global welfare than U.S. national welfare. Read all about it.**

CONTENTS

Chapter One
Some Fallacies Based on Common Sense

The English language abounds with hoary maxims — tidbits of putative wisdom that, upon closer examination, prove to be completely idiotic. — Joe Queenan

FALLACIES are misconceptions, beliefs or myths often accepted as true. An *economic* fallacy is a misconception regarding an economic theory, assertion or policy. Economic fallacies concern production, consumption, income and wealth. Economic and financial institutions are included, as well. Based on faulty reasoning, the fallacy continues to enjoy popular acceptance. But, beware: despite this attempt to vanquish certain fallacies, some fallacies *die hard*.

The false prophet. As a basis for policy, an economic fallacy is a false prophet. Government policies based on fallacious reasoning cause considerable harm. Today, unfortunately, many policies have derived from the worship of one false prophet or another. Some policies threaten national security and survival. One such policy concerns so-called "free trade" pacts. Another policy deals with immigration. Climate change is a hotly contested proposition today. Even the generally accepted assertion of **limited resources** may stand accused as fallacious. These and other fallacy laced policies and beliefs are explored in this work.

The element of truth. A fallacy often contains one or more elements of truth, kernels of factual reality. These elements of truth, tempting intellectual morsels, help explain the seductive appeal, popularity, and deep rooted nature of many a fallacy. However, seductive and appealing as they are, these fragments of truth cannot override the predominantly fallacious nature of the proposition.

Look for the element(s) of truth in the fallacies discussed in this volume.

Let's get started. Fallacious reasoning begins at home, in our personal, common sense view of the world.

1. FALLACIOUS ECONOMICUS: With the advance of science and technology, common sense has been nearly forgotten as a guide to every day decisions. Common sense ought to be brought into more everyday decisions.

Correct Reasoning: Many folks still revere common sense and use it to guide everyday behavior and help in decision making. Is this a mistake? Is common sense a good guide? Could some elements of common sense be good sense while other elements are nonsense?

What is common sense? Common sense derives from what your senses tell you. Your five senses are: sight, hearing, taste, touch, and smell. Included is the reasoning ability that processes the sensory data. (Intuition, the sixth sense, plays a role, as well). Much common sense is based on experience and intuition. It is what you know without being formally instructed. It is what you have come to believe by processing the world around you. At a young age you learned through your sense of touch not to stick your hand in the fire. You did not need a degree in chemistry to learn that fire will burn you.

But, what is learned through common sense is not always correct. Some mistaken beliefs or mistakes in reasoning occur due to reliance on sensory information, i.e., what your senses tell you. The following myths, based on common sense, were once generally accepted:

> ➢ The Earth is flat. After all, that is what our senses tell us. We cannot see the curvature of the Earth.

> ➢ The Universe or the sky revolves around the Earth. Our senses tell us that as we watch the sky "move" over us each night.

> ➢ There is nothing to see beyond the scope of the human eye. There are no x-rays, no gamma rays. There is no spirit world. If the human eye cannot see it, then it does not exist.

> ➢ There are no such things as germs or germ caused disease. Malaria is caused by stagnant water.

> ➢ There are no sounds beyond the range heard by the human ear.

> ➢ Drop a bowling ball and a golf ball at the same time from the same height. The bowling ball will hit the ground first. Its heavier weight and greater mass dictate that it be first to hit the ground.

Our senses gave us the wrong signals in the cases cited above. But, do not rule out all the learning from common sense. There are many correct signals given to us by our common senses! Jump out of a plane without a parachute, we all know what will happen. So, **be wary of common sense**. In some instances an accurate future guide is found and in others it is not. Doubters and experimenters such as Francis Bacon and Galileo, armed with extreme curiosity and new technologies have helped distinguish fallacy from reality. Still wondering about the bowling ball and golf ball?

[1. Don Ulin, "Which Hits the Ground First: A Golf Ball or A Bowling Ball?" 17 June 2014 <http://indianapublicmedia.org/amomentofscience/ground-golf-bowling-ball/>]

2. FALLACIOUS ECONOMICUS:

2. FALLACIOUS ECONOMICUS: As the world becomes more complex and bewildering to some folks, they seek answers in homespun wisdom passed down through the generations. Indeed, much common sense wisdom is embodied in popular sayings, idioms, metaphors and proverbs. This wisdom provides a good guide for daily living. We can learn much from common sense.

Correct Reasoning: Many of these old sayings and kernels of wisdom are in conflict. How can they be a guide when they often take **opposite positions**? For example:

"He who hesitates is lost," versus "look before you leap." Which is the correct guide? Or,

"Birds of a feather flock together," compared to "opposites attract." Here are more conflicting pieces of advice or observations:

1. Actions speak louder than words ... BUT... The pen is mightier than the sword.
2. Ignorance is bliss ... BUT... Knowledge is power.
3. Nothing ventured, nothing gained ... BUT... Better safe than sorry.
4. Two heads are better than one ... BUT... If you want something done right, do it yourself.
5. Many hands make light work ... BUT... Too many cooks spoil the soup.
6. The bigger, the better ... BUT ... The best things come in small packages.
8. Absence makes the heart grow fonder ... BUT ... Out of sight, out of mind.

Well, how does one reconcile these valid but conflicting bits of wisdom and common sense? **One must recognize that these ideas, urging contrary actions, cannot be used as guides _before_ an action.** "He who hesitates is lost" versus "look before you leap" are both valid in one instance or another but not at the same time. It is one or the other. As such, these maxims make poor guides for future actions. **They are more appropriately applied _after_ the fact**, as confirmation or reinforcement. Instead of using these ideas proactively (_before_ acting), consider using one of them _retro-actively_, to re-affirm an outcome.

So, common wisdom as a guide to future decisions leaves much to be desired.

The problem is not uneducated people. The problem is that they are educated just enough to believe what they have been taught ... and not enough to challenge what they have been taught. -Unknown

Chapter Two
The Free Lunch Fallacy

Imagine the opportunity cost of the Pyramids, China's Great Wall and the Panama Canal.

THIS is an old favorite maxim of economics professors: **There Ain't No Such Thing As A Free Lunch (TANSTAAFL).** TANSTAAFL introduces the idea that nothing is free. **Everything has a cost.**

Opportunity cost. Produced goods involve a cost, a sacrifice. Even if there is no out of pocket (cash) cost, there is a lost opportunity to use the resources elsewhere. The best of those lost opportunities is called *the opportunity cost.* Breathable air is an exception, it has no opportunity cost. It does not have to be produced, therefore does not consume resources ... (Breathable air on a submarine must be produced and has an opportunity cost.) To avoid the fallacy, i.e., thinking and acting *as if* goods and services are free, one must search for opportunities that will be lost due to the chosen option. For example, watching TV means that swimming will be sacrificed. Evaluate each alternative and rank them, most to least important, top to bottom. The next best alternative to the chosen pick is the **opportunity cost.**

1. FALLACIOUS ECONOMICUS: I was walking by the movie theatre. They were giving away tickets to the 4 PM showing. I could not say no, it was free!

Correct Reasoning: If you had gone to the movie there would have been a cost. You would have lost all the net satisfaction from whatever else you could have done with your time: play tennis or sleep or play your guitar. Yes, entering the movie you would not be charged any money. But, you lost a favored alternative! Identify the *best* of those alternatives.

The best alternative passed up is what an economist would call the **opportunity cost** of going to the "free" movie. Suppose the next best activity is playing your guitar. If so, that is the cost of attending the movie. Realizing there is a cost "grounds" you and discourages frivolous choices you may regret later. Indeed, *realizing there is a cost helps steer you into making the right choice.*

Your ultimate choice must have benefits *in excess* of costs, including lost benefits from sacrificed alternatives. If not, the choice makes you worse off, not better off. Sounds stuffy and academic, but unexamined alternatives lead to suboptimal choices!

2. FALLACIOUS ECONOMICUS: Imagine a fairytale world where a do-gooder ruler mandates goods be distributed for free. Then, everyone would be happy!

Correct Reasoning: Free goods, for all people, all the time, would be a destructive reality. Soon there would be no goods to distribute! Consider the origins of a *produce and sell* economy. Ancient peoples discovered that making all goods they desired was an impossible struggle. So, **to get ahead**, they specialized, generating personal surpluses, hoping to lower acquisition costs through trade. Specialists traded their surplus goods for the surplus product of others, at a lower cost than making it themselves. Thus, the shoemaker made a surplus of shoes and traded for the baker's surplus bread.

With this arrangement folks could *make* more, *sell* more and, therefore, *buy* more. But, there must be a selling price for one's surplus! **The selling price was the incentive to produce a surplus, sell more, then buy more.** Zero prices work only within the family. No zero price to outsiders, no incentive to produce a surplus. All kinds of wrong signals go to buyers and sellers if a zero prices are **mandated**. Ultimately, **zero pricing** destroys incentive, prosperity and collapses the standard of living. Given free goods, demand skyrockets while production ultimately shrinks to household level. Read all about it:

Chaos Ensues Absent Law and Order

Phase I: Apportioning existing stock of goods. At first, the stock of **already produced goods** on store shelves must be given away at zero price. Civic order is threatened as buyers' aggressively compete for free goods. Civility vanishes as people battle one another for the available goods. (Think outside Macy's on Black Friday, before the store opens!)

Background. In economics lingo, **WANTS are pure desires**, based on wishful thinking. Wants don't need purchasing power backup; they exist without it. Easily created, wants are, in total for all peoples, considered unlimited. **Demand** is another story. Demand is a subset of want, involving one's affordable wants. DEMANDS are wants **backed by purchasing power**. Unlike want, demand is limited, as everyone has limited purchasing power. But, when goods are free, price and limited income constraints are removed and wants alone rule buyer behavior.

Phase I: Distribution of existing inventories of goods

The limited available-for-free quantity must be subdivided (rationed) over the hyped up customers. How would a moon colony, cut off from resupply, money being meaningless, distribute goods? To avoid rioting, if price is zero other methods of subdividing goods must be used.

Nonprice methods include:

1) Social hierarchy, custom or command may dictate the order of consumption. For example, the tribal chief, gang leader, or pharaoh gets first choice, and then dictates how the remainder is distributed.

2) First come, first serve may be instituted. But, what happens when the front-of-the-liners hog so much of the good that deserving end-of-the liners get nothing? Problem: **misuse and overuse** is encouraged among the front liners.

3) Quotas (or mandatory rationing) may be instituted to deter hoarding by the front-liners, guaranteeing some left over goods. A quota provides a *fixed maximum* amount of the good to each buyer. But, are shares fair?

4) A lottery allocates scarce goods, creating lucky winners and unlucky losers. This is an irrational system as needy folks may be unlucky and get shut out.

5) Favoritism. Producers serve only favored customers, e.g., friends, relatives.

Beware: The problematic **nonprice methods of distribution** discussed above will distort the allocation of resources and distribution of goods. Economic welfare will decline. (N.B: surpluses dry up in the long run due to zero price).

Phase II: Existing stocks of goods are exhausted ... now what?

What happens when existing stocks of goods run out? Production collapses to the household level while demand soars on expectation of continued free goods. Starvation and devastation abound amidst a resource rich modern economy! This is economic collapse of the highest order. Read all about Phase II, in Diagram #1:

Diagram #1: If Goods Were Free (distributed at a zero price)

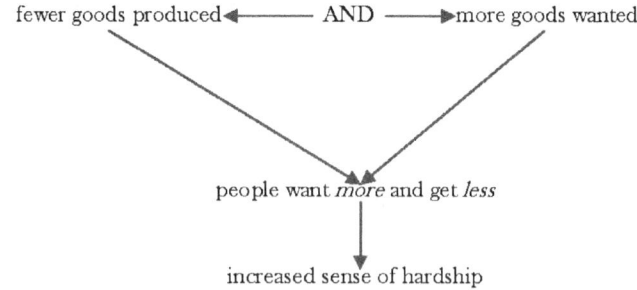

fewer goods produced ◄——— AND ———► more goods wanted

people want *more* and get *less*

increased sense of hardship

Impact of free goods on sellers: Production collapses, shortages emerge in the face of mammoth demand and diminished incentive to produce surpluses for trade. Free riders abound but fail to get goods. The gift of goods on this scale destroys incentives to work, create and produce beyond your household's needs. The standard of living (SOL) falls to subsistence levels.

When goods become unavailable government may ORDER people to use their *private* property to produce, hire and fire workers. Government may dictate wages and prices. This is called **FASCISM.** Private property remains but freedom of enterprise is suppressed. Inefficiency reigns and injustice prevails. This fantasy of *free goods for all* should remain a fantasy! As seen, any attempt to realize this fantasy is utterly destructive.

The Effects of Zero Pricing: Abuse, Misuse, and Overuse

Zero price "rationing" methods lead to the misuse and/ or overuse resources. For example, in first come, first serve, resources may be **misused and/or overused.** Some "free" local resources are totally used up (water and timber supplies) or driven to extinction (the passenger pigeon and Eastern buffalo.) This propensity for overuse and misuse typifies the unpriced, common property waterways, timberlands, fish stocks, American bison and wild game to this day. In general, **underpriced resources tend to be misused and overused,** in comparison to priced resources. See diagram #2 below.

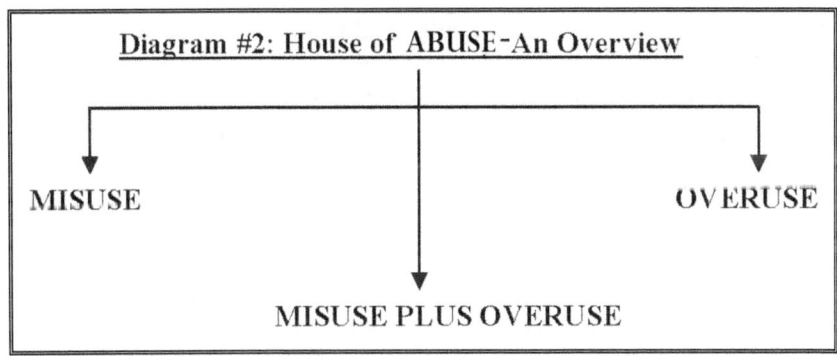

1. **Misuse (misallocation) of resources.** Misuse is one form of abuse. Resources are misused when they are put into **lower value uses** than their full potential would allow. For example, a plastic surgeon is employed as a janitor even when openings exist for plastic surgeons. Or, a computer engineer works as a truck driver when engineer jobs are open. Economists call this **underemployment,** a mis-allocation or misuse of resources. Natural resources and real capital could be misused, as well. Examples of misuse include overbuilding a *more* valuable cornfield with *less* valuable apartment houses. **Misuse is common in all economic systems, but least in the private property, market system.   In a private property system, waste costs money and cuts**

profits and is strenuously avoided ... but, zero pricing encourages waste by taking the financial sting out of it.

Example: Let's say the zero priced, common property lake - **a limited resource having multiple uses** - is allocated first come, first serve. All comers cannot be served at the same time. A waiting line of users develops. Let us say the first user in the waiting line starts dumping non-degradable solid waste. Eventually, continued dumping ruins the lake for higher value uses such as drinking water, swimming and fishing. The lake as "garbage can" is not getting it into the **highest and best use**. Smoke recycling is not the highest and best use of the air mantle. **Nonprice rationing invites misuse**. Allocation by first come, first serve is the way wild animals divide their prey, the strongest being first. With respect to allocating a resource *first come, first serve,* or by any nonprice method, it is sheer luck the resource will be allocated to its highest and best use. Indeed, misuse is the story of Lake Erie in the early 1900s.

[1. Doug Jeanneret "Lake Erie Water Quality" 13 July 2014 *Ohio Sea Grant Program* <http://tinyurl.com/nahja2o>]

Market pricing of resources improves allocation. Market advocates assert economic welfare, i.e., satisfaction of wants, would expand under private property and market pricing. With private property, owners of resources would deny use to those unable to pay the price. If the lake were private property and (market) priced, then the **higher value users would likely outbid the lower value users** (the destructive garbage dumpers) for the use of the lake.

Collectivists, including Socialists, assert communal ownership with **central** command of all resources and goods to be superior to the market. This assertion contradicts the economic record, especially as to economic growth. **Collectivist systems excel at subdividing the "pie" but not making it grow.**

2. Overuse of resources. Destructive *overuse* can occur in ordinary use, whether or not the resource in misused. **Overuse** may be triggered by the zero price. Markers for overuse find a resource unable to regenerate itself or permanently damaged or depleted. Rivers drained dry due to irrigation, depleted fishing grounds due to overfishing and overgrazed grasslands are examples of overuse. The resource is simply over worked, unable to regenerate to return to its previous level of productivity. Even the seed corn is taken. On a personal level, tennis elbow and carpel tunnel syndrome indicate overuse.

Where private property dominates, **selected** commonly owned resources may be rationed by professional managers, in government, to avoid overuse. For example, Alaskan crab fishermen and Colorado River water users are issued quotas specifying their maximum share of the resource.

Misuse plus Overuse

Overuse may be combined with **misuse.** Slaves were subject to misuse (craftsmen, warriors and hunters became field hands and domestics) and overuse (long hours, shortening their lives). Today, slaves are an outlawed human resource in most countries. (However, callous, ignorant and incompetent employers of free labor still may misuse and overuse their *hired* workers.)

In the case of the mis-used lake cited above, overuse comes when other dumpers follow the leader and also dump their trash in the lake. Not only is the lake misused as a trash dump, it is misused excessively. At some point the lake cannot recycle all the waste dumped in it, as its "circuits" have been overloaded. **Misuse and overuse of resources are the direct effects of zero (or artificially low) prices.** In fact, any artificially low price – such as **rent control** – results in misuse and overuse of the controlled good, the apartment rental.
[2. "Overuse and misuse" 10 July 2014 *FAO*
<http://www.fao.org/docrep/005/y3918e/y3918e05.htm>]

Did the Iraq war involve the misuse and overuse of the American military?

RECAP: Production and **distribution of *free* goods in an un-policed world of unlimited want is chaotic, leading to more misery than necessary.** Zero prices ignite a stampede of customers. Civility disappears as shelves empty. The social order is threatened. Shortages abound! Each person's share is likely to be determined irrationally. Consider lots of hungry people in an *all you can eat* buffet, but with *limited availability of food.* The earliest diners tend to over consume. Little food is left for those deserving buyers arriving later.

Alternatively, **rationing by price** invites *flexible prices*, subject to change, based on supply and demand. Market determined prices of resources and goods discourage waste. Gain motivated resource owners sell (or rent) to the highest bidder. Market determined prices of consumer goods discourage their overconsumption. Hoarding is discouraged. In general, **one willingly offers to pay more for a resource or good the more value it creates *at the margin* for the user.** Economy minded buyers – aren't they all? – manage their budgets to get the most "bang for the buck." Market advocates argue this arrangement channels resources and goods toward their highest and best uses. Distributing goods for free disengages *rationing by price*, leaving the resource "pie" and the goods pie to be divided by irrational means.

3. FALLACIOUS ECONOMICUS: My friend took me to lunch and paid the bill. I had a free lunch!

Correct Reasoning: The most commonly committed fallacy is the free lunch fallacy. A free lunch (or any meal, for that matter) is a fallacy, a myth, does not exist. Do not be fooled by the absence of a dollar price. There is no Santa Claus and no Tooth Fairy. (Sorry, no Easter Bunny, either). Economists are fond of saying, "there is no such thing as a free lunch," or "there are no free lunches." Ordinary folks nail it when they say, "you don't get something for nothing." For the economist, nothing is free; everything has a cost. Why all the commotion? Surely someone has bought you a lunch at some time in your life, no? Was it not free?

Let's explore the free lunch as a metaphor for all actions and activities. Okay, so your friend picked up the bill for lunch. You suffered no financial penalty. But, your friend suffered financially. Is that the cost economists are talking about? No, that is a sacrifice in money terms, not real goods. Actually, two costs can be identified here.

First, you and your friend lost all the other nice things you could have done (leisure) or could have produced with your time spent at the lunch counter.

Second, society lost all the other nice things that could have been produced with resources that provided your lunch. The labor, bread and whatever other ingredients that went into the lunch had an alternative use.

So, the lunch was not free. Someone, somewhere had to sacrifice the enjoyment of the other goods which could have been made. **Opportunity cost** is the *best of the alternatives,* i.e., the highest valued of the sacrificed or un-chosen options. Think of the opportunity cost as the **best opportunity lost.**

TANS WAFFLE?

A truly free good is one that a. has no opportunity cost and b. is obtained at the point of delivery without payment of any kind, by any one. Free goods are rare. Breathable air is a free good.

---

4. FALLACIOUS ECONOMICUS: Free or not, acquiring more and more goods is the sure path to a happy life. Nothing else matters in life.

Correct Reasoning: Many folks would argue against this statement. Sure, goods are *good* (sorry!) but some people reject them entirely, vowing to live in poverty. Most religions frown on an obsession with acquiring goods. According to the New Testament, "man does not live by bread alone." Indeed, in Christian theology greed (or avarice) is condemned as one of the seven deadly sins. (Can you name the other six?). The implication is that the acquisition of more and more *goods* is no guarantee of true, lasting happiness. Family, friendship, companionship, love and freedom are legitimate human wants often forgotten in the pursuit of more goods and money (claims to goods).

Is Life Wonderful?
George Bailey, the main character in the film *It's a Wonderful Life*, has an epiphany. He realizes a wonderful life depends on satisfying the **noneconomic wants** of love, family and community support.

5. FALLACIOUS ECONOMICUS: I pay no taxes and get all these free services and goodies. "No skin off my nose."

Correct Reasoning: No skin off *your* nose but others have their noses "skinned." If one individual or group gets something free, others end up paying for it, bearing the financial cost. In addition, society at large loses the other goods that could have been produced, the real opportunity cost.

Approximately one half of the American population pays no Federal Income Tax, receives food stamps and numerous other "free" goodies. **Somebody must pay for those "free" goodies!** Despite hundreds of billions of dollars spent on anti-poverty programs and temporary dips, the official poverty rate has stubbornly hugged the 13% level for nearly fifty years.

The financial burden of benefits to low income people is borne by the upper income taxpayers. The top 20% of taxpayers supplied nearly 69% of tax revenue while the top 1% of earners contributed 24%. The income and goods transfers to the low income folks enable them to purchase or receive goods and services otherwise beyond their reach. Indeed, a government study showed that income of the *typical household* must exceed nearly $80,000 before it *pays* more in taxes than it *receives* in the value of government benefits. **In other words, the typical household doesn't "carry its own weight" in paying for benefits received until its taxable income exceeds $80,000. Given the median household income (2014) is approximately $54,500; more than 50% of the populace is being subsidized for government services!**

[3. Review and Outlook, "More Redistribution and Less Income" 24 November 2014 *Wall Street Journal* A1 < http://tinyurl.com/z3v99en>

Fallacies Associated with the Affordable Care Act (2013)

6. FALLACIOUS ECONOMICUS: "Thank God I will finally get free medical care with the passage of The Affordable Health Care Act."

Correct Reasoning: THERE ARE NO FREE LUNCHES!

[4. See Milton Friedman video speech, Sept. 28, 2015 "There Are No Free Lunches" <https://www.youtube.com/watch?v=YmqoCHR14n8>]

One must abstract from the details and minutia of the Affordable Care Act and see it for what it is. The immediate target is medical insurance, not medical care. ObamaCare, in effect, is a giant **mandatory medical insurance** redistribution plan. Presumably, once the **insurance** is wide spread and operative, medical **care** will be re-distributed from the haves to the have-nots.

Some folks resent the **compulsory nature** of the plan. Millions of people are being conscripted, i.e., forced to buy overpriced insurance – under penalty of fine, for some people. Some folks, mostly young and healthy, are forced to buy coverage they would never choose for themselves. Presumably, the monies are to be spent on providing insurance to the formerly uninsured millions of people who will get a discounted or free ride. Regardless of the details of the Act, three basic points are clear. (BTW: for a time, at least, the act will co-exist with the older Medicare and Medicaid systems.)

Rube Goldberg would be envious of this convoluted setup. Meanwhile, here are some general remarks concerning Obamacare.

1) **Dollar cost per insured person** will be adjusted through insurance premiums. The price (of medical insurance) to upper income folks will be *raised* through tax and rate hikes. The price (of medical insurance) to lower income folks will be *lowered* though subsidy and tax break.

a. Upper income folks will pay more and get less coverage.

b. Lower income folks will pay less (or nothing) and get more coverage.

This is the re-distributive aspect of the program.

2) **Medical care is not free**, never has been, never will be. Medical care administered to any patient in any income level may involve **no out-of-pocket cost to the patient**. But, the service *consumes resources that have other uses.* Society does without those "other uses." It is there one finds the cost, those lost opportunities people must live without. [Note: economists do not consider money to be a resource]

3) **Shortages will emerge**. There will be unintended consequences to **the ACA: it will stimulate demand and discourage supply**. Experience shows this leads to *persistent* shortages and waiting lines and waiting lists that do not resolve themselves via higher prices. There are folks who are left without medical treatment as they wait on lines. Treatment delayed is treatment denied.

In short, the excess of demand over supply created by the program guarantees there will permanent waiting lines and waiting lists for all kinds of medical service.

Triage is inevitable. This brings a clamor for *mandatory government rationing* to expand the distribution of the limited medical services. However, everyone cannot be served. In this context, this pre-emptive rationing may take the form of screening to decide what coverage person is entitled to. Again, treatment delayed is treatment denied.

Rationing costs. Essentially, middlemen, bureaucrats and wanna-be omniscient government functionaries will reshuffle the "deck" of medical care. **Free choice – "you can keep your doctor" - of doctors and insurance plans is severely restricted, despite promises to the contrary.** System payments to medical servers are capped.

Over time, low dollar compensation discourages medical resources from entering or continuing to render medical service. Shortages will increase as a result. Will these "all knowing" rationers determine who lives or dies by how they allocate health care resources? Are these the infamous "death panels" critics warned of?

Rising cost. No doubt the cost of the program will increase as the population ages, in-migration of the world's needy proceeds, real wages are ground down and insurance companies drop out. Taxes will need to target a wider swath of the economy. Where will the additional tax monies come from? As Margaret Thatcher observed about socialism: What do you do after you have soaked the rich or chased them out of the country? Then, you must assault the middle class taxpayer.

7. FALLACIOUS ECONOMICUS: I am a young, healthy individual without a company medical plan. I may not have medical insurance but I get medical care at the emergency room. Now, with Obamacare, if I do not buy health insurance I will have to pay a fine!

Correct Reasoning: Are you sitting down? Good. Technically, it is not a *fine*. It is a *tax*. Yes, the Supreme Court of the United States (SCOTUS) has ruled that the monetary charges for *not* joining Obamacare are **taxes, not fines**.

> The Supreme Court ObamaCare ruling was a 5-4 ruling to uphold the Affordable Care Act. The final Ruling on ObamaCare had a few implications ranging from ObamaCare being defined as a tax and not a mandate and a choice for States to Opt-Out of Medicaid Expansion....ObamaCare will no longer be a mandate (meaning Americans must buy health insurance, which keeps the cost down for all Americans) instead *Obamacare will be a tax, meaning that those who opt out don't pay a tax and those who opt in will receive tax breaks.*
>
> [5. Italics mine "ObamaCare Supreme Court Ruling UPHOLDS Health Care Reform" 5 November 2014 *Obamacarefacts* <http://obamacarefacts.com/supreme-court-obamacare/>]

Legal View: Gruber or Grubber? An architect of Obamacare has admitted he deliberately crafted the bill to avoid calling it what it was, a tax bill, because it would not have passed Congress labeled as such. Moreover, he and the other writers did their best hide the redistributive income effects of the bill.

> In his now infamous talk at the University of Pennsylvania last year, Professor Gruber argued that the Affordable Care Act 'would not have passed' had Democrats been honest about **the income redistribution policies embedded in its insurance regulations.** But the more instructive moment is his admission that 'this bill was written in a tortured way to make sure CBO did not score the mandate as taxes. If CBO scored the mandate as taxes, the bill dies.' [6]

> [6. "Jonathan Gruber's 'Stupid' Budget Tricks" 19 November 2014 *Wall Street Journal Opinion Online* <http://tinyurl.com/nt4ppm9>
> See, also: Gruber: "Lack of transparency is a huge political advantage." 10 November 2014 *Real Clear Politics Video* <http://tinyurl.com/nehncxy>]

Mind you, it was not written as a tax law. According to the Constitution, tax laws must originate in the House of Representatives. SCOTUS ignored that requirement and approved the law by a 6-3 decision.

Question: If the Affordable Health Care Act is basically a tax as dictated by the Supreme Court, why did it not originate in the House Ways and Means Committee, as required in the Constitution for all tax legislation?

The Negative Employment Effect of ACA

A number of economists have predicted the full implementation of the ACA will not increase the number of workers covered by health insurance. First of all, from the employer's point of view, the mandatory coverage expense acts as a compensation increase, as if an employee had been given a raise. But, what if some workers do not deserve a raise? Sounds very cold, but in the labor market **some workers are worth the increase in compensation, some are not.**

Some economists believe the greatest negative employment effect will fall on low income workers, the ones who contribute the least value, as assessed by the firms. Those concerned with the negative employment aspects of the ACA may refer to the Mulligan article cited below.

[7. Casey Mulligan, "Effects of the Affordable Care Act on Economic Productivity," November 2014 *Imprimis* <http://tinyurl.com/nc39rkb>]

Question: What if *two year* college graduates were admitted to condensed *three year* medical school programs? Would that increase the supply of doctors at lower societal cost per doctor?

My <u>Right</u> Implies Your <u>Duty</u> or Your <u>Right</u> Implies My <u>Duty</u>

8. FALLACIOUS ECONOMICUS: Health care is a right -- I demand my rights!

Correct Reasoning: Life, liberty and the pursuit of happiness are the sole unalienable rights proclaimed in the U.S. Declaration of Independence. **Be careful in asserting economic rights, rights that require resources to fulfill.** To be effective, **every established right imposes a corresponding duty on others in society to fulfill it.** A right is a claim on society to provide the right. Rights and duties go together. The right is meaningless unless there is a duty to deliver it. But, what happens when the imposed duty violates the rights of the provider?

> Every right of an individual imposes a *corresponding* duty of others. *Rights and duties go together, like two sides of a coin.* You cannot mint a coin with one side. Rights and corresponding duties often bind strangers in social arrangements. **The right is meaningless unless others have a duty to deliver it.** For example, my right to life implies that others should give protection and security to my life.
>
> [8. Bold mine. "What is the Relationship between Rights and Duties?" 13 June 2014 *Preserve Articles* < http://tinyurl.com/qe8a8cg >]

So, a right without a corresponding duty is like a brand new car without any gas: useless. Economic rights, i.e., rights to goods and services, impose a duty on other folks to provide those goods!

"When you see that in order to produce, you need to obtain permission from men who produce nothing - When you see that money is flowing to those who deal, not in goods, but in favors - When you see that men get richer by graft and by pull than by work, and your laws don't protect you against them, but protect them against you - When you see corruption being rewarded and honesty becoming a self-sacrifice - You may know that your society is doomed."
Ayn Rand,
Atlas Shrugged, 1957

Chapter Three
The Cost and Benefit Fallacy

Every Front Has a Back   - ancient Chinese saying

THIS fallacy is committed when one forms a judgment or makes a decision looking only at one side of an issue, the good or the bad. In reality, most issues and actions have two sides, the good AND the bad. Pessimists see only the downside while optimists are captivated by the good side. Realists see both sides. So, actions, policies ... and people ... have two sides, the good AND the bad, the positive AND the negative. Economists label one side *benefits* and the other side *costs*. (**Sunk costs are not counted**!)

Unfortunately, in most circumstances, the bad cannot be detached and discarded. If only that were possible! Most of the time the good and bad come as one, an inseparable package. One must accept the bad with the good! (Sometimes a package has good, bad ... and ugly, as well).

To improve decision-making, economists encourage examining both sides in terms of *values* sacrificed (the costs) and *values* created (the benefits)!

1. FALLA<IOUS <<ONOMI<US: My life would be much better if I would embrace all the choices that have benefits and avoid all choices that have costs.

Fallacious Reasoning: It is common sense, no?

Correct Reasoning: This is a common mistake in reasoning. You were warned about common sense, right? Be careful! In the economic way of thinking there are no free lunches. *Every action, activity, and thought costs something.*

Remember: every choice has costs! If you avoided all choices having costs you would not do anything! You would not get out of bed in the morning. Hopefully, costs have a corresponding benefit.

"To make an omelet you have to break some eggs." You gain the omelet but you must lose the eggs (or whatever else could have been produced)!

Most choices have some benefit, if you search thoroughly. Consequently, the fallacious rule cited above would also tell you to embrace most every choice in your life. But, you are also told to reject choices having costs. Then, what do you do when the rules conflict, when a choice has costs AND benefits? You are supposed to reject choices with costs and embrace those with benefits, no? Your rule tells you to simultaneously embrace and reject all your options in life! How do you resolve this conflict?

Balance Cost against Benefit

One period process. TANSTAAFL instructs that us that benefits come with costs. They are inseparable, two sides of the same coin.

If every choice has good and bad, benefits and costs, what do we do and what do we avoid? Consider the expansion of an activity, like bites of an apple, miles of a journey or hours on the beach. Recognize that each extra step has its own segmented, measurable good and bad effects, benefits and costs. Here is an idea:

Keep taking extra steps (expand the activity) as long as the extra benefits exceed the extra costs. Do not take the steps where the costs exceed the benefits. They hurt more than help. (Doctor, it hurts when I do this!)

This is common sense that works for you. Stop when the next step involves more costs than benefits.

Applications: One Period Model

1. At the ballpark, keep buying and eating hot dogs as long as the extra satisfaction exceeds the cost.

2. In medicine dosage, stop expanding the dosage of medicine when the side effects overwhelm the health benefits.

3. Keep adding sales outlets as long as the profit exceeds the cost.

Most folks stop short intuitively, instinctively without a long rumination process. But, the principle can be applied in nearly every aspect of life.

But, not all activities begin and end within one period. Some projects overlap many years, like number three above. What then?

Advanced treatment: the Multi Period Model (or Capital Budgeting)

Consider multi-period projects at large institutions. Suppose a decision is to be made today, e.g., building a power plant, that will create a stream of *mismatched* benefits and costs over *future years*. **Projected benefits and costs do not synchronize in each future year.** In these cases, a strict application of the one period benefit-cost rule could lead to wrong decisions, premature shutdowns in odd years where costs exceed benefits. *The entire life of the project must be scrutinized for costs and benefits.* Payments and receipts are expected and forecasted at various non-synchronous future dates.

Time impacts value. Investors believe payments and receipts change in importance as they move back and forth along a future time grid. A given amount, moved closer, becomes more important and gets more weight. The same amount, moved further out on the grid, becomes less important and gets less weight. **It is human nature to value earlier dollars, in or out, more than**

later dollars, in or out, just as we value current enjoyment over future enjoyment. Earlier availability means the dollar can be reinvested or utilized sooner ... and sooner is better. Sooner looms larger than later.

Economists have developed an amazing procedure – **discounted cash flow (DCF)** analysis – to deal with mismatched streams of future incoming and outgoing dollars that vary in importance. Built into the procedure is a weighting scheme that recognizes the **time value of money!** Discounted cash flow techniques automatically revalue inflows and outflows to account for the time value of money coming in and going out.

[1. Ben McClure, "DCF Analysis: Introduction" 5 Dec. *Investopedia* <http://tinyurl.com/7yxlqxr>]

So, before making long view decisions economists, accountants and finance professionals follow this mathematical procedure, outlined below:

1. Use formal discounted cash flow methods to **compress a series of future benefits and costs into their equivalent one number present values.**

2. Compare the one number *present value of benefits* to the one number *present value of costs.*

3. An accept or reject decision is made, based on which number is greater, PV of benefits or PV of costs. [In addition, a stock or bond theoretical value can be derived by *discounting* future cash flows. A basic course in accounting or finance explores the complexities of this approach!]

2. FALLACIOUS ECONOMICUS: The availability of expensive imported crude oil over the past forty years has been a blessing, despite the high price.

Correct Reasoning: Remember, **things or people are not all good or all bad.** Our dependence on imported crude oil has been both a blessing and a curse for importers, world over. Yes, a curse for the extortionist level pricing and the enrichment of a criminal enterprise, OPEC. But, oil's many products have been a blessing for all the satisfaction they have provided. And it has been a blessing for Big Oil, as they partnered with OPEC extortionists to transport, refine and distribute its products. (In addition, the higher OPEC price has given life to some American high marginal cost producers.) An unofficial "surcharge" on the already higher price will come when the oil dollars in foreign hands come back to buy American assets and influence.

Note: The countries of **OPEC,** the Organization of Petroleum Exporting Countries have run the most successful criminal conspiracy and extortion racket the world has ever known. Their open, in your face collusion to rig the oil price is criminal behavior, at least according to U.S. standards of ant-trust law. In short, if companies domiciled in the U.S. conspired to fix prices like OPEC, they could be prosecuted for violations of Federal anti-trust law.

3. FALLACIOUS ECONOMICUS: Dump free market capitalism. It is destroying the environment, i.e., destroying unpriced common property.

Common Property: Seeds of Environmental Abuse

Overuse and misuse of the environment occurs in a free market with common property (unprivatized property owned, in effect, by all citizens and frequently available at a zero price). Selected areas of the environment possessing scarce mineral resources are, when discovered, quickly privatized. But, venture capitalism does not privatize all environmental resources. Government retains ownership and control of extensive mineral resources in the U.S. Privatization is impractical for some resources. How do you privatize and maintain exclusive use of the middle of the Pacific Ocean? It appeared limitless, so why bother? The air mantle, the oceans, the fish stocks, most rivers and lakes, grazing lands were once abundant *relative* to demands. But, arguably, privatization resists exhaustion of the resource, thereby prolonging its availability.

Over the years population growth turned abundance into scarcity, yet the zero prices persisted for much of the common property. For some resources, quotas were put in place to avoid resource exhaustion.

Recall from Chapter Two: **zero prices lead to abuse — misuse and overuse - of those unpriced resources.** Misuse means using it for an improper end, below its full potential. For example, using a lake as garbage can is *misuse*. Overuse suggests permanent depletion of the stock, as in overgrazing or overfishing.

Market to the rescue? As **a privately** owned resource becomes more scarce, approaching exhaustion, its market determined relative price *rises*, sparking a search for substitutes. [Economists would call this a **supply induced shortage**. Ed.]In the 1800s, whale oil rose in price relative to kerosene, a substitute. The price rise sounds an alarm, activating a search for substitutes by buyers and sellers. 1) For buyers, the higher price encourages *economizing on the resource,* i.e., using less of it and using the remainder more carefully. 2) For suppliers, the higher price and profit prospects spark a search for new, cheaper substitutes. End result? Substitutes are sought, found, and brought in. So, the market system activates the brakes on the usage of a market priced scarce resource and sparks a search for substitutes.

Thus, exhaustion of a resource is more problematic in non market systems where prices are not free to reflect increasing scarcity.

Chapter Four
The Sunk Cost Fallacy

The Moving Finger writes; and, having writ, Moves on: nor all your Piety nor Wit Shall lure it back to cancel half a Line, Nor all your Tears wash out a Word of it.

Rubaiyat of Omar Khayyám

Why Cry Over Spilt Milk?

SOMETIMES a project, activity or relationship should be abandoned regardless of how much cost, energy, time or effort has already been expended. Not only have those costs been expended but they are also unrecoverable; have no salvage value. **What's done is done; you cannot undo it, you can't change the past, you can't get back what you used up.**

Sometimes people justify increased investment in a decision, based on sentimental attachment. People sometimes justify *additional* investment in a course of action by pointing to past commitments. "We've already committed X dollars to the project, so we cannot abandon it now. If we do, those X dollars will have been wasted." For most decisions, the prior commitment is irrelevant as the project will "live" in the future. **Irretrievable earlier costs are considered sunk**, like the Titanic. Further investment should be based on *future* events, costs and benefits. After all, "why throw good money after bad?"
[1. "Escalation of commitment," 5 May 2014 *Wikipedia*
<http://en.wikipedia.org/wiki/Escalation_of_commitment>]

Beware the psychological aspect. "When somebody's sacrificed or invested a great deal in a cause or project, they tend to become irrationally dedicated to it."
[2. "Sunk Cost Fallacy," *TvTropes* 5 May 2014 < http://tinyurl.com/l4r4jod >]

1. FALLACIOUS ECONOMICUS: I have gone out with Bill for four years, but now our relationship is on the rocks. But, I will stick with Bill because I don't want those four years to have been wasted.

Correct Reasoning: Those four years are gone, whether they were good or bad. They are irretrievable, no matter what you do. Therefore, those years should not figure in your current plans. *Ignore the time sunk in the relationship.* You should continue the relationship only if the **future holds more good times than bad.** And the bad excludes those irretrievable four years of sunk costs.

2. FALLACIOUS ECONOMICUS: I've invested $10,000 in this stock and I've had it for five years. I've followed and studied the company for years. Hell, my brother-in-law works for them. Lately, the stock has declined to $6,000. But, I think it might come back. I feel a sense of loyalty to the company, as well. I think I'll keep the stock, maybe I'll recover the $4,000. price drop.

Correct Reasoning: Make as firm a prediction as possible of the future movement of the stock. You have lost $4,000 already and you are sentimentally attached, an unwelcome bias. Those factors are irrelevant now. Those factors should be ignored. The critical question is: **what does the future hold?** The $4,000 of the $10,000 has already gone "bad," is lost. Should you hang in and risk the other $6,000? If the stock declines further you will be "throwing good money after bad," a loss that could be avoided by selling the stock now. Still like the company but think the stock is overvalued right now? Then you might sell the stock now and buy it back later after the price falls.

> Can you un-smoke a cigarette?

3. FALLACIOUS ECONOMICUS: I've deployed 50,000 troops and we are losing the war. Should I throw in the 10,000 reservists, too? The war is lost, either way, but I want to show support for the first 50,000 soldiers.

Fallacious Reasoning: We can't quit now, we've already committed 50,000 troops. To quit now would be to dishonor them.

Correct Reasoning: If the 10,000 added troops will not bring victory, why throw them into the fray? To paraphrase, you would be, "Throwing good troops after bad." In other words, the 50,000 have already gone "bad" in the sense of not producing a victory. Now, you want to up that by another 10,000 soldiers? It will only raise your losses and ... you still lose the war.

4. FALLACIOUS ECONOMICUS: I've bet $500 so far on this hand of poker and need to put on another $100 to stay in the game. As I look at the cards on the table I am not confident that I will win the hand. But I have already put in $500! So, I'll put up the extra $100.

Correct Reasoning: If the pot and your $500 is likely already lost, why lose another $100? Cut your losses and fold your hand.

Question: How is the sunk cost fallacy related to the cost-benefit fallacy?

Your Final Answer Is ...?

An answer marked on a multiple choice question is not "sunk" or final until the answer sheet is turned in to the proctor. Prior to that, an answer can be changed. But, is it wise to change your initial answer, your first pick? See fallacy # 5 below.

5. FALLACIOUS ECONOMICUS: When taking a multiple choice test, and doubting your first quick pick answer, resist the temptation to change that first pick. Trust your first instinct, usually it is correct.

Correct Reasoning: The fallacy contradicts the available evidence. An extensive study has shown that changing a first, answer is, more often than not, a change for the better. The first answer is not "sunk" until the exam is turned in. Although some changes are mistakes, **more changes are from incorrect to correct than vice versa.**

The fallacy derives from the idea that, after the test, the test taker remembers more keenly the instances when the answer was changed for the worse. Diminished in memory are the changes for the better.

So, ignore the advice offered in the fallacy and improve your grades!

[3. Justin Kruger, Derrick Wirtz and Dale T. Miller "Counterfactual Thinking and the First Instinct Fallacy" May 2005 *Journal of Personality and Social Psychology* < http://tinyurl.com/nvztjju >]

You can't put the toothpaste back in the tube.

Don't look back, something might be gaining on you.   –Satchel Paige

Chapter Five
the "Too Much of a Good Thing" Fallacy

Moderation in All Things ...   – Aristotle

THE wisdom of the ancients can help to expose many a modern fallacy. Ancient wisdom calls for *moderation in all things*. Failure to respect this admonition leaves one susceptible to *fallacious economicus!* ☹

1. FALLACIOUS ECONOMICUS: If a little of something is good, then more of it must be better and the most must be best.

Fallacious Reasoning: It seems like common sense. Try to get the most you can of a good thing. Why not, it is a good thing, right? There is an old saying, "You can't get too much of a good thing."

Correct Reasoning: Chapter one contained warnings about the improper application of common sense in guiding behavior. This chapter deals with an exception to those warnings. This common sense adage is most appropriate and valuable. Common sense also tells us: "too much of a good thing" can backfire and become a bad thing. The explanation lies with the wisdom of the ancients and summarized in one word: **EXCESS**. One cannot live without water but too much, an excess, would make the stomach explode.

Excess can manifest as a deepening, widening or extending of an activity.

Negative Marginal Utility: Too Much of a Good Thing "You can't get too much of a good thing," an old saying goes. But, that old saying is a fallacy. Actually, you can get too much of a good thing, and when you do, that "good" thing backfires on you ... and becomes a bad thing. Ask doctors about giving medicine, as too much could kill, not cure, a patient. Economists assert that continued consumption of one good ultimately leads to **negative marginal utility. This is overconsumption.** So, Judy feels worse off *after* potato chip #137 than before she ate it. Unit #137 enters the stage of overconsumption and reduces the *total* satisfaction from all prior units.

Obviously, not enough of a good thing hurts, depriving us of full benefits. So, too little of a good thing is a bad thing. Too little may leave us in harm's way. Not enough medicine and the illness persists. Too much medicine and it turns poisonous. So, too much of a good thing or too little of a good thing becomes a bad thing. **Quantity changes quality.**

Read All About it in Aristotle's Words

Both excessive and defective [deficient] exercise destroys the strength, and similarly drink or food which is above or below a certain amount destroys the health, while that which is proportionate both produces and increases and preserves it. So too is it, then, in the case of temperance and courage and the other virtues. For the man who flies from and fears everything and does not stand his ground against anything becomes a coward, and the man who fears nothing at all but goes to meet every danger becomes rash ... **temperance and courage, then, are destroyed by excess and defect, and preserved by the mean.**
[1. (Bold mine) Aristotle, *Nicomachean Ethics* p.22 (trans. 1999) (Ross W.D., Trans.). Kitchener, Ontario, Canada: Batoche Books.]

Recommendation from Aristotle: practice moderation in all things.

Recall the story of the *over* confident Icarus, from Greek mythology, who failed to follow the middle way:

Icarus, seeking to fly across the sea, was ordered by his father neither to soar too high nor fly too low, for, as his wings were fastened together with wax, there was danger of its melting by the sun's heat in too high a flight, and of its becoming less tenacious by the moisture if he kept too near the vapor of the sea. But he, with a juvenile confidence, soared aloft, and fell down headlong.

[2. Francis Bacon, "The Fable of Icarus," *The Wisdom of the Ages* 29 Nov. 2012 < http://tinyurl.com/qglu9zh >]

Major Concept: The message from the ancients is clear: avoid extremes of too much or too little. **Avoid excess and avoid deficiency**. Find the middle path.

A Home Too Far: the Sub-Prime Mortgage Debacle

Good intentions are not enough to guarantee a good result! Overdosing on a good thing violates the caution for moderation or avoiding excess. Home ownership is considered a good thing, part of the American Dream. Misguided good intentions overtook do-gooders in Washington.

The government in Washington pushed mortgage lenders to lower lending standards significantly below traditional levels. Unbelievably, so-called NINJA (no income, no job, no assets!) mortgages were issued to some home buyers. As an asset, holding such a mortgage would be high risk, to say the least! Banksters [sic] assembled these highly risky, sometimes worthless mortgages, and securitized (packaged) them. Then they sold the "packages" on the secondary market, worldwide. These packages also carried, in effect, insurance against default. The market collapsed when it became apparent that too many "packages" contained too many likely defaults. The institutions offering insurance were overwhelmed with claims and were unable to make good on their commitments. The packages were bounced back to the packagers who were unable to make full refunds. The process culminated in the sub-prime mortgage debacle of 2008-2009, which nearly destroyed our financial system.

2. FALLACIOUS ECONOMICUS: For good health, especially blood pressure regulation, try to eliminate or minimize the use of sodium in your diet.

Correct Reasoning: Minimizing or eliminating salt from one's diet can seriously damage one's health! Many healthy bodily functions depend on sodium. Although one study does not establish a fact, a recent large study indicated health problems multiply if a diet is *too restricted* in salt. Read all about it:

> The new study, which tracked more than 100,000 people from 17 countries over an average of more than three years, found that those who consumed fewer than 3,000 milligrams of sodium a day had a 27% higher risk of death or a serious event such as a heart attack or stroke in that period than those whose intake was estimated at 3,000 to 6,000 milligrams. Risk of death or other major events increased with intake above 6,000 milligrams.
> [3. Ron Winslow, "Low-Salt Diets May Pose Health Risks, Study Finds," 13 August 2014 *Wall Street Journal*<http://tinyurl.com/lqzo5cx>]

A Little Bit of a Bad Thing Can be ... a Good Thing!

A substance generally considered harmful in large doses may, in fact, be beneficial in a small dose!

> Nobody wants to breathe dirty air or drink dirty water. But, if either becomes 98 percent pure, 99 percent pure or 99.9 percent pure, there is some point beyond which the costs skyrocket and the benefits become meager or non-existent. If the slightest trace of any impurity were fatal, the human race would have become extinct thousands of years ago.
>
> [4. Thomas Sowell, "Too much of a 'Good Thing' is bad," 19 July 2011 WND *Commentary* <http://tinyurl.com/p44f979>]

Humankind can survive, even thrive, given a minimal level of pollution.

> Not only does the body have defenses to neutralize small amounts of some impurities, some things that are dangerous, or even fatal, in substantial amounts can become harmless or even beneficial in extremely minute amounts, arsenic being one example. As an old adage put it: 'It is the dose that makes the poison.'
>
> [5. Ibid.]
> [6. See also Laura Landro, "In Treatment, There Can Be Too Much of a Good Thing: Aggressive lowering of blood pressure may put patients at risk for harm," 4 August 2014, *Wall Street Journal* <http://tinyurl.com/okhjot4>]

Beware: Ordinary folks depend on good scientific research to tell them at what level excess sets in!

3. FALLACIOUS ECONOMICUS: Consider the beneficial impact immigration has had on this country. More immigration would have brought even greater benefits. Therefore, anyone who wants to enter the U.S. should be allowed in.

Correct Reasoning: That is a very noble -- but naïve and dangerous -- assertion. **How many folks can fit in Lifeboat U.S.A. without sinking it and drowning everyone?** This is open borders run amok. Recall, an *excess* of a good thing, i.e., immigration, that backfires and becomes a bad thing. If allowed, it would be ruinous to the U.S. *and* the new entrants.

Critical questions: The world is nearly a bottomless pit of poor, destitute and oppressed people suffering in other countries. What are their numbers? Five hundred million? A billion? Three billion? **How low would wages be driven and services shared before an inflow stops or the U.S. bankrupted?** On the cultural side, how much diversity can the "nation" absorb and remain a distinct nation? Has *excess diversity* been weaponized, i.e., used as a weapon to destroy the common core of the nation? Can the nation remain intact as a true nation of people if it morphs into a Balkanized "stew" of cultures and a Babel of languages? Can **Lifeboat U.S.A.** accommodate all of them?   Sleep lightly, my friend!

Economists Deal with Pollution

Pollution results from an abuse (misuse and overuse) of natural resources. Involving resources as it does, pollution is an economic as well as an scientific phenomenon.

> Pollution is defined as the presence of impurities or pollutant substances in sufficient concentration levels, causing harmful effects on human beings, animals, plant life or material resources when exposed for a sufficient duration of time, thus reducing the quality of life in the environment.

> [7. Puja Mondal, "Pollution and Pollutants: Classification, Causes, Effects and Sources" 19 February 2015 *Your Article Library* <http://tinyurl.com/p7b7nn9>]

4. FALLACIOUS ECONOMICUS: Every last bit of pollution ought to be eliminated from the environment. We deserve a spanking clean, *pristine* environment for ourselves, our children and grandchildren.

Correct Reasoning: First of all, rule out the goal of an *absolutely pristine environment.* Chasing down those last bits of harmless pollutant might require excessive cost or be technologically impossible. **The challenge pollution presents is twofold.** 1) Resources will be needed to clean up the existing **stock** of pollutants, and 2) reduce or eliminate the **flow** of new pollutants. As to 1), *excess* resources need to be used to create a *pristine* environment. Is a pristine environment worth the cost in terms of other valuable goods lost, i.e., the real opportunity cost?

The onion model. Consider that each layer of pollution removed makes the environment somewhat cleaner, one step at a time. Cleaning the environment is similar to peeling an onion, one layer at a time. The removal of each layer involves a cost and a benefit.

The environment has a built in ability to reprocess biodegradable wastes. However, that capability is limited and frequently exhausted. An excess of pollution at first *over burdens* and then *shuts down* the capacity of natural environmental forces to recycle and detoxify wastes. **Remember:** there are two tasks with respect to dealing with pollution.

> ➤ Clean up the **stock** of pollutants enough so that, hopefully, the natural recycling ability is re-kindled and becomes operative.

> ➤ Reduce the **flow** of pollutants. The pollutant flow need not be reduced to zero, only to a non lethal level.

Remember: at each stage in pollution fight, balance extra benefits against extra costs! The pollutant flow need not be reduced to zero, only to a non lethal level. This idea is central to the economists' handling of pollution problems. (Toxic and hazardous materials present a special problem).

Thus: excess must be avoided in tackling the pollution problem. **Maximizing** the production of a clean environment may involve an inappropriate *over allocation* of resources to the cleanup or deterrent effort. From an economics perspective, there is an **optimum** (or best) amount of pollution that is allowable! Yes, read it again! There is an optimum amount of pollution that is allowable!

Better to OPTIMIZE than MAXIMIZE
The Optimum Amount of a Good

Excess destroys. A good thing destroys itself when taken to excess! Excess cheap labor, excess cheap goods, excess cheap money, excess immigration, excess work, excess free time, excess demand for free goodies and on and on. Excess desire for real and financial wealth is destructive.

Too little hurts ... so does too much! We are all agreed that goods satisfy wants. So, too little of a good causes hardship; but, so does too much! Consider salt, as discussed above. Economists are concerned with *maximizing well-being*, satisfaction or utility. This is not accomplished by maximizing production of every good.

The Incremental Approach Is Best

These ideas are depicted in the diagram below.

Area of Overproduction: Beyond Q_2 in the Diagram #1.

In this range, an expansion of output imposes a net cost on society. Some units already have added more to costs than to benefits, reducing society's welfare. In the diagram below, *overproduction* occurs beyond level Q_2.

Action: *reduce output* to the point of intersection, optimum output.

Area of Underproduction: Below Q_2 in the diagram below.

In this range, there are gains to be gotten from expanding output. This is the land of unexploited opportunity! Additional units are worth more than they cost. In diagram #1, *underproduction* occurs at levels of output below Q_2.

Action: expand (or contract) output to the point of intersection, Q_2, the optimum output and stop! There are net losses beyond Q_2.

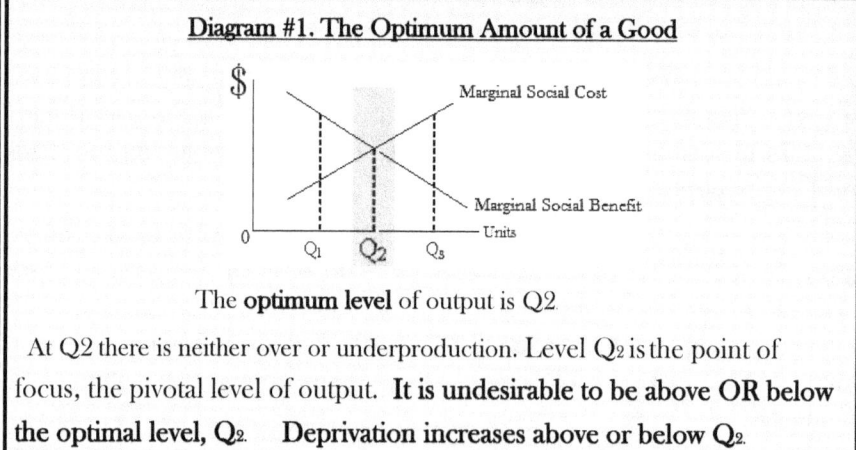

Diagram #1. The Optimum Amount of a Good

The **optimum level** of output is Q2.

At Q2 there is neither over or underproduction. Level Q_2 is the point of focus, the pivotal level of output. **It is undesirable to be above OR below the optimal level, Q_2.** Deprivation increases above or below Q_2.

No matter what the nature of the good, there is a level of production so great that the extra costs *exceed* the extra benefits for those units. In short, there is overproduction, excess production than hurts society more than it helps. Any desirable "good" can be overproduced: vaccines, heat in the winter, and air-conditioning in summer. *Goods of greater value are being given up to create units of goods with lesser value.* This is uneconomic, given the general scarcity of goods. Tear down the luxury apartment to put up some tents. Really? From the point of view of resource utilization this is the forbidden zone! Do take production to this level! Reduce production to Q_2, the optimum. **Do not maximize, optimize!**

Excess in the Creative Arts

The warning to avoid excess extends to the creative arts.

A musical composition can have too many notes, a novel too many characters, a ballet too many movements. Minimalism may not be aesthetic, as well.

***Excess* reduces or destroys the effectiveness of a creative work.**

The creative artist must seek the *optimum* combination of creative elements, not the maximum.

The great creative geniuses know where the line of excess lay and do not cross it.

EXCESS at the Gym

Excess could manifest itself as a **deepening, widening** or a **time extension**. For example, at the gym: too many squats (deepening), too many different exercises (widening), or too long a workout (extension of time). Each reduces the effectiveness of the workout. An example of excess in **economic policy** is giving laissez-faire too much latitude (deepening), in too many areas (widening), and extending laissez-faire into the off shoring and open borders era. Laissez-faire helped build the American economic colossus.

Is it now helping to tear it down?

The Middle Path

The message from the ancients is clear: quantity changes quality.
Avoid extremes of too much or too little.
Avoid excess and avoid deficiency.

Chapter Six
The Environment and the Free Market

POLLUTION was not a worry to ancient, hunter-gatherer, nomadic peoples. Once they despoiled or exhausted a location they escaped to a new unspoiled location, of which there seemed to be an endless number. In the relatively under-populated pre-history world this cycle could be repeated endlessly by nomadic peoples. The attitude was something like this: "All the trees cut down on this mountain? Well, then we'll move to the next mountain and 'gather' those trees. And when we have exhausted that mountain we'll move on to the next and so on. There is an unlimited supply of mountains and trees!"

Not so today, given population growth *relative* to the environment. Today, the **ecologists** tell us we're running out of mountains and trees, game animals, waters and fish, mines and ores. Breathable air is threatened. Exhaustion and pollution of the environment presents economic as well as technological problems unknown to the ancients.

Historically, many resources we now consider scarce were relatively abundant. So, there was no need to assert private property rights and spend to exclude others. The forests, buffalo herds, the rivers, wild game, the fish stocks and the oceans were so abundant **everyone could take his share without diminishing the share of others.** So, there was no "gatekeeper" or "ticket taker" to charge admission. Who would want to bother, who would want the job? These resources belonged to everyone *in common* and there was enough for everyone, with more leftover. This is the origin of the zero price tradition that later became law for some resources.

But, this practice lingered too long for some resources! Recall, an excess of a good thing is a bad thing! Even as population grew some of these resources remained communal, not private property. Witness the open range policy in the Western states. Today we know that communal ownership, gain seeking and zero priced resources are a toxic brew. As population demands increase the resource becomes relatively scarce. This likely leads to abuse, namely **misuse** and **overuse**. The passenger pigeon, once numbering in the millions in the 1800s, was over hunted to extinction by 1900.

Some species were lucky and survived. Consider the near demise of the American bison, the beaver and the sperm whale. Overharvesting was the dominant threatening factor. The communal nature and zero price of bison promoted overharvesting by profit seeking buffalo hunters (for robes, meat and bones) and food seeking plains Indians alike. The same fate befell the beaver, which had been trapped for its pelts. The repeating rifle and railroad expansion overwhelmed and doomed the Bison before they could be saved by substitutes. Hunters and trappers exhausted the local resources for profit and then moved to more abundant locales, eventually nearly exhausting the bison and beaver.

There is no argument, overuse and misuse of the unpriced, available for "free" environment are negative side effects of profit oriented, free market activity. But, is the free market the only bad guy in this story?

1. FALLACIOUS ECONOMICUS: The plains Indians lived in harmony with the buffalo, killing only was what was necessary for survival. Killed meat was shared communally within the tribe. There was little, if any, waste.

Correct Reasoning: New historical research challenges these contentions. Of course, the Indian did not kill on the scale of the white man, but they were not such careful guardians either. They, too, considered the buffalo to be an inexhaustible resource. They would kill *in excess* to deny sustenance to an enemy tribe. They boxed in herds with fires or drove them over cliffs. These practices created considerable waste. No matter, the herds were inexhaustible! Storage of any surplus was considered impractical for a nomadic people.

[1. Larry Schweikart, "Buffaloed: The Myth and Reality of Bison in America" 01 December 2002 *The Freeman* <http://fee.org/the_freeman/detail/buffaloed-the-myth-and-reality-of-bison-in-america>]

> As for communal sharing, if killed by bow and arrow, the hunter's mark on the arrow gave the killer priority in consuming the animal. Yet, the braves who rode their horses into the thundering herds marked their arrows so it was clear who killed the bison. The marked arrow gave the shooter rights to the best parts of the animal. Tribal members who specialized in butchering the kill also received a share as payment for processing the meat...rewards were distributed in accord with the contribution that each had made to the overall success of the hunt.

[2. Miller, Roger Leroy, et. al. *The Economics of Public Issues*, 14th Edition, Boston: Pearson, Addison-Wesley 2005 pp.180-181]

So much for an equal distribution of goods in the romantic notion of life as a plains Indian. And so the reality is told about the old West.

2. FALLACIOUS ECONOMICUS: The free market has problems, its ugly side. Look at how those greedy capitalists overuse and misuse "free" environmental resources by exhausting some and polluting others ... and for what? Profit? Get rid of the profit system! It's simple: pollution is undertaken to raise profits. Outlaw profits and pollution goes away.

Correct Reasoning: The cost-benefit principle must be applied here. Of course the profit oriented, free market has problems, an ugly side. It has excesses, as the ancients would say. What system doesn't? Yes, the pursuit of profit can make a mess of the environment. But, free market capitalism should not be labeled the only bad guy in this story. Furthermore, free market capitalism can create the means for cleaning up the mess it creates.

Profit Not the Only Motive for Despoiling Environment

Communism banned free enterprise, most private property and profits but forgot to ban pollution. A startling discovery was made when the Iron Curtain fell in 1990s and we could look into Eastern Europe and Russia as never before in the Cold War. What did the free world see: the worst pollution in the world, where profit, free markets and private property were severely restricted, if not totally prohibited. Much worse pollution than in the free market, capitalistic West. How did that happen?

> Clean air has become a luxury here and in the industrial zones of Central Europe, where poisonous gases and toxic dust roam freely. As the secrets of the Eastern bloc's formerly Communist nations become known, this one may be the saddest. In the years when Soviet-bloc rulers claimed that they were forming "a new socialist man," they were in many instances condemning this man and his family to severe lung and heart disease.

> [3. Marlise Simons, "UPHEAVAL IN THE EAST; Rising Iron Curtain Exposes Haunting Veil of Polluted Air" 8 April 1990 *New York Times* archives < http://tinyurl.com/ow4epzk >]

But if the profit motive is the primary cause of pollution, one would not expect to find much pollution in socialist countries, such as the former Soviet Union, China, and in the former Communist countries of Eastern and Central Europe. That is, in theory. In reality exactly the opposite is true: *That socialist world suffered from the worst pollution on earth.*

[4. Italics mine. Thomas J. Dilorenzo, "Why Socialism Causes Pollution," 01 March 1992 *The Freeman* < http://tinyurl.com/nqmdqfc >]

It happened because **profit is not the only motivation for abusing the environment.** Aside from profit, pollution may be caused by carelessness, ignorance, political chicanery, bureaucratic neglect and callousness toward the environment. The last four had to figure into pollution behind the Iron Curtain. One must assume those motives would be active in the U.S. **even if profits were outlawed** and full blown communism was instituted! But, remember, by ending the profit system you would lose all the good created by it. In effect, you would be throwing out the baby with the water!

Communal resource ownership coupled with zero usage prices makes a toxic brew. **Misuse** and **overuse** of scarce resources are likely consequences.

Costs and Benefits of Wealth Creation

Profit and Development of New Technologies

The accumulation of wealth gives an economy the means of cleaning up polluted waterways, oceans and land. **If U.S. capitalism creates a mess, it has the productive punch to clean it up.** Economic growth and development create the means of dealing with the waste thrown off in that growth process. Beyond that there must be the willingness to apply resources to the problem. (If communism creates a mess, does it have the ability and willingness to make the correction, given its woeful record on production?)

Private property provides an incentive (profit!) to properly manage the *privately* owned resources and promote their longevity. Failure to do so hits home in the form of lower profit and/or higher cost.

Of course, the richer and smarter we become the easier it is to deal with many problems. The bigger the economy, the lower the *relative* burden of clean-up.

Beware: Government management or oversight of resources is not a panacea. Government officials are not omniscient. Many are vulnerable individuals, subject to the influence of undeserving, concentrated special interest groups

Creative Destruction: Relief from Limited Resources?

Revered economist **Joseph Schumpeter** developed the doctrine of economic growth/business cycles via **creative destruction**. For him, capitalism progresses and an economy grows by a continual birth and death of industries in a grinding struggle for profit.

Creative destruction means a new industry cluster is created and embraced by opportunistic entrepreneurs, creating a surge in economic growth. At the same time the emergence of the new industry signals the destruction or diminution of an older, competing industry cluster. New technologies fuel this process. The telegraph replaced the pony express. Audiotapes replaced vinyl records, in turn replaced by compact disks that were replaced by ... and on and on. Coal gave way to oil as the dominant fuel. Nuclear made a surge. Will oil and nuclear give way to renewable solar, tidal and wind generated power? New technologies, spurred by profit seeking, guided by consumer sovereignty-

    a) enable more economical use of existing resources,

    b) aid in the discovery of new resources.

    c) fuel the creative destruction process.

    d) spur the growth of new industry clusters.

Technological optimists argue that *the capacity of the human brain to develop new technologies has no limit.* This is an astounding assertion! Read it again! Note: other resources (land, labor, capital) are considered finite, i.e., limited.

But, optimists believe human ingenuity is *unlimited and will provide when sparked by the profit motive.*

Today, we look at a new horizon of budding technologies hoping to expand our understanding of new resources. We look for technology advances to enable us to do more with less, to do it faster, to make it stronger, and most of all, do it cheaper. As part of a dynamic growth process, this would increase productive capability. Improvements in technology have unveiled a world of new resources and taught us how to extract more from traditional resources. Examples of how improving technology would raise the productive potential:

- ➢ Innovations that would make coal burn clean.
- ➢ The same size solar collector improved to be ten times more effective.
- ➢ Sea water – already a transportation and fishing resource – may contain source material for fusion energy generation.

Take note of the interplay between technology, freedom of enterprise and resources. Technology and resources go hand in hand. Improved technology may allow alert producers to recognize new resources and assert private property rights over them. They may find new uses for old resources, and apply old medicines to new diseases.

The Economics of the Spaghetti Western

One must consider all the good derived from market capitalism: a well-regulated, free enterprise/free market system respecting private property. Yes, market capitalism produces a variety of outcomes: the good, the bad and, unfortunately, even the ugly. But, here is how they stack up in significance:

THE GOOD .... THE BAD .... and .... THE UGLY

Warning: Beware the commission of one fallacy while unmasking another. In short, **beware the totally unregulated market.** Remember: An excess of a good thing – the free market – becomes a bad thing! Freedom becomes license. The latter can spark an exploitive, rapacious and destructive rampage as in the destruction of American Bison, passenger pigeon and the American Eastern buffalo. The market needs a degree of effective and honest regulation to hold in check the crapitalists [sic], banksters [sic] and brokesters [sic].

Question: Could artificial intelligence, a.k.a. AI, involve more costs than benefits?

Evolution of a Free Enterprise, Modern Market Economy

Government provides the "rules of the game:" legal framework by preserving the rule of law, enforcing property and contract rights, making trade agreements and discouraging monopoly. Then, the "race is on" between entrepreneurs. Yes, taxes and subsidies can sway resource allocation. However, those actions only apply to certain sectors of the economy. Otherwise, **freedom of enterprise** prevails.

Creative destruction theory of Joseph Schumpeter (1942). How does a free enterprise economy develop? A free market economy evolves and grows much like **the human body.** As to the body, each day cells die and new cells replace them. Your body today is not the same as yesterday's body. As to the economy, each day firms die and new firms are born. Each day dawns on a new economy. Occasionally, new industries emerge (creation) and competing industries die off, i.e., *destruction.* Schumpeter argued this pairing of creation with destruction goes on continuously, providing the engine for economic growth.

The guiding force is the search for excess profits (a rent) and consumer sovereignty.

Competition within an industry, **intra-industry competition**, is expected. But, there is the often overlooked fierce competition between whole industries, inter-industry competition. Creative destruction derives from/causes intense **inter-industry competition** for greater profits (iron vs. steel, then steel vs. aluminum, then aluminum vs. composites, trucking vs. rail freight hauling). Usually, creation precedes destruction. Early on it was the wheel or domestication of animals spurring economic activity. Later, the automobile industry was created, destroying the mass market for horses. Indeed, the horse *industry cluster* was nearly destroyed. Gaslight and then electric light were cheaper and superior to whale oil and kerosene lamp light. Electricity enabled the digital revolution, enhancing our lives in so many ways. So it goes, creation of the new, then destruction of the old.

Profits spur progress. On balance, private sector, consumer and profit driven creative destruction has brought more benefits than costs and helped create the U.S. economic miracle. Creative destruction, driven by the profit motive, improves resource use *over time* (dynamic efficiency). In turn, improved resource use over time enriches the satisfaction of wants, e.g., traveling is more comfortable by automobile than stagecoach, TV more enjoyable than radio. After all, more value is created – and income paid out - in the production of car compared to raising of horses. The U.S. standard of living soared to become the envy of the world.

Creative destruction has its problems, as well. Worker skill obsolescence and dislocation is foremost. The blacksmith had to study auto mechanics and the typist had to master word processing. But, thus far, wages and standards of living have improved with their new occupations, new industries and new goods.

Question: But, the situation may be changing in the 21st century. **Is creative destruction still an engine for driving higher U.S. standards of living? What if most of the destruction occurs in the U.S. and the creation in off shore economies?**

Cap and Trade. Government policy today focuses on *cap and trade*. The latter system involves the issuance and trading of pollution rights, essentially, "licenses" to pollute, hoping not to eliminate pollution but to make it more efficient. The policy acknowledges environmental waste is an inevitable by-product of many industrial processes and ordinary human activity. **The major issues with respect to environmental abuse are *overuse* and *misuse*.**

The *cap* relates to the absolute amount of pollutant to be allowed, addressing the *overuse* problem. Polluters are issued licenses to emit a maximum amount of pollutant. Firms unable to hold down emissions to the licensed level can buy additional rights from firms operating below their pollution quota. Ostensibly, this relates to the *misuse* problem. *Cap and trade* provides a firm with a financial incentive to reduce pollution below one's quota. The unused pollution rights can be sold to a polluter in need.

This policy recognizes the ability of the environment to absorb and recycle some pollutants. The determination of the cap size is subject to heated international discussion. It should not be treated lightly by the U.S.

[5. "How cap and trade works: Learn how this key mechanism works to reduce emissions." 2 Sept. 2015 *Environmental Defense Fund.* <http://tinyurl.com/p9dp6qy>]

A Sunny Day in Pollutionville

It's hard to win an argument with a smart person, but it's damn near impossible to win an argument with a stupid person. –Bill Murray

Chapter Seven
The "Half a Loaf Better than None" Fallacy

The sky is the daily bread of the eyes. — Ralph Waldo Emerson

IS half a loaf really better than none? Or, should you switch to a totally different good? The simplistic logic of the fallacy does not stand up to scrutiny.

FALLACIOUS ECONOMICUS: If I cannot have the whole loaf of bread, then I'll take half. Half is the next best thing to the whole.

Fallacious Reasoning: This idea is so logical and reasonable it needs no explanation ... it is self-explanatory!

Correct Reasoning: Yes, the idea is tempting and may be valid if bread, your first choice, is the only item available. Then take the half loaf. But, suppose there are other goods available with greater satisfaction than half a loaf? Your first choice now being unavailable changes your options. Now, you compare the other choices to the half loaf. Then, you re-evaluate your options and you may re-order your list. Frequently the "half loaf" is outshined by your original second best choice.

Examples of cases where "half a loaf" will not suffice:

1. The Chinese restaurant cannot give you a pair of chopsticks. Should you ask for one or ask for a fork?

2. You cannot find the pants to your favorite blue suit. Should you just wear the jacket with slacks that don't match or should you wear the black suit?

3. Suppose there isn't enough of a dosage of the most effective medicine. Should you take half a dose of it or a full dose of next best medicine?

4. A military target must be rendered ineffective. The most effective battle strategy would be to deploy all twenty bombers in your command. But, only 8 are operational. Should you deploy the 8 or switch to the more effective second best strategy, a ground assault?

5. You arrive at the multiplex theatre in the middle of your number one movie choice. Should you go in any way or see the other complete movie, what had been number two on your list? That former number two now comes out on top when compared to half of the first movie.

6. Your first choice is apple pie a la mode. But, there is no ice cream. So, rather than have the naked apple pie you pick the brownie, what had been the second best option. The utility of the brownie outweighs that of the naked apple pie!

What was *second* best now is the *very* best when compared to "half a loaf."

So, when you cannot get all of your first choice, perhaps,
rather than settle for some of it, take the second best option!

Leonardo DaVinci, *Head of A Woman,* Galleria Nazionale di Parma

*DaVinci's impression of a young lady contemplating
a difficult choice involving a half loaf of bread.*

Chapter Eight
The Scarcity or Doomsday Fallacy

The sky is falling.
—Chicken Little (aka Henny Penny)

THE scarcity or Doomsday fallacy has been bouncing around in various forms for hundreds of years. The most prominent historical incarnation was conjured up by Robert Malthus, a British parson, writing in the 19th century. He wrongly predicted population growth would eventually outstrip growth in food production, leading to mass starvation. Today, unproven and still debatable global warming (a.k.a. climate change) is the current boogieman threatening mankind.

Ecologists vs. Economists in the War of Environmental Paradigms

First, consider the viewpoint from ecology.

1. FALLACIOUS ECONOMICUS: Mass starvation and suffering are inevitable as world population expands and resources, especially **land (the gifts of nature),** are gradually overused and inevitably exhausted. Even if we wanted to, we will not have enough resources to feed, house, clothe and medicate a massive, growing population. Moreover, as we strive to expand goods availability we are using up increasingly scarce, nonrenewable resources, polluting the air and exhausting the bounty of the seas. Potable water supplies are threatened, especially in Third World nations.

The earth is finite, limited. The current stock of natural resources is all there is, and we are using it up at rapid rate. It stands to reason someday these natural resources will be used up, followed by an economic calamity.

Correct Reasoning: It is questionable population growth is moving the earth beyond its sustainable carrying capacity. The fallacious reasoning has convincing elements, but the **doomsday scenario is not guaranteed.** How can these forces of doom be overcome? Short answer: **the green revolution,** involving improved productivity of fewer farm workers, working with better tools for weather forecasting, planting, irrigating, land reclamation, harvesting, storing and transporting crops. New pest resistant crops - hybrids - have helped, as well. Also, international markets have grown, accelerating crop specialization. **Containerized shipping** has helped ease the cost of transport.

Malthus: Better Mathematics than Economics

Malthus' theory of economic advance and decline relied heavily on the assumption of a slower rate of expansion in food supply relative to exponential population growth. **Exponential growth** is expansion by the same *percentage* each period. With the same *percentage* growth applied to an expanding base, a larger and larger *absolute amount* is added each period. The rate of growth is constant but the amount of growth is greater each period. **Arithmetic growth** increases by the same *absolute amount* each period. An exponential series will eventually catch up to and then *surpass* a series growing arithmetically. **Malthus asserted** that the food supply grows by an arithmetic process whereas population grows exponentially. Eventually, population growth outstrips the growth in food supply and mass starvation ensues. He was wrong.

Standard Stages of Population Growth ... or ...Lifeboat Economics

Enter Stage 1. Under-population. An under-populated area may want and benefit from population growth. Immigration is acceptable and desirable. The standard of living (SOL) improves for most folks as population and labor force grows.

Lifeboat status: There is much unused room on the lifeboat. U.S. up to the 1970s.

End of stage 1. Optimum population reached. The (SOL) peaks. It is all "downhill" from this point.

Lifeboat status: The lifeboat has reached **optimum** capacity. The U.S., middle 1970s.

Enter Stage 2. After **optimum population is reached**, resource exhaustion kicks in. Further population growth does not bring immediate starvation, but degrades the SOL. Additional population absorbs more goods than it contributes. As more folks are carried, the SOL continues to degrade throughout Stage 2.

End of stage 2. Maximum carrying capacity reached. **Lifeboat status: More folks are aboard but are uncomfortable, no spare space left. The U. S. today.**

Enter Stage 3: Maximum carrying capacity surpassed! Sound the alarms! With the SOL already falling, population growth beyond this point **threatens subsistence**. This is Malthusland. A nation or economic region is flooded with excess immigrants or native population explosion. Economy fails to generate a subsistence level of food and other goods. The SOL sinks *below* the subsistence level. Eventually, population shrinks by deprivation and net emigration.

End of Stage 3. SOL crashes. **Lifeboat status: The lifeboat sinks.**

Today, some nations or regions may be threatened in this manner and enter Stage 3. However, study of the problem sees neither **the world as a whole nor the U.S. to be near this fate**, given the Green Revolution and improvements in public health. Malthus failed to see the resiliency, inventiveness and dynamism of a population challenged by growing scarcity.

Mass starvation may be avoided, but as population grows, so does the great panoply of wants. Around the world, the gap between wants and capabilities – **unsatisfied wants or the economic problem** – expands relentlessly.

[See Chapter Twenty, Fallacy #6 for a partial list of factors impacting standard of living.]

Overcoming the Forces of Doom

Optimum population concept. What happens as population growth nears Malthus' doomsday level? How much population growth through immigration and native fertility is best? One argument focuses on the impact on the standard of living (SOL). It goes like this: **population growth (from immigration and natural growth) *exceeds* optimal levels when it reduces (or stalls) the (pre-growth) current and future standard of living for most folks.**

Labor needs land, capital and know-how to be productive. As population grows, other factors constant, the *optimum* population (peak standard of living) will be reached prior to the *maximum* population. In the short run, perhaps population growth (including immigration of the indigent and dependent) should be discouraged should it threaten to *exceed* the optimum level. Is this a lesson for immigration policy?

The **Ecologist view is static.** For the **ecologist,** most nonhuman resources are limited and nonrenewable. There is only so much land, water, oil and minerals...that's it. Ecology generally does not deal with how people would respond to the hardship of dwindling resources. The economist' view is more dynamic, more optimistic. It accounts for human capacity to adapt to change. **For economists, the Malthusian peak (and optimum population level) can be maintained as long as productive capabilities expand along with or faster than population growth. The history of the last three centuries proves this argument!**

Economists' perspective. Yes, there is a scarcity of goods at any moment. But, in a broad sense, **there are no nonrenewable resources!** Experience tells us that resources – even land -- are not fixed in the long run. They are made variable by human imagination and inventiveness. Those in this optimist school, mostly economists, believe human ingenuity, creativity and inventiveness are boundless **as long as market incentives are in place!** We use up one resource, we find another. Any resource we exhaust, we can replace. That seems to be the historical pattern, as production tries to catch up to want.

The Dismal Science and the Economic Problem. This production deficiency is known as *the economic problem*, namely, we can't have everything we want and likely never will! Day one in Eco 101: at the moment total **human wants exceed output capabilities. Unsatisfied want (scarcity) is ubiquitous.** Output comes up short even when the economy is operating at top efficiency and full employment. So, even when production is maxed out, even at our best, we are not satisfied. Most folks still want more goods than they are getting. **Even at**

our best, there is unserved want, resulting in hardship and deprivation. Such is the economic problem, the origin of labeling economics **the dismal science.**

But, perhaps ecology is the dismal science and economics the optimistic one!

From Economic Problem to Population Crisis

The economic *problem* is not a new idea. The idea of an economic *crisis* magnifies the economic *problem* and grabs the headline. The crisis variation is not new either. "We stand on the edge of doom!"

Modern Malthusians abound. They contend overpopulation leads to resource exhaustion (from overuse and misuse). The assertion of an exhaustible environment is thrown in, as well. Food production will not keep pace with population growth. Today, energy, clean air and water are added to the doomsday list. Essentially, this is a rehash of original Malthusian, jacked up a few notches. Doomsayers seem to pop up in every generation. For these doomsayers, the end is nearing. Malthus preached a similar gospel hundreds of years ago.

We not only have a problem, modern doomsayers cry, we have a **crisis** that threatens to destroy civilization and perhaps humankind along with it! Yet, the world has prospered since his warning of the cataclysm of population growth outstripping the expansion in food output. Why were Malthus and his cohorts wrong?

Scarce Resources and Know-how

Let us examine the roots of these predictions. A resource is anything useful in producing a good. Land, labor, real capital and entrepreneurial ability are the usual suspects on the resource list. Entrepreneurs, using their technical know-how, apply labor to land and capital in order to produce. The scarcity of goods derives from the scarcity of resources and a lack of knowledge of better ways to use those resources (inadequate technology).

Human Ingenuity, the Profit Motive and the Free Market

Breaking the finite resource "sound barrier." So, having resources and knowing how to use them – know-how or technology – makes production possible. Unfortunately, resources are scarce. Technical know-how is limited but capable of advancing. So, the means of creating goods are scarce. All of those statements are true, *at any moment.* But, experience shows that those limitations and potentialities can be expanded over time, even those thought to be finite! De-fusing this apocalyptic time bomb requires a slowdown or a halt in population growth and/or an expansion in production capabilities The former has not happened world-wide. **Technology gives birth to new resources which were previously unrecognized. So, the main engine of change has been the profit based surge in production capability based on technological advance.**

The Cavalry to the Rescue

Natural resources are not, "here today, gone tomorrow." They gradually decline, causing the market price to rise. Like a beacon piercing the night, the rising price signals buyers and sellers of a widening (supply induced) shortage. This 1) prompts profit minded firms to economize on the resource (seek cheaper production methods) and search for (existing and new) substitute resources. 2) On their end, buyers use less while seeking cheaper substitutes.

Thus, **the free market price mechanism helps the economy avoid the shock of sudden exhaustion of a resource.** It smoothes the transition from old resource to new, as whale oil transitioned to kerosene. **Any effort by the government to limit the use of the declining resource will only short-circuit the market mechanism and delay the transition to newly found substitutes. It would be like pulling a tooth slowly. (Ouch!)**

The working of the free market private enterprise/private property system has repelled the forces of apocalypse for hundreds of years since Malthus sounded his warning.

Want to squeeze the most out of a resource? Privatize it. Give someone a reason to economize on it, to use it, perpetuate it but not abuse it. The persistent search for lower cost/higher profit production methods led to improved technologies that enable more goods to be gotten from the same resources. (For example, see the Green Revolution discussed below). For the most part, *creative destruction* of industries has improved production and efficiency for the U.S. **But, creative destruction in the globalist era seems to assign most of the destruction to the U.S. while the creation goes off-shore. Whale of a tale: saved by the profit motive!** When a resource starts running low or running out, its price is free to rise. The price rise signals profit motivated, free firms to search for new resources and users to cut back.

Creative destruction. Firms are encouraged to substitute newly found resources for dwindling supplies of older resources. **Advances in technology enable production facilities to be better, faster, smaller, denser, stronger and best of all, cheaper, thereby economizing on resources.**

The gradually rising price of an increasing scarce resource signals the firm to search for substitutes, lest its profit decline. The rising price of whale oil in the 1800s encouraged firms to substitute the cheaper kerosene coming onto the market. If the price of whale oil did *not* rise and users did react by buying less, would the whale have been hunted to extinction? An argument against quotas! (More *creative destruction* coming up in later chapters). This response from the free market has sparked economic growth and kept the hungry wolf from the door.

➢   Was the system perfect for all participants? No, of course not.

➢   Perfection is not to be found on this earth.

4.   No doubt the need to replenish increasing scarce local resources led to exploration and the spread of humankind throughout the world. The settlement of the New World was spurred by growing overuse of European lands for farming and grazing animals. A surplus labor force *relative* to other resources (mainly, land) was also a factor in encouraging European emigration.

2. FALLACIOUS ECONOMICUS: Consumer sovereignty is absolute: firms are so greedy they will supply *any good* someone is willing and able to buy.

Correct Reasoning: True, consumers signal producers by buying or not buying goods in the marketplace. Naturally, firms pay attention to this behavior. In the *Wealth of Nations* (1776), Adam Smith called this process **consumer sovereignty: firms obey their paying customers.** So, the paying customers are king. They ultimately decide what the producers make. But, consumer sovereignty is not absolute. There are limits to what a free market will "deliver." Firms have other opportunities, other profitable uses – their opportunity cost – for their resources. **To be served, the goods consumers seek to buy must be *more* profitable than other goods the firm could produce.** Those goods which are *most* profitable get made. Red umbrellas, when more profitable than green, are the ones that get made. Next year, fashions could be reversed and the green ones are made. This leaves out many wanted goods that *could* be made but are not profitable enough to be made.

Creative destruction, redux. Human ingenuity is not finite, say the economists. They point to the power of the market and a process called **creative destruction.** In creative destruction a new industry cluster is born from invention and innovation. The new industry provides a new product or a new way of performing an old function. That new industry may destroy an old one. Cars replaced horses, refrigerators replaced ice harvesting and deliveries, trains replaced stagecoaches, kerosene lamps replaced whale oil, **electricity** and the light bulb replaced kerosene lamps. Consider three major advances in technology:

1. Kerosene from petroleum. In 1849, Dr. Abraham Gesner, a Canadian geologist, devised a **new technology** where kerosene could be distilled from petroleum. Gesner's kerosene was cheap, easy to produce, could be burned in existing lamps, and did not produce an offensive odor as did most whale oil. It could be stored indefinitely, unlike whale oil, which would eventually spoil. And so the American petroleum boom began in the 1850s. By the end of the decade there were 30 kerosene plants operating in the United States. The cheaper, more efficient fuel began to drive whale oil out of the market.

[1. "Lighting" 6 May 2014, *Wikipedia* <http://en.wikipedia.org/wiki/Lighting>]

And so the whales were saved from the extinction suffered by the passenger pigeon and American Bison. What saved them? Goodwill? A Save the Whale Movement? No. One might argue that the pursuit of self-interest on the part of consumers and producers saved the whale. Saving the whales was a side effect of their profit pursuit, not their intention.

2. The Green Revolution: New technology on the farm. Agricultural production got a tremendous boost from the spurt of invention and innovation led by Norman Borlaug, the "Father of the Green Revolution." Borlaug is credited with saving over a billion people from starvation, involved the development of high-yielding varieties of cereal grains, expansion of irrigation infrastructure, modernization of management techniques, distribution of hybridized seeds, synthetic fertilizers, and pesticides to farmers. [2]

[2. Green Revolution 6 May 2014 *Wikipedia.*
<http://en.wikipedia.org/wiki/Green_Revolution>]

3. Fracking is a controversial **new technology** for drilling and extracting rock encased oil deposits. Fracking is expanding the stock of known oil and gas reserves in the United States. Yes, there are hazards with fracking. But, the technology is relatively young and adjustments are expected to minimize harmful side effects. Fracking can possibly free the U.S. – and the world – from dependence on OPEC oil extortionists. Indeed, the U.S. can soon start exporting natural gas. Gasoline exports are emerging after a forty year hiatus.

If one goes further back in history one might cite other inventions and innovations such as the domestication of farm animals, harnessing the power of fire, rivers, steam and the cultivation of crops. According to Greek mythology, Prometheus gave fire to the humans and he was punished for an eternity for it. The invention of the wheel added to the production capability of early man. Ancient peoples used crude tools to make crude tools!

As the human brain grew, humans developed greater capacity for reasoning. Tools improved, enhancing the availability of nourishment and other goods.

This aided human physical development, aiding reasoning and so on, in a virtuous circle.

Legislating Fuel Economy

The **Corporate Average Fuel Economy** (Café standards) are regulations in the United States, first enacted by the U.S. Congress in 1975, in the wake of the Arab Oil Embargo. They were intended to improve the average fuel economy of cars and light trucks (trucks, vans and sport utility vehicles) sold in the United States.

[4. "Corporate Average Fuel Economy" *Wikipedia* 17 July 2014
<http://en.wikipedia.org/wiki/Corporate_Average_Fuel_Economy>]

3. FALLACIOUS ECONOMICUS: Raising automobile fuel economy requirements will cut gasoline usage.

Correct Reasoning: It depends. There is no guarantee gas usage will be cut. Gasoline usage may even expand!

No doubt, if the price per gallon of gasoline is constant, raising miles traveled per gallon reduces the cost of traveling each mile.

Initially, assume the driver wants to travel 100 miles.

> ➤ A $10 tank fill up may yield 100 miles of travel *before* the fuel economy improvement. Each mile costs 10 cents.

> ➤ A $10 tank fill up may yield 125 miles of travel *after* the fuel economy improvement. Each mile costs 8 cents.

No question, after the fuel economy improvement, the *gas cost per mile* drops from 10 cents to 8 cents.

Now here is the line of reasoning leading to *greater* gas usage:

> ➤ Basic demand theory predicts that, other things unchanged, *a lower price spurs extra buying.*

> ➤ The price per mile of travel has fallen, predicting an increase in demand for additional *travel miles*. But, will that translate into greater demand for *gas*? It depends on how many additional travel miles are demanded.

Consider: how many additional travel miles will be demanded?

     a. no extra miles?

     b. less than 25 extra miles?

     c. 25 extra miles?

     d. more than 25 miles?

Outcomes:

I. If drivers choose *a, b,* or *c* there will be no additional gas usage and the standards will have succeeded in lowering gas usage.

II. On the other hand, if that increase in demand is *d*, more than 25 miles, then the driver will use *more* gas than before.

In case II. the legislated higher fuel economy standards resulted in more gas used, not less.

Another consideration is the entry of new drivers, attracted by the lower cost per mile. If new drivers enter, attracted by the lower cost per mile, their miles must be added to each alternative. Their new participation could push overall usage into the *more than 25* miles column.

So, there is no guarantee that higher fuel economy standards will save fuel. There is even the possibility this fuel conservation act may prompt fuel use to expand!

4. FALLA<IOUS <<ONOMI<US: Climate change is worldwide and manmade. Therefore, it could be efficiently dealt with by one worldwide government.

Correct Reasoning: The Globalists are a clever bunch. But, manmade climate change is a debatable issue, despite Globalist chants to the contrary! Nevertheless, Globalists see it as an opportunity to push for their final goal: one global government overriding the sovereignty of nations. With one world government all manmade barriers to trade could be minimized or eliminated. Of course, this clears the path to greater profits as the big corporate "fish" deploy their economies of scale to gobble up the small "fish."

Climate Strange

One of the world's leading meteorologists is a global warming – er, excuse me, climate change – denier. John Coleman, who co-founded the Weather Channel, insists the theory of man-made climate change is no longer scientifically credible. In an open letter attacking the Intergovernmental Panel on Climate Change, he wrote: "The ocean is not rising significantly. The polar ice is increasing, not melting away. Polar Bears are increasing in number. Heat waves have actually diminished, not increased. There is not an uptick in the number or strength of storms (in fact storms are diminishing)." The assertion of global warming or climate change persists nevertheless. It is the favorite scare tactic of Globalists who advocate a global solution. That may be true, but **could global cooperation be accomplished by treaty among sovereign nations and not require one overarching world government?**

[5. Jason Taylor, "Climate change PROVED to be 'nothing but a lie', claims top meteorologist," *The Express* 9 June 2015 <http://tinyurl.com/m2cfsbw>]

Perhaps one global government would be more efficient at dealing with the problem and others, as well. But, operating efficiently, i.e., using the least amount of resources in achieving some objective, is not the highest virtue in economic lore. Global government would require the surrendering of national sovereignty, self-rule and perhaps the nation's way of life.   In reality, **the constitution would be subservient to international treaty.** (Globalists would be smart to leave Americans the *illusion* of self governance under the U.S. Constitution and Bill of Rights.)

The dominance of big firms is likely to accentuate the unequal distribution of income between and within countries.

Those costs would be too high a price to pay to deal with a problem which may not even exist!

Freeman Dyson's Position

Highly respected American physicist Freeman Dyson has criticized climate change models as too simplistic and conceptually flawed.

> In a nutshell, he [Dyson] thinks the computer-generated models being used to predict long-term climate consequences are flawed because scientists have too little information about many of the variables that must be taken into account.

[6. "There is no Scientific Consensus on Global Warming," 24 April 2015 *NoConcensus.Org* ‹http://noconsensus.org/scientists/freeman_dyson.php›]

Question: Why do so many scientists subscribe to so-called climate change?

Answer: They may all be referencing the same deficient studies, i.e., drinking from the same contaminated well.

"My choice early in life was either to be a piano player in a whorehouse or a politician. And to tell the truth, there's hardly any difference."
Harry Truman

Chapter Nine
Fallacy of Composition

Don't lose the forest ... for the trees

W E frequently change the scale of an activity and assume an unchanged outcome. Errors in reasoning pop up here because sometimes changing scale impacts the outcome and sometimes it doesn't. **The Fallacy of Composition and the Fallacy of Division deal with the outcome of changing the scale of an activity.** The fallacy of composition is committed when one *wrongly assumes* the combining of many similar, small actions - or the simultaneity of those actions - will not change the outcome. So, when one mistakenly assumes the outcome does *not* change - when, in fact, it does - one commits the fallacy of composition.

1. FALLA<IOU∫ E<ONOMI<U∫: I see no reason why a small scale action cannot be duplicated on a large scale with the same results.

Fallacious Reasoning: Large scale is just a bunch of small scale episodes added up. The fact that there are many does not change the result. So, in a bag of oranges each orange retains the same identity as when each was considered on its own, outside the bag, right? An individual match creates a small flame and a book of matches would create a large flame as the match book is ignited.

Correct Reasoning: It gets tricky when starting from a small scale and then projecting the same activity on a large scale. *Some small scale actions will have the same result when tried on a large scale ... but, some small scale actions will not.* One cannot generalize. Instead, one must study the process involved to determine if expanding the scale changes the nature of the outcome. Sometimes enlarging the scale changes the outcome ... and sometimes it doesn't. One must analyze each case to see what works and what doesn't on a large scale.

But, beware: enlarging the scale of an action or event and getting a different result goes against common sense. It is like putting an orange into a bag and it morphs into something else when combined with many other oranges. Yes, it goes against common sense. But, yet, that is what can happen! That is why the fallacy tricks many a thinking person.

For hundreds of years most economists succumbed to the fallacy with respect to **money and the economy**. After years of study and fallacious analysis, a few economists realized that some actions have one result on small scale (or in one market) and a different result when tried on a large scale (in many markets operating across the whole economy.)

Example 1. The group, saving as would an individual, cannot get the same result. This is the paradox of thrift, in a closed group: if *group* spending drops in order to increase savings, so does *group* income, which reduces the ability to save the amount originally planned. A few workers can plan and succeed in saving more of their salaries each week without threatening the size of those salaries. But, if *all* workers planned to save more and started to do so, their salaries will likely fall after a time, preventing them from realizing those savings. Remember, **in the macro universe, the "big" economy, what goes around comes around**.

In the macro universe *spenders create their own incomes* in a feedback loop pattern. What goes around (spending) comes around (as income). Intended higher savings are not realized when the great bulk of savers act simultaneously. Hence, the paradox of despite *trying* to save more, the plan cannot be realized.

Example 2. Everybody gets educated as cure for poverty. Get an education, a college degree or higher, and you will end up in a higher income bracket. Empirical studies prove this. So, this has proven to be correct advice ... as long everyone doesn't do it! If everyone does it then there will be a wage depressing surplus of workers and one would likely earn more as a day laborer.

So, the strategy to get everyone educated, into higher paying jobs and out of poverty is bound to fail. Interestingly, it will be a successful strategy for a small group. Oddly, the success of the few depends on the failure of the many!

The Fallacy of Composition and Immigration

If a few immigrants enhance and enrich a nation, then why not remove any and all barriers to entry to facilitate maximum entry and the receipt of maximum benefits? When a few immigrants are let in they can be screened and checked for diseases, skills, criminal background and likelihood of ending on the public dole. In other words, the country of entry can "fine tune" whoever gains entry.

Is there a world where *two plus two equals minus one?* Yes, one such world is the world of *excess,* and the world of *excess* immigration, in particular. Consider if any and all barriers to entry are removed, the border safeguards are eliminated. Then, anyone can enter without being checked for undesirable background, criminal records, health status and the like.

Do not assume large scale, unchecked helter-skelter immigration will bring the same benefits as small scale monitored immigration. In fact, it will likely be a bad. *The outcome will not be a larger good* than when immigration was small scale. Indeed, at some level of excess immigration it will be a smaller good than when immigration was smaller! This is the world where two plus two equals one, at least in terms of benefits. Or, perhaps even minus one. **An excess of a good thing becomes a bad thing!** *Excess* turns sweet to sour.

A few thousand immigrant workers per month can be absorbed into the labor force with undue downward wage pressure. However, an immigrant army of hundreds of thousands per year cannot be absorbed without competing American wages downward to get jobs.

A few thousand immigrants per month can be absorbed into the society without extra taxes to finance overwhelmed schools, hospitals and other social services.

It is a different outcome if there is an **unassimilated immigrant flood,** legal or illegal, of hundreds of thousands per year, from many different cultures and ethnic groups, speaking many different languages, lacking modern skills, many illiterate in their own language. They absorb public services and bump Americans from jobs. They cannot be absorbed; perhaps they choose not to be absorbed. They do not embrace the nation's common core of values and beliefs. In short, they do not become part of the nation. The nation is threatened with Balkanization. So, the individual or small group can do ... what the large group cannot!

(See Chapter Twelve, p.74 for an in depth discussion of immigration).

Wage Differences

2. FALLACIOUS ECONOMICUS: I am a profit seeking entrepreneur with a large staff of workers. Recently the National Women's Law Center reported that, "American women who work full-time, year-round are paid only 78 cents for every dollar paid to their male counterparts." Great! **I am going to fire all my male employees and hire all females ... Then my profits will soar!**

[1. Equal Pay and the Wage Gap National Women's Law Center 4 October 2014 <http://tinyurl.com/k2znwcd>]

Correct Reasoning: Aside from the legal issues involved, the plan could work if a) only a small number of firms are involved and if b) men and women were perfect substitutes on the job. However, if large numbers of firms are involved, the added demand for women workers may cause this wage gap to narrow and even vanish. The Fallacy of Composition would kick in. Economic theory predicts: demand for male workers falls, creating a demand induced surplus. This drives *down* the wage. As that demand shifts to the female worker market, a demand induced shortage emerges, leading to wage increase. Economic theory suggests the falling and rising wages would meet somewhere in the middle. A small number of firms could execute the movement as planned, with the planned results: lower labor costs. But, if all firms tried that move at the same time, then it is doubtful all firms could lower labor costs.

Background For The Next Fallacy, Fallacy Number #3

The need to avoid committing the fallacy of composition provides the rationale for dividing the field of economics into two subfields: **micro**economic and **macro**economics.

Microeconomics Perspective: The "small" economy

Microeconomics is a modern term applied to the oldest form of systematic economic analysis. Through the centuries thinkers have pondered the questions of what today is called *microeconomics.* The micro lens is comparable to the lens of a microscope. It is the economics of the small unit of analysis, as small as one typical consumer or one producer.

In micro we study price, output, income and employment in individual markets, taken one at a time. We ignore the rest of the economy as we examine this fragment. We might view the market for bread in a small town or gasoline in NYC. These are fragments of the whole economy. We might even look at an entire industry, say, the U.S. market for chicken. We ignore the rest of the economy as we do this.

Macroeconomics Perspective: The "big economy"

What goes around, comes around. In the macro world, everyone, everywhere is viewed at the same time. All the spending done on all products creates all the income received from the sale of those products. What goes around, comes around, in a gigantic loop. **Spending generates income when the whole economy is in play,** in what economists call a **circular flow of income.**

This does not operate on a micro scale. Your spending on bananas does not impact your income. In fact, your spending on all things has no impact on your income. **There is no circular flow of income in microeconomic analysis.**

Micro and macro are alternative lenses through which we view the very same economy! The macroeconomic approach is different from the micro. It employs a wide angle, broad view lens to view the same economy viewed through the narrow lens of microeconomics. The macro lens focuses on the economy *taken as a whole.* "Lose the details," macro says. It is the big screen, not the postage stamp of microeconomics. The macro lens ignores any tiny fragment of the economy. Individual prices, products and markets - the meat and potatoes of microeconomics - are ignored. They lose their independent identities, as when weekly salaries are added to get the annual amount. The weekly numbers, in effect, get lost in the total. So, in macro look only at **grand totals** of output, income and employment. Look at the average price level and ignore individual prices. So, where is the fallacy here? The fallacy awaits just below.

So, as the next fallacy is discussed, keep in mind that micro and macro deal with the *same* economy from *different* perspectives.

3. FALLA<IOUS <<ONOMI<US: There is no need for a macroeconomics if we already have a microeconomics.

Fallacious Reasoning: If we have explained an economic process on a small or micro scale, why wouldn't it work the same way on a large or macro scale? Large scale is just bigger small scale, no? An adult is just a big child, no? In microeconomics we identify the factors that make the price of bread rise. A *general* price rise is the events of the bread market being duplicated in many markets all across the economy, no?

Correct Reasoning: The large scale may or it may not work like a small scale situation. *It depends on the circumstances.* Some small scale results can be duplicated in the same manner on a large scale. Some cannot. Study of the process involved reveals which small situation can be magnified without impacting the outcome. **Economic activity is particularly sensitive to changes in scale.** Care must be taken not to commit the Fallacy of Composition. Again,

the factors that make one price rise are not sufficient to create a general price rise. A general price rise requires additional ingredients not needed on a small scale: more money and/or higher rate of utilization of money.

Two Sets of Rules

It was a hard lesson to learn but it eventually sunk in. **The "big economy" and the "small economy" operate by different rules.** Economists have divided the economic universe into two parts - micro and macro - to avoid committing the fallacy of composition. Each universe has its own set of rules that dominate within. They deal with the same subject matter, differing only in scale, the perspective of the lens. One price could rise or all prices could rise. Different rules apply! Oddly, all markets behaving the same way at the same time (macro perspective) may give a different result from any single market acting alone (micro perspective).

Recap: to assume a small-scale result can be duplicated on a large scale when, in fact, it cannot is to commit the fallacy of composition, an error in reasoning that should be avoided!

Extended Discussion

Somewhere around 1900 some economists began to recognize that Microeconomics was inadequate to analyze economy wide forces and changes. For example, the forces that made the price of tobacco go up were inadequate to explain all prices rising at the same time. The micro approach committed errors in explaining and predicting for the large scale.

The inadequacies of **Micro** were driven home by the Great Depression of the 1930s. Macro emerged in response to the failure of Microeconomics to deal accurately with economy wide moves. Macro emerged mainly in the 20th century on work done by John Maynard Keynes. He emphasized that some small-scale activities (micro) do not have the same result when tried on a large (macro) scale.

Since then micro and macro have become specializations unto themselves. Each branch demands arduous study.

Macro deals with the determination of price, output, income and employment in the economy **TAKEN AS A WHOLE!** The economy, taken in totality: forget the details focus on the big picture! Recession, depression, inflation, deflation and unemployment are grand scale issues and are studied in macro.

4. FALLACIOUS ECONOMICUS: Micro analysis can analyze a macro problem. Macro analysis can be applied to a micro problem.

Correct Reasoning: Just as the plumber has one set of tools to work on large pipes and another set of tools for small pipes, so the economist must one apply set of principles to small scale, isolated actions and another set to economy wide all-at-once activities.

Major Idea: Do not apply micro rules to a macro situation or macro rules to a micro situation. Know the situation you are investigating and apply the appropriate set of rules for analysis.

Plumber's tools are for plumbing problems and electrician's tools are for electrical problems. Similarly, modern economic analysis involves two different sets of analytical tools, one for micro problems and one for macro problems. Correct analysis requires matching a problem with the corresponding tool, e.g., macro analysis for macro issues, and microanalysis for micro issues.

Appendix

Basic Question: Consumer or Corporate Sovereignty?

Freedom of enterprise at work: **Consumer sovereignty.** Consumer sovereignty is a worldview that asserts consumer buying determines *what* is produced. It was expounded by Adam Smith in the **Wealth of Nations**, 1776. The argument went like this: profit seeking firms must cater to their customers' whims and tastes or lose sales. If it is rye bread customers want, then bakers compete to produce and sell them rye bread, not whole wheat. That is the road to greater profit – and greater customer satisfaction.   Indeed, bakers insisting on whole wheat will find themselves out of business. **The consumer is King or Sovereign: firms bow to and serve their paying customers.** In behaving this way, Bakers are serving the public interest, even if it is not their intention. But, that's okay, as it ends well. In pursuing their private, self-interest (profit) firms unintentionally promote the public, i.e., customers, interest and produce rye bread for them.

Excess profits and losses signal firms as to customers' changing desires.

Smith called this free market process the **Invisible Hand of Self-Interest**, profits guiding resources to where they are most in demand. Smith approved of this allocation process compared to government directives or allocation by custom. He argued *consumer guided allocation of resources*, though not without problems, generates the most satisfaction from limited resources.   Those systems do not give priority to the wants or demands of ordinary folks. So, consumer sovereignty is the idea that customer buying ultimately determine **what** is produced. **Customers rule, firms follow.**

Corporate sovereignty – a world view alternative to consumer sovereignty. Here big corporations largely ignore consumer preferences. These corporations decide what is most convenient and profitable for them to produce. Then, repetitive persuasive advertising is used to practically brainwash consumers into demanding these products.

In this world **firms rule, customers follow**. (Think TV images of families in SUVs on their dream vacations). But, in truth, most corporations only wish they had sovereignty over the customer! Life would be much simpler!

Experience shows customer rejections of attempted corporate sovereignty abound. Failed products include: New Coke, the Edsel car, Sony Betamax format, and HD DVD (lost out to Blu-Ray). **Most new products fail, even advertised ones**. Advertising may get you to try a product once but, if it is not to your taste, you do not become a repeat customer. Another path to the assertion of corporate sovereignty is to get government to eliminate competing firms and their products. Legal anti-trust remedies against giant firms should narrow this approach. **Beware, so-called "free trade" agreements**. A more pernicious brand of corporate sovereignty threatens to emerge in international trade agreements. Arcane legal language can be found allowing corporations to assert sovereignty over national laws!

BEWARE THE GREAT CAUSE!

"Every great cause begins as a movement,
degenerates into a business and ends up as a racket."
—Eric Hoffer

Can you name a cause that ended up as a racket? Name two? How about three?

Vincent Van Gogh: Landscape in Stormy Weather Amsterdam,
Van Gogh Museum.

Van Gogh's vision of the Earth under assault from Nature's fury.

Chapter Ten
Fallacy of Division

Don't lose the trees ... for the forest

THE fallacy of division is the opposite twin of the Fallacy of Composition. Recall, the Composition fallacy is committed when *wrongly assuming* the same result when going from small to large scale. The Division fallacy is committed when *wrongly assuming* a large scale activity can be subdivided without disturbing the outcome.

1. FALLACIOUS ECONOMICUS: What works on a large scale also works on a small scale. Why not? If a bath cleans my whole body then washing my hands cleans my hands, no?

FALLACIOUS ECONOMICUS, VARIATION: What is true for the group is true for each member.

Correct Reasoning: Some large scale activities are capable of duplication on a small scale with the same result. Some activities cannot, as causative factors change going from large to small scale. In those cases, reducing the scale changes the outcome. One commits the fallacy when one assumes, incorrectly, the same result on small scale.

Example 1:   **Division of labor.** The division of labor and specialization of labor would greatly magnify the productive potential of a group of people. But, that doesn't mean an individual would create more if he divided his time and switched from job to job, each time concentrating on the one task at hand.

Example 2:   **Interest rates.** Low interest rates are considered good for stimulating the whole economy, but are not good for each member. For the individual, low interest rates reduce income from savings.

Example 3:   **Scale economies**. More *specialized workers* working with more *specialized equipment* create economies of scale. As output expands there are cost savings due to the use of bigger, higher tech equipment, coupled with greater division of labor. Those savings cannot be realized if one tries to construct a smaller scale version of the same machine. (Economists call these impossibility **technological indivisibilities,** a horrible piece of economic jargon!) The savings are lost when one tries to divide the machine and its technology.

Sometimes an observer fails to recognize that a technology is indivisible and attempts a smaller, little brother version. To think one could build a smaller model as efficient as the bigger one would be committing the Fallacy of Division. Giant oil refineries and steel mills cannot be "miniaturized" and still produce each unit at the same low cost. A smaller container ship raises the shipping cost per container. **The technology cannot be divided – downsized or small scaled – without destroying its productivity.** This painful lesson was learned by Mao Zedong in the 1950s as he pushed for backyard steel furnaces and iron works. The scale of "plant" was much too small, holding steel production down relative to large scale steel works. Eventually, he abandoned this hair brained scheme.

[1. See photos of a backyard steel "mill" in "Great Leap Forward" 3 May 2014 *Wikipedia*<http://en.wikipedia.org/wiki/Great_Leap_Forward#Backyard_furnaces>]

Going Deeper: From Micro to Macro?

2. FALLACIOUS ECONOMICUS: Micro events have no macro impact. Each "universe" is sealed off from the other.

Correct Reasoning: Usually this is a safe, valid assumption. But, the micro and macro universes are NOT "sealed off" from each other in reality. They can interface. A micro event can trigger a macro change. Is there a magical portal between the two universes that allows a micro event to invade the macro universe? The answer is YES, but these are rare instances and special circumstances. Usually, the micro and macro worlds do NOT meet. But, some micro markets are so big or so intertwined with other markets throughout the economy that a micro event can impact the macro economy.

Consider the Examples Below

Examples 1: Crude oil is a commodity with such wide usage that a price change in this commodity (a micro event) could impact the level of inflation in the economy as a whole (a macro event).

Example 2: A **change interest rates** (a micro event). Borrowing and spending is a critical business (and consumer) activity throughout the economy. A micro originated changed in interest rates could have an economy wide impact on spending, production and incomes. Indeed, the monetary policy powers are intending to have a macro impact! MONETARY ECONOMICS is a field devoted to studying these interactions.

Example 3: The **foreign exchange market** or the market for a foreign currency is a huge market, but a micro market, nevertheless. It deals with one on one market exchanges of a one nation's currency for another's. If the U.S. dollar depreciates relative to the Euro, then it takes fewer Euros to buy one dollar. U.S. goods look cheaper to Euro holders. This may stimulate the demand for U.S. dollars AND U.S. goods to such an extent that the U.S. macro economy expands.

In fact, a nation sometimes deliberately cheapens its currency, a micro market event, in order to boost exports and cut imports, thereby stimulating the domestic macro economy. (Still Red) China has used this cheap currency policy as a booster to its macro economy development and further penetrates American markets with its exports.

International finance is a field devoted to studying these interactions.

3. FALLACIOUS ECONOMICUS: Crime statistics show that there has been no terrorist infiltration through the open Southern border of the United States. Therefore, it is safe to conclude that John Q. Border Jumper is not a terrorist.

Correct Reasoning: A variation of the Fallacy of Division called the **ecological inference fallacy** is committed above. At stake is the degree of correlation between group traits and traits of selected members of the group. The fallacy is committed when one *incorrectly* assumes that individual members of the group invariably reflect some group trait. For example, professional basketball players have an average height of 6'3." This exceeds the average height for the general population. Fallacious logic asserts the height of a player selected at random is going to exceed the population average. Obviously, not so. Each member of the team has his own identity and characteristics, including height. Consider the following *fallacious* inferences drawn from group characteristics.

➢ All people living in a low income area will show low incomes.

➢ All people living in a high income are will show high incomes.

➢ All people from a terrorist area will be terrorists.

➢ An individual stock may move contrary to an overall stock index. Major indices are the Dow Jones Industrial Average (30 industrial companies), the Standard & Poor's average (500 stocks), or the NASDAQ index (3000+ stocks).[Of course, all stocks in the index cannot simultaneously move contrary to the overall Index.]

Will all people from a non-terrorist area will refrain from terrorism? To assume that only peaceful, hardworking folks come through the open Southern border is to commit the *ecological inference fallacy.* All members of a group will *not* exhibit group characteristics.

Chapter Eleven
Redistribution of Income: Follies & Fallacies

Our moral obligations cannot exceed our abilities. -Kant

Communism wishes to enslave men by force, Socialism by the vote.
It is merely the difference between murder and suicide.   –Ayn Rand

BUCKLE up, this could be a rough ride. Cure poverty by redistributing income from high to low? Sounds like a no-brainer. Reverse American decline by re-distribution of income? Hardly. Bear in mind that *absolute equality* is too radical for the most radical Communist regimes of Cuba and North Korea. The Soviet Union and Red China gave up on the idea. **Serious concern targets the INCREASING INEQUALITY of INCOMES (recurring remuneration) and WEALTH (collection of real and financial assets at a given moment), tilting to the high end.** Consider the Gini index, the most commonly used measure of income inequality. A Gini score of 0 is *perfect equality* (e.g. each person has exactly the same income) and a score of 1 is *perfect inequality* (e.g. one person has all the income).

Studies using longer time series conclude that **income inequality has been constantly increasing since the early 19th century.** Milanovic (2009), for example, calculates Gini indices 3 over time and finds that global income inequality rose steadily from 1820 to 2002, with a significant increase from 1980 onwards.[See Table #1 below] To further inform the more recent trajectory, Cornia (2003) concludes that inequality increased globally between the early 1980s and 1990s following a review of different studies.

Table #1 Estimated Global Gini Indices, 1820-2002

Year	Gini
1820	43.0
1870	56.0
1913	61.0
1950	64.0
1980	65.7
2002	70.7

[1. Isabel Ortiz and Matthew Cummins , "Global Inequality: Beyond the Bottom Billion – A Rapid Review of Income Distribution in 141 Countries" April 2011 *United Nations Children's Fund (UNICEF)*, <http://www.unicef.org/chinese/socialpolicy/files/Global_Inequality.pdf>]

The rise in the Gini values in Table #1 above indicates that more and more income is being **concentrated in the upper income strata.** In other words, **income distribution is becoming more *unequal* across the globe.**

The U.S. has been dedicated to *reducing* but not *eliminating* income inequality through its progressive income tax, as well as its spending and welfare programs. Generous safety net policies have supplemented purchasing power at the low end. However, critics charge they have proven insufficient to correct for the lopsided distribution of income and wealth.

The embrace of Globalism is the main neglected cause of inequality. Imports of cheap goods and labor, off-shoring of production and jobs dominate. Technological advances have played a role, as well. Other nations have been similarly afflicted! Mandatory redistribution of income is a commonly cited and employed alleged remedy for the mal distribution of income. (Voluntary redistribution via charity is another option). But, questions remain. For example:

> ➢ Is redistribution the correct remedy, even when voluntary?
>
> ➢ How could redistribution *damage* the economy?
>
> ➢ Does dividing the "pie" into more equally sized pieces over the years make the pie smaller ?

Background: Like it or not, income *inequality* has been the real world norm for thousands of years! In other words, left alone, the natural result of human activity and rivalry is that some folks "finish the race" ahead of others. Blame it on a variety of forces, but mainly it is due to an *unequal distribution* of the factors that determine the size of income. Some folks are smarter, stronger, faster, faster learners or more brutal than others. At any moment there are differences in household earner education, experience, native intelligence and abilities, health and initiative. Another factor is geographical mobility of workers and jobs. Opportunities to generate wealth have sometimes been blocked, legally and illegally. Theft and conquest dominated before the modern era. In some societies social stratification blocked upward mobility. (Today, qualifications and experience impact only the **demand for labor.** In a free market economy, **actual wages** are also dependent on how many workers compete for jobs, the **supply of labor compared to demand.**)

Conflict of Rights

Mandatory income redistribution makes the rights of the givers to *retain* their income subservient to the rights of the receivers to *take* it.

Redistribution of income is a hot button issue. Redistribution means, in effect, taking income (or wealth) from the richer Peter to give to the poorer Paula. You love it if you are on the receiving end and hate it if you are on the giving end. Private charity is one noncontroversial form of *voluntary* redistribution. **The heated discussion centers on government being the instrument of forced redistribution.** In other words, the government would play the role of Robin Hood, taking from the haves and giving to the have-nots. It seems a noble gesture and the right thing to do ... who doesn't like Robin Hood? Especially if you are on the receiving end! Understandably, most upper income folks do not consider redistribution to be fair to them.

Professor Good-Guy Destroys Incentives to Learn

Professor Good-Guy wants to help his low achievement students score higher grades. He grades the first exam and adds up all the points scored by all the students. From the grand total of points he assigns more points to the low achievers, in effect taking points from the high achievers. He pats himself on the back, convinced he is doing a good thing for society. Then he is startled by the uniformly poor results of the second exam. Both his high achievers *and* low achievers got low grades! Professor Good-Guy was puzzled as to why. What went wrong?

---

1. FALLACIOUS ECONOMICUS: If income distribution is not *equal*, then it is not *fair*. All same size families should have the same income. Any income distribution short of equality is unfair.

Fallacious Reasoning: Fairness goes hand in hand with equality. Equality is as American as apple pie. Fairness requires equality. Equality among people is a cherished goal for American society. Equal pay for equal work, one man, one vote and so on. Equal incomes fit into the desired pattern. Again, fairness requires equality in income distribution.

Correct Reasoning: Inequality is the historical norm. In the absence of forced or voluntary redistribution, incomes and wealth will be distributed unequally. The fallacious reasoning is an attempt to *prove by assertion,* i.e., *to make it so by simply saying it is so.* Assertion is not strong enough to win this argument. Perhaps in the *political* realm fairness requires equality. One man, one vote, that kind of thing. However, with respect to income distribution, **the notion that fairness *requires* equality is, well, simply an opinion.**

The words equitable or equity provide no precise formula for parceling out slices of the pie. Equitable means *fair* or *just,* period. It means doing what is correct from a right or wrong, moral point of view. As such, fairness is a subjective concept. Also, as such, the notion of fairness could differ from person to person. It seems that fairness, like beauty, is in the eyes of the beholder.

> Socialism boils down to this:
> A and B deciding how much
> C must give to D.

Socialism

Should all earnings be taken by government and then redistributed in some "fair" manner, according to the authorities? Would equal shares be fair shares? Most folks would agree it depends how those shares came to be equal. There would be little objection if equality occurred naturally, without outside intervention. Controversy arises when outside intervention and police power (via taxation) *impose* equality by taking from some to give to others. **Should the street vendor and medical doctor get the same income?**

[Hey, here's an idea: stop importing poverty ... and worsening inequality!]

Most thinking observers reject a strict equivalence between equal and equitable. Under certain circumstances, they argue, unequal could also be equitable. Is it fair for an orthopedic surgeon to have the same take-home pay as a delivery boy or the cleaning lady? Indeed, inequality may be a requirement for fairness when one considers the effort expended to earn the income! Perhaps a generous safety net would defuse much redistributionist rhetoric?

Those on the left of the political spectrum have advocated the redistribution of income from high earners to low to improve the average standard of living. This is a complex issue and a full treatment is beyond the scope of this work. But, some questions must be asked about these policies. Do such policies really impact the distribution? Do people lapse into inequality after a time? Do these policies impact sustainable economic growth?

Demand AND Supply Determine the True Wage Level

Occupational wages depend on the {demand for AND supply of} workers in that occupation. **Willingness to work, talent and the capacity to work hard are not enough to guarantee one a sufficient income if there is an excess of competing workers.** The most heralded surgeon's high income would collapse should the town be flooded with other equally respected and skilled surgeons. Yes, higher education is the path to higher income ... as long as everyone does not follow the same path! But, advanced degrees are irrelevant in, say, the auto mechanic's case. In fact, the auto mechanic's income would soar if competing mechanics left town! **Supply AND demand determine the wage!**

2. FALLACIOUS ECONOMICUS: Government mandatory redistribution of income will correct the underlying cause of an increasingly unequal (and therefore unfair) distribution of income.

Fallacious Reasoning: Higher income Peter gives up $1,000 and $1,000 is transferred to lower income Paula. At the moment (or static) analysis suggests no dollar harm is done *in total;* a zero sum game has been played. Minus $1,000 on one side and plus $1,000 on the other yields a sum of zero. No harm is done to the economy *as a whole* and the end distribution of income is less unequal and fairer.

Correct Reasoning: Remember, unequal distribution is the historical norm. Redistribution is a temporary fix. It doesn't get to the root of the problem. **Redistributing income deals with the symptom, not the cause.** It deals with income *after its initial distribution.* It is a fallacious to think that redistributing income at this point corrects the underlying cause of the initial mal distribution. Factors creating the *initial* maldistribution could be targeted, but will never be totally eradicated. Absent an underlying cure, the redistribution will have to be executed every year, following the movie *Groundhog Day.* At worst, the redistribution strategy encourages **avoidance** and **evasive** actions by the upper income taxpayers. Will the taxpayer be available the following year to assume the burden once again? At the very worst, when taken to excess: forced redistribution dampens incentives all around. It **a)** discourages the creation of income by the upper income folks and **b)** discourages effort by low income folks, and c) encourages the masking of taxable income.

A more effective strategy for dealing with a lopsided or highly skewed distribution of income begins with addressing the underlying causes. The causes lie deeper in structural changes buffeting the economy. **One such monumental structural change was the adoption of Globalism by the United States.**

As tax rates rise, high income folks are likely to seek to avoid and evade higher taxes, as depicted in the **Laffer Curve** (see Chapter Twenty-Seven).

On Board the U.S. Titanic

In the midst of a secular decline like the one currently being experienced by the U.S., redistribution of income is akin to re-assigning the cabins on the Titanic. A cabin on an upper deck provides some additional but temporary comfort. But, "Hey, pssssst! fella ..." take a look at your situation: the ship is still going down! Foremost among the causes of mal distribution of income is the "iceberg" of Globalism, embracing off shoring of jobs, open borders for labor and *de facto* unlimited cheap imports. Labor saving technology worsens the situation. Change course while there is still time!

Redistribution of cabins would not have saved the Titanic from sinking. The **redistribution of income will not save the U.S. from continuing its decline**.

3. FALLACIOUS ECONOMICUS: Involuntary redistribution of income from high income earners to low income earners will *not* hamper economic growth.

Correct Reasoning: It is fallacious to think redistribution of income is a viable strategy for sustainable long term economic growth. Again, this may not disturb economic growth, if practiced in moderation. If carried to excess, mandatory redistribution stifles long term, sustainable economic growth by discouraging a. real capital formation and b. work incentives at the giving and receiving ends! (A complete treatment of this complex issue, including a review of the empirical literature, is beyond the scope of this work.) Let us look at **what redistribution will *not* do:**

> ➤ Redistribution will *not* reverse a cyclical decline, i.e., a recession due to business cycle.
> ➤ Redistribution will *not* reverse a secular i.e., long run decline.
> ➤ Redistribution will *not* make up for the damage to real income done by the embrace of Globalization.

Redistribution policies (higher minimum wages, expanded unemployment benefits, expanded food stamp availability, etc.) have extended the Great Recession of the 2009! So says one economist.

[2. See Casey B. Mulligan, *The Redistribution Recession*, New York: Oxford University, 2012]

A policy should strive to equalize income *upwards*, not downwards. Globalism equalizes income *downward*, merely spreading the misery.

Does inequality promote growth? Perhaps! A twenty year study conducted by the Organization for Economic Cooperation and Development (OECD) found greater economic growth highly correlated with *unequal* distribution of income. "From 2011-13, the five most 'unequal' countries in the OECD grew nearly five times faster than the others."

[3. Matthew Schoenfeld "The Mythical Link Between Income Inequality and Slow Growth" 14 Jun 2015" *Wall Street Journal* < http://tinyurl.com/ox34tp9>]

Growth with *reduced* inequality is preferred. See Fallacy 6 below for as possible explanation for this behavior.

Here is a fresh idea: instead of donating their fortunes to alleviate poverty, can't the rich do even more good by bringing back the jobs they've exported?

4. FALLACIOUS ECONOMICUS: Job availability will encourage able bodied people living in poverty to give up public benefits and seek work.

Correct Reasoning: Only certain jobs would be attractive enough to motivate people receiving benefits to look for work. Poverty dwellers will only be attracted to jobs with wages *far in excess* of jobless benefits that will have to be given up. When prospective wages *equal* (perpetual) benefits, why bother working when the same amount can be gotten without work? Why give up $100 per week in benefits for $100 in wages? There would be no *net* benefits. Even if wages were $200, the net gain would only be $100, which you could get by not working at all! Hence, the idea that jobs must have wages *far in excess* of jobless benefits to attract people in poverty.

At the Pizza Parlor

Remember: when a little of something is good, do not assume more of it is better. An excess of a good thing is a bad thing. If an economy could be delivered in a box like a pizza, the box might include this warning: **Beware, giving everyone the same size piece – or even threatening to do so – will reduce the size of future pies.** Paradise based on equal distribution of income exists only in the minds of dreamers and schemers. Practical folk recognize redistribution from high to low punishes achievement and rewards failure, reducing work incentives for all.

"What's a soup kitchen?" - Paris Hilton

---

5. FALLACIOUS ECONOMICUS: Gifting and charity are benign forms of voluntary redistribution. Gifting deserving people does not hurt their moral fiber, will to excel or character.

Correct Reasoning: risk of moral hazard. Gifting deserving people may have a number of undesirable results. It may create the expectation of a future gift stream. It may create an entitlement mentality in the receiver. It may hazard with their morals by demonstrating they get rewards whether they work for them or not. The receiver may become overly dependent on the givers. Continual gifting may sap one's effort and energy to fight adversity. *If one is rewarded, right or wrong, why should one strive to do right, especially when doing right requires more effort?* If so, it is a manifestation of **moral hazard. In** sum, **gifting, taken to excess, could make a moral, physical and intellectual weakling of the receiver.** Consider the case of the frog's leg and the scientist. It seems that the repeating gift can debilitate or cripple the recipient, but the persistent challenge could activate a "fight back" response, ultimately strengthening the recipient. **Do smooth seas and fair winds make poor sailors?**

The Frog's Leg and the Scientist

The story goes like this: a scientist wanted to find out how long it would take for the leg of a frog to degenerate after it was tied down and immobilized on the lab table. The other leg was allowed complete freedom of movement. The scientist expected the bound leg to deteriorate and the free leg to strengthen. When the scientist returned weeks later he got a surprising result. Against his expectation, the leg which had been tied down actually grew much stronger than the free leg.

Does repeated, excessive gifting weaken the receiver?

Does struggle build character and strength?

Question: Affluenza? Could an undeserved, unconditional, repeated gift, made regardless of behavior, destroy a young man's concept of right and wrong? Affluence has been used as a defense/excuse in court for wrongdoing!

6. FALLACIOUS ECONOMICUS: Equal distribution of income will not interfere with real savings and real capital formation.

Correct Reasoning: Upper income people usually save more, a higher fraction of their income, than lower income folks. After all, how many yachts or homes can one own? Income forcibly redistributed to low income spenders is likely not available for savings and investing in capital formation, threatening the size of the economic pie and its growth. Low income folks usually spend all their income ... and more, thanks to the use of credit. (This is called dis-saving).

How capital investment feeds back to improve living standards. Impairment of the stock of real capital hurts economic growth, worker productivity and living standards. Generally, **workers are more productive working with better tools and equipment,** the result of real savings and real investment. Other things unchanged, this makes the workers more valuable to the firm and puts them in a position to demand and get higher wages – assuming the supply of labor is not swamped by new additions. This is how capital investment feeds back to improve living standards.

Thus, redistribution of income from higher to lower income people is likely to reduce real saving, real investment and capital formation below what it would have been otherwise. Worker productivity sags as they are left with obsolete or worn out equipment.

7. FALLACIOUS ECONOMICUS: Upper income people will dutifully keep paying taxes, no matter how high the income tax rates!

Correct Reasoning: The statement seems to be based on wishful thinking rather than solid analysis or empirical study. As tax rates continue to rise, eventually a point comes that is so onerous that most folks try to avoid and evade higher taxes. Could there be a tax revolt? See Prometheus the taxpayer, below:

Prometheus the Taxpayer?

In Greek mythology, Prometheus was a Titan who stole fire from Zeus and gave it to mortals. Zeus then punished him for his crime by having a great eagle eat his liver every day, only to have it grow back to be eaten again the next day. Why didn't Prometheus pack his bag and move to a different mountain? Because he was unable to, bound in chains to a rock. **Unlike Prometheus, high income taxpayers are not bound in chains to a rock or a country.** When the eagle (Uncle Sam and The Internal Revenue Service) shows up and eats his liver (seizes his income via tax) the taxpayer gets the message and changes his circumstances: he hires a fancy tax lawyer and/or moves to a lower tax jurisdiction.

The trouble with socialism is that sooner or later you run out of people with money. — Margaret Thatcher

---

Prometheus could not change his circumstances; he was locked in to this fate. But, the taxpayer doesn't have to stick around against his will, as he is not chained to any rock or any country. Why get hurt when you can avoid it? Similarly, a pedestrian crossing the street dodges that truck barreling down on him. High income taxpayers, when taxed too heavily, seek to evade and avoid further payments.

"A tax so high." Experience shows that as tax rates are hiked, there comes a tax level *so high* that **evasion and avoidance** behavior kick in. Emigration is one form of avoidance. Emigration may be of people or corporations. In **tax inversion** the legal domicile of the corporation is changed to another, lower tax country. This results in less tax revenue, despite the higher rates! [see Chapter Twenty-Seven for a discussion of the Laffer Curve. Ed.]

Unfortunately, that precise high level of tax rates that backfires in the form of lower tax revenues remains unknown. The U.S. experience in the early 1980s showed that as tax rates were *cut,* economic activity was stimulated to the extent that tax revenue rose when a decline had been expected. The budget deficit worsened in spite of more tax revenues because expenditures grew more than the revenues!

In sum, **redistribution of income from high to low, forcible or voluntary, is not a strategy for growing the "pie."** It is a formula for cutting up the pie, not a recipe for creating a larger pie. Indeed, if fashioned poorly, the policy may backfire, actually discouraging incentives to produce and work, thereby "shrinking the pie" for those who follow.

Major Warning: Are they are coming for YOU? What do redistributionists do after they have impoverished the wealthy through over taxation and other transfer schemes? Then they go after the middle class big time and or run up massive deficits financed by monetization of the debt. They might declare a national emergency, seize savings and pension funds, as have a number of foreign nations.

8. FALLACIOUS ECONOMICUS: There is only one way for low income people to get ahead in America. They must be given gifts from Uncle Sam: foods stamps, public housing, free medical care, free college and so on.

Correct Reasoning: There is another way, a transformative way that will, in effect, create people with new attitudes, behaviors and outcomes in life. It is called, "WORK YOUR WAY UP." In order for this path to be followed successfully, one must transform oneself. One must develop the behaviors associated with success: responsibility, good deportment, a courteous and respectful manner. One must be friendly but business-like. A diplomatic carriage, neat personal appearance, and proper speech must be cultivated. The smallest task, at the bottom of the ladder, must be accepted, mastered, and executed with enthusiasm and, dare I say, joy.

Schools used to foster these beneficial behavioral and attitudinal postures. Schools today have been sidetracked into nurturing victimhood and celebrating diversity. One must avoid considering oneself a victim, waiting for restitution from society. Instead, working at improving character/behavior traits eventually changes the person into a better member of the community, shedding the yoke of victimhood and creating upward mobility.

Of course, the success of this *work-your-way-up* plan depends on the existence of good jobs available at the end of the struggle! **Unfortunately, Globalism excel at shrinking U.S. high quality job availability, not expanding it!**

Wrong Path to Achievement? Merely taking low income people and *giving* them the trappings of middle class life is not sufficient to change their behavior/attitude/achievement pattern.

Beware: Formal degrees/professional licenses aid one's advancement. But, they are neither necessary nor sufficient for success in much of the world of commerce. **The kind of person you are ... counts the most.**

9. FALLACIOUS ECONOMICUS: Ditch the whole capitalist system. Get rid of profits, prices, free markets and private property. Let's try a different approach: Communism. The economy should boom and the distribution of income becomes more equitable.

Correct Reasoning: Pooling goods and communal sharing are age-old (suboptimal) solutions to the economic problems of unlimited want, limited capability and an equitable sharing of goods. The modern communal political system is known as Communism. It was once tried in an early American colony!

Quick tour of communism: Communism is the political system. **Authoritarian or command socialism** is the economic system counterpart. Government central planning permeates the whole economy, aimed at *what* and *how* a good is made, *where* it is made and *who* makes it. (Alternatively, a private property, free enterprise system disperses economic power).

Pure Communism. By government command property, resources, and goods are pooled and belong to the community as a whole. **Market determined prices are replaced by commander (government committee) invented prices.** The "commanders" decide how goods/incomes are distributed. There is very little private ownership or freedom to choose the use of resources. Unless allowed by the "elite" self-appointed commanders, one's *productive* contribution plays no role in determining one's share of the output, i.e., income. Producing more doesn't get you more ... and producing less doesn't reduce your share. **Consumer sovereignty is replaced by commander sovereignty.** Unlike a free market economy, producers are not free to respond to consumer preferences. Producers follow government orders.

The Marxist ideal. Ideally, worker and other users of resources work up to their full potential, producing as much as they capable of. Ideally, the command authorities have the knowledge and the wisdom to distribute goods fairly, according to need. **This is the famous Marxian prescription: *from each according to his ability, to each according to his need.*** Produce up to your potential, but take back only what you need. Sounds compassionate and sensible, but in reality was plagued by problems.

The Reality. The reality of Communism falls short of the ideal. Experience and history demonstrate that **folks work hardest when their reward matches the value of their effort.** Working to contribute to a common pool might work for a family, tribe, or village where folks know one another. But, enlarge the group and "working for the common good" proves a poor incentive, especially as a community swells in population and most folks are strangers. Also, not surprisingly, *needs* tend to expand once one discovers that needs are rewarded with goods. Abilities shrink as folks learn they will not be rewarded for producing up to their full potential. Consequently, **authoritarian socialist systems are chronic underachievers due to misallocation of resources and distorted incentives for their use.** Production cannot reach its free market potential. There is more misery than necessary.

Colonial Jamestown: Communism in Colonial America?

The lost goods from Socialist resource misallocation can mean the difference between life and death. Believe it or not, such was the early arrangement in colonial Jamestown in the early 1600s. They tried a form of communism!

> The problem was that all the men who were sent were bonded labourers. They had no stake in what they produced. They were bound by contract to put all they produced into a **common pool** to be used to support their colony as a whole. This was communism in its purest form. Everyone was supposed to work according to ability and take according to need.
>
> [4. Bold mine. Rakesh Wadhwa, "When US tried Communism: History of Jamestown: 1607 to 1611" 24 Jan 2005 *Free Republic*
> <http://www.freerepublic.com/focus/bloggers/2120669/posts>]

The abandonment of Communism, the institution of private property, worker *reward for effort* **and** the help of native American Indians rescued the colony ... and helped found the holiday of Thanksgiving.

Beware, no one is contending market based private enterprise capitalism is perfect. Arguably, it is the least imperfect and most perfectible of all economic systems. In market capitalism there is the good, the bad and the ugly!

Want to reduce poverty? Start by bringing back jobs to Fathers, and Fathers to families, and tender but tough love to child rearing.

Jesus the Socialist?

10. FALLACIOUS ECONOMICUS: Jesus was a Socialist.

Fallacious Reasoning: Jesus preached on behalf of helping the poor. In today's political terms he would be a socialist, no?

Correct Reasoning: Did Jesus believe in redistribution of income from rich to poor? Yes, but, apparently, not in *compulsory* redistribution. In short, Jesus was not an authoritarian socialist ... or a Marxist. His name is often invoked attempting to justify governmental forced redistribution policies. A review of the scriptures reveals that Jesus believed in **voluntary redistribution** from rich to poor, via private charity. That is how a person "scores points" with the Almighty. (Jesus also believed in expanding goods availability when needed. Remember the multiplication of the loaves?)

There are no biblical references of Jesus exhorting the Roman or Judean rulers to forcibly take or tax from the rich and give to the poor, although the Roman state was not averse to giving **free bread (the *anonna*) and circuses** to its' citizens. In Catholic theology the dominant characteristic in evaluating an act of charity is **intention**. **An involuntary, compulsory transfer of income or wealth, without consent and intention by the giver, scores no points in Heaven!**

GLOCIALISM equals Globalism PLUS Socialism

Glocialism is an amalgam of Globalism and Socialism, ultimately concerned with redistribution of income and wealth ... worldwide! On the one hand are the academics, eggheads, **guilt-ridden Utopians** and all around "do-gooders." Include here the Catholic Church, international agencies, Ivy League Universities, the immigration lobby and assorted progressive think tanks such as the Council on Foreign Relations and the Brookings Institution. They seek to *reduce* income and wealth disparities, worldwide. They favor mandatory, government enforced redistribution of income, wealth, *and jobs* from rich to poor nations. They make no secret of their goals. American Presidents since John F. Kennedy have been part of the movement.

Another wing of the movement is occupied by **transnational corporations**, the "trannies." They seek to alter the current distribution of wealth and income by *increasing* worldwide income disparities *in their favor.* Here you have the multi-national corporations and financial institutions that have global reach. "Big Oil" and "Big Pharma" is found here. Here you find (Bill Clinton's) World Trade Organization, China trade, and NAFTA. At times these two groups are working in opposition to one another.

One world government: Wings over the World. A common goal is a unified world government, which would serve the interests of both wings. **World government would make it easier to redistribute income and wealth on a world scale.** But, the trannies would try to covertly control it! A world government and one world money could remove trade barriers between nations and harmonize legal systems, promoting trade and enhancing profits for the "big fish." Beware: resistance is futile. Secretary of State John Kerry advised graduating students at Northeastern to be ready to live in a borderless world!

[5. Tim Brown, *Freedom Post,* 9 May, 2016 <http://freedomoutpost.com/john-kerry-pushes-new-world-order-agenda-to-university-grads-prepare-for-borderless-world/>]

Another issue that serves both causes is open borders and unlimited immigration to the U.S. The U.S. is the big "nut." Crack it and the whole world will follow. **The U.S. is the leading importer in the world ($2.76T 2015) and the number two exporter ($2.26T 2015) on the overall balance of trade account.**

Already well underway are open borders, one way to advance Glocialism. With open borders the needy of the world are brought to the U.S. and given access to its income, wealth, and jobs. This is one form of Glocialism. U.S. Glocialists are using the command mechanisms of taxation, social service subsidies to and affirmative action for immigrants to execute their plan.

American Manufacturing Diaspora. A key tool for worldwide income redistribution is the American manufacturing Diaspora. If you can't bring them in to take the jobs, then **take the jobs to them**. This is the off shoring of production facilities, research and development operations, and their attendant jobs. This is carried out with the blessings of Uncle Sam, committed to Globalism. **The one two punch of open borders and off shoring of manufacturing jobs has decimated the American middle class.**

> If unequal income distribution and the accumulation of wealth come to be generally accepted as *inherently immoral*, then the intellectual groundwork has been laid for making government seizure of wealth and income morally acceptable.   –Theo Dosius

Socialism is A and B telling C how much to give to D.

Taxpayer being mugged ... by government!

Chapter Twelve
Some Immigration and Population Fallacies

I think everyone who wants to enter the U.S. should be allowed in.
–Kirsten Powers, Fox News "Expert" Commentator

Author's note: Nowhere in this work is there a condemnation of immigration *per se*. Nor does the author endorse such a position. Immigration, in general, like population growth, is beneficial to a nation ... up to a point. Population expansion from immigration eventually reaches a critical benchmark, *the optimal population.* Population growth beyond the optimal level degrades the current and projected standard of living (SOL) for the great majority of people. So, *excess* immigration changes the impact of immigration from beneficial to harmful, constructive to destructive.[Please re-read page 40] Income inequality increases and real wages fall. [See Chapter 7]. *Note that the economic literature on optimal population is colorblind.* As with immigration, native population growth may present similar problems of too little or too much growth. However, unlike uncontrollable native population growth, a sovereign nation can choose whatever level of immigration it wants. Then it enjoys (or suffers) the consequences thereof.

RECALL that Glocialism is the merger of Socialism and Globalism. Its goals are the redistribution of wealth and income on a global scale. The large transnational corporations wish to *increase* the inequality in their favor. The Utopians wish to *reduce* world-wide income inequality for the sake of humanity. Each uses the rhetoric of Glocialism to advance its agenda. Transnational corporations get their cheap labor and Utopians get their raised wages for immigrants. As Glocialism takes hold, there is a price: lowered wages and a lower standard of living for native-born American workers and earlier immigrants. **Glocialism is an amalgam of Globalism and Socialism, vigorously pre-occupied with redistribution of income and wealth ... worldwide.** It has made for strange bedfellows.

1. On the one hand are the *left-wing academics,* eggheads, guilt-ridden Utopians, "one worlders," pointy-headed intellectuals and professional do-gooders. They seek to redistribute jobs, income and wealth from rich to poor populations, worldwide.

2. Critics charge Leftist *intellectuals and academics* advocate unlimited immigration. But, *without* traditional assimilation, unlimited immigration is a weapon to de-nationalize America. They assert there is no need to make more traditional Americans.

Indeed, critics seek the destruction of Western Civilization through an educational core promoting diversity, multiculturalism, and denigration of American accomplishment, pride and patriotism. The culture becomes an indigestible stew. Pass the Bromo-Seltzer!

3. Critics charge that Left wing *politicians* advocate immigration because they want to import dependent populations in need of government services and goodies. In return, grateful legal and illegal immigrants will vote for them.

4. Transnational businesses lobby for *excessive* immigration and more work VISAS. An unhindered inflow of labor keeps wages down in the U.S. and enhances profits. Also, firms hopscotch the world, in a **"Race to the Bottom,"** for the lowest wage country to locate production.

1. FALLACIOUS ECONOMICUS: There are no illegal aliens, only undocumented workers or immigrants.

Correct Reasoning: Immigration is a privilege, not a right. There is no "Universal Human Right to Immigrate to the U.S." When a foreign national is in the U.S. *without* proper authorization, i.e., either by 1) receiving either temporary (non-immigrant) admission or 2) permanent (immigrant) admission, then that person is in the nation *illegally.* Since that person was foreign born that person is an *alien.* Combining the two concepts yields the term *illegal alien.* Estimates of illegal aliens in the United States range from twelve to twenty million people. Of course, *illegal alien* is not descriptive of the person *as a person.* It is descriptive of the legality of one's presence in a foreign nation. The Department of Homeland Security [DHS] sugarcoats the alien status by referring to them as undocumented immigrants, a less threatening but also less informative term. **Remember: every illegal alien has broken U.S. law at the border.**

Read the convoluted description from Homeland Insecurity [sic] :

> Permanent residents are also commonly referred to as immigrants; however, the Immigration and Nationality Act (INA) broadly defines an immigrant as any alien in the United States, except one legally admitted under specific nonimmigrant categories (INA section 101(a)(15)). An illegal alien who entered the United States without inspection, for example, would be strictly defined as an immigrant under the INA but is not a permanent resident alien.
>
> [1. "Definition of Terms" 21 August 2014 *Department of Homeland Security* <http://www.dhs.gov/definition-terms>]

True immigrants seek permanent residence and membership in the family of the new nation. They want to join the stream of history associated with their new nation

How does DHS divine that *all* illegal entrants seek permanent residence, thereby justifying the label illegal immigrants? Does it have psychics working the border areas? Even more presumptuous is the label *undocumented worker.*

If one enters the nation without legal permission or sanction, one is illegal, no? One has broken the law of that nation, no? To label them undocumented is imprecise. It begs the question, which documents do they lack? A bus pass? A library card? Perhaps a Rotary Club ID? Also, to characterize all of them as "workers" presumes they came to seek jobs. In short, characterizing illegal entrants as undocumented workers is misleading, inaccurate and an attempt to mask the complex of reasons for their arrival.

Oh, but when stopped and questioned at the border *they say* they are coming here to work. Oh, I see. But, are their responses truthful, considering what is at stake? What do you expect them to say? Are the following statements likely to be heard at the border crossing?

> ➢ "I am coming to steal a job from an American."
> ➢ "I am coming to get a free operation."
> ➢ "I am smuggling drugs in."
> ➢ "I want my baby born in America and automatically become a citizen." (The annual number of so-called *anchor babies* is nearing 400,000!)
> ➢ "I am coming as part of a terrorist jihad."

Many illegals are well coached, no doubt. To call them undocumented workers smacks of thought control through language as elaborated in George Orwell's *1984*. It is a corruption of language endemic to political correctness.

2. FALLACIOUS ECONOMICUS: Well, we owe a favor to Mexico. After all, they are our ally. So, we'll absorb some of its surplus population.

Correct Reasoning: Undeniably, Mexico is our neighbor, and its population is larger than optimal. But. it certainly is not our ally. Mexico has never fought side by side in any war the U.S. has fought, including World War II. In fact, they were invited to ally with Germany before World War I. *Friend* would also be a questionable descriptor. *Economic parasite and sometime partner* is a more accurate term. But, our ally?

3. FALLACIOUS ECONOMICUS: The NAFTA trade agreement between the U.S., Mexico and Canada had nothing to do with the flood of good and bad illegals coming across the Southern border.

Correct Reasoning: NAFTA bears some of the responsibility. NAFTA did create unemployment in the Mexican **small farm** sector. NAFTA enabled larger, more efficient and subsidized U.S. farmers to undercut Mexican prices. Small, family size Mexican farms, unable to compete, were driven out of business. So, did NAFTA inspire a surplus agricultural labor force in Mexico, one eager to cross the border into the U.S. in search of jobs? Researchers say: YES!

> NAFTA removed Mexican tariffs (but not subsidies) on agricultural goods, with a transition period in which there was a steadily increasing import quota for certain commodities from the U.S. The transition period was longest for corn, the most important crop for Mexican producers, only ending in 2008. Critics charge subsidies went to border manufacturing, not farming.

> Not surprisingly, U.S. production, which is not only subsidized but had higher average productivity levels than that of Mexico, *displaced millions of Mexican farmers....*

> The job loss was in family labor, employed in the family farm sector.

> Between 1991 and 2007, there was a 19 percent drop in agricultural employment, or about 2 million jobs.

> According to Mexican national statistics, Mexico's poverty rate of 52.3 percent in 2012 is almost identical to the poverty rate of 1994. As a result, given population growth, there were 14.3 million more Mexicans living below the poverty line as of 2012 (the latest data available) than in 1994. This, after twenty years of NAFTA!

[2. Mark Weisbrot, Stephan Lefebvre, and Joseph Sammut, "Did NAFTA Help Mexico? An Assessment After 20 Years" February 2014 *Center for Economic and Policy Research* >http://tinyurl.com/ubvb5gw >]

The impact on agricultural unemployment was similar to the impact on England of the Enclosure Acts (circa 1720-1840), which threw many peasant farmers off the land. Arguably, those Acts, in effect, led to the creation of a factory workforce for the emerging Industrial Revolution in Britain.

The magnet for immigrants to the U.S. One must be realistic in evaluating new arrivals. The group includes job seekers eager to take advantage of the **huge** *relative* **wage and relative** *benefits* **gap** between the U.S. and third world economies. Workers' annual **wage remittances** back home to Mexico regularly exceed $20 billion, accounting for over 2% of Mexican GDP.

Unfortunately, in addition, aside from job and benefits seekers, arrivals likely include some drug cartel members, re-conquerors, disease carriers, illiterates and maybe even a terrorist or two. Because of the group's relative size (millions of people each year) and the U.S. obsession with preserving and expanding diversity once inside the U.S. - **this movement is** *de facto* **more like colonization than immigration.**

Colonization via open borders threatens the common core of the nation. It also threatens the U.S. economy and, by extension, national security.

4. FALLACIOUS ECONOMICUS: Indigent immigrants are a burden to society.

Correct Reasoning: It depends on the number of entrants. Encouraging, welcoming and social servicing indigent immigrants, legal or illegal, is a manifestation of *Glocialism*, the U.S. economic policy advocating the *international* redistribution of income. Beware that not all of the newly arrived are potential workers and taxpayers. Some are too old to work. Others are too ill, some are too young. Yes, some are criminal types or terrorists. The country of emigration is relieved of the burden of social servicing those people, i.e., providing medical care, schooling, clothing, housing and food. The financial and real cost burden is shifted onto the people of the country of immigration, the U.S.A. How much of a burden is there? It depends.

Phase I

Servicing the new arrivals may not involve significant incremental costs *if the alien numbers are relatively small*. For example, hospitals and schools may have excess capacity and be able to accommodate a small number of new people at minimal additional cost.

The same reasoning may be applied to immigrant labor's impact on wage levels and job availability. A growing economy usually involves a growing number of jobs. Some of those jobs may be filled by immigrant workers *without* having a depressing effect on the overall real wage level.

Phase II: Quantity changes quality

Phase I is over. We have entered Phase II. Problems arise with sluggish economic growth and an absence of idle capacity. Job growth slows with slow growth in the economy. Social servicing a large cohort of new arrivals may impose significant incremental costs (real and financial) on the nation of immigration. Hospitals, schools, prisons and other social services are being overwhelmed in the Southwestern United States. In addition, providing services to illegals rewards law breakers and shortchanges Americans.

When immigration is moderate, immigrant workers can be absorbed without significant harm. The U.S. average real wage and standard of living rose from 1945-1975, a period of relatively modest immigration, around 600,000 per year.

Again, failure of new arrivals to assimilate threatens the nation's common core, leading to the nation's fragmentation. Swamping low wage workers with foreign competition makes a bad situation worse.

In sum, immigration is a good policy and has a net positive impact *as long as immigration is not excessive.*

5. FALLACIOUS ECONOMICUS: I need cheap labor, even illegal immigrants, to work for me or I will go out of business. Americans won't do these low paying, distasteful jobs.

Correct Reasoning: Employer Strategy, Whine and Wait. This is typical whining from profit grubbing firms. They hope Uncle Sam will deliver cheap labor to them by widening immigration quotas, expanding VISAs and ignoring illegals. And, like it or not, it has been a successful strategy.

1. The U.S. already has the largest immigration quota of any nation in the world, approximately one million people per year. Mexico has the largest national quota. Special visas add tens of thousands to that number. Visa over-stayers constitute a large but unknown proportion of illegal immigration. The lifeboat is becoming overloaded!

2. There are dirty, dangerous and distasteful jobs for which there is *no shortage* of eager native worker job applicants ... as long as they pay decent, American standard wages! Firefighter, police officer, sanitation workers, bridge builder and skyscraper window cleaner are occupations that come to mind.

3. Read "The Grapes of Wrath," by John Steinbeck, and learn who did those agricultural jobs before the arrival of new immigrants.

4. Forget dirty and distasteful. Legal and illegal immigrants have entered many semi-skilled and skilled occupations *not* considered distasteful and dirty. Many are in the construction trades. Consider, are these distasteful and dirty: carpentry, plumbing, landscaping, house painting, cooking, waiting and bussing tables, auto mechanic, building porter, truck driving, delivery van worker and handy man? These are fast becoming the occupations of immigrant workers.

But, are their incomes self-sustaining, given their remissions to the home countries? Many of these workers put added pressure on government services for themselves and their families.

Come on, Mr. Fallacy, stop whining ... pay a decent wage and you will attract plenty of native born workers to baby sit, mow your lawn, drive your truck, do day labor, cook in your restaurant, "bus" tables and clean your hotel rooms.

Excess Immigration, the Weapon

Generally, moderate immigration is a good thing for a nation. Like water and a **sponge,** a nation can absorb a certain amount of new folks without a problem. At some point the sponge is full to capacity and cannot absorb more water. It is the same with a nation. **A flood of diverse peoples from alien cultures can destroy a nation's common core.** Even if the flood is composed entirely of "good," hard working immigrants such an excess could depress working conditions for all in the destination nation. That is, excess could damage the pre-existing and future **standard of living.** Thus, even the "good" immigrants, *in excess,* can harm the pre-existing American standard of living.

Christian Father Tertullian, writing circa 250 A.D. advocated colonization for a few reasons. He and Machiavelli recognized the power of colonization.

> Tertullian used a moral argument about reducing redundant populations caused by lechery who could be sent to the colonies to ease the stresses of overpopulation in the homeland; while, Machiavelli advocated using them to **spearhead an invasion force** directed against the overthrow of the ruler of an existing principality or as a force to maintain power once the ruler had been overthrown.
>
> [4. Whitecrow Borderland, "Nicolo Machiavelli: *The Prince*: On Colonization." 04/10/2001 <http://tinyurl.com/p5jewax>]

---

1. Immigration WITHOUT assimilation threatens Balkanization.
2. Excess immigration WITHOUT assimilation EQUALS colonization.
3. EXCESS immigration under either circumstance may be a Nation Killer.
Colonization is a common weapon of ultimate conquest. To be effective, the colonizers must limit the degree of assimilation with the local population. Colonizers do not give up their culture, i.e., language, literature, holidays, religion, heroes, food, and other cultural practices to embrace that of the occupied territory. They wait for their numbers to swell and then the occupied territory conforms and adapts to them. **The British, Americans, Russians and Spaniards all have used the weapon of colonization to "nail down" a conquest of foreign land.**
Moslems and Mexicans are at it today. The colonizers must remain loyal to their home nation, its native tongue, religion and political leadership. In fairness, all immigration is not colonization. There is a tipping point beyond which benign immigration becomes so excessive that it morphs into colonization. **COLONIZATION IS A NATION KILLER.** Immigration morphed into colonization is a significant weapon used to infect, fragment and destroy the common cohesive core of the target nation. Where successful, it suppresses and overrides the original indigenous, dominant culture. **Once the nation's common core has been destroyed the nation is ready for morphing into a new mother country or a One World Governance scheme.**

6. FALLACIOUS ECONOMICUS: It's those profit hungry *businesses* that hire cheap immigrant labor. The law ought to crack down on them.

Correct Reasoning: It is not only businesses. Every employer on a budget, looking to save a few bucks is a candidate to hire illegals. That includes homeowners, non-profit institutions and even ... get the digitalis ... the Federal government itself! Yes, everybody wants to get into the act and save a buck! In 2007, illegal workers were found working on U.S. military bases! Read all about it:

> Nearly 40 illegal immigrants hired by contractors working on three military bases in Georgia, Virginia and Nevada were arrested over the last three days by U.S. Immigration and Customs Enforcement agents, the agency said Friday.
>
> [5. Associated Press, "Almost 40 Illegal Immigrants Rounded Up at U.S. Military Bases" 19 January 2007 *Fox News* <http://tinyurl.com/qznbtwu>]

Example: Day labor for small construction jobs. Here is a common strategy of employers: The employer does not scrutinize every worker, only the chief, the general contractor. If he checks out as legal, then no matter his subcontracted crew is made up of illegals. The employer looks the other way. If questioned, the employer will claim ignorance and blame the contractor. That is how employers try to shield themselves from liability or culpability.

7. FALLACIOUS ECONOMICUS: Immigrants are a cross-section or typical of the 'back home' population.

Fallacious Reasoning: Why not?

Correct Reasoning: Do not assume if the immigrants are good (or bad) people, they are matched by the folks back home. In general, immigrants are a self-selective sample, a *subgroup* of the country-of-origin population. They are a group of volunteers and volunteers usually are not typical of the parent population. In most countries, no authority designates that some people will emigrate and others will not. The emigrants decide for themselves whether to leave or not, i.e., they select themselves for the journey. (Cuba and North Korea are notable exceptions to this freedom of movement).

Immigrants Not a Cross Section

Legal, as well as illegal immigrants, are *not* a cross section of the parent population. Again, they are a **self-selective sample**, essentially a group of volunteers. The legal cohort is further filtered through a judgment process dictated by immigration law in the destination country. Illegals enjoy no such filtering out of sick, criminal or otherwise undesirable. This screening process rules out some potential immigrants as undesirable. Criminals, the seriously diseased, "dole seekers" and political radicals are good candidates for exclusion. Family reunification works highly in favor of the applicant for entry. Once again, illegals receive little or no screening.

If immigrants were a cross-section the group would include people from all segments of the origin population, a much wider variety of people: old, young, feeble, able minded and able bodied, the sick, women, men, educated and uneducated, rich and poor. An immigrant group rarely has this variety.

Immigrants are usually younger, more aggressive, sturdier, poorer, and healthier than those folks in the parent population. In addition, the immigrants have initiative and, yes, courage to leave their homelands.

However, before we start to award them medals for bravery, understand that immigrants usually follow the "beaten path" of earlier immigrants into foreign enclaves in the new country. Like a home away from home, these foreign enclaves in the U.S. ease the arrival and settlement of the immigrant.

The enclave offers a comfort zone of familiar food and companionship. In addition, one may find newspapers, TV and radio in the immigrant's language. Add social workers, free public services, private charities and professional do-gooders to the list of immigrant helpers and coddlers.

Does Chain Migration Bring the Best and the Brightest?

A tough critic charges: Family reunification - favored by U.S. in granting legal immigration status -- is not about admitting the spouses and children of immigrants we're dying to get. We're bringing in grandparents, second cousins and brothers-in-law of Afgan pushcart operators - who then bring in their grandparents, second cousins and brothers-in-law, until we have entire tribes of people, illiterate in their own language, never mind ours, collecting welfare in America.

[3. Ann Coulter, *Adios, America*, Washington, D.C.: Regnery, 2015, p.15.]

Immigrants Stealing American Jobs? Driving Down Wages? ... I'm Shocked!

8. FALLACIOUS ECONOMICUS: Immigrant labor does not drive down wages in the U.S. nor take away jobs held by native Americans and earlier immigrants.

FALLA<IOUS <<ONOMI<US, VARIATION: Immigrant workers do not steal jobs from Americans by undercutting going wages.

Fallacious Reasoning: In the U.S. there are plenty of jobs for everybody.

Correct Reasoning: Numerous studies have shown immigrant workers – currently at excessive levels – to be guilty on several fronts: bumping Americans from jobs, grinding down U.S. wages and absorbing public services!

First of all, employers usually do not care who they hire as long as it is at the lowest wage. (Secondly, the number of jobs is not fixed. See following fallacy). Indeed, they are eager to employ illegal workers if money is to be saved. At first, hardworking but illegal workers are not concerned about earning standard American wages, whereas American workers are. Consider the "reservation wage" of immigrant labor, the lowest wage they would accept to work. Their "reservation wage" is lower than the Americans. Illegals do not have an American standard of living to try to support, with mortgages, college tuition, car payments, and expensive vacations to meet ... and puppies to feed.

[6. See Elise Gould, "2014 Continues a 35-Year Trend of Broad-Based Wage Stagnation"19 February 2015 *Economic Policy Institute* <http://www.epi.org/publication/stagnant-wages-in-2014/>]

Stagnating Real Wages: the Real Story

1) Wages (and prices) eventually rise due to shortages. **But, how will wages rise if, every time a labor shortage emerges and wages threaten to rise, an alarm sounds in Washington and immigrant workers are dispatched to fill the shortage?** Given this response, *rising wages cannot get any traction.* This is one reason *real* wages have stagnated since the 1980s. They have been torpedoed by immigrant workers.

2) Another *wage depressing force* has been the Trojan horse of cheap imports, galloping into the U.S., escorted (in the 1970s) by an open economy and Globalism. U.S. employers – even patriotic ones – complained that in order to remain competitive with foreign producers they must lower wages in America or off-shore production to a lower wage country.

3) A third reason has been the loss of high paying job openings due to the American manufacturing Diaspora, ushered in by the total embrace of Globalism.

As wages fall *relative* to capital, profit seeking employers are encouraged to substitute labor for capital. For example: why buy an electric dishwasher when the job can be done by three, low paid illegal workers? In Manhattan, sit down restaurants are morphing into food delivery outlets, with small armies of bicycle delivery boys parked outside. – Well, why not, given the availability of low wage food delivery workers?

Studies show low wage jobs are the most impacted by the entry of foreign semi-skilled and unskilled workers.

The Fixed Number of Jobs Fallacy: Do Illegals Create Their Own Jobs?

9. FALLACIOUS ECONOMICUS: The number of job openings is fixed. More immigration means more unemployment.

Correct Reasoning: First of all, the number of job openings is not fixed in a dynamic economy such as the U.S. It changes daily as jobs open up and jobs are terminated. It changes with wages and available workers. The help wanted listings change daily as businesses close and others spring up. [One factor in this dynamic is **the business cycle,** the ebb and flow of general business activity. The number of unfilled jobs varies with stages of the business cycle, falling with recessions and rising with expansions. Creative destruction (birth of new industries and the death of old) also impacts job and occupational demands.]

Firms make substitutions. Immigration is another factor, encouraging firms to alter their mix of labor and capital. Here is the chronology: American employers, on a perpetual search for cheaper labor, petition Washington to open the immigration "floodgates." Washington accommodates these wishes and a flood of legal and illegal immigrants' results. Thus, surpluses develop in various labor markets as immigration and expanded visa programs fuel labor force growth. The surpluses put downward pressure on wages.

After a time, **employers adjust** to the greater availability of lower wage workers, re-organizing production by 1) substituting labor for capital, and 2) substituting lower cost labor for higher cost labor.

New business model emerges taking advantage of the greater availability of cheaper labor. However, note that more jobs are created in this process!

1. *Lower cost labor is substituted for higher cost capital* (machinery and equipment). Consider the example of the restaurant returning an electric dishwasher and hiring three immigrants to do the work. This registers as three additional jobs created solely due to access to lower wage workers.

2. *Lower cost labor is substituted for higher cost labor* (through special visa programs.) This happens as working American are bumped and replaced with lower cost immigrant labor. But, since immigrant labor is cheaper, more workers might be hired than fired. These adjustments by employers result in more jobs than before the immigration surge.

So, immigrants not only bump native workers from jobs, they sometimes lead to the creation of additional jobs. For example: an auto repair shop fires the $300 per week auto mechanic and hires two new arrivals willing to work at

$100 per week as replacements. The added number of workers makes up for the lower *quality* of immigrant labor. The firm created an additional job but still saves $100 per week in salaries. Employment conditions look improved, until you look at the degradation in wages. On the negative side one finds an overall degradation of occupations, real wages, and the quality of the entire labor force. In addition, what of the injustice done to native-American labor ... by their own government? [see also Fallacy #10, below]

[7. Patrick Thibodeau, "H-1B visas produce net IT job boost, trade group says: Compete America argues that Congress's refusal to hike H-1B caps hurts IT job creation," 19 March 2014 *Computerworld* <http://tinyurl.com/pkd2zn4>
See also, Ron Hira, "Outsourcing in America,"16 March 2015 *The Hill* <http://tinyurl.com/mvh4pyz>]

Example: To add insult to injury, some high tech workers have been required to train their lower wage, immigrant replacements!

10. FALLACIOUS ECONOMICUS: Cheap foreign labor, legal and illegal, is bad for American workers, bumping some of them from their jobs. It is bad for American jobs, all around.

Correct Reasoning: Yes, some Americans are bumped and their jobs are taken by newly arrived workers. However, *new* jobs may be created in two ways:

1. **Wages are driven down for all workers** in the industry by a **supply induced labor surplus.** This encourages profit seekers to substitute now cheaper labor for capital *and* higher priced workers. Here is a hypothetical case: A farmer returns a harvesting machine to the vendor. Then, ten migrant farm workers are hired to do the machine's work. That registers as an increase of ten new jobs, ten new workers in the employment stats. In a sense, the surplus workers *created their own jobs by their eagerness and availability.* Had they not been there to work at the lowered wage, those jobs would not have been opened, i.e., created, by the employer.

2. There may be **added demand for inputs that complement the new, lower skilled jobs.** Those ten new workers need different complementary inputs than the machine required: uniforms, hand tools, bushels, housing and such. And they need taxpayer funded public services for themselves and their families: roads, extra hospitals, more schools, additional sanitation, and more police. In this way, **the overall employment level expands but degenerates in job quality and wage level.**

Sanctuary Cities Violate Federal Law

The unmolested employment of illegal aliens betrays a misconceived and unsustainable underground business model perpetuated by tacit collusion between three groups of law breakers: employers, illegal employees and local governments. In the process, real wages and the standard of living of native workers are degraded.

---

11. FALLACIOUS ECONOMICUS: It is comforting to know that law enforcement officials at all levels, including Federal, State and Local, are enforcing immigration laws and apprehending illegal aliens.

Correct Reasoning: Do not get too comfortable. They look the other way if you are in the nation illegally. Many States and cities have declared themselves sanctuary cities. In a sanctuary city, law enforcement deliberately ignores the immigration status of people who brush up against the law for parking violations, apartment disputes, and signing up for school. Perhaps in voting, too. Sanctuary cities are designed to shield illegal aliens from local law enforcement. But, **recall: every illegal alien has broken U.S. law.**

Have sanctuary cities become a modern Hole-in-the-Wall, a refuge from the law for immigrant lawbreakers? But, what if there are some bad guys in the sanctuary group? What if they are not all former altar and choir boys (and girls)? What if they are not all earnest, hard working folks, just looking for work or a hand out?

Haven for Murderer(s)?

Five-time deportee, seven-time convicted felon Juan Francisco Lopez-Sanchez said in a new interview Sunday with a local ABC News affiliate that he came to San Francisco because he knew the sanctuary city would not hand him over to immigration officials. Lopez-Sanchez has confessed to shooting Kathryn Steinle last Wednesday at Pier 14.

[8. Michelle Moons, "Murderer: I Chose SF Because It Is A Sanctuary City" 6 Jul 2015 *Breitbart.com* < http://tinyurl.com/pphzcr5>]

The reason for sanctuary cities is more economic than humanitarian. For example, New York City and San Francisco are sanctuary cities, under the mistaken belief that small businesses, hospitals and the hospitality industry would suffer in the absence of illegal alien workers. How would take-out restaurants deliver a pizza to Upper West Side residents if not for (illegal alien?) delivery boys on bicycles? The same issue applies to San Francisco or Reno,

Nevada where hotels employ huge amounts of (illegal alien?) restaurant workers, room attendants, janitors, Red-Caps, and landscapers.

Employers complain they would be unable to do business without the illegals. Do these employers deserve sympathy from the general public? **No, why cry for a business dependent on illegal workers? The workers and the employers are all lawbreakers. Why support this warped business model?**

Is the security of the city or nation being put at risk so some deli owner or hotel can save a few bucks in wages? Is this smart or stupid? Duh? All the wages saved by New York City employers of illegals would pale in comparison to the damage done by one "sanctuaried" illegal terrorist deploying a weapon of mass destruction.

12. FALLACIOUS ECONOMICUS: A declaration of amnesty will end illegal entry into the United States.

Fallacious Reasoning: None.

Correct Reasoning: Amnesty will accelerate the inflow of illegals aliens.

First of all, amnesty is an undeserved reward to lawbreakers.

Secondly, it is likely to send the signal of free entry, a "green light" at the border, and trigger additional illegal entry!

Third, it disrespects and does injustice to those legal immigrants who have waited for years or are waiting on line, following the rules.

Fourth, amnesty creates *moral hazard* among the illegals that get "something for nothing." Illegals broke U.S. law, committed a wrong ... and were rewarded! Which other laws will they bend and break, on the expectation of a reward?

Fifth, beware *chain migration*. In **chain migration** an immigrant worker later brings in Mom, Dad, Grandma, Grandpa, baby brothers, sisters and on and on. Those latter folks, very old and very young, cannot work. If unsupported by their relative, they simply feed off American generosity.

Sixth, a declaration of amnesty will likely not reduce the wage and social service gaps the between the U.S. and countries of emigration. Those gaps are the magnet drawing people here.

Again, if amnesty is declared *without* control of the borders it will send a signal for more folks to enter ... and who will stop them? Realistically, how can there be verification of who they are and when they arrived? There may be twenty million or more of these folks! That is why closing the border must come first, then talk of amnesty follows.

TRADE AND IMMIGRATION POLICY

Trade and immigration policy are controlled by Congress and the POTUS.

Monetary and Fiscal Policies Unable to Combat Globalism. The stabilization policies (monetary and fiscal policy) generally do not impact the *long run secular trend* of the economy. They act on the underlying economy; they do not determine it. They underlying economy is determined mainly by growth in resource quantity and improvement in quality, incentives for resources utilization, advances in production technology, and an honest and effective legal framework. **Oh, and yes, international trade policy is a major determinant of the long term (or secular growth) trajectory. It can affect the birth and death of entire industries!**

Monetary and fiscal policy cannot undo the damage done by an unwise trade policy such as free trade or Globalism. They cannot correct the harm done by open borders and unlimited immigration to living standards, social services, tax burdens and national security. Tax policy, part of fiscal policy, might help to deter off shoring and even encourage a return of ex-patriot firms. **Instead, tax policy has encouraged the off shoring of production.**

Fundamentally, the cure for relative decline must lie with the removal of the cause: Globalism.

> **Globalism** is a policy advocating the unabashed and unashamed adoption of inbound free trade, open borders and abandonment of trade barriers, *even as other nations remain protectionist*. It has political as well as economic aims.
>
> It has been official policy of the United States for the past forty years.

Whine and Weep ... then Wait

13. FALLACIOUS ECONOMICUS: Legal immigrants, special VISA entrants and illegal aliens are needed to work in occupations where there would otherwise be unfilled jobs openings (worker shortages). How would work get done without the necessary workers?

Correct Reasoning: In many low skill occupations there are worker shortages because wages and benefits are too low and employers are unwilling to raise them. Raising wages would induce more native workers to fill those openings. Instead, employers defer hiking wages. **Employers have another strategy to**

grind down wages and get more workers. It starts with wining and then waiting. It involves immigrant workers and accommodating politicians.

Here is how it works: whining employers run to Washington, complaining of labor shortages. They are hoping for more *willing-to-work-cheaper* immigrant laborers to fill the openings. It is no surprise Washington complies, given its intoxication with Globalism and a less caring attitude toward home-grown American workers. If not through higher legal immigration, then Washington complies with a *look the other way* policy on the borders and visa over-stayers. This approach started with unskilled and semi-skilled labor. Now, it applies up and down the talent scale, especially in information technology and medical occupations. American wages and standard of living are being decimated. So, who cares? Not Uncle Sam.

---

14. FALLA<IOUS <<ONOMI<US: Paying their own way. When illegals are legalized they will "come out of the shadows," go on the books and pay their fair share of taxes. They will not have to be subsidized by other taxpayers for government services they absorb. They will start "carrying their own weight" and relieve the burden on other taxpayers.

Correct Reasoning: According to the government's own Congressional Budget Office, all taxpayers must reach an income in the middle $80,000s before they begin paying their way in taxes, i.e., *carrying their own weight,* paying for government services, Federal, State and local. Up to that income level a taxpayer, legal or illegal, absorbs services and goods worth more than taxes paid!

So, if illegals are legalized but go on the books with incomes *less* than $80,000 or so, they **still eat up a greater value** of government services at all levels than they pay for with taxes. They will still *not* bear the financial burden of the services they receive. They will still have to be subsidized to a degree by other higher income taxpayers. They stop being a burden when their incomes approach $90,000. How likely is that income level would be earned for legalized agricultural workers, domestics, truck drivers, delivery workers, day laborers, landscapers, nannies, grocery clerks, delivery boys and dishwashers?

In effect, taxpayers are subsidizing the employers of illegals!

---

15. FALLA<IOUS <<ONOMI<US: Send all the illegals home and many businesses could not operate and would have to shut down.

Correct Reasoning: What is so sacred about employers who break the law? Who cares if these lawbreakers have to shut down? If those businesses depended on off the books, low wage, tax evading, law breaking workers, then maybe those shady operations *ought to* go out of business. Some businesses have gotten quite comfortable with their supply of *off the books* or "cooked" books cheap labor. Some take unfair competitive advantage using their illegal labor, driving out honest enterprises.

If those employers of illegals wish to operate, let them offer higher, legal wages to legally available native born and legal immigrant workers. Some businesses may not be able to survive operating within the law. Well, then, if they were so dependent on breaking the law to survive, are they socially desirable entities? *Those unable to change their ways should be terminated.*

Border Fence/Wall

16. FALLACIOUS ECONOMICUS: Many anti-immigration folks have recommended the construction of a border fence along the full length of the Mexican-American border. It will not stop illegal entry into the U.S.

Fallacious Reasoning: A border fence would be an expensive failure in keeping out border jumpers on the southern border. Aliens could tunnel under it, ladder over it, cut holes in it and otherwise degrade it. It would be a waste of money. Moreover, it will not stop those who overstay visas and become illegal.

Correct Reasoning: Do not let the *perfect* be the enemy of the *good.* Agreed, the erection of a border fence would not be a *perfect* solution. By "hook or by crook," some illegals will overcome it. (And **visa over-stayers** will not be impacted). Some successful walls: Great Wall of China, Hadrian's Wall in Roman Britain, the Berlin Wall and ... the fence around the White House.

Illegal Aliens Not Paying Their Way

In terms of public policy and government deficits, an important figure is the aggregate annual *deficit* for all unlawful immigrant households. This equals, for all unlawful immigrant households: (total benefits and services received) *minus* (total taxes paid) by those households). Under current law, all unlawful immigrant households, altogether, are **not paying their way**. They enjoy annual benefits in the amount of **$54.5 billion** *in excess of taxes they pay.* An amnesty would perpetuate this burden for an unknown period of time.

[13. Robert Rector and Jason Richwine, "The Fiscal Cost of Unlawful Immigrants and Amnesty to the U.S. Taxpayer," 3 Sept. 2014 *The Heritage Foundation,* <http://tinyurl.com/cka7htx>]

Is Proposed Mexican Border Wall Racist?

A wall at the Mexican border is *not* an expression of racism. It is an expression of frustration over the negative *economic* impact of **illegal** immigration. Consider:

1) Sovereign nations have the right to resist invasions without being labeled racist. Would it have been fair to label Great Britain racist against Germans when it resisted the attempted Nazi invasion of World War II? Did the Brits resist because of race? No, they resisted the behavior. Germans peacefully entered Britain before and after the war.

2) "Mexican" is not a race or single ethnic designation, anymore than American denotes a particular race or ethnic identity. Mexican is a nationality. Mexico is somewhat diverse ethnically. Yes, there is a racial profile. Mexicans are Mestizo (Amerindian-Spanish) 60%, Amerindian or predominantly Amerindian 30%, white 9%, other 1%.

[9. CIA Factbook, "Mexico" *Migration Policy Institute* 1 May 2016
<http://tinyurl.com/jzwbk3m>]

3) "The United States is home to the second-largest Mexican community in the world, second only to Mexico itself, and comprising more than 24% of the entire Mexican-origin population of the world."

[10. "Mexican-Americans" 30 April 2016 *Wikipedia* <http://tinyurl.com/zcl56zd>]

Mexico is fast emptying into the U.S. If racism is so rampant in the U.S., how did nearly 20 million Mexicans sneak in, overcome "racism" and make a life in the U.S.?

[11. "Immigration to the United States" 30 April, 2106 *Wikipedia* <http://tinyurl.com/h7xwf2k>]

4) Mexicans are *favored* - not discriminated against - by U.S. immigration caps and nonimmigrant visas. Mexico has the **largest single national, legal immigration** cap for U.S. entry, nearly 170,000. In addition, in 2015, Mexico was granted nearly 1.5 million nonimmigrant visas to enter the U.S.! That number is second only to China's 2.6 million nonimmigrant visas. Those numbers do not pass the racist "smell" test. BTW: In 2015, total nonimmigrant visas approached 11 million! (Who is monitoring all visa holders?)

[12. <http://tinyurl.com/hwd68pu]

5) The wall is a **passive restraint** for stopping illegal crossers having **undesirable economic profiles – regardless of race or nationality.** Illegal crossers have an entitlement mentality: job seekers, indigent public benefits seekers, drug smugglers, and re-conquerors. In *excess numbers*, they are **a)** threatening the current and future standard of living of American workers and their families, **b)** not paying their way for public services absorbed, thereby **c)** helping to bankrupt American local political districts, **d)** sheltering criminals and possible terrorists in sanctuaries. **In sum, they threaten American *economic* and *national* security.**

6) The southern U.S. border has become the entry point for illegal guns, drugs, runaway criminals, terrorist wannabees and other undesirables from all over the world.

7) The wall will have a monitored "door," allowing **legal passage** between the two countries. Migrants will enter as legal immigrants. Temporary, seasonal workers would enter, work the season, and then return to Mexico. If racism ruled, those entrants would be banned, no?

If the wall were motivated by racism, wouldn't it block ALL Mexicans ALL the time?
Racism does not rule ... Economics rules

Progressives, Prosperity and the Pill

17. FALLACIOUS ECONOMICUS: There is no way to reverse the slow growth and aging of the native U.S. population.

Fallacious Reasoning: There is no way to reverse or halt the shrinking and aging of native populations in the U.S., Western Europe, Russia and Japan.

Correct Reasoning: There may be much truth in this fallacy. These demographic trends may be an uncomfortable truth, leading to expanded immigration quotas in the afflicted countries. However, the *irreversibility* of those trends may be the fallacious element. One observer commented, "Dying nations are usually defined as those with fertility rates of 1.5 or lower. By any measure, 30 European countries are either dying today or like France [are] seeing their cultures and populations transformed by growing ethnic and religious minorities."

[14. Gunnar Heinsohn, "Babies Win Wars," 6 March 2006 *Wall Street Journal Online* <http://tinyurl.com/o8w9jlo>]

Rational Argument for Limiting Immigration

18. FALLACIOUS ECONOMICUS: Immigration (legal and illegal) is so beneficial and diversity is so strengthening that we should just open the borders to all comers. Anyone who wants to come is in!

Correct Reasoning: Less Immigration Now Could Mean More in Long Run!

If the U.S. is overwhelmed with indigent and needy folks it runs the risk of becoming indigent and needy itself. The world is steeped in poverty and poor nations. Must the U.S. be added to the list? There are probably 3 billion folks in the world that would eagerly break our laws to come into our country. We are currently experiencing a first wave.   Can the U.S. – can any nation – let *outsiders* decide who enters and who does not enter? **A nation without effective order on the border is no longer a sovereign nation, ruling itself.** The outsiders are at the controls. Such a nation is doomed for takeover (from political manipulation of the immigrant cohort) and impoverishment (through social service overuse and wage degeneration). We don't deserve to be doomed and we don't deserve to be impoverished. We have many good people here – aren't you? – many of whom were earlier immigrants. **Why let the U.S. be destroyed economically, fiscally and electorally by disorder on the border?** Don't kill the goose that lays the golden egg!

Consider, if the nation is doomed by hordes of needy border crossers, then who could we admit in years to come? The world's lifeboat will have sunk! What would be left to offer them after the U.S. relative wage advantage had been crushed and public services drained the Treasuries dry? If we had legitimate, monitored but limited immigration we could rescue and give opportunity to a few knocking at the door. But, without order on the border hordes of people would, in effect, come on board and sink the ship, taking all hands with it.

Don't Kill the Goose

Overloading the borders today threatens the economy and viability of the nation. Order on the border today could allow even more immigrants in future years. Remember, Kant cautioned:
"Our moral obligations cannot exceed our abilities."... Immanuel Kant

---

You've been there before. Add too much sugar at once to the coffee and it cannot dissolve. **Add a little at a time and it will "assimilate."** Reversing these current trends would be difficult and multi-generational. Here are some ideas. First, from the Japan Times editorial staff:

> Employment opportunities for young people must be expanded and working hours should be shortened. A sufficient number of day-care facilities for children should be established. Companies must offer job opportunities to mothers who wish to re-enter the workforce. They must also lessen the burden of working parents, such as permitting more flexible work schedules.
>
> [15. "Reversing Population Decline" 19 June 2012 *The Japan Times Opinion* <http://tinyurl.com/o8bvgey>]

The Russian Case. The Russian population has been shrinking and aging. Deaths exceed births. Russian President Vladimir Putin has called for the three child family to become the norm in Russia. In addition, Russia has adopted official policies designed to discourage homosexuality. Proselytizing to minors and gay pride parades are forbidden. Consider:

> Lesbian, gay, bisexual, and transgender (LGBT) people in Russia face legal and social challenges and discrimination not experienced by non-LGBT people. Although same-sex sexual activity between consenting adults in private was decriminalized in 1993, there are currently no laws prohibiting discrimination on the basis of sexual orientation or gender identity and expression, and households headed by same-sex couples are ineligible for the legal protections available to opposite-sex couples.
>
> [16. "LGBT rights in Russia." 4 November 2014 *Wikipedia* <http://en.wikipedia.org/wiki/LGBT_rights_in_Russia>]

Solution from the 1400s

The Russian approach of today had little firepower relative to the European solution of 600 years ago. Sociologist Heinsohn recounts how a similar population challenge was dealt with in an earlier age:

> This isn't the first time Europe has found itself tottering on the edge of extinction. Throughout the 1400s, outbreaks of bubonic plague and pressure from conquering Muslim armies reduced Europe's population to 40 million from 70 million. In 1484 Pope Innocent VIII responded to the crisis by decreeing the death penalty for 'persons of both sexes who by accursed charms and crafts, enormities and horrid offenses, slay infants yet in the mother's womb (or who) hinder women from conceiving.' Midwives, who were also experts in birth control and abortion, were prosecuted and killed.
>
> [17. Heinsohn, op. cit.]

Those radical measures worked and Europe was repopulated.

> [18. Heinsohn, op. cit.]

Modern solution

Turkish President Recep Tayyip Erdogan seems to be bordering on implementing a similar policy ... in the 21ˢᵗ century!

> Turkish President Recep Tayyip Erdogan described efforts to promote birth control as 'treason', saying contraception risked causing a whole generation to 'dry up', reports said today. He told the newly-weds that using birth control was a betrayal of Turkey's ambition to make itself a flourishing nation with an expanding young population....To make our nation stronger, we need a more dynamic and younger population. In this country, they (opponents) have been engaged in the *treason of birth control* for years and sought to dry up our generation.... Lineage is very important both *economically* and spiritually.
>
> [19. "Turkey's President Slams Birth Control as 'Treason' " 22 December 2014 *NDTV* < http://tinyurl.com/m2f4wl6>]

As of this writing, Turkey has yet to officially declare birth control to be treasonous.

Solutions for the U.S.

Open borders has been the policy up to now. But, what are the alternatives? Ban the pill? Ban abortion? Instead, the native born fertility drop and population decline will likely be addressed by deploying the usual suspects: tax breaks and subsidies for parents and longer working careers for the aging. Last but not least, the easiest and quickest of all remedies: a drastic increase in legal and illegal immigration. Get people in by "hook and by crook."

However, **the survival of the nation and it common core is put at risk.** *Excess* immigration spikes diversity while avoiding real inclusion via assimilation. Too much diversity threatens the survival of the nation by threatening "the ties that bind," its common core. Remove the common cultural core and the nation is effectively dissolved. If these trends are irreversible, then *the future of Western civilization belongs to high fertility peoples,* mainly Muslim, as they emigrate to low fertility nations, nations eager for labor, customers, entrepreneurs, taxpayers ... and babies!

Recap: It does not matter if a border crosser commits a crime, looks for work, seeks free social services or is about to win a Nobel Prize. No outsider has a right to settle here without permission. Immigration is a privilege that must be granted by lawful authority. It is not an outsider's right. Entering illegally is a violation of U.S. law. U.S. immigration policy should be based on what the U.S. needs to survive and thrive as a nation, not on the needs of outsiders.

Unemployment Games

19. FALLACIOUS ECONOMICUS: U3 is the baseline official monthly unemployment rate. It gives the true condition of the labor market.

Correct Reasoning: The government maintains SIX definitions of unemployment! U3 is the most commonly cited version. It is a very simple formula, based on a monthly sample. It starts with the **potential labor force** (all those who *could* work), which breaks into three components:

1) The **EMPLOYED** - people with jobs, even part timers who want full time jobs.

2) The **UNEMPLOYED** - people who are a) without jobs and b) who actively seek work. These workers constitute **involuntary unemployment.** (BTW: running out of insurance benefits does not remove one from the unemployed roles if one is still actively seeking employment).

3) **NOT IN THE LABOR FORCE.** Eligible workers *without* jobs and *not* looking are not in the labor force. They are not part of involuntary unemployment and frequently are overlooked in labor market analysis.

The Unemployment Rate (U3)
EQUALS
[involuntary unemployment]
DIVIDED BY
[the actual labor force]

So, if the actual labor force is 100 and 10 workers are involuntarily unemployed, the
U3 rate of unemployment is 10%.

[20. U.S. Department of Labor, "How the Government Measures Unemployment,"
21 October 2014 <http://www.bls.gov/cps/cps_htgm.htm>]

Beware the One-Number-Tells-All Trap

Changes in U3 give an incomplete and sometimes distorted view of labor market conditions. The fallacious reasoning tells the correct story – in a mechanical sense. That is, it depicts the correct computational procedure. However, *it may lead to a misinterpretation of labor market conditions.*

Many observers charge that U3 – the stat that gets all the press – actually *understates* the hardship being endured by *part timers, discouraged workers* and others *marginally attached* to the workforce. Consider that some unsuccessful job seekers get discouraged, stop looking for work and leave the labor force. They are assigned *discouraged worker* status. Others take part time jobs in lieu of full time work. All would have preferred full time employment. *U3 rules with a fine point and does not officially recognize them as involuntarily unemployed.* Each part time worker is counted as one *employed person,* given equal weight with full timers. The discouraged workers are considered to have left the labor force out of despair. They are not classified as unemployed.

Yet, these reluctant part timers and discouraged workers are indicative of a labor market unable to accommodate all those seeking work. If they were added into the official pool of U3 unemployed, the unemployment rate would rise, indicating worse labor market conditions than the official rate implies.

Beware: There is such a broader measure of unemployment called U6.

U6 = U3 plus (discouraged workers) plus (unhappy part-timers)

Beware: U6 is a complement to U3 but is still only one number. It is recommended to assess the change in total employment along with observing the unemployment rate month to month.

Exporting goods is fine, exporting jobs is problematical.

UNDERemployment

U3 may mask worker displeasure. Though employed, workers do not always work at jobs they prefer or qualify for. Enter the concept of underemployment. **Underemployment is an important labor market indicator.** Those part time workers wishing full time jobs are considered underemployed. Also, a worker is considered underemployed if one is working at a job below one's ability level. A plumber working as a janitor or a history professor driving a cab are examples of underemployment. This type of underemployment is masked by U3, as those workers are counted employed.

Other indicators: **CHECK THE LEVEL OF *TOTAL* EMPLOYMENT**, the unemployment rates (U3 and U6), and the *change* in real wages. As **indicators go, total employment rules over the unemployment rate, U3.**

1. If unemployment rate (U3) rises but *more* people are working, then the labor market is improving, despite the rise in unemployment rate (U3).

2. If unemployment rate (U3) falls but *fewer* people are working, then the labor market is deteriorating, despite the fall in the unemployment rate (U3).

3) **The capstone is the movement in real wages.** Real wages add perspective to the labor market are the spoiler. Real wages should trend upward, but have fallen and stagnated in the past 35 years, signaling an ongoing degradation of income and economic security for workers – despite job growth!

[21. Elise Gould, "2014 Continues a 35-Year Trend of Broad-Based Wage Stagnation" 19 February 2015 *Economic Policy Institute* <http://tinyurl.com/o8hhnv9>]

What is full Employment?

Full employment does *not* mean zero (involuntary) unemployment. At full employment there is little *cyclical,* i.e., demand deficiency, unemployment. However, at full employment there is *noncyclical unemployment.* There are still discouraged workers counted unemployed who want to work. U3 might be 4 or 5%. Even in the best of times there are folks between jobs, re-locating, searching want ads and the internet, and re-training *while still job hunting.* This unemployment is always there, unrelated to the business cycle, and part of normal business life. Noncyclical unemployment includes seasonal unemployment, location mismatches, skills mismatches and lack of info on job openings. The mismatch may be temporary (creating short run or **frictional unemployment**) or persistent (long run or **structural unemployment**).

---

20. FALLACIOUS ECONOMICUS: Numerous studies show women are paid less than equally qualified men for the same jobs. Given the management imperative to minimize cost, soon these higher paid men will be fired and lower paid women hired in their places.

Correct Reasoning: There is no hard evidence of a mass firing of men and hiring of women in the same job descriptions. There are numerous reasons, objective and subjective, so-called "equally qualified" are not viewed as perfect substitutes. For example, in some occupations some women choose to work fewer hours. Some shun *salary hiking promotion* to bear and raise children. Others may low-ball their initial salary requirements. These individual behaviors depress the *average* women's salary. A more complete discussion *can* be found at Ogle, cited below.

[22. Ara Ogle, "If there is a real gender pay gap, why do firms hire men at all?" 23 May, 2016 *Quora* < http://tinyurl.com/zt9lo2m>]

Appendix One
Dec. 2015 Seasonal Job Adjustment: From 11,000 to 292,000

Time series data, say, reported weekly or monthly, are subject to seasonal variations. Seasonal variations are movements – bumps or slumps - in the data caused by seasonal forces, say summer heat or winter cold. When identifying trend, statisticians seek to re-imagine data, i.e., seasonally adjust the data, to what would have been assuming *no seasonal impact.*

Seasonally adjusted data are not actual observations of the variable being studied. They are contrived, invented, manipulations of the actual observed value. The seasonal adjustment process starts with the actual observations, the raw data, which were subject to seasonal forces. Then, the raw data are pushed, pulled and squeezed (mathematically, of course) to eliminate the impact of typical seasonal forces.

The *seasonally adjusted value* is (an estimate of) what the *actual value* would have been had not the usual seasonal forces intervened. So, if a) experience shows seasonal forces cause an observation to *double* in July, then seasonally adjusting the data reduces the raw observation by one-half. If b) experience shows seasonal forces cause the actual datum to *fall* by three quarters, then the S.A. raises the raw data value by a factor of four.

1) Want to spot trends or cyclical movement? Use S.A. data. Seasonal adjustment is used to help observers identify cyclical or trend movements in time series, mainly monthly data. For example, unemployment usually rises in the summer. But, is an observed bump normal or abnormal for this season? Seasonally adjusting the data removes the typical seasonal bump (or sag), and then inserts the seasonally adjusted, artificial number into the monthly sequence. This helps the researcher spot trends and cyclical movements without seasonal factors clouding the issue.

2) Want the real skinny on what's happening *at the moment?* Use the raw, not seasonally adjusted number. Here's why:

> ➤ It is actual amount of rain that impacts the crops in a given month, not the contrived seasonally adjusted figure.
> ➤ It is the actual amount of money supply growth that impacts the economy, not the artificial seasonally adjusted amount.
> ➤ It is the actual amount of unemployment that causes hardship, not the concocted seasonally adjusted amount.

But, can the seemingly benign seasonal adjustment process have a significant effect on the datum's value, so much so that it distorts the current picture? Well, you be the judge. The Bureau of Labor Statistics reported December, 2015 **SEASONALLY ADJUSTED** job growth at 292,000. The *not seasonally adjusted* (N.S.A.) number – the *actual* number – was closer to 11,000, a considerably smaller number for this hot button economic series!

[21. David Stockman, "Only 11,000 Jobs Last Month, Not 292,000" 9 Jan. 2016 *newsmax* <http://tinyurl.com/hpah6hp]

Appendix Two

Note that average wages are reported only for *employed* workers. If low wage jobs are destroyed, average wages rise, signaling an improvement in the labor market in spite of higher unemployment! BTW: unemployed workers' wages – zero – are *not* averaged in.

Appendix Three

Observe changes in U1 through U6 in the article cited below:
[23. Jo Craven McGinty. "What the Unemployment Rate Shows" 4 March 2016 *Wall Street Journal* at <http://tinyurl.com/z83f3dh>]

Appendix Four

Development of the American Southwest

Land and labor, with scant capital equipment, is the ancient and medieval model for production. Nomadic, tribal hunting and gathering wild game dominated prior to agriculture and domestication of farm animals. But, agricultural productivity, i.e., output per acre, stagnated. Millennia saw little or no growth in real income and the standard of living. Except for tiny elite, living standards were low or subsistence and showed no promise of improvement. Life expectancy was short by today's standards. Such was life for most of the people in most of the world, including the American Southwest, for thousands of years before the Industrial Age was born in the 1700s.

The Treaty of Guadalupe Hidalgo, signed by Mexico in 1848, conveyed Texas and Western states to the U.S. for $15 million. Ambitious and energetic American entrepreneurs changed this pre-industrial model in the great Southwest after the Mexican-American War. As part of the U.S., huge amounts of financial and real capital flowed in: railroads, mining and agricultural equipment, and irrigation systems. Human capital, technology embodied in workers, augmented the physical capital influx. Later, airports, highways and information technology – moved into those "stolen" states. The rule of law enforced private property rights.

Real capital was made possible by resources released in real saving, the temporary sacrifice of consumer goods, mostly by Americans. British financial investment played a role, as well. This astute combining of land, labor AND capital sparked economic growth and a higher standard of living for millions of people. Natural resources could be developed and properly managed. This created a vast amount of real and financial wealth likely unachievable by those states had they remained in their prior neglected state as part of Mexico.

Appendix Five

Case Study: Brits Blitz Nit Wits

England is also in the cross-hairs of globers seeking to de-nationalize England. In response, some old style patriots are pushing back. They have formed the English Defense League (EDL). Naturally, they been criticized and labeled *fascist* by small minds who cannot muster a split pea of a real argument against them. Well, no wonder, when one checks out their beliefs and demands in their Mission Statement. The reader can judge whether or not their platform is radical, oppressive, racist and fascist.

Here are some outlandish demands from their mission statement.

Demand 1. "The EDL believes that English Culture has the right to exist and prosper in England."

Comment: Shocking and totally outrageous! How dare they make such a demand! Off with their heads! To the Tower of London they should be sent! Duh? How dare people demand they be allowed to be what they are *in their own country* without the permission of the high exalted mystic rulers! These gritty Brits are not surrendering to the social engineers barking at their heels. Does America need its own demand #1 for Americans?

[24. "Mission Statement" 30 Mar 2012, *English Defense League*, <http://englishdefenceleague.org/about-us/mission-statement/ >]

Demand 2. "We recognize that culture is not static, that over time changes take place naturally, and that other cultures make contributions that make our shared culture stronger and more vibrant. However, *this does not give license to policy-makers to deliberately undermine our culture and impose non-English cultures on the English people in their own land.*" [Italics mine].

Comment: This demand very eloquently speaks for itself. How dare the representatives of the *nation* tell the people of the *nation* they should give up their *national* identity and pride! Does the car tell the driver where to go? Here multiculturalism is actually designed to suppress the native culture, not function on an equal basis with it. Actually, it should not be a surprise that the British government would take such steps. Remember that Dr. Jekyll and Mr. Hyde, as well as Frankenstein's monster and Dracula all came from the minds of British authors. So did Adam Smith and David Ricardo.

Demand 3. "If people migrate to this country then they should be expected to respect our culture, its laws, and its traditions, and not expect their own cultures to be promoted by agencies of the state."

Comment: Aren't the guests at a party expected to follow the "rules of the house" they are visiting, and not vice versa? Why should the guests be allowed to run the party? They didn't buy the food, drink, buy the house and pay insurance on it. This is an eminently reasonable expectation and should not even have to be requested. So, the state is asked *not* to promote the cultures of immigrants. Golly, how unreasonable, racist and xenophobic can the EDL get? The EDL believes that in the natural course of things, "The best of their cultures will be absorbed naturally and we will all be united by the enhanced culture that results."

Demand 4. "The onus should always be on *foreign* cultures to adapt and integrate. If said cultures promote anti-democratic ideas and refuse to accept the authority of our nation's laws, then the host nation should not be bowing to these ideas in the name of 'cultural sensitivity'."

[25. "Mission Statement" 30 Mar 2012, *English Defense League*, <http://englishdefenceleague.org/about-us/mission-statement/ >]

Outsourcing vs. Off Shoring

Outsourcing is the delegation of a business activity or function to an independent productive agent outside the firm. Example: Samsung outsources the production of its smart phones batteries to an independent supplier.

Off shoring occurs when the firm outsources to a foreign platform.

There are more of us coming off the ships each day. I heard 15,000 Irish a week. And we're afraid of the Natives? Get all of us together ... we ain't got a gang ... we got an army. And all we need is a spark. One spark, to wake us.

–Amsterdam Vallon, *Gangs of New York*

"My dream is a hemispheric common market, with open trade and open borders...."

Hillary Clinton in a speech to Banco Itau, a Brazilian bank, on May 16, 2013.

<http://www.lifezette.com/polizette/wikileaks-dump-hillary-dreams-open-trade-open-borders/>

Chapter Thirteen
Shakespearean Fallacies

Brush Up Your Shakespeare!   –Cole Porter

Folks revere Shakespeare. But, arguably, he gave some questionable advice. Shakespeare wrote at a time when England was an economic backwater. It had yet to discover the wealth producing power of mercantilist trade policies, policies that have been resurrected in modern dress by America's major trading partners.

"Neither a Borrower nor a Lender Be" Fallacy

1. FALLACIOUS ECONOMICUS: The owners must invest all the money necessary to start a business. Borrowed money is not recommended.

Correct Reasoning: What if, without borrowed money, businesses could not start-up and generate a return to the owners? Is that desirable, Mr. Shakespeare, to miss profit opportunities due to lack of start-up money? In truth, few entrepreneurs have enough money to finance the entire needs of a business startup. Funds could be solicited from a) other investors who become, in effect, co-owners, b) lenders, who become, in effect, passive investors without management prerogatives, or c) donors (of cash, property, or other assets) who relinquish all claims to the donated assets. The status of the co-owner would be partner or fellow stockholder, depending on the legal form of the organization. Lenders become creditors of the firm.

2. FALLACIOUS ECONOMICUS: The owners could borrow money to start the business. This would contradict Shakespeare's famous caution about borrowing or lending money. Don't do either! To be wise, one should follow Shakespeare's advice and "neither a borrower nor a lender be."

[1. From the soliloquy by Polonius in Act I, Scene 3 of William Shakespeare's Hamlet.]

Correct Reasoning: Meaning no disrespect to old Uncle Will, but there are situations when it is advantageous to borrow money ... or lend money. Of course, unlike invested *owner* money, a business would have a legal obligation to repay money to the lenders. (Lucky and most rare is the owner who accepts borrowed money without being required to repay ... that is called a gift!)

Yes, of course, the owners, too, may someday wish to get back the money invested. Ending the business and liquidating the assets is a quick way to get some cash out of the business ... *after* creditors have been paid. But, there is no legal obligation of the business to repay the owners for money invested. The **corporate** form is problematic for owner cash withdrawals. (See Chapter Sixteen for more information on the legal form of a business enterprise).

3. FALLACIOUS ECONOMICUS: So, let's see. If a startup business needs extra cash there are two ways to get it: borrow from folks who become creditors or seek additional ownership money. Other than the commitment to repay the loan there seems to be no difference between the two sources of funds.

Correct Reasoning: Pay attention, there are significant differences between borrowing and soliciting ownership money.

Extended Discussion

If bonds, i.e., long term debt, were issued to evidence the borrowing, there likely is semi-annual interest to be paid. Failure to pay the interest and/or the principal of the debt constitutes default, an outcome with serious legal consequences.

In the extreme, **corporation** ownership money NEVER has to be paid back, no matter how profitable the business, **as long as the corporation operates**. If the corporation ceases operations and is dissolved legally, noncash assets are sold and creditors paid off. Any remaining funds go to the owner(s). One must be sure to meet the obligations assumed when a debt is created. Debt money may bear periodic interest and must be repaid at maturity. Failing to do so puts the issuer in default. Default may lead to bankruptcy proceedings, which may lead to the dissolution of the business and the liquidation of the remaining assets. (See Chapter Sixteen for how the legal form of the business impacts the distribution of owner money).

The Folger Shakespeare Library Prints
THE DROESHOUT ENGRAVING OF SHAKESPEARE, ON
THE TITLE-PAGE OF THE FIRST FOLIO, 1623
(From a proof state of the engraving in the Folger Shakespeare Library.)

Another way. Raising money by taking in partners or additional stockholders creates other issues. As co-owners, those folks will have the right to share in the earnings *and* management decisions. Original owners may object to sharing control.

Now for the good news. There is good news about creditors is this: 1) if they are paid what is due on the date due, then creditors have no legal right to hassle the borrower. For the most part, creditors are passive investors who normally have no control over business management or activities.

2) The second piece of goods news concerning borrowed money is the interest payable is usually fixed. No matter how profitably the firm invests the borrowed money or how high the market rate of interest goes, the lender gets that fixed interest and principal obligation. 3) Interest expense is a legitimate tax deduction for business. (Payments to stockholders are *not* deductible.)

Leverage effect is the **use of borrowed money to increase returns to the owners. Sometimes it is referred to as *financial leverage.* It is** a common tool for increasing profits – and risk. The borrowed money is put to work in the business, and, hopefully, raises profits. Then the fixed, limited interest is paid on the debt. **The excess earned *above* the interest due, however large, all belongs to the owner(s).**

A down home example of leverage: a gambler borrows $100 to play the horses and wins $1,000. He returns the borrowed $100 and is $900 ahead ... on someone else's dime! Not one dollar of his own money was put at risk. To leverage is to use the other guy's money to boost the owners' return on a project.

Buying Stock on Margin

Expect a stock price to rise? Then, magnify your return with a margin purchase. Buy *more* **stock by buying on margin,** i.e., with money borrowed from a broker. If the initial margin (down payment) requirement is 50%, you can borrow half your required outlay. So, you can **double** the number of shares bought and your return without doubling *your* investment. But, this leverage effect has a potential downside. Suppose the stock pice crashes. The borrowed money, as well as your money, is lost. Then, your losses are doubled, as your money and the borrowed money are lost. The **borrowed money must be repaid**, with interest, out of your remaining funds!

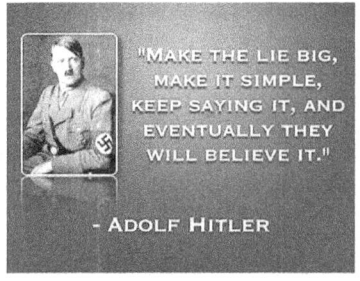
"MAKE THE LIE BIG, MAKE IT SIMPLE, KEEP SAYING IT, AND EVENTUALLY THEY WILL BELIEVE IT."
- ADOLF HITLER

4. FALLACIOUS ECONOMICUS: "What's in a Name?"

Fallacious Reasoning: The name says BUY CHEAP, so they must be the best buys, no?

Correct Reasoning: Public relations and advertising folks will tell you there can be plenty of punch in a name of a product or firm. But, the name does not create the reality. This popular spin fallacy is committed when one wrongly assumes that an organization's name truthfully describes its philosophy, goals and behavior.

Many names are "foolers." The names are deliberately slanted to ensnare or confuse those dealing with it, to create an image contrary to its true purpose.

> ### The Control of History
> #### He who controls the past controls the future.
> #### He who controls the present controls the past.
> #### – George Orwell

Political Correctness: Orwell recognized how words could be twisted and used to control thought. In the fictional work, 1984, George Orwell imagined an oppressive nation where words were twisted and meanings turned upside down. For example, the Ministry of Peace was in charge of making war and the Ministry of Justice was engaged in oppressing people. Slogans included freedom is slavery, ignorance is strength. Political correctness (PC) ruled. Winston Smith, the protagonist, worked daily at re-writing history, thereby "controlling" the past. The government was creating a new vocabulary called Newspeak, eliminating words like love from the old lexicon. All this helped the government, incarnated as Big Brother, control the thinking – as well as the behavior – of its citizens.

> ### Good Ship Lollypop is Sinking
> Is political correctness a threat to national security? Words affect thoughts and thoughts effect actions. Under President Obama, F.B.I. procedures and practices have been purged of any perceived negative bias toward Islam. The terms *radical Islam* and *Jihad* have been stricken from training manuals, along with any "offending" language portraying Islam or Muslims in a negative light. Profiling, a useful intellectual tool, is prohibited. **Question:** is this the equivalent of keeping one's head in the sand? How would humanity have survived if people did not profile their food for toxicity?

Beware: (PC) is a destructive practice and ideology, focused on using language as a means of thought control. But, **control thought, thereby control behavior.** So, contrary to Mr. Shakespeare's dictum, there is a lot in a name or a label. "A rose by any other name would smell as sweet" is a commonly quoted part of a dialogue in William Shakespeare's play Romeo and Juliet. Juliet agrees. Shakespeare asserts the *names* of things do *not* matter, only what things "are." Big Brother disagrees with Shakespeare: everything is in a name.

Change the name, solve the problem. An entire political, academic, social and legal movement seeks to distort and, in some cases, eradicate truth. That movement is called **political correctness.** Up to a point, by avoiding offensive speech, political correctness may be a positive process.

Has **1984** become a guidebook for today's unsavory politicians? Visit **1984 Doublespeak in the 2000s:**

> ➤ "Comprehensive Immigration Reform" really means open borders.
> ➤ "Free Trade" really means the whole Glocialist/Globalist agenda.

Is Uncle SAM Really Uncle SCAM?

American nationalists resent that anti-American revisionist history is a key tenet of Globalism. That interpretation of history involves the de-glorification of American institutions, heroes, and actions, at home and abroad. Orwell had great insight into this process of deliberate nation destruction: **"The most effective way to destroy people is to deny and obliterate their own understanding of their history."**

They charge that America has bullied and exploited many of its own people as well as those in other countries. The Globalist propaganda wing includes elite, Ivy Fatigue – sorry, that's Ivy League- universities – big transnational media, and progressive *stink* tanks – oops, sorry, again – that is, *think* tanks). They must get Americans to hate and reject traditional America. Globalthink must take precedence over patriotism and Nationthink! Controls on school curriculums and textbooks are essential to this effort.

Renaming and relabeling are key tools in this mind control game. So, in the lexicon of political correctness, illegal aliens become "undocumented" immigrants and lazy people become "initiative deficient."

> Americans must feel guilt and shame over America's behavior, here and abroad, past and present. Christianity, the Constitution and traditional American history must go. In reality, the American story is full of racism, xenophobia, and exploitation.
>
> [2. John Smith, "Manipulation of The People – The Rudiments of Propaganda"
>
> September 2003 *EnergyGrid* <http://tinyurl.com/pn6sgpe>]

Could it be, once convinced of America's evil, the good people of America will absolve their guilt by voluntarily surrendering their nationalism, patriotism and sovereignty to a worldwide governance system ... and Glocialism?

Chapter Fourteen
Government Meddling

I don't make jokes. I just watch the government and report the facts.
—Will Rogers

Firms often pay lip service to government laissez-faire or hands off policy. But, very often their behavior indicates a preference for government interference.

1. FALLACIOUS ECONOMICUS: It's a free country. I can produce what I choose and the government cannot meddle in my affairs.

Correct Reasoning: That might have been true back in the 1850s, but certainly is not true today. Government has tremendous powers to stimulate or discourage your economic activity.

Government can be supportive in the following ways: it can ...

1. ... become your customer.

2. ... give you a tax break.

3. ... give your customers a tax break should they buy from you.

4. ... give you a subsidy, i.e., refund part of your cost, on domestic sales or exports.

5. ... give your suppliers, transporters or vendors a tax break, subsidy; or government becomes their customer, increasing their viability.

6. ... impose trade barriers (tariff, quota or regulation) on imported competition.

7. ... mandate everyone to buy some of your products, e.g., health insurance.

8. ... outlaw your competition.

The above measures represent examples of *crony capitalism.*

Crony capitalism is a term describing an economy in which success in business depends on close relationships between business people and government officials. It may be exhibited by favoritism in the distribution of legal permits, government grants, special tax breaks, or other forms of state interventionism. In many cases, the term is used interchangeably with corporate welfare.

[1. "Crony Capitalism" 18 June 2014 *Wikipedia*
<http://en.wikipedia.org/wiki/Crony_capitalism>]

Government can make life tough for you in the following ways: it can ...

1. ... stop buying from you.

2. ... regulate your price.

3. ... if applicable, raise your license and insurance fees.

4. ... impose special tax on your product, its transporters and vendors (think excise taxes).

5. ... tax your suppliers to raise their cost to you.

6. ... allow competition from foreign imports.

7. ... in the extreme, outlaw your product.

2. FALLACIOUS ECONOMICUS: Businesses do not want government regulation or other meddling in their affairs. They want non-interference from government (a.k.a. fallacy of business favoring laissez-faire).

Correct Reasoning: This fallacy is committed when one wrongly assumes that business owners always prefer noninterference from the government.

Businesses are fond of paying lip service to free enterprise and government non-interference. But, in fact, the government hands-off approach, called laissez-faire, is sometimes favored and sometimes opposed by business. In reality, business attitudes toward government interference depend on the position the business is in. They prefer whatever works best for them in a particular context. Sometimes they prefer interference on their behalf.

Despite what they say, most businesses today prefer government not as a passive observer but as an active ally every step of the way from outside to inside of the industry!

There's more

Before entry into the industry. The business firm before entering an industry: Call for more competition and lower barriers to entry! Firms as outsiders generally want no government interference blocking entrance into the target industry. Indeed, they may seek government aid in easing entry barriers erected by firms already in the industry. Such aid may include loans (at below market rates), direct subsidies, reduced legal barriers, suppression of market power of firms already in the industry, in some cases, call for more diversity in industry.

After entering an industry. The firm calls for less competition and higher en-try barriers. After entering an industry, firms may seek government involvement to expand market power and discourage other outsiders from entering. Policies may include: seeking government contracts and subsidies, encouraging government to erect barriers to entry to keep out new firms. This may include the erection of barriers (e.g., tariffs and quotas) on competing imports.

Invite government in to regulate the industry, thereby preventing intra-industry competition from reaching the destructive phase. (See CAB example below). In times of crisis, seek a government bailout. (See banking example below). **Encourage government to increase the pool of available labor by adopting relaxed immigration policies.**

Government noninterference sought when one firm seeking to merge to eliminate competition or pursue another path to eliminating competition.

Example 1: **Codex**. Pharmaceutical companies and MD's have sought to bring vitamins and nutritional supplements under prescription only sales. Critics charge the World Trade Organization (WTO) is being used as a backdoor approach to government regulation of the U.S. nutritional supplement and vitamin industry. The vehicle device is called a proposed regulatory instrument called the Codex Alimentarius, another murky trade deal concocted in secret.

[2. "Codex Alimentarius" 26 June 2014 *Alliance for Natural Health*
<http://tinyurl.com/o6y7ch6>
See also, John Hammell **"Are Vitamins by Prescription Only Coming to The U.S.?"**
April 2015 *Monitor.Net* < http://tinyurl.com/q9bkaaj >]

The Codex seems squarely aimed at the freedom enjoyed to purchase vitamins and supplements as one pleases in the U.S.

> Should the Codex Commission approve the Draft Guidelines for Vitamin and Mineral Supplements on its agenda, 300 of the 420 basic vitamin and mineral products commonly used by European consumers will be banned from manufacture and trade inside the European Community. **The ban will seriously impact the export business of U.S.-based supplement companies and could eventually result in similar product restrictions being implemented here.**
>
> [3. Bold mine. Peter Byrne "The History of Codex and The Fate of Vitamins" 2 January 2015 *smart-publications.com*
> <http://tinyurl.com/ptrfqpm >]

Example 2: **"Save us from ourselves!"** The Civil Aeronautics Board (CAB).1938-1978. A government agency created by the 1938 Civil Aeronautics Act. The CAB was a Federal government agency that, essentially, eliminated freedom of enterprise in the airline industry by regulating competition among interstate airline carriers. Routes and rates were CAB-regulated to discourage "destructive" competition.

Destructive competition occurs when entry barriers are relatively low and so many firms enter an industry that minimum or normal profits are threatened for all firms. In such cases, as with the airline carriers in the 1930s, the firms may welcome government regulation to bring stability and profits to the industry. In a way, the firms are saying to the government, "Please come in and save us from ourselves!"

Example 3: **Please arrest the other drug dealer!** Illegal drug dealers have a selfish interest in having the government arrest rival drug dealers, thereby reducing competition. Taken by itself, this removal of competition may raise sales and profits of the remaining dealers.

Example 4: **"Mother hen" to banking system.** No laissez-faire here! One of the main purposes of The Federal Reserve System is to manage money and credit for the economy as a whole. In addition, it supervises and regulates the banking system in order to discourage bank failures. In emergencies, the Fed stands by as a **lender of last resort,** a kind of bankers' bank, to advance funds to banks in times of extreme distress, as when there is "bank run." A **bank run** occurs when many depositors make a mad dash to withdraw their money,

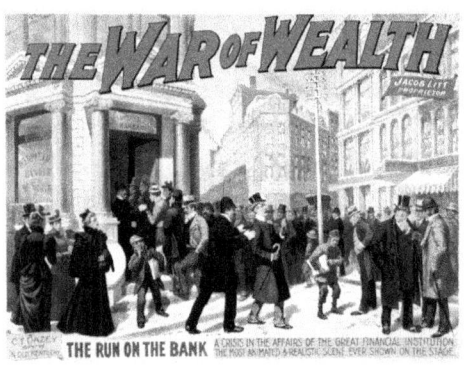

THE RUN ON THE BANK A CRISIS IN THE AFFAIRS OF THE GREAT FINANCIAL INSTITUTION THE MOST ANIMATED & REALISTIC SCENE EVER SHOWN ON THE STAGE

fearing the bank has squandered or somehow lost the money. (In truth, even the most well managed, sound bank does not have cash on hand to satisfy withdrawals during a run. The bank will have loaned or invested most of their cash.) This government "interference" (a.k.a. government to the rescue) is welcomed most heartily by the banking system!   Working alongside the Fed, the Federal Deposit Insurance Corporation (FDIC) insures deposits up to $250,000. Critics have charged that this rescue posture leads to **moral hazard.**

Beware: The FDIC would be overwhelmed in a large scale bank run, as in 2008. Also, merging a failing trillion dollar bank with a healthy trillion dollar bank is impossible? Let us say, such a merger is problematic.

3. **FALLAⳫIOUS ⳫⲤONOMIⳫUS:**   All I have to do is create (or buy) a patentable invention, then patent it with the U.S. government. This gives me a monopoly and I can live on easy street ever after.

Fallacious Reasoning: The patent grants me a legal monopoly over my invention. If anyone tries to imitate it I can marshal the law to my side to outlaw illegal theft of my intellectual property.

Correct Reasoning: Yes, a patent gives the holder a *legal* **monopoly** over the product but does not guarantee an *economic* **monopoly**. The patent assures only one firm can legally exploit the making of the product. Only rarely does a legal patent create an economic monopoly. For economic monopoly, the product must be viewed as unique or nearly unique in the eyes of the customers. Legal barriers to competition may help but do not guarantee the emergence of monopoly. Patents, trademarks, copyrights and franchises are neither necessary nor sufficient to create monopoly. There are millions of patents extant, not millions of (economic) monopolies created thereby.

Close Substitutes. An economic monopoly is consistent with a single seller of good having no close substitutes. A monopolist can set its own price, without fear of retaliation from close rivals ... there aren't any! A monopoly could be local, regional, or national. But, having absolutely *no close substitutes* is a tough standard to meet. That would constitute pure monopoly. Lawyers, economists, judges and juries constantly debate what constitutes a close substitute. Absent some licensed and regulated **legal monopolies,** mainly public utilities, pure monopoly is rare.

Monopoly power. The supposed evil of monopoly derives from its **monopoly power**. It allows a firm to **underproduce and overcharge**, relative to a more competitive industry. Monopoly exists in varying degrees. It can extract higer prices and *excess* (above normal) profits from its customers, without fear of retaliation from rivals. A monopolist has no close rivals. More competitive environments do not allow for monopoly power. (The entity discussed here is not the legal variety of monopoly, the licensed and regulated public utility).

Question: Who had more monopoly power when pricing a concert?

a. Elvis b. Sinatra c. the Beetles d. Madonna

A **monopsonist** is a single *buyer* who may extract price reductions from sellers.

In **Oligopoly,** a small cluster of *interdependent* large firms dominate an industry. Illegal cooperation is an everyday temptation when there are so few firms. Firms are hyper rivals; executives may know each other personally. They possess and exert monopoly power, as well. Commercial and investment banking, autos, aircraft manufacture and computer chip production are examples of non monopolies exerting ... monopoly power! Dominating their industries are Amazon versus Wall-Mart in retailing, or Apple versus Samsung in smart phones.

Oligopolists usually shun *price* competition, preferring product improvements and promotional practices. They tend to conspire to fix prices and/or divide markets. Oligopolies outside the U.S. often morph into **cartels,** witness the phenomenally successful OPEC cartel. **Cartels are illegal in the U.S.**

An **economic monopoly** is, in effect, "conferred" by customer behavior – not the government – who *buy as if there are no close substitutes for the product in question.* Once customers signal there are no close substitutes, the monopolist is given nearly free rein in setting price, an option a *regulated* legal monopolist may not possess.

Recap: *economic* monopoly need not be based on a patent, trademark or copyright! One does not need a patent, a *legal* monopoly, to enjoy an *economic* monopoly! A unique talent as an artist or performer may confer monopoly power. Local monopolies are numerous, e.g., the only pharmacy, gas stastion or dentist in a small town. But, the public and anti-trust authorities are most interested in the more rare nationwide monopoly. *Unregulated monopoly* enables the holder to exclude close competition, charge higher prices and earn higher profits – at least until competitors enter the industry!

But, beware: Unregulated monopolies or near monopolies may be potential rivals, e.g., Samsung and Apple smart phones, keeping each other's price in check. Product innovation is the main weapon of competition for those two companies. In addition, there is possible prosecution by anti-trust authorities at the Federal and state levels.

4. FALLACIOUS ECONOMICUS: Monopoly is evil. It charges the highest possible price, **earns excess profits, stifles competition and retards innovation.**

Correct Reasoning: Why would a profit seeking entrepreneur charge *the highest possible price?* Why chase away customers? Wouldn't it be more prudent to charge the **profit maximizing price**, likely a lower price than the absolute maximum? There is no award for charging the highest price. Indeed, there might be a penalty in terms of lost customers, profits and prosecution. Anti-trust authorities may be attracted. Remember, there are no close substitutes, but there may be distant substitutes. An unregulated monopolist may set a price lower than maximum, low enough to **limit entry** of new firms yet high enough to earn excess profits. The prospect of losses deters competitors.

Reasons for lower price: First of all, even a monopolist can have a bad year and not earn excess profits. But, that may be acceptable in keeping a low profile. **Excess profits and high prices could be self–destructive**. They could draw potential competitors and ant-trust authorities to the activity. Creative destruction may arise. On a positive note, excess profits of a high tech near-monopolist could be reinvested in research and development (R&D), leading to new products and technologies. Apple, Samsung, Boeing, DuPont, IBM, Intel and Big Pharma rely on a constant stream of new inventions, innovations and discoveries. **Creative destruction** can provide a potential check on monopoly behavior. When a new industry is born, it could destroy an old monopoly. Consider that the automobile ended the 4000 year reign of the horse for personal mobility.

Some oligopolies reinvest significant excess profits in R &D to fuel creative destruction and progress!

Moral Hazard

Little Tommy spills milk on the floor. His mother says, "Good, Tommy!" and gives him a kiss. Is Tommy learning right from wrong? Is Little Tommy deterred from spilling milk again? Is his mother teaching him right from wrong or is she corrupting his morals? Is the Fed doing the same by bailing out failing banks time and again?

5. FALLACIOUS ECONOMICUS: Those big banks learned their lesson after the big bailouts of 2008-2009. They will not engage in shady banking practices as in the subprime mortgage lending crisis.

Correct Reasoning: TBTF. Yes, the subprime mortgage lending crisis was instigated by government **redistributionist policies, pushing home ownership for low income, nontraditional buyers.** Yes, banks tried to capitalize on the mortgage mandates. Yes, the banks misbehaved and yes, most of them were bailed out by Uncle Sam. *But, no, they are not necessarily changing their behavior to avoid new crises.*

You see, the folks who run Big Banks have realized that they are *too big to fail* **(TBTF)**. The U.S. government would not let them fail, regardless of their behavior! For example, a failure of Citibank, J.P. Morgan or Goldman Sachs would threaten other banks and, indeed, the entire U.S. economy. Yet, they have a history of reckless business ventures that get them into trouble, threatening insolvency. Ventures undertaken are seen as win-win. Either the venture plays out as expected or it doesn't. Either way, the bank and its stockholders are protected! Arguably, the bankers no longer know right from wrong. Their morals have been "fried" by the successive bailouts. So, why should they stop the bad behavior? If they win, they win. If they lose, they win via bailout!

Question: Licensed to kill? Are TBTF banks, in effect, 007 banks, licensed to kill the economy?

The bailouts are hazarding with the morals of the bankers. Their morals are put through a ringer so they no longer know right from wrong. They get rewarded either way. Usually when you reward bad behavior you get more of it. The lesson is this: we can expect these pampered monsters to get into trouble again as Uncle Sam rescues them from failure.

The Living Will

Under the Dodd-Frank Financial Reform Act (2010), banks deemed "too big to fail" must submit detailed plans as to how they would, *with their own resources*, deal with another financial crisis like the one in 2008. The plan is known as a living will. As of 2014, regulators have not been satisfied with the living wills presented by the giant institutions.

[4. Kimberly Amadeo, "Dodd-Frank Wall Street Reform Act, A Summary of its Regulations" 26 June 2014 About.com. U.S. Economy <http://tinyurl.com/ccfhlgk>]

Question: Can the Dodd-Frank law rein in rogue banksters and brokesters?

Other Business Fallacies

Workers Mimic the Behavior of Firms

6. FALLACIOUS ECONOMICUS: Workers in licensed occupations want minimal government interference.

Correct Reasoning: Consider workers in licensed occupations, before and after they enter a licensed occupation. They want help at all stages of the licensing process.

Workers before they enter the occupation. As outsiders, workers usually prefer a lowering of government imposed license qualifications to ease their path to entry.

Outsiders are likely to advocate lower license requirements, the reduction of academic prerequisites and shorter apprenticeship training.

Workers after they enter the occupation. As insiders, workers usually prefer a rising of government imposed license qualifications to discourage further entrants into the occupation. This is done to reduce competition among workers to protect and, hopefully, enlarge the incomes of the insiders. As insiders they are likely to advocate higher license requirements, the raising of academic prerequisites and longer apprenticeship training, all stumbling blocks for those still outside the occupation.

7. FALLACIOUS ECONOMICUS: Put the critic in charge. He seems to know what is wrong and probably can fix it.

Correct Reasoning: Do not mistake the critic for an expert fixer! Criticism is easy because everything has a fault (see cost-benefit fallacy). Negative criticism is easy because everything has a problem, as in "every rose has its thorns." People criticize the Sistine Chapel Ceiling and the Mona Lisa. Has any critic done any better?

Don't think that because someone is "right on" with the criticism that the critic can do any better. This fallacy is committed when one wrong assumes that the perceptive critic would do better if put in charge. Being a good critic does not mean we should put the critic "in charge." **Good critics are not necessarily good fixers or have better ideas.**

8. FALLACIOUS ECONOMICUS: Hey, I could make any claim I want in my advertising. After all, it is my product and I am paying for the advertising.

Correct Reasoning: The law says you must be able to back up express or implied claims that are made in your advertising.

> ... You need to substantiate (i.e., back up) the claims in your advertisements (utilizing expert testimony, extrinsic evidence, tests, studies, etc.). And this is so whether the type of claim you're making, or plan to make, is express or implied.
>
> [5. JLCom Publishing Co., LLC, *Advertising Substantiation.* 20 May 2014 <http://www.advertisingsubstantiation.com/>

The Buy One, Two Free Suit Store

9. FALLACIOUS ECONOMICUS: I went to the store, bought one suit for $750 and got two free! Man, did I get some deal!

Correct Reasoning: If this vendor consistently offers this "deal," then one must conclude that the $750 covers the cost of all three suits, plus profit. So, the seller takes a suit that would be profitable at $250 and raises the price to $750. When the buyer (over)pays $750 for the one and two "free" it amounts to $250 per suit, the original price per suit. Recall: there are no free lunches!!!

10. FALLACIOUS ECONOMICUS: It doesn't bother me if you do illegal drugs. To each his own, "no skin off of my nose." Law enforcement should let them be.

Fallacious Reasoning: You are you and I am me. We are separate people, no? What you snort or stick in your veins does not go into my body. So, go for it!

Correct Reasoning: Your buying of illegal drugs can provide financial support to drug gangs who could hurt society in different ways. Here are a few: gangs engage in other criminal activities, overcrowd the jails, require more social services and overburden law enforcement. Dealing with these effects requires more tax dollars and resources drawn from other uses. The cost rises if one adds the value of lost production from drug dealers and users due to drug use.

Consider: Illegal drug use is not a victimless crime. If illegal drugs become legal there may still be many harmful side effects. Legal drug use also may harm innocent bystanders.

Government Price Controls

Failure and unintended adverse consequences dog government attempt to control prices. Government price controls are a favorite corrective when the market malfunctions. For thousands of years, Emperors, Kings and governments of all kinds have tried to control prices by law. And **for thousands of years these efforts ultimately failed.** Critics charge government intervention often has side effects that create more serious problems.(See Diagram#1 below for an overview of price controls).

Diagram #1: Overview of Price Controls

```
                  ┌─────────────────────────────┐
                  │  Government Price Controls   │
                  └─────────────────────────────┘
                       │
        ┌──────────────┴──────────────────────────┐
        ▼                                          ▼
┌───────────────────────┐            ┌──────────────────────────────┐
│ Selective Price       │    VS.     │ General Price and Wage       │
│ Controls              │            │ Controls                     │
└───────────────────────┘            └──────────────────────────────┘
        │                                          │
        │                                          ▼
        │                              A **macro** tool for price and wage control
        │                                 applied to most markets
        ▼
applied to only a few markets
a **micro** tool for price control
        │
   ┌────────────┬──────────────────┬──────────────────┐
   ▼            ▼                  ▼
price floor   VS.    price ceiling          pegging
   │                   │                      │
legal minimum price  legal maximum price   fixing a single price
   │                   │                      │
minimum wage         rent control   gold price, fixed exchange rate
   │                   │
*surpluses*          *shortages*
```

[6. See "Price Controls, Price Ceilings, and Price Floors" 5 April 2014 *Economics Library* <http://www.econlib.org/library/Topics/College/pricecontrols.html>]

Supply and Demand

Selective price controls: Diagram #2 (below) shows the typical placement of the price floor and price ceiling in a <u>micro</u> market. Note that the floor is above and the ceiling is below the free market, natural wage.

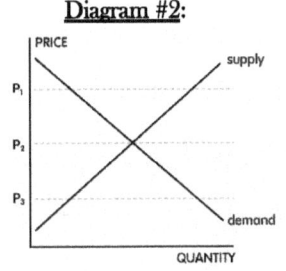

Diagram #2:

Price floor, P1: If free price, P2, is too low, a floor would be set *above* it at P1, as with minimum wage or farm price supports. A **persistent surplus** emerges due to the drop in demand and hike in supply.

Price ceiling, P3: If the free price (P2) is deemed too high to be fair, the **legal ceiling** price is put *below* it at P3. Some lucky buyers get the lower price but some deserving buyers are shut out by the now limited quantity. For example, rent controls or ceiling medicine prices. A **persistent shortage** emerges due to the drop in supply and hike in demand.

Example of a Price Floor: the Legal Minimum Wage

11. FALLACIOUS ECONOMICUS: Raising the legal minimum wage will improve the incomes of low wage workers.

Fallacious Reasoning: Are you kidding? Does there have to be reasoning? This isn't rocket science!

Correct Reasoning: This is another hot button item. In reality, the legal minimum wage will have a number of effects, some good (1/3) and some bad (2/3). A legal minimum wage is one placed *above* the natural wage rate which market forces would establish. So, it is an **artificially high wage.** This sets in motion a chain of events which eventually sabotages the goals of improving worker welfare and the standard of living. Consider the following chain of events:

Demand Side: Cut in Demand for Labor

Pick up any mainstream economics text and it will tell you most economists agree: raising the **legal minimum wage is a *net job killer*,** at least in the short run. The *artificially* high wage requirement will reduce the quantity demanded of **legal labor.** This is a normal reflexive business reaction, i.e., to reduce the use of a now higher cost factor of production. Some workers will be discharged, furloughed, retired and otherwise removed from the payroll list. Or, planned hiring will be scaled back. Hiking the legal minimum will kill some jobs. (Hiring may increase in the uncovered sector ... **illegal labor.** See discussion below on **uncovered sector activities!**)

Those dismissed will be the workers who do not produce enough value to justify receiving the higher minimum, say $15 per hour. These jobs are lost. In effect, the jobs are destroyed unless 1) the firm hires with new workers at illegal, below minimum rates or, 2) workers facing dismissal agree to accept the pre-hike, now illegal wage. There is nothing personal involved.

Simple Solution

Want to raise wages and living standards in the U.S.? No need to raise the legal minimum wage! Simply expel all workers who are in this country illegally. Yes, labor shortages will result. Eventually, employers will be forced to pay higher wages to a smaller workforce enjoying a higher standard of living!

Some workers helped. Some workers, usually higher up the skill and/or managerial scale escape the ax, are retained and earn the new minimum. They are the beneficiaries of the higher legal minimum. One might argue they were underpaid before the hike in the minimum and merited the raise.

Operations re-organized, jobs eliminated. Having reduced its labor force, the firm will have to replace the effort of the laid off workers. This is done in two ways. 1) The production process is re-organized and workers re-assigned. Employers will try to get more effort from the remaining workers. Economists call this increased **productivity!** 2) Real capital (machinery, equipment) will be **substituted** for the dismissed labor.

Supply Side: Jump in Supply of Labor

Unfortunately, movements on the labor *supply* side worsen the unemployment situation. More workers, enticed by the higher minimum wage, enter the labor force and seek employment in the sectors covered by the minimum wage. Lured by the higher wage, these job seekers persist regardless of the decline in job availability.

 **Uncovered sector activities**. Compounding the problem for legal workers is the ready availability of **illegal workers**, native and immigrant. These are workers willing to work *below* the new minimum. Employers may seek illegal workers to avoid the minimum. Unemployed workers may seek work in the *uncovered sector*, the sector not covered by the legal minimum. This includes the so-called underground economy of illegal activities. Day labor in construction, landscaping and hospitality come to mind. Also, *uncovered* includes the self employed.

Will a rush of job seekers to the uncovered sector drive down wages there, or will increased demand (transferred from covered sector) prevent that drop?

Mixed bag of results from the minimum wage: ceteris paribus

➤ Those workers *retained* in spite of the higher wage will earn a higher wage. Union contract workers are likely to get raises.

➤ Legal employment will *fall*, illegal employment will likely rise in the low skilled occupations.

➤ Uncovered, "off the books" sector will thrive.

Illegal Labor Force. There is an illegal, **shadow labor force** in the U.S., willing and able to work at subminimum wages. And it numbers in the millions. When the minimum is raised, some unscrupulous employers may turn to this pool of uncovered workers, viz., illegal workers, and increase hiring there. For obvious reasons, these low profile, illegal workers do not demand the legal minimum wage. (Conspiracy theorists might argue the minimum wage hike was really a "make work for illegals program"). Was the law intended to help these workers?

Some legal job seekers may be forced to join this shadow work force, take lower wage jobs, work "off the books," just to have a job.

Hiking the minimum wage produces a mixed bag of outcomes. It does not help all low wage workers nor does it hurt them all. *First of all, realize that the minimum wage applies to less than 5% of the hourly workers in the economy.* One cannot conclude unequivocally that "raising the legal minimum wage will improve the incomes of low wage workers." Why not raise minimum to $50? Yes, the retained workers are helped, but others are thrown out of work as their positions are eliminated or re-configured.

Additional Notes: robust economic growth with increasing labor demand and restricted added supply, could temper some of the ill effects of a minimum wage hike. However, the U.S. is unlikely to experience robust economic growth, e.g. above 4%. Moreover, the supply of labor is continually augmented by the entry of legals and illegals, refilling the pool of workers not requiring the minimum!

Does Higher Minimum Wage Alleviate Poverty?

First of all, most folks in poverty do not have a job. **More than two-thirds of the folks in poverty are either too young or old to work and feel no direct effect from a minimum wage hike.** There is no immediate benefit for these folks unless they live in a household with a worker retained after the wage hike. In fact, if they are low skilled workers, the higher minimum makes it harder for them to be hired.

> **Fascist America?**
>
> Perhaps government should hike the minimum wage AND freeze employment. Then, no one will be thrown out of work. But, that is a degree of command and control over freedom of enterprise most Americans would reject.

Boosting the minimum wage as a weapon in a war on poverty is **dealing with the symptom** instead of the underlying cause: the decimation of higher wage and salary occupational and job opportunities.

Boosting the minimum wage is like putting a finger in the dike about to break. Remember, Globalism attacks **personal economic security** through a pincer movement of 1) cheap imported labor and 2) cheap imported goods. Those cheaper imported **goods** put downward pressure on U.S. wages, as U.S. firms struggle to keep costs low and remain competitive by shaving wages and benefits. Recall, **trade is a substitute for migration**. Both depress the demand for native born labor while shifting demand to lower wage, imported workers. 3) Off shored manufacturing and service jobs put downward pressure on labor demanded for those jobs. From the kick-them-when-they-are-down department: American consultants troll corporate halls counseling companies how to ... off shore American jobs!

Macro Stimulus From Higher Minimum Wage?

Proponents of raising the legal minimum wage assert raising the national minimum will provide enough stimulus to the macro economy to spur robust economic growth. The reasoning is as follows: The implied assumption is that workers will have additional income and are likely to spend the additional amount. But, is this a valid assumption? But, laid off workers will likely cut spending, an offset.

Yes, consumer spending accounts for about three quarters of total spending. And, yes, worker earnings are a key determinant of consumer spending.

Check total earnings, not wage per hour. But, the worker earnings at issue in a macro context are *not* the wage *per hour* of micro analysis. In macro view, **total earnings of all workers is more relevant than wage per hour**. With fewer workers on board after the minimum wage hike, and despite the higher minimum per hour for retained workers, it is uncertain whether *total wages* will increase. Total wages for the firm may fall or, in some circumstances may rise. For firms with a highly sensitive demand curve for labor the total wages may, in fact, decline. If **there is no expansion in total wages, then there is no extra fuel to create an expansion of total spending.**

Beware: It is problematic to forecast a change in <u>total</u> wages, economy wide, based on raising the hourly minimum wage per worker.

More research needs to be done under controlled conditions where, in effect, the minimum wage is changed while other determining factors are held constant. This is not an easy task!

Remember: robust economic growth with increasing labor demand could temper some of the ill effects – layoffs and mechanization – of a minimum wage hike. However, the U.S. is unlikely to experience robust economic growth, e.g., above 4%. Moreover, **the supply of labor is continually augmented by the entry of illegals, refilling the pool of workers willing to accept *subminimum* wages.**

So, it seems that raising the minimum wage will not provide enough stimulus to the macro economy to spur robust economic growth.

[7. "The Minimum Wage Debate" 2 September 2014 *the Cato Institute*
<http://www.cato.org/joining-the-minimum-wage-debate>]

Union Wage: Another Price Floor

12. FALLA<IOUS <<ONOMI<US: Raising the union wage will improve the incomes of union members.

Correct Reasoning: Again, a tough call on a complex, emotional topic. First, see the minimum wage case above. The cases are similar in that both use legal means to impose a wage *above* the prevailing, unregulated market wage. Such artificial intrusions cause adjustments on both sides of the market. At first, one is tempted to predict the higher union wage will result in a smaller workforce, i.e., less demand for labor. In these cases some employers reduce their workforce through early retirements, fewer new hires or increased long term furloughs/layoffs. The remaining workers are asked to be more productive to make up for the loss of their colleagues. Thus, other things unchanged, employment may fall in unionized industries.

On the other hand, some union contracts can cause added hiring or retention of unneeded surplus workers in spite of the higher union wage/benefit package. This is called *featherbedding*. **Featherbedding** is considered highly inefficient, given that it employs more resources than needed to do the job, an over-allocation of resources to this activity. This imposes unnecessary opportunity cost on the economy. Indeed, it may retard the implementation of new, beneficial production technologies. But, featherbedding is the exception, not the rule.

Final blow: union membership has been shrinking in the United States, mirroring the manufacturing Diaspora and the decline of the middle class standard of living.

Price Ceilings, Rent Controls and Government Rationing

Selective price controls are not imposed to fight inflation. *Selective* price controls are imposed to restrain an *individual* market price from rising too high or falling too low. Controls to fight inflation are called **general price controls**. Oddly, it is possible for a *selective* price controls to contribute to a general inflation, in a micro meets macro 3D horror movie! Consider the price floor technique discussed below.

13. FALLACIOUS ECONOMICUS: Well, if the price of rent or gasoline threatens to go too high, the government can rule those to be illegal. The government can put a legal price ceiling, a *legal maximum price* on the good. Then no one gets shut out by a free market high price.

Correct Reasoning: A **price ceiling** is intended to keep a price *lower* than it would be on the free market. A **price floor** aims to keep a price *higher* than it would be on the free market. Are they tampering with Mother Nature?

These tools are not used widely and **not at the same time in the same market**. Imposing a legal price ceiling (a legal *maximum* price) or price floor (a legal *minimum* price) interferes with where the free market price "wants to go." Floors and ceilings interfere with "Mother Nature" and sometimes create unexpected, adverse side effects. Read all about it:

Unintended consequences. Buyers and sellers will react to the ceiling, altering their behavior in ways not intended by the price control. However, the reactions should not be unexpected. Indeed, the reactions are consistent over thousands of years of experience with price ceilings! Microeconomics has codified how buyers and sellers will react. Read all about it.

Price ceiling. The free market, in equilibrium, may exclude **deserving buyers**. For example, unable to pay free market rent, low income folks may also be shut out of rent controlled apartments.Well-intended do-gooders gin up the idea of imposing a price ceiling to help those excluded renters.

Buyers and Sellers React

Imposition of the ceiling below the free–market level distorts the market. Typically, demand and supply take off, but in opposite directions!

The artificially low ceiling price will **raise** demand while **lowering** supply of the most costly units. Availability of the good *declines* after the price ceiling is imposed. A **persistent shortage** results from imposition of the ceiling. Those previously excluded deserving buyers who were supposed to be helped by the ceiling may still be excluded at the ceiling price!

The shortage emerges. So, a ceiling price of $80 is imposed on a market which would have yielded a free market price of $100. It is argued that the $80 will enable left out buyers to acquire some product. But, apportioning the product among buyers is no longer orderly. Now, more is demanded, say, 500 units, than is supplied, say 400 units. Waiting lines and waiting lists develop as the artificially low price has stimulated demand *beyond* the free market level. Moreover, no help from the supply side as production of highest cost units is discouraged. **More folks look for rent controlled apartments while fewer folks move out and housing is withdrawn from the market ... or not built.** The housing shortage worsens! There is no way all buyers can go home with some of the product. Well, then, who are the lucky buyers ... are they deserving?

Is it fair? Remember, 500 units are demanded but only 400 units are supplied. Who gets to share in the available output, lower than the free market amount? A substitute rationing system has to be put in place of the price mechanism to keep order during distribution of the product.

Four alternative rationing methods. Each method gives no guarantee of goods getting to "deserving" buyers, compared to free market pricing.

1) First come, first serve. Waiting line formed; last liners get little or nothing.

2) Seller decides. Friends and relatives come first. Are they most deserving?

3) Mandatory government quotas. Everybody gets a little. In government dictated rationing, do cronies and donors get more coupons?

4) Lottery. But, do deserving buyers get lucky?

These solutions are imperfect, fallacious "solutions" to an equitable distribution of goods. None of the alternative rationing systems *guarantee* a share to those leftover, yet deserving buyers, unserved by the free market. As long as the legal ceiling price is in place a **persistent shortage** arises. **Speaking of fairness: how fair is a price ceiling to the seller?**

[8. See: Robert Schuettinger and Eamonn F. Butler *Forty Centuries of Wage and Price Controls*, Wash., D.C.: Heritage Foundation, 1979]

14. FALLACIOUS ECONOMICUS: The private market is an ideal, perfect arrangement. No government interference is ever needed.

Correct Reasoning: Most market advocates admit **the private market is not a perfect solution to the economic problem.** If left alone, the market *underproduces* some goods, *overproduces* others and produces none at all of a third class of goods. Government may be needed to:

a) encourage production of *underproduced* goods, such as education, low rent housing and public health facilities,

b) discourage the output of *overproduced* goods (having negative side effects such as excessive pollution) and,

c) produce what the market will not because exclusion is impossible (national defense system), the projects are risky, long term and expensive (space exploration). In some instances government supplements production in the private sector: schools, hospitals, roads and homeless shelters.

Subsidies, tax breaks, tax hikes, zoning regs, licensing and jawboning may be used by government to.

Equilibrium (or Balance) in a Micro Market

Under constant conditions and left alone by government, a free market will gravitate to a balance of opposing forces, supply and demand. Economists call this *equilibrium.* In equilibrium, price and quantity do not change as supply and demand are in balance, i.e., equal. **A balance of opposing forces creates and maintains the equilibrium.** There are no unhappy left out buyers or sellers to initiate change. **An equilibrium will remain as long as underlying conditions do not change.**

A change in underlying conditions creates imbalance, "reshuffles the deck," and brings about a new equilibrium, new price and new quantity. The **actual price** is "programmed" to seek the new equilibrium price; like homing pigeons seek home or politicians seek donations.

At the beach. Consider the power of equilibrium to rule in a free market. Take a beach ball into the water, submerge it and let it go. It pops up to the surface. Throw the ball in the air and it falls to the surface. Where is equilibrium for the ball? Floating on the surface of the water. When the ball is *left alone,* free to move as it pleases, it seeks and finds it own equilibrium level, natural under the conditions. The ball did not have to be directed to the water's surface. It went there on its own, as if it has conscious will.

Similarly, in a free micro market, surpluses and shortages usually "self-destruct" (resolve themselves), as follows:

➢   An **actual price** above the equilibrium will fall.

➢   An **actual price** below the equilibrium will rise.

Beware: While equilibrium may be efficient, questions of fairness may remain.

For example: How fair is the minimum wage to the employer?

>   **How fair is a price ceiling to the seller?**

>   **Are price floors to the farmers fair to the consumer?**

Beware: The phasing out of price ceiling rents is an implicit recognition of their failure to bring fairness to the housing market. In New York City, traditional rent control covering 27,000 apartments is being gradually being phased out and replaced by rent stabilization. "Newer" apartments (post 1947 for rent control and post 1971 for rent stabilization) are not controlled or stabilized.

Chapter Fifteen
Fallacies about Money and Wealth

A bank is a place that will lend you money if you can prove that you don't need it.   Bob Hope

MONEY and wealth are the subject of a multitude of myths and fallacies. A few of them are considered here and more are discussed in later chapters.

1. FALLACIOUS ECONOMICUS: Money is wealth.

Correct Reasoning: If wealth is something of value, then money is one form of wealth. Money originated with private individuals (traders/producers) who tried to improve their lives by overcoming the problems of **barter** (swapping goods for goods). Barter requires the synchronization (or coincidence) of wants between the parties to exchange, a difficult barrier to overcome. Yet, barter works for some people, some of the time and there are barter clubs that ease the way. However, **barter is destructive if tried for all people, all the time.** (Fallacy of composition kicks in!)

Unlike barter, money is compatible with specialization and the division of labor, both force multipliers of resources. Other things being equal, an economy using money exchange **(a monetary economy)** is more productive, facilitates more exchanges, and create higher standards of living than a barter economy. Government dominates modern money, called M1: currency, token coin, and checkable deposits (private bank money subject to government regulation). Modern money is not backed by or convertible into gold, silver, or any precious metal. It is **fiat money, i.e.,** money by government decree, and intrinsically worthless. Its value lies in its acceptability, its ability to command goods in exchange. Without goods to buy, and sellers to accept it, today's **token and fiat money** is worthless.

Money is the generally accepted means of final payment. It is a *claim* to real wealth: goods and services in general, land (improved or not improved) and other nonhuman resources. The U.S. monetary unit - the dollar – functions as a baseline **standard of value** or yardstick for measuring value. It provides the monetary unit for measuring and labeling wealth. In the Euro zone the monetary unit is the Euro.

In addition to being an abstract concept, a measuring rod for wealth, the monetary unit also incarnates as a physical means of payment, a **medium of**

exchange, the money itself! (More precisely, money is a medium *for* exchange.) As such, an accumulation (or stock) of money in a safe, wallet or bank account is *financial* wealth. Money also serves as an imperfect **store of (real) value**, i.e., future buying power.

The Primary Functions of Money

Money serves as a) medium for exchange b) standard of value c) perfect store of *nominal* value d) an imperfect store of *real* value.

Today's money is not real wealth. Money belongs to the **financial wealth** family. Financial wealth denotes money or claims to money. That family includes stocks, bonds, and retirement annuities. **Real wealth** indicates actual consumer and capital goods. For example: food, furniture, cars, real estate, jewels and yachts, real things with value. Traditionally, gold, silver or some other useful commodity led a double life. It served as a commodity and also as a medium for exchanges. But, modern money in the form of currency, coin and checkable deposits has very little if any value as a commodity. Its value is in *exchange*, for today's or tomorrow's goods.

Money gives its possessor command and control over goods and resources. But, what good is money without resources and goods, i. e., real wealth, to command?

Preview of Financial Accounting

2. FALLA<IOUS €<ONOMI<US: Assets are the sole or best measure of wealth. It's what you got that counts. And it doesn't matter how you got it.

Fallacious Reasoning: As a fallacy, this proposition is debatable. Assets are things of value in your possession: cash, your house and car, property you own. This is what makes for a comfortable life. One might argue that the more assets, the better. So, who cares how you got them?

Correct Reasoning: This is a tough one. Yes, assets are all that. But, from an outsider's point of view perhaps **Net Worth** is a better one number measure of one's wealth.

Net Worth is {your assets} minus {outside claims to those assets}

Net worth (or, Net Assets), is that part of your assets that belong to you, which no one else can legally claim. Net worth (or owners' equity) is that part of your assets you own outright, not obtained by going into debt. In accounting, Net Worth is synonymous with Capital. Again, assets are the stock of things of value a person has at a given moment. Assets are a source of good things, benefits. Assets include a house, a car, a bank account, antiques, even Uncle

Ezra's IOU for the $1000. Outside claims on those assets might include a mortgage payable to the bank, credit card debt or money owed to a brother-in-law. Then, there the most versatile of assets, the king of assets: **CASH!**

Cash for solvency. Cash is the most versatile asset. Adequate cash is needed to remain SOLVENT, that is, pay bills as they come due. If one does not pay one's bills when due creditors may force an **involuntary bankruptcy** proceeding. The bankruptcy proceeding may lead to a court ordered seizure of some assets to make pay off those creditors. So, **cash is king**; use it to pay maturing debts, keeping the business alive by forestalling involuntary bankruptcy. Other assets such as building, land and inventories may not be convertible into cash quickly enough to pay bills as they come due.

Yes, certainly, there is an element of truth in the idea that assets are the best measure of wealth. After all, assets are available for use and enjoyment, regardless of where the person got them from. Assets are important, but they are only one dimension of a person's (or a business's) financial and material well-being profile.

First line of defense against losses. It matters how assets are acquired! In business practice, **owner money is the first money considered "eaten up" when operations have losses**. Creditor money is second and last in line to absorb losses.

Observers caution that the manner in which assets are acquired may impact the degree of happiness derived from the asset package. Assets may be acquired by **investing one's own money, re-investing earned monies, borrowing or receiving a gift.** Borrowing creates liabilities, interest and debts that must be repaid, usually on a regular basis. For example, borrowing to buy a house creates the obligation to repay the debt with interest. This is called a (monthly) mortgage payment. Surprise: borrowings must be repaid! Yes, shocking! This gives sleepless nights to some borrowers. Sometimes lenders put restrictions on how the asset (borrowed money) is to be used.

On certain occasions, the law restricts how owner claimed money is dispensed in corporations. These restrictions reduce the utility derived from assets. Owner money can sit in the firm for a long time. In a corporation owner money can sit forever, as the corporation has an infinite legal life. Owner money gives a fledgling business a little more "breathing room," more flexibility to invest long term. Long term debt plays a similar role. **Debts usually carry a fixed repayment schedule involving interest and/or principal.** Those sometimes kick in quickly and must be met with cash outlays.

Owner money carries no immediate commitment to repay. As such, it is ideal to finance long term projects with delayed pay-offs. Long term borrowed money may be considered as substitute for or complement to owner money. **Borrowed money may substitute for owner money, using the *leverage effect* in an attempt to magnify the returns to the owners.** Going into debt permits expansion perhaps unavailable absent the debt. So, income producing assets may be acquired by owner money or borrowed money. Just make sure those debt payments are made on time or creditors could force a firm into bankruptcy proceedings.

Fundamental Equation of Accounting

The fundamental equation is among the finest inventions of the human mind....
- Goethe

3. FALLACIOUS ECONOMICUS: Too bad there is no simple framework to logically integrate the terms assets, liabilities and what is leftover when liabilities are deducted from assets.

Correct Reasoning: There *is* a way to integrate all three concepts. It is called the **fundamental equation of accounting.**

Classic accounting version:

Assets are identically equal to [Liabilities PLUS Capital (or Net Worth)]

> **The Fundamental Equation of Accounting**
> This is the legal view
> $$A \equiv L + C$$

This is the financial management view:

{Assets [identically equal to] Sources of Assets}

The Net Worth formulation:

{Assets [minus] Liabilities $\equiv$ Net Worth, Net Assets or Capital}

Net Worth or Capital is that part of assets claimed by the owners or belongs to the owners. Outsiders – creditors - have no legal claim on these assets.

But, beware: **Net Worth may be a clue to over or under used financial leverage.**

If one wants to gauge business *operating* capabilities then all assets at the command of the firm may be a better measure than Net Assets (= Net Worth).

The fundamental equation is reported as The Balance Sheet, a formal statement of assets, liabilities and capital at a *point* in time.

Distribution of cash upon business dissolution and asset liquidation: If push comes to shove in a bankruptcy proceeding and assets are liquidated, claimants to the assets get in line. First in line are the **creditors**, represented by the liabilities on the Balance Sheet.

They stand in front of the owners in the line.

In bankruptcy (or even voluntary liquidation) the liabilities are paid off first and the owners get the amount left over. (Taking priority: Assets that had been pledged as specific collateral for specific debts are liquidated and the proceeds set aside to pay off these specific obligations.) The more debts there are, the further back go the owners in the repayment line! Do not expect the liquidation value of assets to equal their book value. So, after debts are repaid there is no guarantee the leftover cash equals the Net Worth on the books!

4. FALLACIOUS ECONOMICUS: I owe $100,000 on my home mortgage. I only have $10,000 in cash. I am done for! I cannot pay off this mortgage. The bank will seize my house and I will lose everything!

Correct Reasoning: A debtor may appear overwhelmed when *total* debt, right now, is compared to the available means of payment, right now. This **static perspective** is unfair to the debtor.

The *total* amount of debt is rarely due on a single day. A fraction may come due each month, as in a home mortgage. In nearly every situation, as long as a debtor keeps paying his bills *when due* he is solvent and not in default, *regardless of the total amount of debt.* This is the concept of **dynamic (through time) solvency**. To remain solvent the debtor must pay only the amount due on the due date.

Mortgage default. By the way, you may not lose everything if you default on your mortgage and the bank seizes your house. The bank will auction the house off, take what is owed to it and return any leftover monies to you. When the auction fails to yield enough cash (say, only $50K, the market value of the property) to pay off the mortgage (say, $80K), it is an **underwater mortgage.**

5. FALLACIOUS ECONOMICUS: Wow, good news! Now all I have to do is pay the minimum payments on my credit cards.

Correct Reasoning: Yes, pay the minimums and you remain solvent in a legal sense. Yes, there a floating amount that never seems to come due. But, it is a costly strategy, in a financial sense. The interest rate you are charged on unpaid credit card balances is double digit, sometimes over twenty percent! By paying only the minimum called for each month interest will be charged on unpaid interest, over and above the principal! Take on lower interest loan to consolidate credit card debt into one lower but longer payment.

Chapter Sixteen
Fallacies Concerning
The Legal Footprint of a Firm

Where there is no law, there is no freedom.   — John Locke

very commercial venture, from sidewalk hot-dog vendor to transnational enterprise, has a legal identity or standing. It has a status before the law indicating its rights, responsibilities and powers. The three traditional (or legacy) legal forms are: sole proprietorship, partnership and corporation. These are the old-timers, well established and familiar. But, recently a parade of alphabet soups entities has arrived, lead by the LLC, a limited liability company. **Beware: LLC law and practice is still evolving, so double check with a lawyer/C.P.A. in your state before getting involved as an owner (called a *member*), creditor or customer of an LLC.** [The general case is discussed at the end of the chapter.]Read all about it:

1. FALLACIOUS ECONOMICUS: The legal form of business organization of a borrower is irrelevant to a lender contemplating a loan. All borrowers are equally responsible to repay debts, regardless of their legal status.

Fallacious Reasoning: It doesn't matter who you lend money to. If they owe it to you, then they have a legal obligation to repay regardless of their legal form.

Correct Reasoning: Do not ignore the legal status of a borrower. It DOES matter who you loan money to. If you lend money to a corporation or an LLC, it is only liable to re-pay loans from *business* monies and other assets. The corporate creditors do not get repaid if the corporation is unable to pay its debts from *corporate* funds. No matter how wealthy they are, the corporate owners, called stockholders, do not have to dig into their personal cash and assets holdings to repay corporate debts. This feature of a corporation is called **limited liability, meaning limited responsibility.** Stockholder responsibility for corporate debts ends when business assets have been exhausted by pay out or loss. In general, **business owners enjoying limited liability are not required to use their personal assets to satisfy unpaid business debts.**

So, beware in lending to a corporation or an LLC. Scrutinize their financial statements. When dealing with a corporation, focus on the debt paying ability of the business, not the wealth and glamour of the owner(s). The debts of big corporations bear credit ratings from (supposedly) independent agencies and some are insured by private insurance companies.

2. FALLACIOUS ECONOMICUS: Limited liability applies to partners and sole proprietors as well as corporate stockholders.

Fallacious Reasoning: Well, if stockholders have limited liability, then to be fair, partners and sole proprietors must have it, too, no?

Correct Reasoning: General Partners and sole proprietors do *not* have limited liability for business debts. On the contrary, they have **unlimited liability** for debts of the business. Personal assets cannot be shielded from business creditors. Should *business* assets be exhausted in paying debts, then *personal* assets may be sought legally for repayment. [Owners of an LLC are referred to as *members*. They enjoy limited liability.]

More Info on the Corporate Form

A separate business, accounting and legal entity. Like a partnership and sole proprietors, a corporation is a *separate business entity* for accounting purposes. It has its own set of books, its own reckoning of assets, liabilities, capital and income from activities specific to it and separate from its owners personal affairs. However, *unlike* a partnership or sole proprietorship a corporation is a separate, free standing *legal entity* with rights and obligations spelled out in law. (Likewise, an LLC is a separate legal entity.) **An LLC has reduced "red tape" relative to a corporation.**

A separate taxable entity. In addition, a corporation is a separate *taxable* entity, taxed separately from its natural person owners. Alternatively, the sole proprietorship and partnership are *not* taxed as entities separate and apart from their owners. For those entities, there is no separate business entity that is taxable for its income.

Unlimited life. As a separate artificial legal person, the corporation has an unlimited life. Shares of ownership pass to new owners on the death of a stockholder. [Note that an LLC terminates upon the death of a member.]

Double taxation. Corporate taxable income is taxed, after which cash dividends may be paid. Once dividends are paid, a personal income tax is levied on the recipient of the dividend income. This is the often denounced double *taxation of corporate earnings*, a significant disadvantage to the corporate form. By contrast, income on partnership or sole proprietorship "passes through" the business to the owner(s)' personal tax return. No double taxation here.

Contract capable. The corporation has contract making power, i.e., it can enter into contracts and own property in its own name. (Of course, a natural real person or persons are empowered to act on behalf of the corporation!)

Limited liability. Stockholders have limited liability for corporate debts. Personal assets are legally shielded from business debts. When it exhausts its assets in paying debts, the corporation and its stockholders are discharged from further debt payments. In fact, the most a stockholder can lose is what was invested. This contrasts sharply with a sole proprietorship or partnership where the owner bears **full personal legal responsibility for business debts**. The owner (or one partner) could be responsible for all the business debts to the full extent of one's personal assets: the house, the car, the dog!

Created at the state level. Nearly all corporations are created by State governments. Delaware is the favorite for large firms. But, business activity is not limited to the state of incorporation. Only a handful have a Federal charter, such as national banks, the Federal Reserve Banks and other Federal agencies. Laws governing corporations may vary from state to state. Corporations are relatively easy to set-up. In most states a nominal fee and formal papers filled out and – boom! – you are a corporation in less than a week.

[1. An excellent survey of legal forms of business can be found on the Small Business Administration website. "Choose Your Business Structure," *13 March 2014* Small Business Administration <http://tinyurl.com/l5ndpey>
Also see, "Use Your Business Structure to Limit Liability," 13 March 2015 *BizFilings* <http://tinyurl.com/bnzww9k >]

Q. Can I avoid corporate income tax by reinvesting my profits?

Yes. First of all, in a real sense a firm does not re-invest profits, an accounting measure. It invests **cash** in inventory, building, equipment or intangible long term assets. Accounting rules allow some of these investment costs to morph into expenses as the accounting year progresses. For example, a part of overall equipment cost becomes tax deductible depreciation expense. Then, at year end, tax deductible *expenses* are deducted from *revenues* to determine **taxable income**. You are taxed on your taxable income (Earnings before Tax) for the year. If you re-invested cash equal to expenses, such that your expenses eat up all the revenues, then you have no net profits and pay no taxes! So, yes, your reinvestment of what would have become "profit" allowed you to avoid taxes on that reinvestment. Astute expense/asset management can lead to at least some reduction in corporate income tax due to re-investment.

---

3. FALLACIOUS ECONOMICUS: I guess that decides it for me. I don't want liability from some small business I start. I have to shield my family assets. I

must become a corporation to get limited liability and protect my family's assets from bad results in my business.

Correct Reasoning: That statement is not strictly true. There are other ways a business owner can shield personal assets from business debts. For example,

> ➢ A storeowner/sole proprietor could buy **liability insurance** against lawsuits, much as a driver gets liability insurance for car accident settlements. For example, if a passerby slips on snow the storeowner failed to remove and sues for a large cash amount. The storeowner/sole proprietor should carry liability insurance which, hopefully, would cover any settlement costs.

> ➢ Structure the business as a partnership and become **a limited partner**. A business may be structured as a limited partnership with one general partner and other limited partners. The limited partners have limited liability but the general partner retains unlimited liability. There is a price to pay for this protection: Limited partners are usually passive investors with no say in the management. TANSTAAFL!

> ➢ If qualified, investors may form a **Limited Liability Company**.

Related **FALLA<IOUS <<ONOMI<US**: A corporation cannot shield its assets from claims by creditors.

Correct Reasoning: 1) A well-known corporation may wish to hide its identity due to legal or ethical concerns about some of its activity. A legally formed *subsidiary* corporation, a separate entity, named differently could provide that secrecy. 2) Perhaps a corporation (the parent) is about to venture into a high risk area involving substantial liability. It may create another wholly owned corporation (the subsidiary) to absorb and limit liability, thereby shielding the assets of the parent. 3) A foreign branch may be incorporated separately.

Under the parent-subsidiary arrangement, any liability arising from the subsidiary activity is *limited to the assets of the subsidiary* corporation, thereby shielding the parent company assets.

4. FALLA<IOUS <<ONOMI<US: Corporations pay the same tax rate on income as do partnerships and sole proprietorships.

Fallacious Reasoning: It only seems fair to treat them equally.

Correct Reasoning: The specter of **double taxation** haunts the corporation. The specter makes no appearance at the partnership and sole proprietorship doors. Corporate Federal income tax is applied to corporate taxable income on a graduated or progressive rate basis. As of 2014 the brackets ranged from 15% for the lowest layer of income to 35% for the highest income layer. This is known as a C corporation. If the remaining income is paid out as a dividend, the dividends count as personal income to the stockholders and liable to the personal income tax. This feature is referred to as the **double taxation of earnings.** In 2014 the highest marginal tax bracket for individuals is 39.6%.

[2. Business Owners' Toolkit, "S and C Corporations Create different Tax Consequences" 6 February 2014 *Bizfilings* <http://tinyurl.com/njyms84>]

In an S Corporation, a filing status not available to large, industrial corporations, there is no corporate income tax. The entire amount of income can be passed through to the stockholders and taxed as personal income.

Deferred Tax on Foreign Earnings

Most other developed countries employ a **territorial tax system.** In that system, only *domestic* profits are taxed. Foreign earnings are basically earned tax free as to the home country. Alternatively, the U.S. follows a **worldwide tax system.** In principle, profits earned anywhere in the world are subject to U.S. corporate income tax. However, the U.S. allows its firms to **defer** federal tax on their overseas earnings, *as long as the earnings remain offshore.* Foreign taxes paid are credited toward the ultimate U.S. obligation. This gives American corporations an incentive to leave foreign earned profits reinvested overseas.

---

5. FALLACIOUS ECONOMICUS: Leaving cash from unremitted profits overseas has left many U.S. companies strapped for cash to pay dividends, undertake real capital expansion and meet expenses back home.

Fallacious Reasoning: If you don't have the cash, you don't have the cash, no?

Correct Reasoning: American corporations dusted off an old cash raising strategy in lieu of repatriating dollar profits and paying the U.S. income tax on them. **Borrow the money!** Read all about it:

> Since 2008, the Fed's easy cash policies have allowed companies to buy back stock, pay dividends and make acquisitions largely *without tapping cash from overseas subsidiaries* ... Among more than 240 companies disclosing increases in unremitted foreign earnings in 2013, those with bigger increases tended to also see bigger increases in corporate debt, according to data from research firm Calcbench.
>
> [3. Theo Francis and Ted Mann "America's Business Puzzle: Record Debt and Record Cash: Tax-Avoidance Logic" 3 August 2014 *Wall Street Journal Online* <http://tinyurl.com/pbu89vn>]

Consider a corporation in need of cash. Given a low interest situation in the U.S., a U.S. domiciled corporation needing cash considers borrowing money in the U.S. as a substitute for bringing home foreign earnings. The cost conscious corporation must crunch the numbers to figure which is the cheapest way to acquire cash. If borrowing is chosen, the corporation must conclude borrowing money at home (and paying interest thereon) is cheaper than repatriating foreign profits (and paying taxes thereon). The interest burden is less than the tax burden, so let's borrow!

A "wrench" is thrown into the Federal budget process. The U.S. Treasury loses the tax dollars, for now. Other taxpayers (or U.S. bond buyers) must pick up the slack left by unpaid and deferred taxes on the foreign earnings. The equity of the tax system is called into question.

Tax Inversion

A more radical approach to avoiding American tax on ALL earnings, foreign and domestic, is to give up one's legal identity as an American corporation. This is referred to as *tax inversion* or *corporate inversion*. Implementing the strategy changes the corporation's official, legal residence to a lower tax nation.

The move is a pure tax gambit, not intended to re-organize or re-structure operations. Most or all of the operations remain located as before the switch. Even so, this is radical surgery. The corporation sheds its national identity as an American corporation. Perhaps it adopts a new national identity as a Bermuda or Irish Corporation. One way to accomplish this is for the American Corporation to merge with a foreign corporation domiciled in the foreign land. **Many foreign nations have NO corporate income tax!**

Although tax inversions are legal, they do not sit well with the American people and present a public relations challenge to the corporation involved.

6. FALLACIOUS ECONOMICUS: Limited liability is meaningless.

Correct Reasoning: Limited liability is a plus. The limited liability feature of the corporate ownership is the most attractive factor enabling large amounts of money to be raised from a diversified group of **stockholders**. One can invest as little or as much as one wants in a corporation. The maximum, worst case scenario is a stockholder's **losses are limited to what was invested**, even if corporate creditors are left "high and dry." Becoming a limited partner will cut liability to the amount invested, as with corporate stock.

7. FALLACIOUS ECONOMICUS: The sole proprietorship and partnership forms are just as attractive as the corporate form for raising large amounts of money.

Correct Reasoning: The divisibility of ownership available in the corporate form gives it a huge edge in raising large amounts of money.

Ownership in a corporation may be divided into many small pieces or shares. This enables a large number of moderate income people to buy as many (or as few) small "pieces" of ownership as they prefer. Potential losses are limited to the amount invested. Bundles of shares can be gathered in "customized packages" of 100 shares per bundle (a **round lot**) and multiples of 100. This encourages a wide range of risk taking by investors.

Beware: Again, the most a stockholder can lose is what was invested. Not so with a sole proprietorship or partnership. Be very careful entering a partnership! A very small investment could potentially bring all the debts down on **one partner**, who then has to give personal assets to settle the claims! One's ownership share is not easily transferred in a in an ordinary partnership. Compared to partnership interest, corporate shares are easily transferrable.

Master Limited Partnership (MLP)

Normally, acquiring or disposing of a partner's ownership interest is a cumbersome legal process. Read all about it:

Partnerships generally lack the ease of changing ownership found in a corporation. Partnerships generally lack the ease of buying and selling stock in a corporation. The other partners could block the entry of a new partner or block the sale of an existing partnership interest.

A *master limited partnership* (MLP) is a special form of partnership allowing change of ownership interest, similar to trading stock in a corporation.

> **Master Limited Partnerships**, or MLPs, are tax pass through entities that derive 90 percent of their income from the exploration, development, mining or production, processing, refining, transportation, or the marketing of minerals and natural resources. Their ownership consists of one or more General Partners (GPs), which have managerial and administrative control over an MLP, and many Limited Partners (LPs), which provide capital to an MLP and are entitled to periodic distributions, but have no control over operations. Investors can access an MLP by buying LP 'common units' on an exchange or by purchasing shares of publically traded General Partners.
>
> [4. Globalxfunds, "AN OVERVIEW OF THE GENERAL PARTNERS OF MASTER LIMITED PARTNERSHIPS" 15 Oct. 2014<http://tinyurl.com/oda7wwj]

8. FALLACIOUS ECONOMICUS: When a business is dissolved, the owners take their money out first. The remainder is there for the creditors.

Correct Reasoning: As discussed earlier, upon the dissolution of a business the assets are sold and converted into cash (liquidation). Legally, the creditors are paid first. Any remaining cash goes to the owners. This is true for sole proprietorships, partnerships and corporations. Partners and sole proprietors are *personally* responsible for debt not covered by the asset liquidation cash. Corporate stockholders are not responsible for leftover debt.

9. FALLACIOUS ECONOMICUS: In bad years, a corporation can skip paying dividends to stockholders or not pay interest to bondholders. Both are optional.

Correct Reasoning: Dividends are optional, interest due is not. **Semi-annual, contractual interest to bondholders is the highest priority for payout.** Dividends must come after interest commitments are paid. Failure to pay the interest on a bond (or the maturity value at maturity) constitutes default, a breach of contract. Serious consequences may ensue as the bondholders seek legal remedies, including bankruptcy proceedings. It is imperative that the business, especially the large corporation, pay its debts when due!

The worst case scenario for the corporation is **involuntary bankruptcy**. In that case the creditors force the firm to sell off its remaining assets, to raise as much cash as possible. This is the last drastic option for creditors. Owners would try to negotiate a reasonable, extended pay schedule *before* raising cash through asset liquidation. Asset liquidation sales signal the end of the functioning business.

10. FALLACIOUS ECONOMICUS: A corporation must meet its dividend commitments, just like interest due on its bonds payable.

Correct Reasoning: This can get a little complicated, so pay close attention. **Basically, dividend payments are optional**. In general, three conditions must be present for a corporation to have cash dividend "commitments."

1. The corporation must be **financially qualified**, i.e., able to spare the cash. After all, the cash will be paid out and thereafter unavailable for use in the firm. So, either the firm has the cash or can get it.

2. The firm must be **legally qualified** to make a payment to the stockholders. For this the firm must have retained Net Income from this and prior years, called Retained Earnings. (Look in the Stockholders' Equity section of the Balance Sheet to find Retained Earnings). [Note that some states relax this requirement] The corporation may satisfy the first two steps but cannot pay a dividend unless the last step is taken.

3. The corporation's Board of Directors must **vote in favor** of the dividend payment. Then, the amount and timing of the dividend must be **announced**

publicly. A date of record and date of payment must be specified. Only with this last step does the legal commitment arise to pay a dividend. Dividends payable show in Liabilities section of the company's Balance Sheet.

Unlike interest due, **a dividend commitment may be avoided by not declaring them publicly.**

Beware, the first two conditions may be met but the firm chooses not to pay a dividend. Some highly profitable corporations rarely or never pay dividends! Stockholders have little recourse in these cases. Perhaps they could elect a Board sympathetic to dividend payments or hope for price appreciation.

11. FALLACIOUS ECONOMICUS: But, wait a second. I own Preferred Stock. According to the stock share, they must pay me my dividend every year. They cannot omit or "pass the dividend." Passing the dividend would be like defaulting on a bond.

Correct Reasoning: Cash dividends on Preferred Stock, called Preferred dividends, must meet the three criteria spelled out in fallacy #10 above. This means Dividends on Preferred Stock are optional until they have been publicly declared by the Board of Directors. The Preferred feature means Preferred stockholders must be paid first, before any dividends on Common Stock.

Unlike Common dividends which have no dollar limits except Earnings, Preferred dividends are usually capped, limited to a fixed amount. However, like the common dividend, the preferred dividend may be avoided by not declaring it.

Most Preferred issues are **cumulative with respect to dividends**. Should the Preferred dividend *not* be paid, the unpaid amounts usually accumulate year by year. They are said to go into **arrears**. Here is the killer with preferred dividends in arrears: in future years, no dividends can be paid on the Common stock as long as any Preferred dividends in arrears remain.

If dividends are passed for lack of Retained Earnings, then Cash Dividends or Stock Dividends cannot be paid on any issue until the corporation becomes profitable. Two points: 1) Stock splits or reverse splits are permissible in the absence of Retained Earnings and 2) Some states may be more lenient on the Retained Earnings requirement. The source of dividends should be part of a public disclosure by the firm.

By the way, if the Dividend on Common Stock is passed in a given year, they **do not go into arrears,** i.e., create a future obligation. Passed dividends on common stock are *not* cumulative. If the common dividend is passed there is no legal requirement that the passed dividend be made up in later years. In effect, they are gone forever.

Warning: Corporations are creatures of the State governments. Bear in mind that laws may differ from State to State as to the powers and responsibilities of a corporation to the public, its creditors and stockholders. Consult an attorney!

Note that Convertible preferred stock and convertible bonds are usually **callable** as well as convertible into common stock.

Limited Liability or Unlimited Liability?

12. FALLACIOUS ECONOMICUS: I like the limited liability feature of the corporate form. When I set up my small corporation and invest some cash in it I can always withdraw that cash whenever I need it for private, non business purposes. I'll use the corporation as my private automatic teller machine.

Correct Reasoning: Stockholders are free to invest additional cash in the corporation in exchange for more shares. One technique for cash withdrawal would be the payment of cash dividends, at the discretion of the Board of Directors. But, cash dividends cannot be withdrawn unless there are earnings that have not been the basis for earlier payouts. These are called Retained Earnings. In many states, cash withdrawn *in excess* of Retained Earnings would impair the legal capital, violate the legal capital rule and not be permitted.

Legal Capital Rule: Protects Corporate Creditors

13. FALLACIOUS ECONOMICUS: OK, well maybe the corporation cannot pay me a dividend unless there have been earnings. I know they are not legally obligated to do so, but why not have the corporation buy back my stock?

Correct Reasoning: The conditions for buying back stock are the same as paying cash dividends. There must be (positive) Retained Earnings on the Balance Sheet. Then, the Board of Directors must authorize the buy-back. So, do not invest cash in a corporation if you might need it back right away!

Background: These restrictions are reflections of the **legal capital rule**. It is designed to protect the corporate creditors. The rule says the corporation cannot make payments to stockholders that would impair the "legal capital" of the firm. Basically, the legal capital lays claim to assets which cannot be withdrawn from the firm by the owners.

Just because they have limited liability they cannot "loot" the firm of assets and leave the creditors without assets to claim in bankruptcy. **Assets corresponding to the legal capital cannot be impaired (reduced) by returning them to the stockholders.** Those assets are supposed to remain in the firm to be used as a last resort to help pay off creditors. The legal capital rule favors creditors. It is designed to offset the limited liability protection available to stockholders.

[5. "Dividend Payment and the Legal Capital Rule" 2 May *Legal Help* 2014<http://tinyurl.com/q7y34s4 >]

So, once owners invest cash in a corporation the money is, in effect, locked in. Given adverse circumstances, it may never be paid out as a dividend or used for a stock buyback. Beware the promise of cash dividends in the absence of Retained Earnings! Dissolution of the corporation trumps the legal capital rule and – after payback of creditors – allows the return of assets to stockholders.

14. FALLACIOUS ECONOMICUS: I am a stockholder and I am glad there is a **legal capital rule**. It protects me and the other stockholders.

Correct Reasoning: False! The rule is intended to protect creditors by mandating a certain amount of capital cannot be impaired by the owners. But, the legal capital rule doesn't protect creditors from involuntary Net Losses due to bad business conditions or management incompetence. A Net Loss means expenses (which eat up capital) exceed revenues (which raise capital) for the year. So, overall a Net Loss eats up capital and could eat up so much capital it works through all the Retained Earnings and other Surpluses. If losses persist they will eat into the last bastion of capital, the legal capital layer of capital.

15. FALLACIOUS ECONOMICUS: I have a sole proprietorship and resent the fact the legal capital rule keeps me from withdrawing cash from my business. After all, I have to pay rent on my personal apartment and tuition for my kid's college. It is my money, why can't I take it out of the business?

Correct Reasoning: Good news, you *can* take cash out at will from a sole proprietorship or partnership. There is no legal capital rule in those cases. The reason is, sole proprietors and partners have *unlimited* liability for business debts. So, it does not matter where they keep their cash or other assets, in or out of the business. All assets, business and personal, are eligible to be seized by creditors seeking payment.

16. FALLACIOUS ECONOMICUS: If I cannot get cash dividends, then I cannot enjoy any gain from investing in stock.

Correct Reasoning: Cheer up! All is not lost! There are a number of ways you can gain, even in the absence of cash dividends. Here is some general advice [always consult a credentialed investment advisor before acting!]

1. The obvious strategy: wait for a price increase, then sell your shares.

2. Hope for **stock dividends** instead of cash dividends. Stock dividends are free distributions of some small amount of shares of stock. Shares can then be sold. (Retained Earnings are needed to legally enable this distribution.)

3. Hope for **stock split** of 2 for 1 or 3 for 1. Turn in one share and get 2 or 3 in return. No cash exchanges hands. Additional shares may be held or sold. Collective value of stock usually rises. (Retained Earnings are not needed)

4. Write a **covered call**. Sell, for a fee, the right to buy these shares from you at a price above the current one.

[6. Find an excellent treatment of this strategy at: "How to Write Covered Calls: 5 Tips for Success" 3 May 2014 *TradeKing* < http://tinyurl.com/p8gsxsw >]

Other strategies exist – consult your credentialed investment advisor before acting! **The Limited Liability Company-Your Cake and Eat it, Too?**

➢ Beware! A very popular, easily created new legal form of organization has appeared in the last few years. It is called a Limited Liability Company **(LLC).** It is an appropriate form for small companies with a single owner or handful of partners. The owners are referred to as **members** (Note that it is a form open to nonprofits, as well.) A corporation can be a member of an LLC, but not a member of a PLLC. There can be a single member LLC for the solo entrepreneur.

➢ A Limited Liability Company (LLC) is a creature of a State, a business entity having certain characteristics of both a corporation and partnership or sole proprietorship (depending on how many owners there are).

➢ The primary characteristic an LLC shares with a corporation is **limited liability,** and the primary characteristic it shares with a partnership is the availability of **pass-through income** taxation.

➢ "Like a corporation, a **limited liability company** or 'LLC,' is a separate and distinct legal entity. This means that an LLC can get a tax identification number, open a bank account and do business, all under its own name." [7]

[7."Definition of a Limited Liability Company or LLC" 29 July 2016 <http://tinyurl.com/je8r7pf>]

➢ An LLC can elect to be taxed as a sole proprietor, partnership, S corporation or C corporation (as long as they would otherwise qualify for such tax treatment), providing for a great deal of flexibility.

➢ In cases where distributions to members render the LLC insolvent, a *personal* liability may reside with the members.

➢ The limited liability feature may be weakened or nonexistent for **malpractice** suits in licensed LLCs professions of medicine, engineering, accounting or law. These professionals create a Professional LLC, or PLLC.

Beware: Business and corporate law may vary from State to State. The above discussion has been general in nature and not meant to speak with perfect legal authority. Always seek legal counsel before adopting a legal form of organization.

17. FALLACIOUS ECONOMICUS: Net operating losses in any one year are "chiseled in stone." Kiss goodbye forever the lost money.

Correct Reasoning: No! The U.S. tax code allows an operating loss to be carried forward 20 years and applied to the **taxable income** of profitable years, avoiding income tax of later years. This is a perfectly legitimate, long time tax practice! (The same break is available on capital losses versus future capital gains).

Overview of the Net Operating Loss Carryback and Carryforward [8]

When a business reports operating expenses on its tax return that *exceed* its revenues, a net operating loss (NOL) has been created. An NOL can be used in some other tax reporting period as an **offset to taxable income**, which reduces the tax liability of the reporting entity. The basic rules for using an NOL are:

1. Carry the amount back to the preceding two tax years and apply it against any taxable income, which can generate an immediate tax rebate. OR
2. Carry the amount forward for the next 20 years and apply it against any taxable income, which reduces the amount of taxable income, and tax, in those years.
3. After 20 years, any remaining NOL is cancelled.

[8. "Loss Carryback and Carryforward" 2 Oct. 2016 *Accounting Tools* <http://www.accountingtools.com/nol-carryforward>]

Chapter Seventeen
Accounting Fallacies

[The reader is urged to re-read pages 125 and 126 before engaging this chapter.]

THE language of business is accounting. But, that language is often misunderstood and misused. Everyone who handles money or is in business must grapple with technical issues in accounting. Fallacies abound. Of course, **Debits equal Credits** is not a fallacy, but a rock ribbed truth in accounting. Some fallacies are explored below. The Venetian friar Luca Pacioli is generally considered to be the father of modern accounting and the author of the first accounting textbook.

[1. L. Murphy Smith "Luca Pacioli: The Father of Accounting" 14 July 2014 *American Accounting Association* <http://aaahq.org/southwest/pacioli.htm>]

1. FALLA<IOUS <<ONOMI<US: The terms sales revenue, gross profit, net profit, net income, and earnings all mean the same thing.

Correct Reasoning: Unfortunately, sloppy usage has allowed some of these terms to be used interchangeably in the press and business literature. These terms come from a business report called an **Income Statement** or **Statement of Profit and Loss.** (See Exhibit #1 below).

Exhibit #1:   XYZ Corporation
              Statement of Profit and Loss (or Income Statement)
              For the Year 20XX

Sales or Service Revenue (the amount earned) **[THE TOP LINE]**	$10M
minus the **Cost Goods Sold (CGS)**	Minus 6M
(The Cost of Goods Sold is what the business had to pay to acquire or manufacture those sold goods.)	
So, if Revenue is $10M and the CGS is $6M, then **Gross Profit (GP)** is	$4M
Other expenses, (but not interest expense) deducted from GP	Minus 1M
Earnings Before Interest and Taxes (EBIT) EBIT	$3M
Deduct interest expense and that gives	Minus 1M
Earnings Before Taxes (EBT) EBT is	$2M
Deduct **corporate income tax**, and that gives	Minus 0.5M
Earnings after tax (EAT) = EAT [THE BOTTOM LINE]	$1.5M

The Line Gang

The top line. Revenues are the top line. Arguably, Revenues approximate the value *created* during the period whereas Expenses approximate the value *destroyed* in the process of creation.

The middle line. EBIT, sometimes called Operating Earnings is an important "milestone" in the Statement of Profit and Loss. It is an indicator of how well management used the resources available to the firm (without regard to how the firm acquired those resources, borrowing or owner money).

The **bottom line.** The bottom line is found at the end of the Statement. When Revenues exceed Expenses, **Net Income** (or Profit) has been earned. One may loosely conclude the firm's activity added to the wealth of society. Something *less* valuable was transformed into something *more* valuable. **Net Losses** occur when Expenses exceed Revenues. Net Losses reflect the net destruction of wealth. In effect, *more* value was turned into *less* value. The bottom line displays Earnings after Taxes (EAT). EAT is the part of Revenue rightfully claimed by the owners. So, Revenue is the top line and EAT is the bottom line!

2. FALLACIOUS ECONOMICUS: One number, such as Earnings After Tax (EAT), tells an investor all he/she needs to know before investing.

Correct Reasoning: It is best not to focus on any one number. One number can never tell all an investor would want to know. The most commonly cited metrics for measuring profitability are:

> ➢ **Free Cash Flow (FCF):** *Discretionary cash* available to the firm after paying bills and capital expenditures. Also a debt paying measure.
> ➢ **Earnings Per Share:**   EAT / number of common shares outstanding
> ➢ **Price/Earnings Ratio:** Price per share / Earnings per share
> ➢ **Earnings Yield:** Earnings per share / Price per share
> ➢ **Dividend Yield:** Dividends per share / Price per share

Warnings:

1. One number, one measure from those statements should never be used in isolation. One number can never tell all about solvency and profitability. Instead, the various measures form a mosaic, a completed cross word puzzle, giving a more complete depiction of the firm's financial condition.

2. Always rely on data drawn from audited financial statements with *favorable* auditor's opinion! (A company is issued a favorable opinion when the outside auditors conclude the company followed standard accounting rules in preparing the financial statements. The *favorability* of the opinion is not a recommendation of the company as an investment. The results might be profit or loss. In effect, *favorability* means the company did not "cook" the books.)

Standards of comparison. The above calculations should be made for the current year. **To add perspective,** compare the one company, one year results to various standards of comparison. Among them are close rivals' performance, the industry average, prior years' results, internal performance targets and forecasts. Doing so will add much needed analytical depth/perspective.

3. FALLACIOUS ECONOMICUS: In any year, cash received from customers is identical to reported Sales Revenue.

Correct Reasoning: Most big firms and many smaller ones use the accrual method of accounting. Under the accrual set of rules revenue is recorded when the firm performs for the customer, not when cash is received. There is no guarantee cash is received when performance is rendered to the customer.

The **accrual method** is a set of rules governing how transactions and business events are to be recorded. It is considered to provide the best measure of success or failure of the firm. As such, it produces the most useful information for manager and investor decisions. [*Cash forecasting* is advisable for bill paying on time]

In the accrual method, revenues are not recorded when the customer pays. Under accrual accounting rules, actually performing for the customer allows the seller to record revenue. *Performing* for the customer may mean shipping the goods or performing the service. The actual cash receipt may occur before, during or after the firm has performed.

Example: Sales made *on account* (credit sales) in 2015 become revenue for 2015 even though the customer will pay in 2016. Thus, cash from customers fall into one period while related sales revenue fall into another period.

So, do not expect business revenues to be matched by related cash inflows in any single period.

4. FALLACIOUS ECONOMICUS: In any year, reported business expenses are identical to cash outflows connected with serving customers.

Correct Reasoning: Not so with most big firms. Most big firms and many smaller ones use the *accrual method of accounting.* [Accounting students sometimes jokingly refer to it as the **cruel method**] It is a set of rules governing how revenues and expenses are to be recorded. It is deemed to provide the most useful information for manager and investor decisions.

Matching concept: In the accrual method, expenses are not necessarily recorded and recognized when the cash is paid. **Expenses are recorded in the period when the firm benefits (earns revenue) from the expenditure (or cost).** The actual cash payout may occur before, during or after the firm has enjoyed the benefit. The expense is **matched** as closely as possible to the **revenue** it helped to generate.

Example: Let's say sales commissions are paid in 2015 for sales made in 2014. These commissions show as expenses in 2014, the year of the related revenue. That is the year in which the firm benefited. This despite the fact that the cash outlay for commissions occurs in the following year, 2015.

So, in any accounting period, *do not expect reported business expenses to be matched by related cash outflows.*

Accountants following the accrual method apply what is called the *matching principle.* The matching principle requires Revenues to be matched with related Expenses, the expenses that helped generate that revenue.

Example: Sales Commissions are expensed in the same accounting year that the related Sales Revenue is earned and reported. This is true regardless of when the commissions are paid and when cash is collected from the customer.

Diagram #1: Goals for the Firm

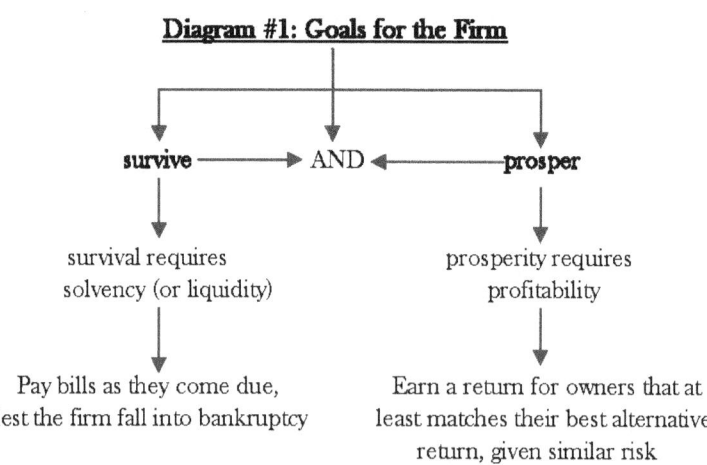

survive ⟶ AND ⟵ prosper

survival requires
solvency (or liquidity)

prosperity requires
profitability

Pay bills as they come due,
lest the firm fall into bankruptcy

Earn a return for owners that at
least matches their best alternative
return, given similar risk

It is prudent for business to focus on the *twin goals* of solvency and profitability. Solvency assumes the highest priority, for without the survival provided by solvency there are no opportunities for profit. (See Diagram #1 above).

5. FALLA<IOUS <<ONOMI<US: Profitable businesses always have enough cash to pay their bills on time. Therefore, lending money to them is a good credit risk.

Correct Reasoning: No! Solvency is an important condition not easily detected. Profitability is no guarantee of debt paying ability. Earning profits is no guarantee a firm will have the cash on hand (or in the checking account) ready to pay a bill when it comes due. In serving its customers, the firm pays out and receives cash in an irregular, sometimes unpredictable pattern. Cash inflows and outflows may cluster or be spread out.

<u>**Diagram #2: Sources of Funds**</u>

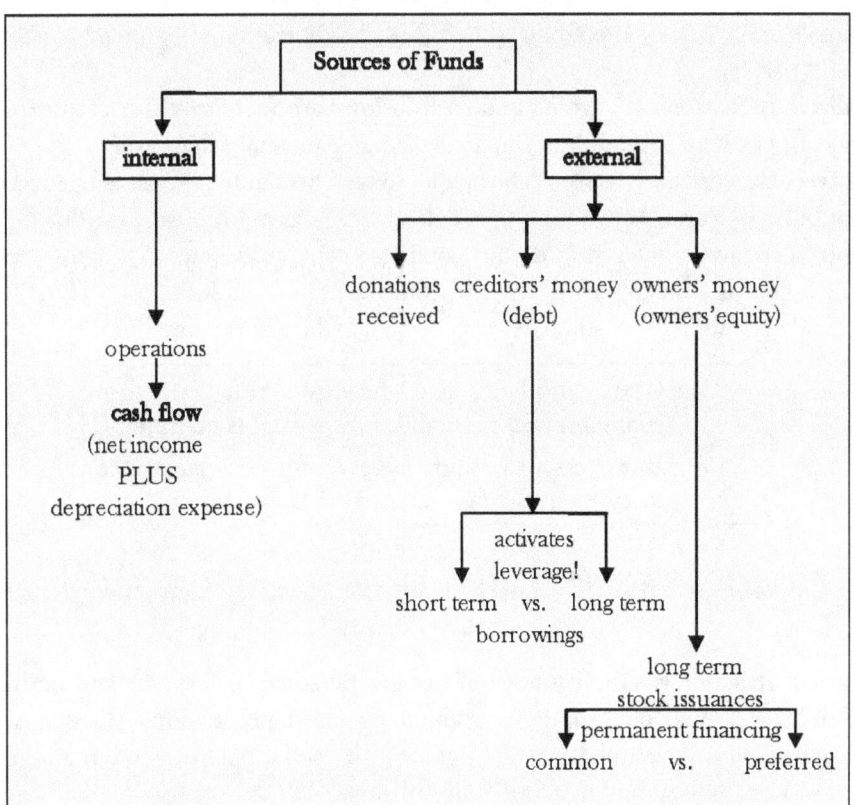

Diagram #2 above gives an overview of the **internal versus external** sources of funds for a firm. Other ways to view a firm's sources of funds are long versus short term and spontaneous versus nonspontaneous. Take a finance course!

Need For a Cash Balance

When cash inflows exceed outflows there is net cash inflow and the cash balance builds up. Under the accrual system of accounting, profits are no guarantee of a net cash inflow equal to bills coming due. This failure of cash inflows to synchronize with cash outflows threatens a cash shortage when bills are due. A cash reserve balance i.e., **a stock of cash, is required to provide for cash outlays not covered by inflows. The more regular (irregular) the cash inflows, the smaller (larger) the cash balance required.** So, a business may have plenty of customers, make lots of sales and have abundant profits. Yet, that business may have inadequate cash on hand to pay bills when due. Profitable business have gone bankrupt due to the inability to **pay debts when due**.

6. FALLACIOUS ECONOMICUS: Unprofitable businesses will likely not have enough cash to pay their bills. Therefore, lending money to them is a bad credit risk.

Fallacious Reasoning: Profits and cash inflows are identical. You earn profit, you can pay your bills, unless you are stealing or mismanaging cash!

Correct Reasoning: Not so, according to accrual accounting! **Cash is needed to pay bills.** Beware: Accounting profit does not guarantee *positive* cash inflow (and cash availability) nor do accounting losses guarantee a *negative* cash inflow (and unavailable cash). A firm could experience a loss (as measured by accrual accounting) but still have cash on hand when bills come due.

> ➢ Good products and healthy Profits do not guarantee *solvency* (ability to pay debts on time).
>
> ➢ Bad products and Losses do not guarantee *insolvency* (the failure to pay debts on time).

7. FALLACIOUS ECONOMICUS: I am exercising my Constitutional right, declaring myself legally bankrupt! Now I do not have to repay my debts!

Correct Reasoning: One cannot self declare personal bankruptcy and be free of debt. Personal bankruptcy is granted by **court permission**, which is not always granted. If granted under Chapter 7, personal bankruptcy relieves one of the legal obligations to pay common debts. A "get-out-of-jail-free" card, almost! **Beware:** not all obligations are discharged (see box below).

Common Debts NOT Forgiven by Legal Bankruptcy
Student loans
Money owed for child support or alimony
Most taxes and debts incurred to pay taxes
Most fines and penalties owed to government agencies.

There are other debts not discharged, as well. Consult a bankruptcy attorney!

[2. "Bankruptcy Frequently Asked Questions" 2 August 2014 *Dixon and Johnston Law Firm*
<http://tinyurl.com/o7m3wqn >]

Beware, also: Although not legally obligated, some bankrupt individuals eventually repay their debts. This is done to display good character and, hopefully, re-establish good credit. Also, borrowers who can prove permanent disability can have **student loan debt** discharged. Consult a bankruptcy lawyer!

Shutting Down Operations: When should you?

8. Fallacious Statement: It is best for unprofitable businesses to close.

Fallacious Reasoning: Duh? This needs explaining? If you are suffering losses, then get out, no? What could be wrong about this recommendation?

Correct Reasoning: Not so fast on closing the doors. Sometimes, yes, sometimes, no. It depends on the match-up between revenues and costs. Under certain conditions a firm would lose less by staying open! Short run vs. long run is important, as well.

In the long run. If losses persist into the long run, liquidate the assets and leave the industry! But, what of the short run?

In the short run. Losses are not always cut by shutting down!

➢   Stay open, despite the losses, if you lose less by doing so.

➢   Shut down if you cut losses by doing so.

Rationale: **Fixed costs live in the short run. Some have an afterlife, even after a business is shuttered and shut down.**   In the short run, rental or lease payments, bond interest payments, payment to executives, property taxes, licensing and franchising fees may persist beyond the cessation of business activity. These are the fixed costs.

In the long run there is enough time to negotiate or liquidate one's way out of the fixed costs.

Fixed costs persist in the short run even if the firm closes and sales drop to zero. Some fixed costs have an **afterlife** that persists even though the business has ceased operations. For example, there are fixed costs of maintaining Yankee Stadium in the off season: security, insurance, property tax, interest on borrowed money, skeleton staff, etc. These fixed costs remain a burden *after* the business has shut down *in the short run*. In a shutdown, without incoming revenue, they will have to be covered with non-operating funds.

Variable costs. Shutting down avoids variable costs such as cost of goods sold, salesmen's wages and delivery charges. They can be avoided entirely if the business is shut down. But, revenue evaporates, too, as those pesky total fixed costs persist. **Variable plus fixed costs gives total cost.**

Shut down rules for the short run:

1) Stay open in the short run if your revenue *covers* the variable cost and at least some of the fixed costs.

2) Shut down in the short run if your revenue *fails to cover* you added variable cost. Then, the firm fails to recover the variable cost and any of the fixed cost.

Digression: Total Fixed Cost, Average Fixed Cost and Overhead

Fixed costs are sometimes referred to as **overhead**. In the short run, *total* fixed costs do not vary with production, sales or business activity. Sales go up and down, and **total fixed costs** (such as rent and property taxes) remain constant. In a short run period, say, less than one year, no matter what happens to production or sales, up or down, the total fixed costs are unchanged. Thus, the fixed costs are always "hanging over your head." That is, they cannot be avoided. [Note: fixed costs may change due to factors *other than businesses activity*. For example, the landlord raises the rent.]

Average fixed cost varies inversely with the level of output, alternately spreading or concentrating the overhead.

Overhead Movements

➢ as output expands: fixed costs *per unit* – average fixed cost (AFC) – fall, **spreading the overhead**, without end ... a *desirable* outcome!

➢ as output contracts: AFC rises, **concentrating the overhead**, an *undesirable* outcome!

[See Appendix One on deciding whether to shut down or stay open while suffering a loss in the short run.]

To earn Accounting Profit:

[Revenues] must exceed [Total Cost = (Fixed plus Variable costs)]

Coming up: economists contend the **required minimum profit** to stay in business is an *implicit - implied* - fixed cost! They even give it a name: **normal profit.**

The World of Breaking Even

9. FALLACIOUS ECONOMICUS: When sales revenue equal expenses the firm breaks even. The investors neither lose money nor earn money. They have neither gained nor lost. Breakeven is a neutral result. No harm, no foul.

Correct Reasoning: This fallacious reasoning fails to consider that the investors most likely could have invested their money elsewhere and earned a return.

The Loss From Breaking Even. For economists, (accounting) breaking even – showing no income or loss on a firm's Income Statement - is equivalent to a loss! Breaking even is not "treading water" or "holding one's own." Breaking even is going down. But, apologists argue, in breaking even nothing was lost, right? Wrong. The resources devoted to the breakeven enterprise were not free. TANSTAAFL! Those resources could have been deployed elsewhere to earn a return. **This implied, best alternative return *not* earned is an** *opportunity cost* **called the opportunity rate of return. It is ignored by accounting rules. This is the loss when breaking even according to accounting rules. By not earning the alternative return, breaking even at this juncture is holding back growth in the firm's Net Worth.**

Normal profit. Now, go beyond the **accounting breakeven level** and assume a profit is earned. The trouble is a small accounting profit may be deemed inadequate and considered a failure by economists. For example, a huge company such as Apple Computer would consider a $1 million accounting profit to be a dismal failure, given the size of the company. Indeed, aware firms have a minimum target accounting profit, arrived at by looking at available alternative projects with similar risk. Economists call this a **NORMAL PROFIT and treat it as a cost of production, to be recovered from sales revenue. A firm must recover its normal profit to stay in business. A firm not earning the normal profit will eventually leave the industry.**

Assume B and A are alternative projects (bearing similar risk) and B is returning 10% profit. Then the firm figures it must earn at least 10% on A ... *or it is losing money.* Failure to attain this standard on a consistent basis would trigger a decision process that might withdraw resources from the A line of activity.

A good corporate finance class can amplify and clarify these concepts!

Therefore, breaking even involves a *loss of alternative return, a payoff* which could have been earned elsewhere. **Breaking even is equivalent to a loss and is not to be tolerated!**

10. FALLACIOUS ECONOMICUS: The firm has one breakeven level, where accounting expenses equal revenues; zero profit, zero loss.

Correct Reasoning: The firm with this narrow, simplistic goal could be missing opportunities to enhance the firm's solvency and profitability. The astute firm recognizes many breakeven points, each a **milestone to be reached and then surpassed** during the work year. In general, *a firm should seek to attain and then surpass the following sales points every year:*

1) The *cash* breakeven point: Cash inflows *equal* cash outflows from operations (dealings with customers). Below this sales point operations are a cash drain on the firm and solvency may be threatened. Beyond this point operations provide more cash inflows than they cause cash outflows.

2) The *accounting profit* breakeven point: This usually lies beyond the cash breakeven level. No loss or gain, according to accounting concepts. This is the traditional breakeven level taught in business school. But, if firm stuck at #2, there is actually an *economic loss* due to missed profit opportunities. The missed profit is called **normal profit, which is required to stay in business.**

3) The *normal profit* breakeven point: The firm has now captured missed profit opportunities, the normal profit, from #2. Normal profit is nice. Without normal profit we quit, i.e., leave the industry in the long run. Normal profit is the cake ... without the icing! When at #3, there is enough accounting profit to constitute the targeted normal profit. In that sense, the firm "breaks even." This is welcome and acceptable, but no "jackpot," no relish on the hot dog here.

Beyond #3, the Jackpot! If sales grow and accounting profit *surpasses* #3, the firm's profits *outperform* its competitors and its own minimum profit requirement. The spillover is re-labeled *excess* profit, a.k.a. *economic or pure or surplus profit or rent.* It is profit *in excess* of what could be earned elsewhere, under similar conditions of risk. It is icing on the cake! Thus, the firm wants to hit target #3 and, if possible, surpass it ... and stay there! But, are these excess profits this **sustainable** if new firms can easily enter this industry?

Diagram #3: Breakeven Sales Levels for the Firm

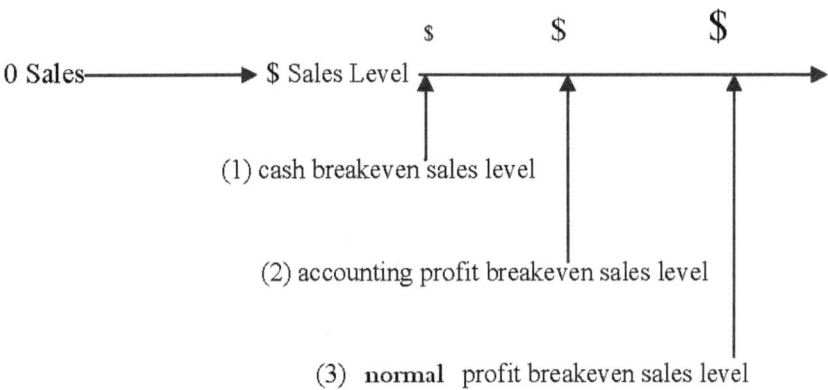

11.**FALLACIOUS ECONOMICUS**: **Tax Avoidance and Evasion.** Evading and avoiding taxes are essentially the same activity aimed at the reduction of a tax bill.

Correct Reasoning: Tax evasion is the use of illegal methods and is, therefore, illegal. Examples of illegal methods include not filing a return and making up deductions. Tax avoidance involves the use of legal methods for reducing taxes due and is, therefore, legal. It is commonly believed that when tax rates get too high, upper income taxpayers seek refuge in evasive and avoidance behavior.

12. **FALLACIOUS ECONOMICUS:** In running my business I do not mind incurring tax deductible expenses as they reduce my taxes, *dollar for dollar.* In effect, these tax deductible expenses cost me nothing! The tax refund is a complete recovery of what I laid out as expense.

Correct Reasoning: Expense acts as a tax shelter. When there is a tax deductible expense there is money saved in the form of reduced taxes, but the saving is *less* than the expense. One dollar of additional expense does *not* reduce tax by one dollar, but by *less* than one dollar. The reasoning is as follows: each dollar of tax deductible expense, in effect, shields (or shelters) a dollar of taxable income from being taxed. So, a company (or individual) saves the tax that otherwise would have been paid on that sheltered taxable income. That saving is, in effect, a *partial refund* of the expense. There is no total refund of the expense; there is still a residual burden attached to it.

Use the following formula to calculate the effect of the tax deductibility.

Consider a $100 expense for a taxpayer in the 30% bracket.

After tax expense = (before tax expense) X (1 – marginal tax rate)

$$= \$100 \text{ X } (1 - 0.30)$$

$$= \$100 \text{ X } (0.70)$$

<u>**After tax expense**</u> = <u>$ 70.00</u>

The $100 of expense "shelters" $100 of taxable income from being taxed.

The tax deductibility feature allowed the taxpayer to recoup $30 (tax not paid) of the $100 expense.

The amount of the tax saving depends on the marginal tax bracket. The higher the marginal tax bracket, the greater the tax saving and, in effect, less the *after tax* burden of the expense. Consider a $100 tax deductible expense undertaken by a large firm in a high bracket versus a small firm.

1) The hundred dollar donation from the *lower* bracket donor proves more of a burden than for the higher bracket donor. Less of the donation is salvaged via the tax deduction.

"The hardest thing to understand in the world is the income tax." - Albert Einstein

2) When compared to smaller, lower bracket corporations, larger, higher income bracket corporations bear a lower *after tax* burden for every extra $100 of expense. They salvage more of the expense as they fall in a higher marginal income tax bracket. Remember, in effect, you "save" the tax rate.

13. FALLACIOUS ECONOMICUS: American corporate "fat cats" are

overpaid while rank and file employees are often underpaid. Bill Clinton remedied this inequity. President Bill Clinton succeeded in getting corporations to limit compensation to top executives, leaving more funds for lower level employees. In his first budget (1993), Bill Clinton tried his best to limit executive pay by creating section 162(m) of the Internal Revenue Code. This limited the deductibility of traditional, salary rooted executive compensation *to the first one million dollars. Amounts paid beyond $1 million would no longer be tax* deductible and firms will be less likely to expand an executive's pay into that range.

Fallacious Reasoning: This would cut overall executive compensation and reduce income disparities in the economy. Compensation *above* one million dollars would no longer be deductible, making the after tax burden equal the before tax burden. In effect, there would be no tax refund on traditional salary payments over one million dollars. Payments in *excess* of one million would cost more, putting a bigger burden on the corporation.

Correct Reasoning: Corporations found a loophole in the regulation. Read all about it:

> The $1 million cap only applied to traditional salaries, bonuses and grants of company stock. Stock options (that is, stock grants that take time to vest and are meant to provide a performance incentive to workers) and other performance incentives are considered performance-based pay and are deductible even in excess of $1 million. So, unsurprisingly, businesses starting paying executives more in the form of stock options, such that fully 55 percent of deductible executive pay was "performance pay" between 2007 and 2010.
>
> [3. Dylan Matthews "Bill Clinton tried to limit executive pay. Here's why it didn't work" 16 August 2012 *Washington Post* <http://tinyurl.com/pppyfmo>]

A side effect of this failed attempt to control executive compensation has been the **executives' near manic focus on performance based measures such as the stock price.** Stock options became the vehicle that translates stock price into executive compensation. Maximizing shareholder value, i.e., the stock price, becomes synonymous with maximizing executive compensation. Rising stock prices rocket up the value of stock options, juicing up total executive compensation. But, corporate actions that cause short term or even momentary surges in the stock price may ultimately prove to be detrimental to the viability and/or profitability of the firm.

So, the good intentions of the Clinton law were circumvented by the creative ingenuity of the corporate legal "brain trust."

Selling Price: Quo Vadis?

14. FALLA<IOUS <<ONOMI<US: Pricing my goods is as easy as pie. Under fixed conditions, if I want to increase sales I *lower* my price. *Raising* prices is always counterproductive as I lose sales as a result.

Fallacious Reasoning: It is an unbroken law in economics that lowering a price encourages increased demand, no?

Correct Reasoning: It would take nearly a whole semester of microeconomics to straighten out all the errors of this fallacy! No doubt, most firms want control over their own price. The rule as stated ignores the general goal of greater profit. Greater sales (quantity) should be pursued only when greater profit results. Moreover, not all firms can control the selling price of their goods. In theory, (the rare) unregulated monopolist can set its own price.

Moving from the monopoly case, **the more competitors there are and the more similar the product they sell, the less control over price by any one firm.** At the extreme, thousands of firms selling an identical product, say, wheat at the farm level, finds each firm a price taker, selling at the going market price.

Control over price? All firms wish they had total control over their selling prices, called **monopoly power.** Firms seek **monopoly power,** if not monopoly itself. A firm's monopoly power – and control over price – increases with its size *relative* to the rest of the industry.

But, back to our fallacy. Lowering one's price is sometimes but not always beneficial. Lowering the selling price may boost quantities sold but reduce sales revenue ... and profit. Economists call this situation **inelastic demand.** More units are sold but the extra unit sales do not make up for the price cut per unit. Expenses increase but total revenue falls, thereby reducing profit.

Broadly defined goods usually exhibit inelastic demand. Bread, milk, and rental payments are examples.   Crude oil is another example. Basic agricultural commodities such as wheat, corn, and soybeans exhibit inelastic demand. Bumper crops on those farms are more of a curse than a blessing, as they reduce revenues and profits! Home heating oil and other goods considered necessities generally exhibit inelastic demand customers.

For example, go from selling 5 units at $3 to selling 6 units at $2. That is a price cut of $1. Total revenue (price X quantity) goes from $15 to $12, despite selling one additional unit!

15. FALLACIOUS ECONOMICUS: I heard on the news that there was a big illegal drug bust last night. Illegal drugs were confiscated. No doubt about it: This hurts drug dealers through lost sales and lost inventory.

Correct Reasoning: It depends on how intense demand is for that drug. It is possible the dealer could actually benefit from the drug bust! Loss of the confiscated drugs leaves the market with a shortage, an excess of demand not being satisfied.

An excess of demand in free markets leads to intense competition among buyers for the limited, remaining supply. Ultimately, this drives up the price. In some cases demand may be so intense the price on the remaining inventory is driven up so high that it offsets the loss of quantity for sale. For example, compare *setting one* to *setting two* in Table #1 below.

Table #1: Inelastic Demand for Illegal Drug after a Price RISE

	(Unit price) x	(Qty) =	(Total Revenue)
Setting one, *before* the drug bust:	$10 x	500 =	$5,000.
Setting two, *after* the drug bust:	$15 x	400 =	$6,000.

Notice how the quantity sold drops from 500 to 400. But, the price rises from $10 to $15. Note that despite selling fewer units, the total revenue to the seller is higher ($6,000) than before ($5,000). So, in this case the drug bust worked in favor of the drug dealer!

When demand behaves in this manner economists label it *inelastic demand.* Demand has this property when there are few or no good substitutes.

16. FALLACIOUS ECONOMICUS: New oil discoveries, brought to the market ... mean more revenues for the oil companies. The rich get richer!

Fallacious Reasoning: Well, *if they lower their price* and sell more goods, they'll make more money. Is that incorrect reasoning?

Correct Reasoning: Yes, that reasoning may be incorrect. This strategy may or may not increase profits. Success depends on the *intensity of demand* for the commodity or good. Repeated research has shown the demand for the commodities crude oil, jet fuel and gasoline tends to be *inelastic,* among others.

Inelastic demand means demand is so intense all the time that when price is dropped folks don't buy a whole lot more. Once again, staples such as bread, milk, rental apartments and other whole commodities and broadly defined goods tend to exhibit inelastic demand.

This property of *inelasticity of demand* does not always favor the seller. Sometimes it backfires on the seller. This occurs when an additional uncontrollable wave of supply hits the market, creating a surplus and driving down the price. The market price falls and sales increase, but sales do not rise enough to "pick up the slack." *Sales volume does not rise enough to make up for the lower price per unit.* The firm is left with selling *more* units but collecting *less* revenue in total ... and earning less profit. (See Table #2 below for an example of these events).

Table #2: Inelastic Demand for a Good after a Price DROP

	(Unit price)	x	(Qty)	=	(Total Revenue)
Setting one, *before* the price drop:	$10	x	100	=	$1,000.
Setting two, *after* the price drop:	$ 5	x	150	=	$ 750.

Note the fall in price (from $10 to $5) but the increase in sales (100 to 150). Despite the rise in sales quantity the total revenue to the firm *drops* ... due to the 50% drop in price.

So, sometimes an inelastic demand works FOR the firm and sometimes it works AGAINST the same firm selling the same good! It depends on the direction of the price change!

So, new oil discoveries may not be brought to the market if the outcome increases sales but hurts profits....

(still Red) China and India Takeover the World?

The plan: drastically slash costs by generating tremendous economies of scale. Then, undercut prices of competitors, enabling a takeover of their markets.

Economies of scale are **cost savings** due to expanding the complex of fixed factors of production such as property, plant, and equipment. Great specialization of labor complements the larger, higher tech equipment. It is imperative these large scale, heavy fixed cost operations (steel, autos, aluminum, tires, shipping, cement, petroleum refining, etc.) serve a large market, to **spread the larger overhead of bigger plants** and **offset diminishing returns** in each plant. Buying in bulk garners quantity discounts from suppliers, further depressing average cost. Fixed costs per unit (average fixed costs) will fall as the market and output expand, **spreading the overhead** in each plant, and, up to a point, lowering overall cost output .

The lower average fixed cost (AFC) yielded by spreading of the overhead permits price undercutting of smaller scale competitors, further expanding the customer base. The larger customer base, in turn, allows for further economies of scale! What can go wrong, go wrong with this scenario?

Economies of scale run out at some point. Thereafter, bigger is not better. Recall: An excess of a good thing is a bad thing. **Diseconomies of scale: Overexpansion of the bundle of fixed inputs can be ruinous.** In pushing the output too high, building bigger and bigger plants yields a sprawling enterprise too big to manage efficiently. Economies of scale end, overall cost rises as **diseconomies** of scale – rising long run average cost – take hold. This leaves room for smaller scale enterprises to be cost competitive, survive and compete alongside giant enterprises. Relax; China and India are not destined to control all manufacturing.

17. FALLACIOUS ECONOMICUS: Well, then, it seems all I have to do is convince buyers that my particular product has no substitutes, demand will become inelastic. Then I'll jack up my price, sell less, make more profit and live happily thereafter.

Correct Reasoning: The short run. That strategy may work in the short run for some firms. In the short run that inelastic demand curve "has our backs" as we jack up the price. But, the more profitable a firm, the more it is a target for potential competitors to gear up and enter the market. Then they undercut our price, seeking to attract some of our customers and steal a slice of the profit "pie." That complicates matters.

The long run. If these new firms enter the industry they introduce competing, substitute goods. The introduction of substitutes reduces the inelasticity of demand, i.e., makes demand less inelastic. Then, the "increasing price, increasing profit" strategy will not work as intended. Jacking up the price will drive customers into the arms of these new sellers, an undesirable outcome.

Barriers to entry. Anticipating these competitors will come knocking at the door of the industry inspires the firm to protect itself by attempting to bar their entry. The firm will try to erect barriers to deter entry. Some barriers are based on legal capacity to produce a duplicate or substitute product. These include: **copyright, patent, license, franchise, trademark, zoning restrictions and control of component or raw material supply** line. Other barriers include strong brand loyalty, product differentiation (real or concocted via persuasive advertising), economies of large scale output (the big firm advantage) and a large advertising budget (for consumer goods).

Conspicuous Consumption: Consume luxury items so as to get noticed! Hello, Thorsten Veblen! Contrary to everyday logic, *raising* the price of some items will *increase* sales! Some shoppers do not want to be seen consuming low priced, "cheap" goods. Such consumption would injure the self-esteem of this type of consumer, especially a peer conscious, well-heeled one who fears the disdain of snobbish friends and neighbors.

Store owners often take advantage of this propensity by overpricing what are, in reality, much cheaper goods. So, the lamp that goes unsold for $200 sells out when priced at $2000. The buyers want to show off their economic success and prowess to their friends, neighbors and the world. This doctrine of conspicuous consumption was developed by the economist and sociologist Thorstein Veblen (1857 - 1929), in his book, *The Theory of the Leisure Class: An Economic Study in the Evolution of Institutions* (1899).

Examples of Conspicuous Consumption: Consume to get noticed: a Rolex watch, a house on Malibu Beach, a Lamborghini automobile – or all three.

Appendix One: the Shutdown Point

Assume the firm has an overall loss: P < AC ... or P< (AVC + AFC). Should it continue producing or shut down in the short run? The firm should take the course of action where it **loses the least.** Under certain conditions a firm with losses will stay open, despite the losses! It does so because it will lose less than if shut down! The simple rule for **shut down in the** short run is:

1. STAY OPEN if **P > AVC,** continue operating in **short run** and lose less.
   If **price** is above **average variable cost** for each unit produced and sold, the firm earns enough revenue to pay variable costs (since price is greater) and leftover revenues to offset some of the **fixed costs.**

2. SHUT DOWN if **P < AVC shut down** in the **short run.**
   If **price** is below **average variable cost** for each unit produced and sold, the firm earns less revenue than the added variable costs it incurs (remember it only incurs variable costs if it produces). In this case, staying open is, in effect, "throwing good money after bad!"

Therefore, the added revenue is less than the added cost, so losses are greater than just fixed costs. **If losses persist into the long run, rule says SHUT DOWN. See:**
[4. <http://www.econweb.com/Sample/PerfectCompetition/ShutDownSR7.html>
    <https://www.youtube.com/watch?v=7XDEo2o-wm0>]

At output = 100 units:

Assume P =$10 AVC = $5 AFC = $9 so each unit sells for $10 but costs $14.
This firm should stay open and lose less.
Price, $10, recoups all the extra variable cost, $5, and some, $5, of the fixed cost.
Losses are $4 per unit, the unrecovered fixed costs.

If losses persist into the long run, rule says shut down. In the long run all costs are variable. There are no fixed costs as the decision horizon is long enough to change all the inputs and their associated costs. *If losses persist,* ultimately the firm liquidates its assets, escapes the fixed cost arrangements and goes out of the industry.

Breaking the rule: a firm might violate the shut down rule and stay open, enduring greater losses than necessary, *if profit prospects are expected to improve shortly.* For example: a huge sales contract is near, competitors are expected to fold, a new patent is expected to be approved, or a suitor is about to buy the company and this location must be held. The firm may stay open even when the rule says ... shut down!

Chapter Eighteen
Investing Fallacies: The Personal Perspective

Bulls and Bears Make Money, but Pigs Get Slaughtered - J.Cramer

THIS chapter focuses on some personal investing fallacies. The reader should peruse the two previous chapters for background understanding. [This discussion is educational and not meant to be taken as advice to be relied on in personal investment decisions.]

1. FALLACIOUS ECONOMICUS: Time is irrelevant in investing decisions. It does not matter *when* one pays and *when* one receives cash. Only the total paid and total received are important.

Correct Reasoning: Time IS money! The passing of time can eat into your stock of money or add to it. Investors and business managers should not be indifferent as to the timing of cash outflows and cash inflows. Time and timing are critical investment and cash management variables. Following proper timing guidelines can improve the well-being of the investor! The guidelines are relatively simple.

Background: The Time Value of Money

The concept of **time value of money** is analogous to the artist's concept of perspective. For an artist, objects moved further away from the viewer appear smaller. The same objects moved closer appear larger. Respecting those differences gives reality to an artist's rendition of objects in a spatial plain. In finance, time replaces distance as the active force.

A person views future money as having different importance, depending where it lies on her *personal* time line. Money, paid in or out, is closer to the current moment is more important. Earlier cash flows – in or out – loom larger than the same amount located further out on the time line. Money closer to the current moment is deemed more useful than money further out. Kids want their allowance the first day of the week, not the last. Landlords want their rent the first day of the month, not the last. Thus, the further into the future are costs *and* benefits, the less important they seem today.

> ➤ *Earlier* cash received is preferable to the same amount received *later*. The sooner cash is received, the sooner it can be invested or utilized. So, the sooner, the better. Therefore, accelerate the inflows.

> Cash *paid sooner* hurts more than the same amount of cash paid later. The later cash is paid, the longer it can be yours to use or invest. So, delay the outflows (without hurting credit rating). So, the later the better.

Get cash as soon as possible ... and hold onto it as long as possible!

These two practices recognize timing as a critical element in successful investing. Observing these practices help build up the **most useful asset: cash**.

The "Stock Market as Casino" Fallacy

Before considering other fallacies in investing behavior and, let us first deal with a grand misconception about Wall Street and the various stock markets.

2. FALLACIOUS ECONOMICUS: The stock market is no different than the casino. I could hit it big or lose my shirt. There is no difference. They could shut the stock markets. We don't need them. At least casinos give free drinks.

Fallacious Reasoning: That is how I see it based on my real world experience as an investor and a gambler.

Correct Reasoning: Correct reasoning looks at casinos and stock markets from the viewpoint of the whole economy, not just one player or investor. In short, stock markets and other securities market are an important link in chain of events leading to **real capital formation** in a complex, modern economy. These institutions, namely, **financial intermediaries, channel savings from savers to investors who build capital.** Capital formation is critical to promoting and sustaining economic growth. Casinos are not financial intermediaries and have no role in facilitating capital formation. Casinos could vanish from the economy and the economy "keeps on ticking." On the other hand, the economy would collapse should the stock and other securities markets vanish. This is why healthy, honest banks and security markets are imperative.

3. FALLACIOUS ECONOMICUS: Stocks, bonds, what is the difference? They are just pieces of paper. I could lose my shirt on either one.

Correct Reasoning: Paying off bonds and bond interest are contractual and mandatory. Those actions take priority over redeeming stocks and paying dividends, which are optional financial actions for a corporation. Remember, in buying a bond you are lending money that the borrower promises to repay. **Stocks do not carry such an enforceable promise to repay.** Therefore, stocks, by their nature, cannot and do not default, as they never promised you anything in the first place. Bonds are different; they have a termination date. You bear the risk of default when buying bonds. Recall, **a debt obligation defaults when the borrower fails to pay at maturity or on interest dates.** Even in default, all may not be lost as some assets may remain. The stronger the issuer, the less likely is default. Some money might be recoverable from the issuer.

Market valued stocks can leave you in a bigger hole. In the worst case scenario a stock's market value could fall to zero. (In the best case scenario, it could soar to the Heavens!) You could lose every penny you paid for a stock and have no recourse against the issuer because you, as a stockholder, agreed to these terms. You could lose your shirt ... your underwear and socks, too.

Chapter 7 bankruptcy is available to individuals, married couples, corporations and partnerships.

4. FALLACIOUS ECONOMICUS: I lose every penny if a bond defaults.

Correct Reasoning: The holder of a defaulted bond may not lose every penny invested. Life gets complicated when a bond defaults. Default is a sign of dire financial distress and threatens the life of the business! The court steps in between the parties and a bankruptcy proceeding is likely.

In **Chapter 7** bankruptcy, a court appointed trustee oversees the liquidation of assets in order to pay off creditors. **Mortgage bonds** are an example of secured bonds. In a secured bond, *specific* collateral underlying a *specific* bond is seized in a legal proceeding and auctioned off. The proceeds are used to pay off those particular bondholders. **Debenture bonds** are unsecured by any specific collateral. The proceeds are used to pay off the bondholders, who may or may not recoup their investment. This loss of operating assets (rail cars, airplanes, trucks, real property, etc.) signals an end to business operations and the business. Most corporate bonds are unsecured (debenture bonds), not backed by specific collateral.

Chapter 11 bankruptcy is more common than **Chapter 7**. In Chapter 11 bankruptcy, courts try to arrange some kind of revised, reduced, and extended repayment schedule to the creditors. Hopefully, the struggling business survives as monthly payments are negotiated downward. If new payment schedules cannot be negotiated the firm likely enters Chapter 7 proceedings. Oddly, bonds threatened with or actually in default, known as **"junk bonds,"** may still trade, but at steep discounts from par.

5. FALLACIOUS ECONOMICUS: With all this talk about rising Federal Debt I am afraid my government bonds are going to default.

Correct Reasoning: U.S. **Government bonds cannot default.** They are direct obligations of the U.S. Treasury, backed up by the full faith and credit of the United States. If a default threatens, the Federal government, together with the Federal Reserve System can, in effect, **print more money** and pay off bonds as they mature. This is done through a process called **monetization of the debt.** New bonds are issued directly to the Federal Reserve which creates the money to buy them. The government gets the money and repays maturing bonds, thereby avoiding default. Bookkeeping wizardry at its best! This practice should not be constrained by the Federal Debt Ceiling. At the end of the day, the new bonds have substituted for the maturing bonds, leaving total bond debt unchanged and the ceiling unchallenged.

Beware: Although an investor in (marketable) government bonds cannot lose holding them to maturity, one can lose principal should the market price drop and the bonds be liquidated. This is called *market* or *interest rate risk.*

6. FALLACIOUS ECONOMICUS: It is comforting to know government bonds cannot default. I own these New York City *general obligation bonds* and would sure not want them to default. My life savings are invested in them!

Correct Reasoning: Be aware, in Wall Street jargon and in financial practice, your "bonds" are not Government bonds! "Government bonds" is a term reserved for direct obligations of the U.S. Treasury. Bonds issued by a State or political subdivision of a State are referred to as Municipal Bonds. There are over 80,000 municipal bond issues United States. They are also known as *munies* or *tax-exempts.* With limited exceptions, interest earned on munies is exempt from Federal Income Tax and any income tax of the state of issuance, should the investor reside in that state.

Beware: *Unlike government bonds, municipal bonds carry risk of default as well as market or interest rate risk.* That being said, defaults are rare. Munies may carry private "default insurance" and be bought in mutual fund "packages."

7. FALLACIOUS ECONOMICUS: Always invest in stocks (or securities, in general) that have zero risk.

Correct Reasoning: Avoiding risk is an impossible directive! Risk is part of living! Even government bonds, without default risk, have market (or interest rate) risk. **Risk** is the *possibility* that something will go wrong, causing hurt, damage or loss.

When a process is subject to risk, something can go wrong. Investment Risk can sometimes be reduced. But, it cannot be eliminated. **All investments, real and financial, have some degree of risk.**

In simplest terms, securities risk is subdivided into default risk and market risk. **Market risk** is the possibility that a traded security like a stock or bond will be down in price at the liquidation date. **Default risk** is the possibility the issuer will not fulfill the legal obligation payments. For example, failure to pay interest when due or principal at maturity on a bond creates default risk.

Risk City

➢ Stocks do not mature and, therefore, have no default risk.
But: stock values could fall to zero on the market.

➢ Bonds mature and pay interest. Therefore, bonds bear some risk of default. But: If default occurs, holders of secured bonds may have access to pledged collateral.

➢ Federal government bonds have no risk of default but have market risk.

Tradable securities, including government bonds, have market or interest rate risk. Generally, **bond prices vary <u>inversely</u> with market interest rates.**
This exposes the investor to possible losses when market rates rise.
(Beware: U.S. Savings Bonds are issued at a discount from face value, are not marketable and, therefore, bear no market risk.)

Risk and return: risk and return are highly positively correlated. They rise and fall in tandem, in direct variation. Higher risk ventures have the *potential* for greater returns ... and greater losses. There is no guarantee of a higher return, given higher risk. Lower returns go with low risk ventures. An analogy with wildcatting for oil: we will drill more dry wells than usual to find oil. But, if we hit, it will be a gusher. **Beware:** Despite the promise of higher returns, do not assume a level of risk that causes you to lose sleep and abuse your pets!

In a *steady state*, i.e., a fixed interest rate structure:

➢ Do not accept a higher risk opportunity it unless it has the potential for higher return.

➢ Do not accept a lower return opportunity unless it is lower risk.

Question: Would a zero risk bond still bear interest? If so, why?

8. FALLACIOUS ECONOMICUS: My stock fell by 50% yesterday. Hopefully, tomorrow it will go up 50% and I will be back where I started.

Fallacious Reasoning: Well, if it fell by 50% then it will have to rise by 50% to get back to the original amount. Simple, no?

Correct Reasoning: Be careful using percentages! Watch the base the percentage is applied to. In this case, the falling percent is applied to a different base, a higher number than the rising percent. So, *on the rise* the same percentage addition (50%) will fall short of restoring the drop.

Example: A stock falls from $100 to $50, a fall of 50%. But, a rise of 50% from $50 is an increase of only $25, less than the drop of $50. That produces a price of $75, not the initial $100. A percentage rise *equal to* the percentage fall does not restore the drop. In fact, a 100% rise is needed to restore the fall of 50%.

What is fallacious about the following statements?

1) "A GDP rise of 6% is needed this year to restore the 6% drop of last year."
2) "The boss wants to take away the 10% raise he gave me last year by cutting 10% this year. This would bring my salary back to where it was."
3) "We are adding 15% to the defense budget this year to make up for the 15% cut last year."

So, be careful! Don't get snookered by a percent manipulator.

The Cardinal Goals: Survive and Prosper

9. FALLACIOUS ECONOMICUS: Financial analysis doesn't seem to lead anywhere. Just a bunch of ratios, percentages and statistical measures. I can't figure out the purpose of all that mumbo jumbo. What does it all lead?

Correct Reasoning: There is a point of view to financial analysis. Before investing one must do homework on the prospective investment. But, what should be the focus of such an investigation?

Can the firm survive? This is the *viability* question, the *live long* part of the Vulcan motto. Survival requires *solvency* or *liquidity* where the firm can pay bills as they come due. Failure to pay bills when due and pay interest could result in bankruptcy, followed by liquidation of remaining noncash assets. The life of the business is effectively ended ... the end of the firm's life ... kaput!

Can the firm prosper? Survival isn't enough for an investor. The swimmer isn't satisfied just treading water. The swimmer wants to win the race. And so the investor is not satisfied just to avoid losses. The investor wants to prosper, to enlarge his/her wealth. This is the prosperity question. But, the *absolute* level of prosperity isn't enough either! The next level of prosperity to assess is *relative* prosperity, prosperity *relative* to some **relevant standard of comparison.** (Industry averages and the firm's own history can provide standards for comparison of the firm's performance). Examining the Profit and Loss Statement (covered earlier) can play a critical role in this analysis. The previous chapter on Accounting Fallacies reviews a few of the numerous measures analysts use for evaluating financial data. See especially Fallacy #2.

The fallacy below instructs on how to interpret those various ratios, percentages and raw figures.

> ### Order Out of Chaos
>
> Financial analysts generate hundreds of bits of information about solvency and profitability of a company. Each bit of information (ratio, percentage, raw figure) is like a piece of a **jigsaw puzzle**. As each piece of the puzzle contains limited information, so a single ratio or percentage cannot reveal everything about solvency and profitability. Some pieces might reveal more of the final picture than others. Each piece will contribute something to the final picture. A complete picture emerges only after all the pieces have been identified and fit into a recognizable image. Education, training and experience guide the financial analyst.

10. FALLACIOUS ECONOMICUS: The One Number Fallacy Let's not go crazy on this financial analysis stuff, with dozens – or even hundreds – of calculations and cross calculations. One number, be it a ratio, percentage, or raw number, contains all necessary information about a firm. One number is all you need.

Correct Reasoning: Do not fall for the "one number tells all" sales pitch. One number taken in isolation can never reveal all the information needed to make an intelligent decision. Here are some "one numbers" about a person: height, weight, color of eyes, age, etc. Is any one of these enough to describe a person? Is any one of these numbers, taken alone, enough to describe survivability or profitability: sales, profits, dividend yield, earnings per share, new product, number of branches, stores or products, etc. These numbers are equivalent to individual pieces of a jigsaw puzzle. Investing or dis-investing based on any ONE of these measures is not recommended!

Just a reminder: for reliable data, always employ audited financial statements having a favorable opinion from the auditors. Interested in a common stock? Consider investing in a related convertible bond instead of the stock. But, first crunch the numbers!

11. FALLACIOUS ECONOMICUS: I don't have to worry about paying bills on time. I've got plenty of assets available to meet my payment commitments.

Correct Reasoning: Simply having assets is not good enough. Many assets are illiquid and cannot be converted into cash in time to pay bills. A firm needs highly liquid assets (cash, checkable bank money) or a bank credit line to pay debts by the due date. It is best for a firm to construct rolling **day to day forecast of expected cash inflows and outflows.** That document is called a **cash**

budget or cash forecast. It could be extended over the following weeks and months. The firm can use this document to pinpoint possible problems of insufficient cash to pay bills. A firm without such a planning document is flirting with insolvency.

Hedge Hogs: High-Rollers, Only, If You Please

A hedge fund is a special class of mutual fund for a special type of investor. It is not for the small investor or the faint of heart.

1) Most hedge funds are *open ended* mutual funds, continuously issuing new shares and redeeming outstanding shares. To "buy in" may cost in the millions of dollars.

2) These funds are not as regulated and supervised as are ordinary mutual funds.

3) Hedge funds are available only to qualified investors called *accredited investors,* including individuals, banks, insurance companies, brokers, and pensions.

4) Unlike ordinary mutual funds, hedge funds are allowed a wider range of investment vehicles. In addition, they can sell short as well as buy long, and use borrowed money to create leverage.

5) Hedge fund shares may be more difficult to cash in than ordinary mutual fund shares. There is an infamous variable "lock-up" period banning cash-ins of shares.

6) Management fees are based on management performance. Critics charge this leads to reckless investment practices which can go boom or bust.

[1. "What is a Hedge Fund?" 20 November 2014 *Barclayhedge* <http://tinyurl.com/lr4lkch>]

Capital Gains Tax

12. FALLACIOUS ECONOMICUS: I want to squeeze every penny of gain I can out of investing. As soon as my stock rises, I am selling, taking my gains.

Correct Reasoning: You seem to be ignoring the tax implications of your action. Your tax situation will impact how much you are left with after settling with Uncle Sam. Selling a stock (or house) is considered the sale of a **capital asset.** The gain will be taxed according to your holding period of the asset. If you have a net capital gain, that gain may be taxed at a lower tax rate than your ordinary income tax rates.

Gains are taxed according to whether they were held long term or short term. In general, sale of capital asset (at a gain) after holding it one year or more is called a **long term capital gain.** That gain is taxed at a *lower* rate than a **short term capital gain,** where the asset is held for less than a year. So, assuming the gain will hold, a greater after tax return will be garnered is one waits for the long term period to expire. As usual with tax laws, it is recognized there are complications and exceptions to the blanket rule. So, tax lawyers, please do not write in! (Net capital losses have an interesting tax impact). A quick check of the IRS website answers most questions (wink, wink!). Here is an excerpt from the IRS website:

> Generally, for most taxpayers, net capital gain is taxed at rates no higher than 15%. Some or all net capital gain may be taxed at 0% if you are in the 10% or 15% ordinary income tax brackets. However, beginning in 2013, a new 20% rate on net capital gain applies to the extent that a taxpayer's taxable income exceeds the thresholds set for the new 39.6% ordinary tax rate ($400,000 for single; $450,000 for married filing jointly or qualifying widow(er); $425,000 for head of household, and $225,000 for married filing separately). For more information, refer to Publication 505, *Tax Withholding and Estimated Tax.*
>
> [2. "Topic 409 - Capital Gains and Losses" 24 November 2014 *Tax Topics* <http://www.irs.gov/taxtopics/tc409.html>]

So, pay attention! Your holding period before sale can impact your after tax gain when disposing of a capital asset. If the anticipated gain will hold, try to get to *long run capital gain* range. Consult your tax expert for more information!

13. FALLACIOUS ECONOMICUS: Investors stand to earn more from buying and holding a low-priced stock than a high-priced stock.

Fallacious Statement Variation: Low priced stocks have more upside potential than high priced stocks.

Fallacious Reasoning: Low priced stocks, such as penny stocks, have nowhere to go but up. Thus, they have more potential for upward movement, more headroom, than stocks already high priced. On the other hand, a stock already high priced seems to have nowhere to go. Therefore, investors should try to get in on or near the "ground floor" of the price range and enjoy the upside gains when they materialize.

Correct Reasoning: Recall, undervalued or overvalued is what counts. Do not assume a low priced stock is undervalued! A low or high price label cannot be assigned to an actual price without first doing some homework. 1) Note the actual price, the market value at any moment. 2)) Investors must try to calculate the true or *intrinsic value* or *theoretical optimum price (true value)* of the security. The intrinsic value is what the stock value *ought to be, based on expert analysis.* A stock is not automatically priced (by the market) at its intrinsic or true value. 3) Then, investors compare the *actual* price to the intrinsic or *theoretical optimum price* to see if the stock is improperly valued by the market.

The implied justification for seeking the intrinsic price is this: the actual price - low or high - will (quickly?) gravitate toward the intrinsic value, up or down. The actual price is always chasing the intrinsic price, up or down. Should the intrinsic price be above (below) the actual, then the actual is expected to rise (fall).

> **Stock Market Visits Animal Farm**
> *Bulls* expect rising prices and are, of course, *bullish.*
> *Bears* expect falling prices and are, of course, *bearish.*
> A bull market has rising prices. A bear market has falling prices.

Investors in stock look for **mis-valued** *stocks*, stocks that have values that a) diverge from their true values and b) are gravitating toward those true values. Most investors look for **underpriced** or **undervalued** stocks. For example, the $100 intrinsic valued stock is selling for $70. According to plan, these stocks have upswing potential when the actual price ($70) "wakes up" and gravitates to the true, intrinsic price ($100).

In general, these mis-valued stocks may or may not have a low price to start. Remember: do not prejudge a stock by its price. Do the analysis! Do not assume a low priced stock is undervalued or a high priced stock is overvalued!

> ➤ A low priced stock may or may not be *undervalued.* It may be overvalued! Although now at a low price, it may go even lower.
> ➤ A high priced stock may or may not be *overvalued.* It may be undervalued! Although now at high price, it may go even higher.

Do not judge a price in an informational vacuum. Do the analysis! Watch recent history of price AND volume for clues as to near term movements.

Intrinsic or True Value: the Holy Grail for Investors

As stated earlier, a stock is not automatically priced (by the market) at its intrinsic or true value. Very often the true, intrinsic value and the *actual* value (or price) diverge. However, most analysts believe the actual value will gravitate (how quickly?) to the intrinsic value. In short, the intrinsic value tells us where the actual value is going, or, at least, *should* be going if everyone has our information. (For those conversant with market behavior, the intrinsic value is equivalent to the equilibrium value).Thus, **the intrinsic or true value of a stock is equivalent to the Holy Grail for investors.** It points the way to the stock price location and possible movement.

However, know that the intrinsic value at any moment as new information hits the market. For example, a new popular product is introduced or a government contract is lost, altering the assessment of the true value. So, the search for the true value is constant.

Finding the Intrinsic Value ... or ... Catch the Wind

In general, short of smoking or ingesting an illegal substance, there are three major tools used in the hunt for the vaunted, elusive intrinsic value of a stock.

Fundamental analysis: This approach incorporates all kinds of data related to the issuing company. Analysts scrutinize the economy, the industry, the competition, the sales history, among other relevant information. Analysts "slice and dice" the financial statement data. **Ratio analysis** is an important tool for adding **perspective** to reported raw numbers. Fundamental analysis may not pinpoint a specific intrinsic value. Fundamental analysis seeks a "ballpark" stock value, to label the stock as under or over-valued, given the current market value.

Technical analysis: This approach ignores most of the information that fundamental analysis studies! Reading the tea leaves is what this is about. It might focus only on the track record of the stock's price, trying to identify its trajectory. Charts and graphs are used to plot hourly/daily/weekly/monthly price and volume data. Technical analysts have been referred to as *chartists*. Sophisticated equations may generate trend lines for analysis. Purely mathematical models may be constructed. (Beware the use of extrapolation!)

Combined Analysis: Fundamental analysis and technical analysis each have their rabid adherents. But, why have to choose? Some analysts first use fundamental analysis followed by technical analysis to time their trades.

[3. See Socrates Alvarez, "What Is The Intrinsic Value of a Stock?" 6 July 2014 *Investopedia* <http://tinyurl.com/nc5znh7>]

[4. See also: "How to Calculate Stock Price by Using the Intrinsic Value Method," <http://tinyurl.com/pv4an2a>]

14. FALLACIOUS ECONOMICUS: With regard to investing in stock, even in the worst case scenario I will walk away with some money. I can never lose every penny I've invested as a stock can never go down to zero. After all, this is America, the most prosperous nation in the world!

Correct Reasoning: Do not commit the fallacy of division. Prosperous or not as a whole stock market, an individual stock can "buck the tide" and take a real beating in the market. *It can become worthless even if its price does not fall to zero!* Read all about it:

First of all, company prospects could be so dim a stock price could fall toward zero. Remember the *current* price is considered to be a *compressed* version of future net cash flows to the stockholder. If investors' opinions of future earnings and dividends "tank," so can the stock price.

Secondly, a stock price does not have to fall to zero to deny a return to the stockholder. All that has to happen is the stock price falls so low the proceeds from selling the stock do not cover the broker commission required by the sale! In that case there is actually a loss from selling the stock. So, one holds it idle until conditions improve. During this period the stock is, in effect, worthless despite having a price above zero. Watch out for this situation with so-called "penny stocks," those selling for pennies a share.

Third, the stock exchange listing the stock (New York Stock Exchange or NASDAQ) may suspend trading or de-list a stock for failure to meet reporting, price performance or other standards required for continued listing. This presents problems in liquidating the stock and problems spell drastic price decline.

Fourth, the Securities and Exchange Commission can force an exchange to suspend trading in a stock if nefarious circumstances are involved. A stock that cannot be traded may be worthless. On the SEC website (www.sec.gov) there is a list of reasons why trading may be suspended.

[5. See "Trading Suspensions," 27 February 2015 *Investor Bulletin*
<http://tinyurl.com/nn7tpcz>
See also, Cory Janssen, "The Dirt On Delisted Stocks" February 27 2015 *Investopedia*
<http://tinyurl.com/yyzupt>]

Expect a falling or collapsing stock price? Don't wait until it starts and then try to sell out. Put in a **stop-loss order,** below current market, to be executed should the price fall to the specified price. (See end of chapter for further discussion of stop-loss orders).

15. FALLACIOUS ECONOMICUS: I'm scared! My stock is selling for $50 per share but I just learned it has a par value of $1. It must be overvalued and is destined to collapse.

Correct Reasoning: Par value is one of those mysterious business concepts generally misunderstood by the public. **Par or stated value is an artificial, arbitrary face value placed on a share when it is issued.** Some states require shares to have a par or stated value. The corporate charter specifies par value, if any. In those states, shares cannot be *issued* below par. Of course, later on shares can *trade* below par. Other states allow the *issuance* of no par, no stated value stock at any price. Today, par value is a mere formality (for common stock) and has no relation to its market value.

Par value is no measure of what the share's market value ought to be, the intrinsic value. High par value stock does not necessarily carry a higher market value than low or no par value stock. There is no correlation between assigned value at issuance (either par or stated value) and market value. Market price or value is determined by the market's assessment of (discounted) expected future net cash flows claimable by the share of stock. Par value is unrelated to future cash flows and, therefore, is unrelated to the current market price.

Par value for bond. Par value does have significance in certain circumstances. Unlike par value for a common stock, par value for a bond is meaningful. It is the amount payable by the issuer at maturity of the bond. Failure to pay the par value constitutes default. Par value *is* meaningful for calculating **preferred stock dividends**. Par value (or its brother Stated Value) is the basis for calculating preferred dividends.

Beware, as well: Below par stock. On a rare occasion, stock may be issued *below* par. Stock issued *below* par may carry an obligation for an owner to pay in the difference between the issuance price and the par value. So, a $100 par value stock issued at $40 carries a contingent obligation for the stock owner to pay in an additional $60 per share should the company run into financial trouble and require funds. Always ask about original issuance price of par stock!

Interesting fact: the par value of Google common stock is $00.001.

16. FALLA<IOUS <<ONOMI<US: The market is tough. It lets you make money only when prices are rising.

Correct Reasoning: Selling short is one technique for pursuing gains as a stock price is falling. Selling short means borrowing stock and selling it. But, you must return or repay the stock in the near future. This means soon you must enter the market as a BUYER of that same stock. In between you hope for a price decline. So, if you borrow and sell stock at $10 hopefully you buy it for $8 and return it. Your gross profit is $2 per share. **Short sales are not allowed on a stock that has already fallen 10% that day. (The Alternative Uptick Rule).**

17. FALLA<IOUS <<ONOMI<US: Diversify your holdings by investing in a pool of securities called a **mutual fund**. In that way you *eliminate* risk.

Correct Reasoning: You may *reduce* risk but no one has found a way to *eliminate* risk without a substantial reduction in return.

Beware: Buying stock on **margin**, i.e., with borrowed money, enables more stock to be bought, creating a **leverage** opportunity. That raises risk, magnifying the potential for gains (or losses) over and above putting up all cash.

18. FALLACIOUS ECONOMICUS: Diversification reduces risk, so diversify as much as possible.

Correct Reasoning: A number of fallacies are in play here. Remember, TANSTAFL! Yes, intelligent diversification reduces risk ... but usually at a price in the form of reduced return. The *excess* fallacy is called into play here. There is such a thing as too much diversification. And too much of a good thing backfires ... and becomes a bad thing.

Individual Retirement Accounts

IRA's have been a popular vehicle for savings.

The I.R.A that Isn't Irish

The Federal government offers legal ways for individuals to postpone, reduce, and even eliminate taxes on part of one's income when saving for retirement. The **Individual Retirement Account (I.R.A.)** offers an arrangement for annual contributions toward a fund with tax reduced retirement age withdrawals. IRAs are of two varieties: Traditional and Roth. Here are the bare bone basics of how they work: Currently, both the traditional IRA and the Roth IRA allow contributions up to $5,500 annually to a retirement fund.

For the **Traditional IRA**, those are *pre-tax dollars*, so no income tax is paid on $5,500 the year it is contributed. The fund monies are invested and earn a tax deferred return. The tax is deferred (or put off) until withdrawals during one's *lower* tax bracket, retirement years. *In retirement, withdrawals of contributions and earnings are taxed* according to the bracket of the low income retiree. Thus, the savings in taxes is realized.

For the **Roth IRA**, the income contributed comes from *after-tax dollars*. All income tax obligations have been paid. As with the Traditional IRA, the fund monies are invested and earn a return. *In retirement, withdrawals of contributions and earnings from a Roth are not taxed.* Unlike tax *deferral* in the traditional IRA, in the Roth IRA retirement fund earnings are *tax free*.

Caveats: In general, the Roth IRA is suited for younger workers. Depending on one's circumstances, there may be legal complexities not discussed above! *See your qualified tax advisor for additional counsel.* A good start is the reference below.

[6. Denise Appleby, "Roth vs. Traditional IRA: Which Is Right For You" 20 Sept., 2014 *Investopedia* <http://tinyurl.com/3e7qz>]

The Expectations Game

19. FALLACIOUS ECONOMICUS: Either the stock market is rigged or highly irrational. Good new comes out about my stock and the price goes down! Bad news comes out and the price goes up! It is driving me nuts!

Correct Reasoning: The market is neither rigged nor irrational. Most *current* valuations are based on market expectations about *future* dividend streams and earnings prospects. Big, listed firms report earnings quarterly. Market observers announce earnings expectations. When the reality is revealed and it differs from what had been generally expected, then market participants revise expectations. Then they act on their new expectations. Those actions move the actual stock price.

Results commonly differ from expectations. Rarely are expectations realized perfectly. Expectations as to the next quarterly earnings report rarely "hit the nail on the head." Moreover, those results form the core of a new set of expectations. And on and on. Rarely are expectations realized perfectly. Consider two cases.

Overly Optimistic Expectations

Example 1: Actual earnings rise, but the stock price falls.

Market reaction: Yes, earnings rose, but less than expected. The stock price had been based on *overly optimistic* expectations before the earnings report and, hence, was too high. As it turns out, the stock was **overvalued.** When the good news is realized the stock price falls. It seems the *actual* good news was not as good as the *expected* good news! Price falls despite the good news of higher earnings because earnings didn't measure up to *overly* optimistic expectations.

Overly Pessimistic Expectations

Example 2: Actual earnings fall, but the stock price rises.

Market Reaction: Yes, earnings fell, but less than expected. Before the earnings report, the stock price had been based on *overly pessimistic* expectations. Earnings turn out badly, but not as badly as expected. It seems the *actual* bad news was not as bad as the *expected* bad news! In retrospect, given the *excessive* gloom and doom, the stock price was **undervalued.** Stock price rises despite the bad news because expectations were even worse!

The expectations game is also played with general economic statistics such as GDP, inflation and unemployment. Are you an investor or a trader? Either way, you must play the expectations game!

[7. American Association of Individual Investors, "Earnings Estimates and Their Impact on Stock Prices" 19 June 2014 *AAII* <http://tinyurl.com/odxmgs2>]

Retirement planning for Middle America has become an exercise in lowered and shattered expectations.

The future ain't what it used to be.   —Yogi Berra

Did You Hear the One about the Stock That Merged with a Bond?

Well, it became a **convertible bond**. A convertible bond is a tradable security with a split personality. Sometimes it trades like a stock and sometimes it trades like a bond. Want your cake and eat it, too? Want the added security of a bond and the potential for appreciation of a risky stock, all in one? If so, then convertible bonds might be your choice. A convertible bond is a traditional corporate bond with the additional feature of being convertible, at the investor's discretion, into a pre-determined number of common stock shares. As such, convertibles are hybrid securities that combine both equity [i.e., common stock] and debt characteristics. Preferred stock may or may not come with the convertible-to-common feature.

Through the equity characteristic, investors in convertible securities have the potential to participate in appreciation of the connected common stock. Meanwhile, the bond feature limits the downside risk associated with the underlying stock. The stock price cannot fall below its conversion value into a bond.

[8. See: "Convertible Bond Primer" 30 August 2014 *Invesco Power Shares* <http://tinyurl.com/naud3ec>]

---

20. FALLACIOUS ECONOMICUS: I have a degree in financial analysis and believe I can correctly assess the impact of events on corporate profits. I can identify and quantify good news and bad news. I will identify and fit together all the pieces, ratios, percentages, growth rates, all the minutia of the financial analysis jigsaw puzzle. The true picture will emerge. Then, I will invest according to my own expert analysis.

Fallacious Reasoning: What could possibly go wrong? My approach follows all the textbooks and is perfectly logical.

Correct Reasoning: The problems are a) not everyone is expert like you and, b) markets are not always rational. What if you are the only one who realizes a stock is undervalued (or overvalued)? **The stock price is not moving without the support of the crowd, the great mass of buyers and sellers.**

The crowd moves markets, not you. Ideally: try to be one step ahead of the crowd. Acquire an investment *before* the crowd and sell in advance of the crowd's exit. So, do your expert analysis. But, try to figure *how the crowd will react* to the same information, the same announcement. Then act. Even if you think you are right and the crowd is wrong, base your strategy how the crowd will act. You cannot turn back the tide ... just understand it and adjust your investment actions accordingly.

21. FALLACIOUS ECONOMICUS: Forget all that analysis stuff. I called a radio show for investment advice and spoke to the host for two minutes. She gave me what sounded like good advice. I am now acting on that advice.

Fallacious Reasoning: The speaker has published a number of books on investing. She sounded like a good, earnest and honest person, knowledgeable and understanding.

Correct Reasoning: How can someone speak to you for two minutes on the radio and, not knowing your financial background, investment history, family situation, temperament, and attitude toward risk, in good conscience make accurate and appropriate recommendations that may impact your whole life?

A worthy, in-depth investor profile requires an extensive in person interview. What of these media experts? Listen to their general counsel but beware their specific investment advice for you.

It's morally wrong to allow a sucker to keep his money ...W. C. Fields

22. FALLACIOUS ECONOMICUS: I want to get rich and will always aim for maximum returns despite the higher risks.

Correct Reasoning: The fallacy betrays a naïve approach to investments. An improved strategy is **the life cycle theory of investing.** Generally, investment risk should decline as one ages. Start here:

1) **Accumulation phase.** The best time for a high risk, high return approach is when one is a young investor starting to build wealth. Young folks have more time than older investors to bounce back from any losses. After the accumulation phase one should alter strategy to consolidate gains. Shift to phase 2).

2) **Consolidation phase.** Reduce risk in your middle years. Seek predictable returns to match regular, predictable outflows. Secure return flows to meet the regular payments of mortgages, property taxes and college tuition for the kids. Next: in one's senior years one should begin enjoying the fruits of both accumulation and consolidation.

3) **Decumulation phase**. Perhaps nursing home and hospital bills loom. At this stage seniors require safety of capital and steady cash inflows. A conservative, low risk, preservation of capital approach involving bond funds and annuities should be considered in that stage.

So, do not stick with one strategy for an *excessive* length of time. Adjust your strategy as your life circumstances change. Everything in its turn.

[9. Ros Altmann "Investing over the life-cycle – building wealth" 11 July 2014 <http://tinyurl.com/nvu56mk>]

Hey, Buddy, Can I Give You Some Advice?

Sound General Financial Advice:

Prepare a realistic household budget to determine what portion can be devoted to savings, in general and stock market investing, in particular. Then, be prepared to lose any monies you put in the stock market! In other words, do not invest the baby's milk money or this month's rent in the stock market. The worst that can happen is you lose every penny ... and have no legitimate claim to a refund. From the *individual's* point of view, the stock market(s) resembles a gambling casino.

As in the casino, there are different "poisons" to choose from, different games to play. It is the same with the securities markets. Explore and study those various investment vehicles: stocks, bonds, convertibles, derivatives and so on.

More Advice:

Borrowing to invest, i.e., using leverage by *buying on margin*, can be a two edged sword that may magnify your return ... or deepen your loss.

Even More Advice:

Investing in derivatives (options, warrants, futures, options on futures, et. al.) and foreign currencies can make you ... or break you ... and do so in a flash! This is living at the extreme edge of risk! This is the casino on steroids. James Bond and Indiana Jones meet the dare devil Evel Knievel!

Even More Advice than That:

➢ Remember: getting back what you invested -- *accounting breaking even* -- is really losing money, given there were available alternatives.

➢ Set investment goals, but don't forget: added return comes with added risk, i.e., higher probability of not realizing that higher return! (TANSTAAFL).

➢ If interested in a stock, look for a related convertible bond or preferred stock as an investment alternative. It can help reduce downside risk.

➢ Avoid individual stocks altogether. Instead, buy into a diversified pool of stocks and/or bonds by purchasing shares of a **no load** mutual fund.

➢ Explore ETFs (Exchange Traded Funds) SPDRs ("Spiders").

➢ Place stop-loss orders to lock in gains or limit losses.

Finally:

Anticipate how the crowd will react to announcements and news stories!

Always consult with a qualified and honest investment advisor.

Don't insist on buying at the very bottom and selling at the very top.

Don't forget: Bulls and Bears Make Money, but Pigs Get Slaughtered.

[10. For more tips, see Jim Cramer. "Cramer's Twenty-five Rules for Investing" 3 December 2014 *The Street* <http://www.thestreet.com/static/25-rules.html>]

23. FALLA<IOUS <<ONOMI<US: A strong *positive correlation* exists between stock market prices and current economic conditions. Good times mean rising stock prices and bad times mean falling stock prices.

Correct Reasoning: One easily embraces this fallacy until checking the data. Oddly, experience shows there are numerous instances of *negative* correlation between current economic conditions and current stock prices. In other words, times may be good, but stock prices are down. Times may be bad, but stock prices are up. That indicates a certain element of disconnect between the American stock market (e.g., Standard and Poor's 500) and the current state of the American economy. There is a simple explanation for this behavior. Read all about it!

The stock price is generally considered a **leading indicator** of economic conditions, not a coincident indicator. That is, prices in the stock market usually do not coincide with the current state of the economy. **The market looks forward and condenses what it sees, good or bad, into a current price, regardless of current conditions.** In that way of thinking, today's changes in the stock price divulge the market's consensus view of the *future* returns to the stock, not current returns. A change in the consensus view registers as a change in the current market value. Of course, that view may be adjusted moment to moment, expressed as current stock price changes. A few points of explanation apply:

1. Reports on economic conditions relate to the current situation or the recent past, not the future. Market values are generally understood to be a composite, condensed measure of *future* economic conditions impacting future earnings. A **stock price may be thought of as a collapsed, telescopic view of market consensus forecasted future earnings,** like a slinky toy in its compressed state. There may be a divergence between current conditions and projected future conditions. The market dwells on the future not the past. **The market is a leading indicator, not a coincident or lagging indicator.**

2. Many of the companies in the stock indices are multinational, deriving earnings from various economies worldwide. In this sense, they are insulated from declines in current and future U.S. earnings.

3. When interest rates are low *relative* to stock returns, investors seeking higher returns may switch from bonds to stocks. They do this despite low current stock earnings, earnings prospects and general economic conditions. This puts upward pressure on stock prices. In the last ten years the Federal Reserve has pushed down interest rates with its **Quantitative Easing** policy, encouraging many investors to exchange low rate bonds for higher risk stocks.

4. On any given day, any stock could go in any direction without any apparent reason! These "out of nowhere" random events drive investors crazy!

24. FALLACIOUS ECONOMICUS: Buy land, you can't miss.

Fallacious Reasoning: They aren't making any more!

Correct Reasoning: The recommendation is fallacious because it is too imprecise. Generally, when one buys, one buys a specific piece of land, not land in general. Lots of specific land values have cratered or stagnated. Any area where population or industry is leaving is suspect. Take Detroit, for instance ... or leave it. Or, land values may be threatened by factors such as:

1) **Natural disaster** (landslide, flooding, erosion or earthquake) or
2) **Man-made disaster** (pollution, toxic waste or radiation leak) or,
3) **Political action** (seizure by eminent domain, unfriendly re-zoning or regulation). In all these cases, investing in land is problematic. (Insurance may cover the financial loss of personal property or damage to an improvement to the land, e.g., a building. However, not all risks are insurable.) Note that even a good piece of land has carrying costs such as property taxes, insurance, and security. Some parcels of land may be illiquid (not quickly saleable at the going price). Improved land may bring troublesome tenants.

Small land parcels are made all the time. The (still Red) Chinese are building islands in the South China Sea! Artificial islands proliferate in *Dubai* and the Middle East. Many cities have filled in swamps (eh, excuse me, I mean *wetlands*) to create living space. A better recommendation: Shop for ANY asset whose price is likely to rise.

New York Society Page: The Streets, Divorce of the Century

After a long marriage, it was announced today that Mr. and Mrs. Main and Wall Street will separate and eventually divorce. The Streets cited irreconcilable differences. No longer will they be seen as a loving couple, always moving in tandem. The divorce was initiated by Mr. Wall Street and bitterly contested by Mrs. Main Street. No longer will prosperity for Mr. Wall Street reflect or guarantee prosperity for Mrs. Main Street, nor will Mr. Wall Street be responsible for the well-being of Mrs. Main Street. In recent years, Mr. Wall Street has sought greener pastures outside the U.S. As a result of a bitter negotiation, Mrs. Main Street will get custody of the U.S. while Mr. Wall Street gets the rest of the world. Rumor has it Mrs. Main Street is considering an offer from the TV reality show The Real Housewives of Wall Street.

Terms are being negotiated.

Chapter Nineteen
Investing Fallacies: The National Perspective

Giving money and power to government is like giving
whiskey and car keys to teenage boys. -P. J. O'Rourke

ECONOMISTS distinguish between saving and investing *money* (financial investment) and saving and investing *resources* (real investment). Tools and equipment are the output of saving and investing real resources. **Real capital** is what economists call these intermediate goods. Just as soldiers need weapons, workers need tools.

Consider, what can one produce with bare hands? Labor needs land, capital and know-how to be productive. Economic growth requires more and better tools. More highly skilled workers are required, as well. Tools include machinery, business computers, and software. Tool making is referred to as *real capital formation.* **Real capital formation requires:**

1) REAL SAVING (setting aside of resources from consumer goods production, obviously causing the sacrifice of consumer goods), and

2) REAL INVESTMENT (using those released resources to produce capital goods).

This is especially difficult and painful for emerging and subsistence economies. The sacrificed consumer goods may threaten levels needed for survival. (Real savings must be distinguished from financial savings, as depicted in Diagram #1)

Diagram #1: Overview of the Savings Process in the Economy

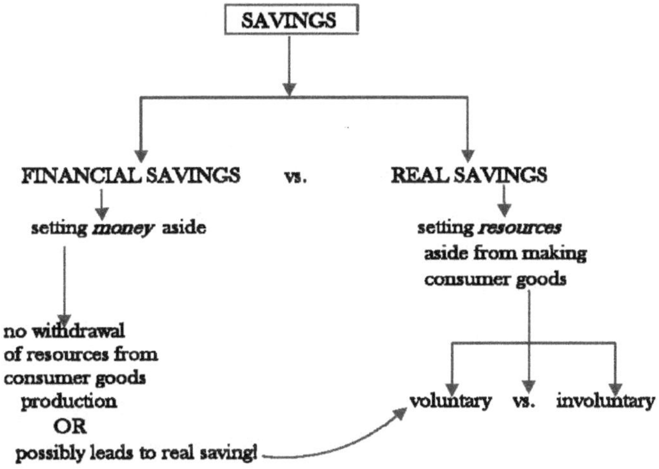

Emerging economies need roads, bridges, electrical grids, power plants, dams, sewage systems, harbors, airports, hospitals and other social overhead capital to support "take-off" of economic growth. They need real capital formation to raise the productivity and incomes of their workers. Again, **producing capital goods requires resources, as they cannot be fabricated out of thin air. The released or saved resources are known as real savings.** Real saving requires the unpopular sacrifice of consumer goods.

To compound the problem, over time capital goods wear out or become obsolete. Those worn out capital goods must be replaced, lest productive potential fall. Indeed, a nation seeking economic *expansion* must produce capital goods faster than they are wearing out (real depreciation). This requires a *higher level of* consumer goods sacrifice, not easy in some countries where most folks live at or near the subsistence level.

I. Voluntary (Unforced) Real Savings

1. FALLACIOUS ECONOMICUS: There is no such thing as *involuntary savings*. All real savings are voluntary. If I do not wish to save, then I do not save. In a free society, no one can force me to save when I do not want to.

Correct Reasoning: Actually, **real savings can be voluntary or involuntary**. Remember, in economics *real* saving is a setting aside and idling of resources. As idled resources, *real* saving is a prerequisite for *real* investment.

You cannot build capital without resources, no? *Real savings* are resources set aside and available for capital construction (highways, power plants, factories, etc.) But, how do resources get set aside or become available in a free market economy? Basically, most *real* saving originates in voluntary *financial* saving, setting the stage for *real* saving. Read more about it:

> ➢ **Step 1:** Income earners, thinking of future consumption, voluntarily give up some consumption today and save *money* in financial intermediaries. In a modern, monetized economy **financial intermediaries** are critical adjuncts to the capital formation process. Financial intermediaries (banks, pension funds, mutual funds, insurance companies, et. al.) serve to channel money from *financial savers* to *financial* investors. Or, savers may reduce consumption, use a direct channel and buy corporate and government bonds directly. (This is a leakage from the circular flow).

> ➢ **Step 2:** The financial intermediary is the conduit for moving money to potential borrowers. Ideally, the bank is willing to lend and a borrower

is willing and qualified to borrow. In this way financial savings are channeled to a borrower.

> **Step 3:** A loan is extended.

> **Step 4:** Borrowers order *capital* goods and spend the money. The resource idles by drawing resources from consumer goods production.

Example: Let us say passenger car sales have fallen. Resources formerly used to produce passenger cars (a consumer good) have now been idled. *Those idled resources are the real savings.* **Real savings are saved resources,** resources diverted from consumer goods production.

Beware: Most financial saving is done by middle and upper income recipients. Lower income people are likely to spend every dollar of income to sustain themselves. Take that one step further: low income people are notorious *dissavers,* using credit to spend beyond their income limit.

It is the capital producers, the real investors, who apply released resources to building capital goods (the real investment). Caution: not all financial saving results in real saving and investment. Sometimes financial saving exceeds real saving.

Note that in today's specialized economies real saving and real investing are carried on by different economic agents. Saving and investing *money* does not necessarily result in *real* saving and *real* investment of resources.

Beware: Some saved money may be channeled to other consumers who spend on consumer goods. If this happens there is no additional *real* saving for the economy. Financial saving, yes, but no *real* saving because resources are not released from consumer goods production.

Example: Instead of the saver buying a new sports car, the saver deposits money in a bank. A borrower comes along, borrows the money and orders an SUV (sports utility vehicle). The auto manufacturer produces an SUV instead of a sports car. There is no diversion of resources, no real saving, from consumer goods into capital goods for the *economy as a whole.*

Is there real capital formation? When money is involved, follow the money to see if there is a saving of *resources*. Then, follow the idled resources to see if they are used to build real capital.

Example: Judy "saves" $50 per week from her salary by depositing it in her bank account. No doubt, Judy is engaging in *financial* saving, saving the *money.* But, money is not a resource.

Question: Is there a setting aside of resources, *real saving*, for the economy as a whole?

Answer: Follow the money. It depends on what happens to the money saved by Judy.

Rumors Can Hurt

Depositor confidence in the solvency of a financial intermediary is critical to its survival. Triggered by a real threat, a diminution of confidence in financial intermediaries – such as occurred in 2008-2009 – further undermines the survivability those institutions, economy wide. Even a rumor can shake confidence and spark a run on healthy institutions throughout the banking system. **If savers lose confidence in the financial intermediation process, intermediaries will collapse.** That collapse could trigger a domino effect from depressed financial saving to depressed real saving, capital formation and economic growth.   The lesson is this: intermediaries must be guarded, sometimes guarded against their own foolish actions! Keep savings out of the mattress! Here stands the Federal Reserve System as guardian (mother hen?) of the banking system.

Remember, when the banking system is threatened, so is the economy. And when the economy is threatened, so is national security. So, connect the dots:

The good health of financial intermediaries is critical to national security!

Variation 1: Financial saving without real saving. Suppose the bank takes Judy's $50 and lends it to Shirley. Shirley uses the borrowed $50 and buys music CDs, a consumer good, for personal enjoyment. Here there is no real saving. (Of course, there can be no additional *real investment* as there are no freed resources available to invest, i.e., no real saving).

Variation 2. Financial saving followed by real saving and real investment. Alternatively, suppose the bank lends Judy's $50 to Shirley, who puts an order in for an instructional CD on sharpening her office skills at the job. This instructional CD is a capital good. The CD company then burns this instructional CD instead of the music CD. This re-allocation of resources away from consumer goods production to capital goods production constitutes *real* saving. The burning, i.e., creation, of the instructional CD constitutes real investment.

II. Involuntary (Forced) Real Savings

2. FALLACIOUS ECONOMICUS: What if *voluntary* saving is too little to expand or even replace the stock of capital? What if earners become consumption "happy" and do not save? Must the economy suffer a decline in its real capital stock and productive potential? Since real savings are critical to capital formation, why doesn't the government force people to save?

Fallacious Reasoning: If real savings are needed for capital building and capital building is needed for a strong growing economy, then too bad - in a free society - the government cannot *mandate* a certain level of real savings, no?

Correct Reasoning: Surprise! The government *can* encourage and even force people to create real savings (free up resources from making consumer goods.) But, they do this in clandestine, unannounced ways folks are unaware of. Understand that *involuntary* real savings is the same as *forced* (real) savings. Government can force people to save by the following methods.

1) Forced saving via higher tax rates. One way to force real saving is by raising tax rates, forcing income recipients to forego consumption, triggering the release of resources by consumer goods producers. This is called *forced (real) savings*. Then government spends the tax money, drawing resources into the production of public capital goods, say, highways, bridges, tunnels, etc.

But, Beware: Increased taxation does not always lead to increased real saving!

Example1: There are no real savings for the economy *as a whole* if the government simply re-directs the tax money to other citizens who use it for consumption, e.g., food stamps.

Example 2: Collected taxes devoted to repayment of debt create no real investment to that point.

Example 3:   Forced saving via higher taxation. Higher taxation is frequently used to force the civilian economy to cut spending, thereby freeing resources, i.e., *saving* resources, to be re-deployed to military efforts. So, as fewer passenger cars are bought resources are freed to produce tanks.

2) Forced saving via inflation. A reluctance to raise tax *rates* may lead the government to *over-expand* the money supply, most likely leading to inflation. Through its central bank the government can create *excessive* monetary growth. Unless velocity collapses, this fuels inflation. **The inflation forces spending cutbacks by income recipients unable to adjust incomes upward to match the inflation.** Those on fixed incomes, e.g., social security and private pension recipients, contractual wages, interest and rentals, suffer a decline in *real* income as the purchasing power of their unchanged money income declines.

Fixed incomes cannot keep up with the rise in prices, causing real income to fall. Consumer spending falls, releasing resources for real investment. Resources are released, i.e., real saving occurs. Uncle Sam steps in to reallocate the released resources. Those freed resources (the real saving) can be hired and brought into government programs.

So, after the inflation, the resources freed from consumer auto production get re-directed into military vehicle production. Such is the *forced* real saving and real investment process via inflation. Therefore, an increase in statutory tax rates is not needed to carry out the transfer of resources from civilian to government/military use.

The result is real investment by way of a hidden tax! Keynes weighed in on this issue:

> By a continuous process of inflation, governments can confiscate, secretly and unobserved, an important part of the wealth of their citizens. By this method, they not only confiscate, but they confiscate arbitrarily; and while the process impoverishes many, it actually enriches some....
>
> [1. John Maynard Keynes. "Keynes on Inflation," *The Economic Consequences of the Peace,* 1919, pp 235-248. <http://tinyurl.com/8anb9ln>]

Examples: In the 20th century Brazil built Brasilia and Lyndon Johnson financed the extra spending for the Viet Nam war using *forced saving* generated by accelerating inflation fueled by excess *monetization of the debt.*

3) Forced savings via command or conquest, e.g., forced labor. Many workers who built the Great Wall of China were peasants taken by force by the Chinese military and used on the construction of the wall. In effect, resources - their labor - was *forcibly removed* from other occupations, say, farming (consumer goods production).

Conscripts helped build the Moscow subway and Trans Siberian railway. The families left behind most likely had to survive on fewer civilian goods. They did the sacrificing. Germany and Japan used captives as forced labor, i.e., slave labor, during World War II.

Question: For many years the U.S. had compulsory military service for males of 18 years and older. It was called *the draft.* Would you consider the military draft an example of forced saving?

3. FALLACIOUS ECONOMICUS: Bolivia, Hungary, Russia, Greenland and

Grenada have all have a version of a flat income tax. Critics charge the U.S. **graduated (or progressive) income tax system is too complicated,** overloaded with brackets, exclusions, exemptions, credits and other complexities. Different tax rates for different folks with different incomes. Some taxpayers get breaks others don't. *The whole system is unfair and unworkable.* Critics say we need a flat tax, where every taxpayer pays the same rate, say, 20% on ALL income. Simple, no? Deductions from taxable income for individuals and corporations would be eliminated. That would improve the fairness of the system.

Correct Reasoning: Yes, the U.S. currently has a complex Federal income tax system based on a graduated or *progressive rate* structure. In that system, taxpayer income is, in effect, viewed as a layer cake. As one adds layers of income, each higher layer is taxed at a higher rate. The situation is complicated by a multitude of loopholes, gimmicks and special treatments not available to all taxpayers. Hence, the lure of the **flat tax – same tax rate for all incomes**. In pure form the flat tax would ditch all deductions and exemptions. Conceptually, a tax return could be three numbers:

[(Income) minus (Tax) EQUALS (Income After Tax)]

[There will be, in effect, a zero bracket, as there is now, for very low income taxpayers. So, there will be two tax brackets, not one.]

The fallacy connected to the flat tax is that it would provide more fairness than the current system. But, aren't rich folks *undertaxed* if they pay the same percentage as low income folks?

Indeed, the flat tax of imposing too light a tax burden on the rich and super rich. After all, a flat tax would mean the $30,000 and the $30,000,000 income are taxed at the same rate, say 20%. Could it be the lower income taxpayer, paying $6000 is actually *hurt more* than the higher income paying $6 million? That leaves mucho after tax income for the $30,000,000 taxpayer. (Actually, after tax income would be $24,000,000). Here lies the counter-argument: the flat tax does not necessarily improve fairness. **Critics argue the flat rate on all incomes is *not* fair as it *under taxes* the high income person and *over taxes* lower income people.** In sum, critics argue that, relative to the graduated rate structure it would replace, a flat tax would create *more* unfairness or inequity.

On practical level, it would take a bomb load dropped from a B-52 bomber to uproot and eliminate all the loopholes built into the current corporate income tax. Lawmakers would be assaulted by an army of lobbyists hoping to keep the loopholes and tax gimmicks that favor their clients. For example, banks and the housing industry would strenuously object to the elimination of the mortgage interest deduction.

[BTW: a flat tax is not to be confused with a tax Universities would like to put on obnoxious fraternities. Yup, you got it ... a *frat* tax ... sorry!]

The flat tax is appealing on some levels but disappointing on others. Yes, it would be simpler than the current system. But it cannot deliver on its promise to *be fairer than the current system. Progressivity has always been the gold standard for fairness in the income tax rate structure.* Ultimately, instituting a flat tax is a political decision.

Appendix

An *individual's* credit score – indicating debt paying ability – may be found at the Big Three different credit rating agencies: TransUnion, Experian and Equifax. FICO scores are based on reporting from the Big Three.

[7. Andy Kessler, "My Tour of FICO Scores, Fido Loans, Whatever" 10 Nov. 2015 *Wall Street Journal* <http://tinyurl.com/pfkcxb6>]

A tax collector at work – from an illustration by Henry Holiday
in Lewis Carroll's **The Hunting of the Snark** (1876)

Chapter Twenty
Some GDP Fallacies

GDP, GDP, Do You Have Something for Me?

G ROSS DOMESTIC PRODUCT (GDP) is the grand total dollar value of new goods and services produced in a year in the U.S. It is a rough measure of welfare (well-being) of an economy for a particular year. Each nation has its own GDP and family of subsidiary numbers derived from it. The GDP "family" is a treasure trove of economic data on consumer and business behavior as well as government activity in the economy. Foreign trade stats are included. U.S. growth in GDP **had been anemic (1-3%) for more than a decade. Compared to other faster growing leading economies such as (still Red) China, U.S. growth rates signal relative decline.**

GDP is probably the most watched number related to the state of the economy. Its quarterly report is eagerly awaited by professional economists, journalists, investors and members of the general public. In general, changes in (real) GDP signal a change in economic conditions. However, beware this one number as there are many misconceptions associated with GDP.

GDP is the Chairman of the Board of Economic Statistics, at least where the general state of the economy is concerned. Beware, there are many misconceptions and improper inferences associated with the one number, GDP. One number cannot tell all, yes, but GDP heads a family of subsidiary statistics such as investment, consumption and trade data. GDP alternatively reveals disguises and omits important information. Read all about it:

> ➢ GDP divided by population yields GDP *per person* or GDP *per capita*. Heroically, one may call this *average income*. But, this is not the actual or average income going to each person. It is simply a mathematical calculation, an arithmetic mean. Its value lies in its simplicity, its ease of calculation. This facilitates comparisons with prior years and other countries.

> ➢ GDP masks the division of GDP between goods versus services.

> ➢ **GDP masks changes in the grassroots standard of living,** which has been in absolute decline.

> ➢ **GDP masks changes in the pattern of income distribution.**

> ➢ GDP masks changes in the *quality* of goods.

➢ GDP masks the obsolescence of some goods and introduction of new ones. Today's computer buyer gets much more for each $100 paid.

➢ GDP does not count the value of hobbies, home production, and underground (illegal) output and incomes.

➢ GDP is insensitive to a shift in composition of output from work clothes to leisure clothes, from overcoats to ski vests, from pickup trucks to sports cars. In short, GDP does not account for the pleasures of leisure time, a major component of individual welfare. However, it does account for the production of the material adjuncts to leisure. These include recreational goods such fishing poles, swimsuits and skiing lodges. These goods are markers for the *quality* of life.

➢ **GDP is amoral** in the sense that $1,000 worth of bombs gets equal billing with $1,000 worth of baby food.

➢ GDP does not properly account for the production of "bads" such as pollutants and non degradable materials that reduce the quality and quantity of life. These "bads" may require the devotion of other resources for collection and disposal. The application of resources to pollution "duty" reduces the availability of other goods which could have been produced. **Some observers have suggested environmental damage and clean up costs are deducted from GDP.**

1. FALLACIOUS ECONOMICUS: More is better. The composition of the
GDP between capital and consumer goods is irrelevant. As long as the grand total increases, life is getting better.

Correct Reasoning: Beware of the devil is in the details. The fallacious statement ignores the importance of **real capital goods**. A GDP devoted only to consumer goods dooms an economy to lower and lower GDP in future years. Here is why: nearly all production requires man made tools, capital goods. Tools do not satisfy wants directly but help make consumer goods. The division of labor, tools, and standardization of parts are **force multipliers**. But, tools and equipment are not indestructible. They **wear out/become obsolete** and must to be replaced lest the stock of tools be depleted.

Used up capital is referred to as **real depreciation**. Production capability will decline if tools are not replaced as they wear out. So, other things being equal:

➢ To *maintain* its production capabilities in any given year, a nation must produce new capital equipment and other tools of production *equal* to capital used up (real depreciation).

> ➤ Failure to replace worn out capital means, other things equal, a drop in productive potential for Guns, Butter and Capital equipment itself.

> ➤ Other factors constant, to *expand* the productive potential a nation must add *more* new capital than wears out in a year.

2. FALLACIOUS ECONOMICUS: Well then, if real capital is so important, why not produce as much as possible?

Correct Reasoning: TANSTAAFL! Real capital expansion is not free! Creating real capital imposes an opportunity cost on the economy. Producing the truck sacrifices the sports car. Building the factory sacrifices the apartment building. Resources must be removed from consumer goods production (a process called real saving) and re-allocated to capital goods production. The more capital goods produced currently, the fewer consumer goods can be produced currently. The sacrificed enjoyment from lost consumer goods must figure into a capital investment decision. However, **if more capital goods are produced today, at greater consumer sacrifice, they enable more of all kinds of goods tomorrow.** Patience and ability to bear sacrifice is required to execute this plan!

Recap: to achieve growth in productive potential requires producing must *more* capital than is wearing out. Ten new machines come online as six are ditched. This is called **net capital formation.** **Private capital** such as factories, transportation and communications equipment, office buildings and equipment are involved. Also included are **social overhead capital** goods such as roads, bridges, airports, communications facilities, power lines and generation stations. These are crucial for the "take-off" stage of economic growth.

Command economies, some using slave labor, extract real saving by force. For example: Ancient China conscripted workers to build the Great Wall.

3. FALLACIOUS ECONOMICUS: It does not matter if military or civilian goods are being produced as long as the total Gross Domestic Product grows.

Correct Reasoning: Pay attention to whether "swords" or "ploughshares" are being produced. This is the famous Guns (military goods) versus Butter (civilian goods) issue. Both are desirable and necessary. Of course it matters whether production is devoted more to Guns or more to Butter and how those proportions change. [But, see the next Fallacy]The division of output between military and civilian goods is important for assessing national defense capabilities. Inadequate national defense could lead to subservience to a foreign power hostile to the American Way of Life. In the extreme, inadequate national defense may lead to conquest by that hostile foreign power. In that case, self rule or national sovereignty would likely end, along with personal freedom.

Producing (or procuring) military goods alone is not enough to maintain a given level of national defense. As with capital goods, each year military equipment simply wears out from use in battle or training. Moreover, some weapon systems become technologically obsolete. The worn out, destroyed and obsolete equipment must be replaced and updated.

Military capital. If the national defense capability is to be enhanced, then procurement must move beyond mere hardware replacement to expansion. Expansion is referred to as **net military capital formation**. Adding to military or defense capital requires *additional* real savings, additional sacrifice, to release the necessary resources. For a stagnant economy, this means a drop in Butter production. Alternatively, a *growing* economy can maintain Butter output while expanding military capability and national security.

Never forget: *the Economy is the Mother Ship of National Security*

4. FALLACIOUS ECONOMICUS: There is a strict subdivision of goods between military and civilian goods. Civilian goods have no military application and military goods have no civilian application.

Correct Reasoning: The division of production into civilian versus military goods is a false dichotomy. **All goods and resources have a military application, direct or indirect.** Automobile factories can be converted to produce tanks; farmland can be converted into airfields and farmers into soldiers. Food, fuel, medicines and clothing can be used by civilians or the military. Even baby food can feed the troops.

> ➤ **Most goods/resources have an indirect as well as direct military application.** Women replaced men in factories during World War II, freeing the men for the battlefront. Women contributed to the military effort even if they stayed home and made sandwiches for their fighter pilot husbands.

> ➤ Of course, civilian resources vary in ease and speed with which they can be converted to military occupations. It is best to have a standing military establishment.

> ➤ Military equipment is convertible to civilian use when war ends. The "swords" are beaten into "ploughshares." Soldiers return to civilian occupations.

Finally, beware of so-called "humanitarian" aid. All civilian or humanitarian aid has a direct or indirect potential military application. For example: helping a country improve crop yields in the agricultural sector is a seemingly benign activity, right? But, improved yield per acre permits fewer acres to produce the same amount of food as before. This permits the release of land, labor and capital to be re-deployed to the military sector!

5. FALLACIOUS ECONOMICUS: An expansion in GDP signals there are more goods and services being produced.

Correct Reasoning: Watch the **real GDP**. It is reported quarterly and, of course, yearly. GDP has two modes of expression, so pay close attention to the precise wording connected with reported GDP. Only when there is growth in the total **real** or **inflation adjusted** GDP is there growth in actual output. That measure neutralizes the effect of price changes. But, beware, as there is a reported GDP measure called **nominal** or **unadjusted** GDP which does not correct the measure for price changes. It changes with price changes, disguising the movement in actual output. Real GDP is the real deal, as it is sensitive *only* to output changing! On occasion, nominal GDP can trick the observer because it changes when prices change. In effect, real GDP pretends there are no price changes, only changes in quantities produced. **Real** GDP tells no lies about actual output! **Production moves in the same direction as real GDP.**

> ➤ If **real** GDP rises, this signals a rise in production.

> ➤ If **real** GDP falls, this signals a fall in production.

Nominal GDP is an unreliable indicator of movements in real output. If nominal GDP rises, the increase may be due to price increases without production increases. Stick with real GDP, up or down.

GDP, Per Capita Income and the Standard of Living

6. FALLACIOUS ECONOMICUS: GDP divided by population yields GDP **per capita, or income per person.** Changes in GDP per capita are a good indicator of changes in the standard of living of ordinary folks.

Correct Reasoning: The calculation is correct but the interpretation is fallacious. **GDP per capita** (or average income) is often cited as a measure of economic welfare or standard of living (SOL). **The GDP per capita is not calculated and then the goods/income distributed according to the calculation.** It is simply a quickly calculated extremely rough measure of economic well-being. However, it has very little relevance to the amount of income *actually available* typically available to a person. Unfortunately, there is no one best measure of the (SOL). Yet, GDP per capita is often trumpeted by those wishing to cloak declines the standard of living, especially as GDP – *total* income – rises but the *distribution* of income becomes more unequal.

GDP and SOL. However, GDP per capita is not to be tossed out. It is calculated quickly and is easy to interpret. However, it is recognized as only a minor component in a basket of indicators associated with the standard of living. A number of measures are needed to make a valid assessment of the SOL. Unfortunately, there is no generally accepted basket of indicators for assessing the standard of living.

> Opinions differ among economic researchers as to the ideal so-called list of ingredients that should make up a standard of living measure. With so many different ways to measure the quality of a country's healthcare, for instance, *there is no single, concrete list of factors that comprise a unified living standards formula.* As a result, there are many different statistics generated by various research groups that may be called standard of living.
>
> [1. Italics mine. Mike Howells "What is Standard of Living?" 06 March 2015 *Wisegeek* <http://www.wisegeek.com/what-is-standard-of-living.htm>]

Two overriding ideas dominate the thinking about the movement of SOL:

➢   Giving up *more* (or the same) and getting *less* is indicative of a *decline* in the standard of living. (One may give up money, effort or leisure.)

➢   Giving up *less* (or the same) and getting *more* is indicative of a *rise* in the standard of living.

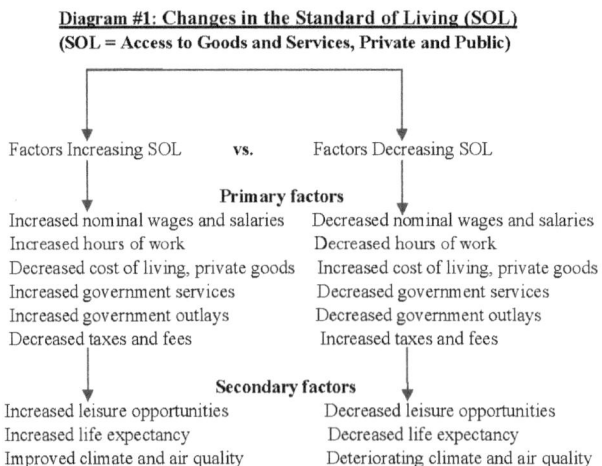

Diagram #1: Changes in the Standard of Living (SOL)
(SOL = Access to Goods and Services, Private and Public)

	Factors Increasing SOL	**vs.**	**Factors Decreasing SOL**

Primary factors

Factors Increasing SOL	Factors Decreasing SOL
Increased nominal wages and salaries	Decreased nominal wages and salaries
Increased hours of work	Decreased hours of work
Decreased cost of living, private goods	Increased cost of living, private goods
Increased government services	Decreased government services
Increased government outlays	Decreased government outlays
Decreased taxes and fees	Increased taxes and fees

Secondary factors

Factors Increasing SOL	Factors Decreasing SOL
Increased leisure opportunities	Decreased leisure opportunities
Increased life expectancy	Decreased life expectancy
Improved climate and air quality	Deteriorating climate and air quality

Diagram #1 above gives a more complete – but not exhaustive – listing of the factors involved. **Each factor is considered to be acting alone, other factors** constant (ceteris paribus). Americans' have lowered their expectations about their future SOL. **For most middle class Americans, "the future ain't what it used to be." (attributed to Yogi Berra).**

Beware: The U.S. SOL has been in slow decline for nearly forty years!

A trade-off: Note that a movement to improve one's standard of living may reduce one's quality of life. For example, one may work more hours per week, resulting in a larger paycheck. But, working more hours reduces the number of hours available for leisure time with spouse and children. (For additional discussion, see Chapter Eleven on Redistribution of Income).

7. FALLACIOUS ECONOMICUS: It is a good thing that GDP keeps soaring upward, year after year. without a break. That means more stuff to enjoy and greater happiness all around. (Assume a nation in autarky, i.e., not trading)

Fallacious Reasoning: *More* is better than *less*, right?

Correct Reasoning: Yes, most folks agree more is better than less. Unfortunately, GDP (the broad economy) does not shoot straight up, more and more every year. In some years there are declines. Actually, **GDP moves in waves, in cycles. GDP follows the twists and turns of aggregate demand.** GDP grows for a few years, then contracts, then grows, then contracts and so on. Unfortunately, it does not grow continuously or evenly. Fortunately, it does not decline endlessly. Every stage has an end, which begins the next stage. Business is good for a while, then bad, then good again and so on, mirroring the aggregate demand cycle. Periods of growth end, as do periods of decline. Two consecutive quarters of decline mark the beginning of an official recession.. This pattern of behavior is called *the business cycle (or, the economic cycle).* The cycle weaves around a **rising trend**, dashed line in Diagram #2, below.

<u>Diagram #2: The Business Cycle Pattern</u>

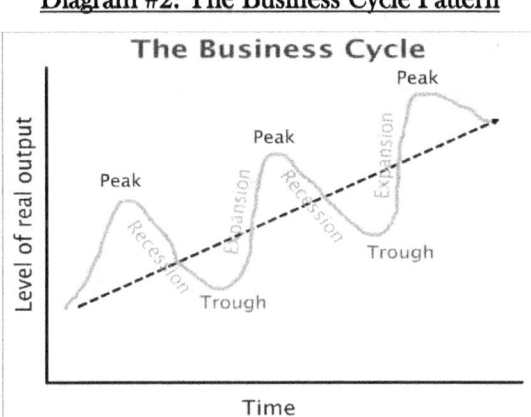

Why Recessions? Kindernomics

Gather round kids! Today we're going to create a recession! We are going to show you one way a recession could be created. (Other paths to recession are possible.)

It goes like this:

1. Overly optimistic sales forecasts cause firms to over-hire and *overproduce* goods.

2. Unfortunately, actual sales fall short of these rosy expectations.

3. Excess, unwanted inventories of unsold goods pile up.

4. After a time, the rosy sales forecast of (1) is dropped and sales expectations are revised downward.

5. Firms cut production (and employment) to work off the unwanted inventories, avoid further additions and match production to the new, lower level of expected sales.

If 1-5 *are widespread throughout the economy, then* real GDP goes into a decline.

Back to Economic Basics: Why Repeated Business Cycles?

In a market economy, **production and employment follow the ups and downs of AGGREGATE DEMAND.**   Firms employ workers and produce goods and services to serve their *paying* customers, those expressing DEMAND. Aggregate demand (AD) is the **grand total** of what people are willing and able to buy. More (fewer) paying customers at the door translates into greater (less) production and employment. Trouble is, aggregate demand itself has its ups and downs, pulling GDP behind it. Put GDP on a slow moving *asymmetrical* Aggregate Demand roller coaster and you get the business cycle pattern. (Diagram #2). Most years, the GDP "train" goes uphill. The path of economic growth shows one business cycle following another on an uphill climb. The steepness of that climb depends on the *underlying growth trend*, shown as the dashed line in Diagram #2 on the prior page. It is the result of structural forces (resource growth, technology advances, and institutional reliability capped by international trade policy).

Diagram #3: The Macro Roller Coaster: One Cycle

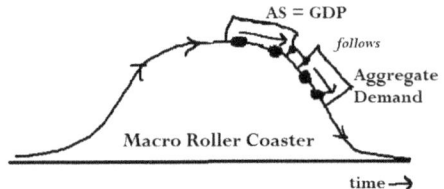

Wherever the lead car (AD) goes, the behind car (GDP) follows. Wherever aggregate demand goes, GDP follows.

Snowflakes and Business Cycles

Snowflakes and business cycles have much in common: each one is unique. No two are alike. Snowflakes come tall, short, fat, and thin. Cycles come long, short, intense, and mild. Each cycle is somewhat different, involving its own cluster of unique circumstances. In particular, cycles differ in their:

a) **Duration**- the length of time it takes to go through all phases of a cycle and get back to square one. Expansions usually last longer (average 5 years) than contractions (average 6 months).

b) **Intensity**- some cycles exhibit more extreme movements. For example, the Great Depression of the 1930s involved a greater decline (40%) in GDP than later, milder declines are called recessions.

c) **Spread**- cycles differ in their geographic and industrial impact. Not all regions and industries are declining in a general recession or growing in a general expansion. There are pockets of contraction in the midst of a general expansion and pockets of expansion within a general contraction.

Remember, in a free market economy businesses do not employ and produce to serve want *per se*. To earn profits they serve *demand*. Demand is want backed up by purchasing power. In this way production and employment rise and fall as (aggregate) demand rises and falls.

➢ Aside from real output, cycles also track the aggregates real income, employment and industrial production.

➢ Cycles are caused by fluctuations in *aggregate demand*. Aggregate demand is composed of Consumer demand (75%), Investment demand (1-2%), Government demand (23%) and Net Export Demand (exports minus imports) (minus 1%).

➢ Government would like to manage aggregate demand in order to eliminate harmful swings, especially recessions. A recession is a mild depression, with unemployment rising but held below 10% of the labor force. Recessions involve lost jobs, incomes, production. Moreover, they threaten national security due to the drop in production of *guns and butter*.

➢ Government "stabilization" tools are monetary policy (controlled by the independent Federal Reserve System) and fiscal policy (expressed in the Federal budget). They are used to coax the economy toward its full potential.

Unfortunately, aggregate demand is like a wild stallion which government has been unable to rope and saddle train on a consistent basis.

Dealing with a Slump in Business Activity

8. FALLA<IOU$ <<ONOMI<U$: It is a good thing government has those **macro stabilization tools, monetary and fiscal policy,** to battle occasional recessions or cure inflations. They activate these policies and - poof! - the problem is solved. This avoids a world of hurt associated with unemployment, recessions and inflations.

Correct Reasoning: If only those policies worked quickly and dependably, without fail! Unfortunately, that is not the case in the real world. The truth is those policies occasionally fail to **stimulate aggregate demand** when needed. The macro (or broad) economy sometimes seems to have a life of its own, a momentum independent of low interest loans, tax rebates, tax cuts and stimulus spending. In other words, there are times when the macro economy does not respond to fiscal and monetary policy ... Okay, let's back up a bit.

Fedmobile. Without getting too technical, think of the economy as a car and the economic authorities as the driver. Cars come equipped with accelerators and brakes. So do modern economies, where the accelerator and brakes are controlled by the driver, namely, government authorities.

The Fedmobile

If the Fed were a car, it would be better at **braking** (slowing money growth and the economy) than **accelerating** (speeding up monetary growth and the economy).

Monetary Policy: A sometime "upper" but a guaranteed "downer." Easy monetary policy is presumed to cause a chain reaction: interest rates fall, loanable funds are borrowed and spent, juicing up aggregate demand. Hopefully, the economy bounces back as desired. Economists call this the **monetary transmission mechanism.** But, the upswing in demand and the economy is **not guaranteed** as the transmission may "slip" and the economy is unaffected. The increased liquidity stays "on reserve," goes into a "holding pattern" without stimulating aggregate demand. Keynes called this a **liquidity trap.** Lenders cannot be forced to lend, spenders cannot be forced to borrow and spend. This situation persisted through the financial crisis and Great Recession of 2008-2009. Arguably, the situation persists to this writing (middle 2016). Lending rates approach zero but fail to stimulate. **Has this exhausted horse - monetary policy – run its last race? Is the stimulatory burden shifting entirely to another worn out nag, fiscal policy?**

Fiscal policy, retired tool? There is a standard remedy for failed monetary policy. It is called **fiscal policy,** controlled by COTUS and POTUS. When monetary policy fails to stimulate it is best to play the expansive *fiscal policy* card. Increase the deficit in the budget and have the government spend the money. Then you know it gets spent. So says the textbook. **But, beware: this path has limits.** As debt accumulates, current deficits become more problematic. Also, **Sequestration** (mandatory Federal spending cuts, 2013 - 2021) is restricting fiscal policy as a stimulus tool.

Braking with monetary policy. The *monetary brakes* work differently. They are reliable! The Federal Reserve can slam on the brakes and pursue a tight monetary policy. Without fail this action grinds the economy into a recession or a deeper depression, as in 1933 and the early 1980s.

Beware: it is easier to dampen economic activity than spark it. Don't always congratulate the economic authorities for booms and don't condemn them for recessions. It could be the economy "doing its own thing," listening to its inner voice and disregarding outside direction.

Special Monetary Policy: Exchange Rate Policy Gives False Hope?

Foreign demand for U.S. goods is a component of Aggregate Demand. Suppose in a slump ordinary monetary and fiscal policies are unavailable or ineffective. Then the nation can try to stimulate aggregate demand by cheapening the *external value* of its currency, its exchange rate with foreign currencies. **A cheaper, i.e., *weaker* dollar** would mean fewer units of the foreign currency are needed to acquire the sought after number of dollars. U.S. goods, priced in $, appear cheaper to those holding foreign currencies. Hopefully, the cheaper dollar (and cheaper U.S. goods) would spark a round of foreign buying, boosting U.S. exports and incomes. But, there is a price to pay: 1) imports would become more expensive! TANSTAAFL! 2) other nations might retaliate by devaluing, to restore the original exchange rate. **Also, there is the possibility that other nations may retaliate and de-value their currencies ... then, back to square one?**

---

9. FALLACIOUS ECONOMICUS: I heard a joke about a man who married his maid, making the GDP drop. That cannot be true!

Correct Reasoning: It is true. The output of hobbies and the homemaking efforts of homemakers are not counted in GDP. A parent makes a bowl of soup for his kids, a woman repairs her living room chair or a homeowner grows flowers and vegetables for personal use. None of this production is counted officially as part of GDP. The reason? Those activities are looked upon as hobbies, performed for personal gratification. Also omitted from official measurement are the outputs of illegal activities, e.g., sale of illegal drugs and incomes derived there from.

[2. Mijin Cha, "What's Missing From GDP?" 29 January 2013 *DEMOS* <http://www.demos.org/publication/whats-missing-gdp>]

GDP versus GNP

The U.S. switched to GDP from GNP in 1991 as the major indicator of aggregate economic activity for the nation. Be careful, do not confuse GDP with GNP.

GDP, or Gross Domestic Product is the value of new goods and services produced **within a nation** in a year. This calculation also equals all income earned within a country, or all expenditures on new goods within the country for the same time period.

GDP is a *territory* centered measure, including value created (and income enjoyed) within the U.S. borders, *regardless of the nationality of the creators.*

GDP is a *territory* centered measure, including value created (and income enjoyed) within the U.S. borders, regardless of the nationality of the creators.

GNP is a *nationality* centered measure of value, as betrayed by the word National in its name. It includes goods created (and income enjoyed) by **U.S. nationals**, regardless of where the production occurs, here or abroad.

GNP, or Gross National Product starts with GDP, but adds income to Americans from foreign sources, including dividends, interest and profit. Then it deducts income paid to foreign citizens and entities. This yields *net income from abroad, which could be positive or negative.*

Both measures as still reported and add up to very similar totals.

[3. Read more: InvestorWords, 1 Oct. 2015 < http://tinyurl.com/ofeo36j >]

Appendix One

10. FALLA⊂IOUS ⫷⊂ONOMI⊂US: The higher the GDP, the more goods that are

made here. And the more goods are available for enjoyment by the American people.

Correct Reasoning: Economists differentiate between goods *produced* in an area, the GDP, versus goods *available for use* in an area, called absorption. In an open economy, one which is importing and exporting, trade impacts the goods *available for use* by the nation. Trade may make absorption differ from GDP.

The Absorption Story. Absorption is the annual value of the world's production of goods (and services) available to the members of a nation. It is calculated this way:

ABSORPTION equals (GDP) plus (Imports minus Exports)

Trade deficit in merchandise. The U.S. is a giant net *absorber* of world goods! The U.S. is the world's second largest *exporting* nation (roughly $1.5T exports of merchandise), behind world leader China and ahead of Germany and Japan, numbers three and four. Trouble is, the U.S. is an even larger -- the largest -- ***importing*** nation in the world (roughly $2.27T imports of merchandise), followed by the European Union and China. The U.S. *takes* more value than it *makes,* enhancing SOL! Imports minus exports gave the U.S. a merchandise **trade deficit of roughly $750** billion.

[4. Source, <https://www.census.gov/foreign-trade/statistics/historical/gands.pdf>]

In 2015, most of the merchandise trade deficit was with China and Japan. Essentially, the trade deficit is the value of imported goods not paid for with from export earnings. **The deficit goods are, in effect, borrowed merchandise paid for with IOU's**, U.S. dollars. Theoretically, absorption could keep expanding as long as foreigners keep accepting intrinsically worthless U.S. dollars in payment. No doubt, however, those nations have their limits as to how many dollars to accept as the U.S. continues to run trade deficits.

Question: Given absorption is positive in America's favor, is the U.S. exploiting the rest of the world ... or vice versa? Read all about it:

The upside of raising absorption. Is raising absorption good or bad for the American economy? Rising absorption benefits the standard of living, at least in the short run, due to greater availability of goods. **In effect, borrowed goods are padding our SOL.**

The downside of raising absorption. Continuing high levels of absorption are putting vast amounts of dollars in foreign hands, sometimes hostile, threatening national security. Has "too much of a good thing"– rising absorption – already morphed into a bad thing for the U.S.? How long will trading partners accept currency IOUs, already exceeding $3 trillion? Japan and (still Red) China have been buying interest bearing securities (including U.S. government bonds). Also, on their shopping list are American real assets (mines, land, and buildings) and stock in American companies (to acquire technologies and strategic assets). Financial institutions are also "in their sights." **The heart of American industry has been targeted for acquisition or decimation.** Political influence in the U.S. is a goal, as well.

Dollargeddon? When foreign dollar holders tire of U.S. acquisitions, they may sell dollars for other currencies. Could large scale dollar dumping precipitate a dollar crash? A dollar crash would spark exports and crush imports. It would be the ultimate insult to the economy – and it's Godchild – national security!

Impact at the street level: SOL. Absorption, like GDP, is a grand total measurement and has little relevance for the typical person. Even **absorption per capita**, though superior to GDP per capita, remains a mathematical calculation with no real impact on any individual. Someday U.S. IOUs to foreigners, now over $3 trillion, will come in and we will be called on to actually pay for all those trade deficits. We will pay with future goods or past goods (properties). Home **command and control** of the American economy – and with it, U.S. sovereignty – will come under a serious threat.

Appendix Two: Balance of Payments Accounting. The annual U.S. Balance of Payments is divided into different accounts. The ***current account*** gets the most attention as it is an indicator of international competitiveness. It displays trade, exports and imports, in goods and services, including investment earnings. This opposition of imports and exports is called the *balance of trade*.

Balance of Trade = (merchandise trade balance) PLUS (services trade balance)
    $500B in 2015   (huge **deficit**, $750B.)   (small **surplus** $250B.)

The **merchandise trade balance** is the main component of the *overall* balance of trade. It is the difference in value between imported and exported *goods or merchandise.* A positive number indicates that more goods were exported than imported. In addition to the merchandise trade balance, there is a balance of trade in services, called the **services trade balance.**

[5. Ibid]

In 2015 the U.S. had a small *surplus* in its balance of trade in *services,* $250 billion. Services include banking, insurance, consulting, travel and transportation. However, that small surplus is overwhelmed by a huge *deficit* in its *merchandise* trade account. In 2015, the balance of merchandise trade deficit was around $750 billion per year. Most of the deficit was and is with Japan and China. Confusion may be introduced when the speaker is not clear about which deficit is in question, the *merchandise* trade deficit or the *overall balance of trade* deficit.

If exports pay for imports, one could accuse the U.S. of living way beyond its means. It is akin to a family continually spending more than its income. The extra spending is financed with debt, IOUs. For now, these IOUs are willingly accepted by our trading partners. The U.S. has been playing the same game with the rest of the world for thirty years or so. Accordingly, foreign holdings of U.S. dollar and dollar asset holdings have grown to around $3 trillion. How long will the rest of the world take our IOUs?

[6. "U.S. International Trade in Goods and Services September 2014 Highlights for Congress" 20 November 2014 < http://tinyurl.com/lnylg7f >]

Appendix Three: Absorption and Aggregate Demand

Given that monetary and fiscal policy are nearly impotent in stimulating the economy, what about trade policy?

➢   When the trade deficit *exceeds* the budget deficit, the net effect is to dampen aggregate demand. Other factors unchanged, the economy slows.

➢   When the budget deficit *exceeds* the trade deficit, the net effect is to boost aggregate demand. Other factors unchanged, the economy is stimulated.

Major point: Consider the trade *deficit* (a net leakage from the circular flow) compared to the budget *deficit* (an injection into the circular flow). Trouble is, the **added spending/demand (injection to circular flow) resulting from the** *budget* **deficit may make up for spending/demand lost (leakage from circular flow) in the overall** *trade* **deficit.** Injections into the flow from the *budget* deficit ($470B in 2015) raise domestic incomes and almost make up for the *trade* deficit leakages ($500B in 2015) from the flow.

Chapter Twenty-One
U.S. Gigantism Fallacies and Fantasies

China's elite wants to build up its own country; the American elite is quite happy to let America gradually decline so long as they can make investments and money overseas. —   Ian Fletcher

REMEMBER the Titanic? The U.S. may well be the nation equivalent of the doomed ship Titanic. Only this time the ship of state has been steered deliberately into an iceberg field by Globalism. Mortally wounded, the ship of state is going down. Face it: **America is in *relative* economic decline, when compared to rivals. Worse yet, at the grassroots individual level, the current and future SOL of middle class Americans is in *absolute* decline.** Titanic's lifeboats are being overloaded! You might be surprised to learn the U.S. is a small country in certain ways. Yes, believe it! Worse yet, according to critical measures, it is shrinking relative to its main rival, (still Red) China. Can it get even worse? Yes, it can. As long as our elites remain enthralled by Globalism, our decline will continue– by *our own hand.*

1. FALLA<IOUS <<ONOMI<US: The United States is still the number one economy in the world and likely to remain in the top slot.

Correct Reasoning: The good news: currently, the U.S. GDP exceeds that of any single rival nation. Now, the bad news: The U.S. annual growth rate is stuck in the "sludge," in the low single digits, a meager 1-2%. Remember, in terms of population, America is a relatively small nation! It has 3-4% of the world's people and 7% of the land. Nevertheless, her achievements have been astounding. But, **Globalism has taken its toll over the last half century.** Once perched at the lofty 50% level, the U.S. percentage of world output is sinking toward 20%. **U.S. GDP, though still growing, will soon be surpassed by protégé and frenemy (still Red) China. This is the *relative* economic decline of** the U.S., inflicted on itself by the adoption of the suicidal Globalism policy.

Who made (still Red) China into an economic powerhouse? Remember, as the economy declines, so does national security. Up for China, down for us. Now, get the digitalis ... Under Globalism, matters are worse on the personal level! Ordinary folks are worried about their current, *wage funded* standard of living. They are concerned about their future standard of living. Shadows gather over social security and private pension funds.

The **Trifecta of debt** (household, Federal budget and trade debt) persists and grows, providing added goods and incomes. Essentially, the economy is **running on fumes. Those practices have expiration dates; they cannot be relied on forever.** The U.S. occupational profile is degenerating. Invasions of cheap goods (the Trojan horse) and cheap labor have hurt more than they have helped. They are the gifts that keep on taking. Thank you, Globalism!

There has been an **American manufacturing Diaspora**. Real wages have stagnated for the last 30 years! Income inequality is widening. American sovereignty has been compromised through trade agreements and giveaways. Recall, a nation's security is best viewed *relative* to other nations.   One gets a better perspective by comparing and contrasting a nation's economic and military prowess to its actual and potential rivals. Continuation of Globalism and its trappings (open borders, free trade, off-shoring, Globalthink) will only reinforce the *relative* decline of the United States, jeopardizing national security. Is there a reason to conclude otherwise? When compared to our protégé, "frenemy" and devoted suckling (still Red) China, the U.S. is in decline. So, stop gloating, my friend!

2. FALLACIOUS ECONOMICUS: There is no cure for the U.S. decline.

Correct Reasoning: Abandon Globalism, restore Economic Nationalism! Well, there is no antidote for the *relative* decline of the U.S. if it continues to follow the policies that put us in decline. That poisonous policy must be abandoned, not expanded. **WHEN IN A HOLE, STOP DIGGING!** The number one disastrous policy has been the total embrace of Globalism by the ruling elites: the President, Congress, transnational corporations, big transnational media, progressive think tanks and elite academia. They must re-balance priorities, reject Globalthink and restore America as the focal point of their policies. No doubt, the U.S. has been scammed by policies prioritizing the global economy. **There must be a return to nation centered policies called Economic Nationalism ... and it must be soon, as Globalists are scheming 24/7 to promote their destructive agenda.**

Let's face it, the song is grossly out of tune. Globalthink has been taken to excess. Under Globalthink, U.S. prosperity takes a backseat to Global prosperity. Duh? **The U.S. decided it wanted to conduct the world orchestra rather than be its star soloist.**

An attitude adjustment is needed in our leaders and their educators.

There must be a resurgence of Economic Nationalism. Restore the policies we followed for 150 years, since independence. Those policies, basically Hamilton's protectionism complemented by Henry Clay's American System, helped create the American economic colossus. Yes, that includes tariffs and other trade/investment barriers, when needed, to guard industries critical to national security. Note that this does not mean isolationism. Nationalism, in this instance, is not isolationism. Trade will be fair, not free.

In sum, Nationthink must replace Globalthink in the minds of the ruling elite. **Lifeboat U.S.A. is becoming overloaded and threatens to go down, along with its standard of living.** Without a policy change, we continue down the road to lower current and future standards of living for the great mass of the U.S. population. A return to Economic Nationalism is *not* isolationism. It is a return to the partner who "brought us to the dance."

Step aside, special interests. Unlike Globalism, economic nationalism elevates the *nation* above the special interests in the economy that would compromise the nation and its way of life for their own selfish ends. The almighty *buck* rules in Globalism. It is the buck, *über alles.* **Under Globalist policies, income inequality has worsened, decimating the American middle class.**

Red Meat Treat

It's no use trying to get corporate globalists to be less greedy. Face it: greed is what they are, greed is what they do. Try an alternative that works __with__ their greediness, not against it. If its profits they want, its profits they will get. Use tax, licensing and regulatory powers to throw them some "red meat." Namely, 1) penalize them for going off shore and staying there and/or 2) reward them for coming home and staying here. Give the greedy buggers a "red meat treat" and have them create prosperity right here in the good old U.S.A.

---

3. FALLACIOUS ECONOMICUS: Forget the rise of China! The U.S. is a giant nation with tremendous resources, it will ultimately dominate.

Correct Reasoning: Americans, beware hubris! Right now, the U.S. is a giant in production capability, but small by other important demographic measures. Small in an absolute sense and in a relative sense, as well. **The U.S. has, at most, 4% of the world's population and an economy growing (in absolute sense) at 1-2% per year.** But, it is aging and shrinking *relative* to the world's peoples. The U.S. has 7% of the world's land.

By these measures – population and land mass - the U.S. is a tiny country! But, there is a giant in the wings, ready to sweep us away: our protégé, our step child. It is a Red giant, but it is not a star, a country with 20% of the world's people. Could the fable of the elephant and the squirrels be a warning of bad things to come?

Fable of the Elephant and the Squirrels

"Oh, please," the little baby elephant begged of the squirrels, "...just a few nuts. Surely you can spare them! Look how rich you are! And I am so hungry, with this big body to feed. It s just not fair."

The squirrels all gathered round for a discussion of the elephant's appeal. Each voiced an opinion. Some, like Sammy Squirrel, were sympathetic to the elephant:

"Yes, the poor elephant...he is starving!" Sam declared, "...and we have so much! I agree with the elephant: it's just not fair. Through our industriousness and ingenuity we have accumulated so much, surely we can spare some nuts for the elephant."

Sally Squirrel, even more eager to be a do-gooder, piped in, "Better yet, why not show the elephant how he can gather nuts for himself...it's only fair! Why should we be the only animals in the forest with the knowledge of how to gather nuts? Once the elephant learns how to gather nuts for himself he won't bother us anymore for charity... and he can never eat so many nuts there would be none left for us!"

Sally's argument appealed to many of the squirrels assembled, who eyed each other and nodded assent. But then, over the chirping, a third squirrel voice arose:

"No, no" squeaked Sol Squirrel at the top of his little lungs, as he nibbled on a tasty little acorn, "...we struggled and sacrificed for many years to learn how to gather and store nuts for ourselves, our children and grandchildren. All the elephants did during that time was to stomp around the forest and ignore their future needs. We squirrels may not be rich but we are secure. Moreover, we are little creatures. If we instruct the elephant he'll grow big and fat... and then trample us!"

"Nonsense, nonsense," the cries rose. "He could never grow so big as to be a threat to us! When he knows what we know, we will all be equal in gathering nuts! Furthermore, I am sure when he grows up he will remember how we saved him from starvation. Trample us? No, he will be forever grateful..."

And so the squirrels debated back and forth as to the wisdom of aiding the elephant. Meanwhile, the elephant grew impatient. He secretly promised the squirrel King that if given nuts from the squirrels' common warehouse, he would secretly return some nuts to the squirrel King's private stores. In this way, the squirrel King would grow rich and fat.

Tiring of debate, and reveling in his new abundance, the squirrel king made speeches, tears in his little eyes, saying how the squirrels should pity the elephant and how all the creatures of the forest would admire the squirrels if they helped the elephant. Then, thinking of his own private stores, he made up his mind. With great fanfare, he directed his subjects to show the elephant how to gather nuts in the manner followed by the squirrels.

The elephant cried, "Oh, thank you, thank you dear squirrels. I don't know of any other animal who would have been so kind as you! I will be forever grateful to the squirrel kingdom! When I grow up I will guard and protect you!"

Soon the elephant mastered the technique of gathering nuts shown to him by the squirrels. And so the years passed and the elephant grew big and ponderous, fat from consuming the nuts he gathered in the manner shown to him by the squirrels. His store of nuts grew to immense proportions and was the envy of all the animals in the kingdom. His friend the squirrel King also grew fat on the nuts "kicked back" by the elephant.

More years passed. The elephant prospered and grew so ponderous he could knock down trees. Increasingly, however, it became more difficult to find any squirrels in the forest.

After a time, no squirrels- not even the King- could be found anywhere in the place now known as the Land of the Elephant.

The End

The Cast

The role of the elephant was played by the (still Red) China, the squirrels by the U.S.A.

Chapter Twenty-Two
National Security Fallacies

Economies win wars. War is not a romantic struggle between soldiers. It is not the strategy or tactics of generals. It is a life-and-death struggle between nations, between societies. The stronger economy wins.   Dana Blankenhorn

NATIONAL security is often confused with national defense. National defense is more concerned with defending the geographical borders of the country, the territory of the nation. National security surpasses territorial security in coverage. Let's being at the beginning: what is a nation?

1. FALLACIOUS ECONOMICUS: *Nation, country* and *State* are the same.

Correct Reasoning: The NATION is the people, the COUNTRY is the territory and the nation-STATE is the governing apparatus. But, a nation conceived here is more than just a collection of isolated, anonymous strangers, living in a work house called the United States. Ideally, the members of the nation are united, bonded by a **collective awareness** of their common values, goals and aspirations ... and, perhaps, their common enemies. Aware of their  commonality and difference from other groups, they have come together to preserve and defend their **way of life**, the so-called **common cultural core**. Enriching and reinforcing the bond may be common blood relations, religion, history, language, food, sports and a historically occupied "homeland." As these common elements meld, a national identity, a certain self aware mind set, is forged. **But, beware: if commonality diminishes and diversity surges, the nation will show signs of impending fragmentation, as is the U.S.**

Nationalism. At its core, nationalism is a political ideology advocating the preservation and perpetuation of a singular nation or the world national system. Nationalists cherish self rule – sovereignty – according to *their* way of life. **Sovereignty – freedom from outside rule – is a high, if not the highest priority for nationalists.**

The strength of the one's connection to the common core progresses from national identity, to national pride to national patriotism, the last being the strongest association of the individual with the nation. Nations can migrate and occupy different lands. World history is rich with epic migrations of whole nations, sometimes founding new homelands.

Country vs. nation. The terms *country* and *nation* are often used interchangeably. However, an important distinction should be kept in mind. Remember, the *nation* is the people, the country is the land or territory. The term *country* relates to the homeland's borders on a map. The term *country* is rooted to a specific geographic area on the Earth's surface. It may refer to the historic homeland of the nation. Note that, unlike countries, nations are mobile!

Stateless nations: nations without countries. History teaches us *nation* and *country* are separable. The nation does not always occupy its homeland territory or any country! Kurds, Chechens and Uyghur, minorities in larger states, come to mind. In fact, most nations do not have a homeland or nation-State of their own! One author cited the 5000 nations of the world squeezed into 200 nation-States. Many are micro nations.[1] Just as there are homeless nations, there are countries encompassing multiple nations. Iraq and Afghanistan are artificial nations composed of multiple squabbling tribes and warring Islamic religious factions. The Soviet Union, Yugoslavia and Czechoslovakia encompassed multiple nations until nationalism sparked their break-up.

[1. George W. White. *Nation, State, and Territory: Origins, Evolutions, and Relationships, Volume 1.* P. 4. Lanthan, Maryland: Rowman and Littlefield, 2004]

Country is defined thusly:

"A tract of land; a region; the territory of an independent nation."

[2. "Country," 20 June 2014 *brainyquote* < http://tinyurl.com/o44g8ju>]

The country is a geographic region, the territory of the nation. It is the homeland of the nation. Maps indicate the geographic boundaries of countries, but not necessarily the boundaries of nations. A map of *nations* would be highly fragmented and not have coincident boundaries with a map of *countries.* Oceans, rivers, mountain ranges and other geographic features often formed the boundaries of countries. Typically, the nation (the unified, much in common, bound together group of people) usually seeks a territory as a homeland, a country (geographic area to occupy) where it can live as it chooses. As stated above, today there are nations without countries and countries made up of multiple nations. Nations aspire to have their own independent homeland.

Birth of the Nation-State. Nation-States may be formed voluntarily or involuntarily. Many *nations* were created spontaneously and voluntarily. Like-minded folks or extended families came together for survival of the people, protection from rival nations, and religious worship. They ceded powers to the

State to maintain order, oversee and protect them. The State is a superstructure, a protective shield, to separate and protect it from rival nations. The military power and police monopoly (ceded to the nation-State from the nation) should shield the nation and protect it from harm, much as a banana skin protects the banana. Ideally, the State protects the sovereignty of the nation, i.e., keeps it free from foreign rule.

Ideally, the nation-State functioned to validate, preserve, protect and reinforce the existence and character of the nation.

National security is the prime function of the nation-State. It deals not simply with securing territory. Ultimately, most people expect the nation-State to guard, nurture and reinforce the commonality that makes the people a nation.

> To the old right, America as a nation and a people already existed by 1789. The Constitution was the birth certificate the nation wrote for itself, the charter by which it chose to govern itself. The real America had been born in men's hearts by the time of Lexington and Concord in 1775.
>
> [3. Patrick J. Buchanan, "Behind the crack-up of the right," *Human Events* 16 June 2012 < http://tinyurl.com/pk6y9yb>]

Recap. Cultural security means locking in the *way of life.* Colonists and early Americans saw themselves as significantly different from other groups of people, other nations. A national shared common identity or consciousness arose, despite considerable diversity. A wide spread common religion and language strengthened the common bond. There was a conscious awareness that this group differed from others. There was an "us" versus "them" attitude. National identity grew into pride and patriotism.

A dual core? The core has always been marked by diversity. But, a **dual core** (oxymoronic, no?) is unsustainable for **one** nation. Indeed, the viability of the dual core was challenged in the 1860s, as the nation suffered a breakup between a disparate North and South. It required a costly Civil War to apply stitches that held the Union together by force. Those stitches still have not dissolved completely. Today, a new cultural core may be emerging as older traditions are wiped away. Deviancy has been defined down. Inclusion and diversity worship wrapped in political correctness dominates public life. **Today, more than ever, the U.S., with diversity rising and common kinship diminishing, requires a common core of values, ideals and aspirations.**

Always remember: The Economy is the Mother Ship of National Security!

and

Oil is the fuel of the Mother Ship.

Are We a Nation of Immigrants?

Well, of course we are, aren't we? Actually, yes and no. The idea that "we are a nation of immigrants" is a fallacy that contains an element of truth. Yes, most Americans are *descendants* of immigrants, some of whom arrived here five hundred years ago, and some before then! After all, the American story is more than five hundred years old. But, to say "we are a nation of immigrants" somehow implies that the entire population was assembled yesterday, "brand spanking new," from all nations of the world. Not so. *We are more than a recent assemblage of foreign born, anonymous strangers.* **We are a nation, a cohesive people bonded by a common core of beliefs, values and aspirations ... or, at least, we were. The core is in transition right now as multiple belief and value systems are commingled without assimilation into the traditional core.**

In the long history of mankind's spreading over the earth, isn't every nation a nation of immigrants and their descendents?

Immigrants to North America developed their own common ideology, rooted in Judeo-Christian and European traditions. They forged a new nation with a common core of shared values, aspirations, goals, ideas, laws and customs. A common language and blood kinship helped cement the bond. Many people died to a) establish the nation, b) keep it united, and c) keep it free. In, mid 19th century a serious fissure surfaced in the core. This lead to Civil War. Union victory in the Civil War kept the nation-State from fragmenting. Later immigrants assimilated and more or less embraced the common core and joined the historical march.

In "we are a nation of immigrants" too much emphasis has been paid to *immigrants* and not enough to the idea of *nation*. This idea is not an intelligent rationale or justification for open borders or unlimited migration. **Arguments for expanding immigration should not be based on the past, but on the future. The past is past; the future awaits.**

Final word, by Marc Levin: "We are a nation of citizens, not immigrants."

2. FALLACIOUS ECONOMICUS: The U.S. has the strongest military in the world and can defeat any nation in a war. We are invincible.

Fallacious Reasoning: The U.S. has more of the best military equipment than any other nation. For example, the U.S. Navy has more aircraft carriers than the rest of the world's nations combined. The Navy and Air Force are leaders in stealth technology and futuristic particle beam weapons.

Correct Reasoning: Goal Overload. It is not only what you have but how and when you use it. Most importantly, are you willing to use it? How is it we have the strongest military but keep losing (or failing to win) so many wars? Iraq, Afghanistan, Viet Nam and even Korea were stalemates at best. Perhaps in fighting those wars we tried to win the war *and* at the same time win the hearts and minds of the enemy peoples and world public opinion. The problem is this: **too many overlapping goals have undermined the military.** This approach may be admirable but has been proven a failure. In trying to win hearts and minds we compromised on the goal of winning militarily, turning soldiers into social workers and then, when they fight, saddling them with ridiculously stringent rules of engagement. (Read Miranda rights to enemy combatants captured on the foreign battlefield? Duh?)

Recommendation: Apply the basic economic idea of division of labor. First win the war, then worry about winning hearts and minds. Yes, in winning the war you may alienate some hearts and minds. So what; expect that. TANSTAAFL, remember? You win them back hearts and minds after the war. Along these lines, Civil War General W.T. Sherman preached the doctrine of *hard war and soft peace*. A "first win the war" strategy – with sensible rules of engagement – is owed to our troops, their families and the rest of the nation. It may not be a perfect strategy, but it has proven to be a successful one.

There was little concern about hearts and minds when we pursued victory in World War II. It was a winning strategy. Seventy-five years after the end of that conflict Germany, Italy and Japan remain pacified, unlikely to once again threaten the world with fascist dictatorship.

3. FALLACIOUS ECONOMICUS: National defense must be kept strong in order to defeat terrorism.

Fallacious Reasoning: Terrorism is the enemy that threatens the United States.

Correct Reasoning: Terrorism is not the enemy; terrorism is a **tactic** employed by the enemy. To say that terrorism is the enemy is like saying tanks or bullets are the enemy. During World War II Japanese zeros and German panzers terrorized our allies. But, were we at war with tanks and planes? In the immediate sense yes, we wanted to destroy them with *our* tanks and planes. **Ultimately, we were at war with the people who employed those weapons.** Misidentification of the enemy can be a fatal error.

Arguably, during World War II we also used terrorism as a weapon! Yes, arguably, we won the war because we out-terrorized Germany and Japan through indiscriminate carpet bombing of their cities. (This was a time when rules of engagement were more permissive and lawyers were not embedded with fighting men). Germany and Japan have gotten out of the conquest business - permanently. Thankfully, in the 1940s our leaders correctly identified those who were out to destroy us. Moreover, they were not afraid to name them, not just condemn their tactics. To mis-identify the enemy is to give an advantage to the enemy. **Can our leaders muster up the courage to name the enemy in today's world of political correctness and political doublespeak?**

4. FALLACIOUS ECONOMICUS: We must be careful in fighting terrorism. We cannot "fight fire with fire." That is, we cannot use terrorist methods to fight terrorism. *That would make us just like them.* We don't want to sink to their level, do we? And, after all, they are the bad guys and we are the good guys, no? Fighting terrorism with terrorist tactics would make us terrorists. That is not what the U.S. is all about.

Correct Reasoning: Remember, terrorism is only a tactic. As stated earlier, we *terrorized* the German and Japanese civilian populations with massive bombings during World War II. Were we terrorists or patriots? Those bombings helped to end the war and bring peace to millions of people. Indeed, an argument can be made that the U.S. should employ soft terrorist methods against outside terrorist groups for two reasons:

1) Americans want more "bang" for their military "buck." The American public will be gratified to see guilty terrorists quickly punished (hung and shot) instead of being "lawyered-up" and catered to at American taxpayer expense. Hanging would be justice in the eyes of many Americans who would then feel more secure. In any event, hanging and the firing squad seem mild compared to beheading, crucifixion, slavery, burning alive, drowning and rape they employ. But, wouldn't that make us just like them, brutal and evil?

2) **A rationale for U.S. terrorist tactics?** Terrorist groups like al Qaeda, Boko Haram and ISIS terrorize in order to oppress people, especially infidels and women. They terrorize to impose *their* ideology and way of life. In their totalitarian world, freedom of choice (religion, speech, and form of government) is suppressed. Opposition to their religion and ideology will not be tolerated. Critics accuse Islam of being a totalitarian ideology, aiming to control every aspect of life of everyone, believer and non-believer.

Alternatively, **we would fight in order to liberate people**, give them freedom of choice, and liberate women. Our goal is to liberate, their goal is to oppress.

The Enemy Sandwich

A deceased prominent liberal Democrat Senator was a vehement opponent of the Vietnam War. However, he piloted a B-24 bomber over Europe during World War II. He was asked if he had regrets about his bombs killing "innocent" civilians. He said that if someone was making a sandwich for an anti-aircraft gunner who might shoot him down, then that sandwich maker was, in effect, part of the military. So, it was a legitimate target. **Every resource and good has a direct or indirect military application.**

National Defense vs. National Security

5. FALLACIOUS ECONOMICUS: There is no significant difference between National Defense and National Security. Once an adequate national defense is mounted, the nation is secure.

Correct Reasoning: As developed here, national defense and national security are related but significantly different terms. History teaches us that an adequately performing national defense does *not* guarantee national security.

National defense is equivalent to a ship repelling borders. National security starts with national defense but extends to how life is lived on that now secure vessel. It includes the management of the ship; the passengers' way of life. (Beware: a nation could be defended but its people brutalized by the same military! Remember the Stalin's Soviet Union or Hitler's Germany?)

The country must be defended and the nation must be secured. The term national *defense* should be understood to apply to securing the *country*, the nation's territory. It is analogous to repelling boarders on a ship: no invaders gain access to the ship. National *security* applies to making secure the people *and their way of life.* **Massive immigration of those *rejecting* our way of life violates national defense and threatens national security.** There would be no threat to national security if the mass of immigrants embraced our way of life. Thus, *national security* is a more inclusive term, encompassing but not limited to defending a geographic area. **National security implies securing the territory, the nation and its common bonds.**

Case: the Soviet Empire. National defense can serve the nation's rulers, even as a people are oppressed. Even despotic nations have national defense. National security serves the nation's people.

The Soviet empire dominated and defended many captive nations during the Cold War of the 20th century. It provided national defense only to oppress the desire of those peoples for personal and political freedom, thereby failing to achieve national *security.*

National *security* is people centered, not ruler centered. Standing alone, national defense is as first step. Consider: of what value is a successful national defense if the rulers treat citizens as subjects and free men as prisoners? If the national defense apparatus repels invaders but does not protect and support the way of life, then there is no national security. **In this view, national defense, if achieved, is no guarantee of national security. The purpose of national defense must be to serve national security, not limit or destroy it.**

> **Military power rests on industrial and financial power.** Countries exist in a world dominated by war and peacetime military competition. It may therefore be suicidal for a country to pay attention only to its *absolute* wealth rather than its *relative* standing among other powers.
>
> [4. Bold mine. Michael Lind, "Friedrich List and Economic Nationalism: A Personal Credo, Part III" 6 September 2012 <http://tinyurl.com/q5doxmf>]

6. FALLACIOUS ECONOMICUS: The strength of the economy has little to do with national defense. National defense is blood, guts and glory.

Correct Reasoning: Blood, guts and glory are no good to an unarmed, naked and hungry soldier. A mighty economy is needed to equip and support a mighty military and, at the same time, support the civilian sector, as well.

In this context, the following points may be somewhat idealistic but are critical, nevertheless.

For national security: Americanism, not Globalism!

Reduce reliance on the Trifecta of debt (trade deficit, budget deficit and household borrowing) to create illusion of enduring prosperity. Re-structure economy to produce genuine prosperity.

1. **Bring home and create good jobs for Americans. Put America first.** Ditch Globalthink and return to Nationthink. Stop thinking of the U.S. as a workhouse manned by strangers. Start thinking of it again as a nation of *people tied to a common core*, a core not shared by outsiders.

2. Stop selling entry visas through the **EB-5 visa program** for individuals who invest in or start businesses. Easy entry for a wealthy terrorist, no? Have we sunk that low, are we that desperate that the path to U.S. citizenship is for sale? Also, develop a tracking system for those entering on **nonimmigrant visas,** nearly 11 million people per year!

3. Seek **fair and managed trade, not reflexive "free trade."** Manage trade to the U.S. advantage. Forget the dopey "level playing field." Roll back trade deals such as NAFTA, the WTO and the Trans Pacific Partnership that impose net losses of the U.S. Avoid new ones with similar outcomes. They ultimately gut the U.S. economy, compromise sovereignty and reduce the American SOL.

4. Adopt policies that build a strong economy, based on manufacturing, human capital and technological advancement. Gradually increase domestic

content of imported materiel. If possible, produce essential military materiel in the U.S., even if imports are cheaper!

5. Restrict imports that destroy strategic, defense related industries.

6. Severely restrict exports of advanced civilian/military **technologies** such as supercomputers. Restrictions should apply to friends as well as potential adversaries. Remember, today's civilian goods and personnel are tomorrow's military goods and soldiers. Boeing plans to sell 80 passenger jets to Iran ... Duh? Note the obvious military application! Military planes are also a planned sale from Boeing to the Saudi Arabia. (Don't forget the kill switch!)

7. Prohibit foreign ownership and control of **strategic public and private assets** in the United States. These assets include: port facilities, airports, bridges, toll roads, railroads, power companies, mass communications facilities, land resources (oil, gas and uranium) and banks.

[5. Portia Crowe, "China is buying up American companies fast, and it's freaking people out" *Business Insider* 21 Feb. 2016 < http://tinyurl.com/h4mlqrx>]

8. Avoid *excess* immigration which depresses the home standard of living, via lowered wages and absorbed public services. Insist on immigrant assimilation.

9. Along with native population growth, encourage the widening and deepening of the nation's stock of **human capital.** Become the relative leader in building human capital, especially cyber technology, basic science, and applications.

10. **Bring home and create good jobs for Americans.** In the long run, limit the employment of foreigners in high tech areas and in-shored firms. This keep job openings Americans can fill. Do not let the **American human capital industry** whither.

11. Do not export a weapon system we cannot defeat. Or, equip the weapon with a destruct button or a kill switch!

A Vibrant Economy Underpins a Potent Military

The *ultimate* power of the United States, then, lies not in its military – potent as that military is, to be sure – but in its wealth, the wide distribution of that wealth among its population, its capacity to create still more wealth, and its seemingly bottomless imagination in developing new ways to use that wealth productively.

[5. John Steele Gordon. *An Empire of Wealth: The Epic History of American Economic Power.* New York: Harper Perennial, 2005, pp. xiv-xv.]

The ideal. There is an ideal minimum target economic marker for national defense and security. It is evidenced by a predominantly self-sufficient and perpetual capability to produce a minimum threshold amount of guns AND butter needed to ensure national survival and sovereignty. **Rarely does a modern nation, the U.S. included, meet this high self-sufficiency standard.**

Never forget: The economy is the mother ship of national security.

7. FALLACIOUS ECONOMICUS: "Guns will make us powerful; butter will only make us fat." Hermann Goering, Nazi leader.

Fallacious Reasoning: If you are going to engage in military operation to defend the country, then you need military equipment, right? Butter cannot help.

Correct Reasoning: Of course, military equipment and soldiers are needed to engage in military operations. But, Butter helps feed/clothe the troops and boosts morale on the home front. Also, there is another use for Butter, as a backup or reserve for Guns! Understand that all so-called "civilian" goods and personnel, i.e., the Butter, have a direct or indirect military application. This fact cannot be overemphasized. Don't be fooled: **There is no such thing as a purely civilian or humanitarian good.** Here are some examples:

> ➤ Land can be farmed or used as a military base.
> ➤ The farmer can be transformed into a soldier.
> ➤ The auto plant can be converted to make tanks.
> ➤ Weather forecasting can target the battlefield.
> ➤ Homemakers can work shifts in the defense plant or make sandwiches for the troops.
> ➤ Food, medicine and clothing can be commandeered for the military.
> ➤ A commercial harbor can accept naval vessels.
> ➤ A civilian airfield can accommodate military aircraft.
> ➤ A senior citizen can take the civilian job of a young, fighting age male.

Speed of mobilization is the problem in converting civilian goods to a military mission. It is best to have a regularly available stock of up to date military equipment. In other words: a standing military.

8. FALLACIOUS ECONOMICUS: The state of the economy is totally divorced from the state of the military and national security.

Correct Reasoning: On the contrary, military capability and national security are heavily dependent on the state of the economy. **A mighty economy makes for a mighty military and supportive home front.** Consider:

1. Soldiers cannot fight barehanded, naked and hungry. They need training and weaponry, if nothing but Molotov cocktails.

2. Supportive folks on the home front cannot be left naked and hungry, lest their morale collapse, dissolving their support for the military.

The economy is the source of food, clothing, medicines and housing for folks on the home front and *weaponry* for soldiers.   Thus, the economy is the source of GUNS (military) and the source of BUTTER (civilian goods).

Again: **a   mighty   economy   makes   possible   a   mighty   military, a supported and supportive home front. This is true for all nations!**

Fatal Tug of War? The problem with this model is that the military and civilian sectors are locked at swords points in a perpetual tug-of-war over who feeds more at the public trough. This struggle heats up in peacetime or the longer a war persists. The struggle accelerates as the U.S. population ages and becomes more indigent, dependent on goodies from Uncle Sam. Enemies of the U.S. love this struggle! One historian speculated on how this struggle might evolve in a democracy:

The Evolution of Democracy?

A democracy is always temporary in nature; it simply cannot exist as permanent form of government. **A democracy will continue to exist up until the time that voters discover that they can vote themselves generous gifts from the public treasury.** From that moment on, the majority always votes for the candidates who promise the most benefits from the public treasury, with the result that every democracy will finally collapse due to loose fiscal policy, which is always followed by a dictatorship.   Quotation from Alexander Tyler, Historian

Question: Could Tyler's dire prediction be America today?

---

9. FALLA〈IOU§ €〈ONOMI〈U§: Building up the civilian sector of a trading partner's economy poses no military threat.

Correct Reasoning: It follows from evaluating the previous fallacy that enhancing a trading partner's so-called "civilian" economy directly or *indirectly* enhances its war making potential.   A mighty economy can support mighty military and civilian sectors at the same time.

Consider the U.S. build up of its protégé and frenemy, (still Red) China. Ever question where so-called humanitarian aid winds up? Remember: **all goods produced, Butter as well as Guns, potentially have a military application.**

Sequestration. But wait! **Stop the presses! Fly in the ointment:** Forget expansion of spending. Both GUNS and BUTTER Federal spending cuts are mandated under the current budget **program** designed to run until 2021!

Crash of Civilizations?

➤ **Fact:** Islam is a world religion practiced by more than one billion people.

➤ **Fact:** The overwhelming majority worships and lives peacefully.

➤ **Fact:** Muslims have made significant positive contributions to American life.

➤ **Fact:** Today, only a tiny fraction of adherents favor radical Islam and practice violent Jihad.

These are facts. Now, consider some fallacies.

---

10. FALLACIOUS ECONOMICUS: Sharia Law will never come to the U.S.

It is in fundamental conflict with market capitalism, profit, wealth accumulation and private property. Moreover, Sharia values are in sharp conflict with U.S. values, moral precepts and freedoms.

Correct Reasoning: Distinguish what could happen form what should happen. Never say never! There is much compatibility between Western capitalism and the Islamic world. There are big bucks to be made engaging the Islamic world, a world of over a billion people. They can function as investors, workers, and customers for Western capitalists. Their lands have generous endowments of natural resources, especially oil. In any event, ordinary Americans will have little say in whether or not Sharia comes to America. **Globalist ideology,** welcoming to all cultures and traditions, especially profitable ones, could **dictate** that Sharia Law be accommodated in America. This, despite numerous fundamental conflicts over basic religious, political and personal freedoms, i.e., the way of life. **Indeed, Sharia has a Globalist, one world vision of its own: the Islamic Caliphate.**

There will be some resistance. Ultimately, profit will overrule prudence and Americans will have no choice other than to embrace Sharia ... no?

Sharia Law allows for private property, profit and wealth accumulation. No "worship the poor" mentality prevails. Some of the greatest exponents of wealth accumulation can be found under its tent. In the last forty years OPEC, the greatest criminal enterprise in world history, has extorted trillions of dollars from oil customers around the world. OPEC is dominated by Saudi Arabia, Iran, Iraq and other Moslem nations. Yes, making a buck is very much within the province of Sharia Law. "After all, Islam is the only religion founded by a trader — one who also, by the way, married a wealthy merchant. The Koran has only good words for successful businessmen."

[6. Gary Sorman, "Is Islam Compatible with Capitalism?" Summer 2011 *City Journal* <http://www.city-journal.org/html/islam-compatible-capitalism-13392.html>]

11. FALLA<IOUS €<ONOMI<US: Do not worry, moderate Muslims will rise up, oppose and restrain radical, Jihadist Muslims.

Correct Reasoning: Yes, moderate Muslims vastly outnumber radical Muslims. Yes, if they stood up they likely could be a restraining influence on the radicals. But, this is a pipedream. They are moderate and will not "change their stripes" and restrain radicals. But, who knows? Islam - without effective restraint from moderates - has been on the warpath with infidels and apostates for fifteen hundred years or so. Moreover, Islam has had a long running civil war in its ranks, Sunni versus Shia. Critics of moderate Moslems have asked the following questions: Would they welcome Sharia law if handed to them by the radicals? Are moderate Muslims passive-aggressive enablers of radical Muslims? Do moderates serve as camouflage for the radical Jihadists?

12. FALLA<IOUS €<ONOMI<US: In a series of unprovoked, malicious attacks starting in 1095 A.D., Christian Crusaders rampaged, pillaged and murdered their way through Muslim lands. To this day Western European Christians bear the burden of guilt for their atrocities. Indeed, if any evil deeds are done to the West by Muslim extremists, those deeds are understandable, even excusable, given the carnage from the Christian Crusades. Western Christian civilization is only getting what it deserves.

Correct Reasoning: Forgotten history. The Holy Crusades must be put into proper historical context. Muslim "crusades" or Jihads into Europe preceded the Holy Crusades from Europe by hundreds of years! Modern Muslim acts of extremism may be understandable but *not* excusable. Neither Buddha nor Jesus embraced militarism, conquest, the subjugation of women and the killing of nonbelievers ... under any circumstances. **Prior to the emergence of Islam** Europe was fragmented politically, but it was Christian land. War started from the time of Muhammad, the early 600s A.D. Thus began a long period of **world war** between the Muslim civilization and all non-Muslim peoples: Christian, Hindu, Buddhist ... and all others! Arguably, that war ended with the defeat of the Ottoman Turkish Empire in 1919, one hundred years ago.

Background: At the birth of Islam, circa 600 A.D., Christendom stretched from West to Eastern Europe. It included much of the Middle East, including Jerusalem. At the onset of the Holy Crusades, Europe had been under constant threat and attack from Muslim marauders and pirates for hundreds of years! Spain had been invaded and colonized. France was nearly conquered. Muslims had conquered the Christian Holy Land. Simultaneously, Muslim armies were murderously conquering most of India, leading to the death of tens of millions! Historian Will Durant asserted, "The Muslim conquest of India is probably the bloodiest story in history."

In the wider view, the Christian Crusades were a response, **a counter-attack to the Muslim Conquests of the prior four hundred years.** Muslims had rampaged, pillaged and murdered their way through the Christian world for four hundred years, starting in the 7th century A.D. The Islamic conquerors crashed the Christian world, bent on a bloody Jihad to spread Islam. Muslim wars of imperialistic conquest have lasted more than 1,500 years against hundreds of nations – East and West – and over millions of square miles. The Jihad stretched from the Middle East to India, Southern France to the Philippines, from Austria to Nigeria, and from central Asia to New Guinea. The Armenian genocide added another million or so dead.

The voyages of Columbus and others were sparked by the need to go around the Moslem world and find new, less restricted and costly trade routes to China! Consider: **at the onset of the Christian Crusades, Muslims had conquered two-thirds of the Christian world.** A Christian response was inevitable. This history cannot be denied or whitewashed.

[7. Dr. Richard Abels, "Timeline for the Crusades and Christian Holy War to c.1350," 10 October 2014 United States Naval Academy<http://tinyurl.com/d8d67gu >]

The Islamic marauding continued for hundreds of years prior to the Christian Crusades. Italy was a victim of Muslim armies and pirates during this period. Read all about it:

> In the 846 a Saracen [Muslim] fleet of 73 ships landed at Ostia [Italian seaport on the Mediterranean], and raided inland, sacking Rome. In doing so, they burnt the churches of St. Peter and St. Paul. The new pope Leo IV (r. 847-855)...formed a naval alliance with the cities of Amalfi, Naples, and Gaeta, which drove off a Saracen fleet in 849.
>
> [8. "Saracen Towers Found Along Both Coasts" 10 October 2014 *Sorrento Coast* <http://tinyurl.com/pffos9l >]

For hundreds of years the Islamic **Ottoman Empire** occupied parts of Eastern Europe and threatened the rest! Hopefully, that threat finally ended in 1919 with the defeat of the Ottoman Empire in World War I.

In sum: the Christian Crusades were launched as a response, a counter-attack, to the earlier ravages of Muslim Jihad. Today's Christians need not exhibit regret and guilt over the Holy Crusades, any more than the allies deserve guilt over crushing murderous fascism in World War II.

Related **FALLACIOUS ECONOMICUS:** Look, get real. There are over a billion Muslims in the world, including many millions of fighting age males, more than the west could ever muster. Should they choose, they could muster armies capable of burying the Western world. So, surrender now, convert and maybe they will be merciful.

Correct Reasoning: There are several misconceptions here.

1. **The economy:** Soldiers cannot enter a battle unarmed, naked and hungry. There must be an underlying, supportive economy to arm, clothe and feed them. The U.S. may have fewer fighting age males but still has the biggest economy in the world, able to support its troops as no other nation can. Most of the Islamic world is pre-industrialized agricultural. Without an abandonment of their Jihadist ideology, Muslim economies pose a greater military threat as they grow and industrialize.

2. **Technology.** The U.S. is the leader in weapons technology, a tremendous force multiplier. War today depends not on numbers in the field but strategies and technologies to undercut the enemy's command and control system, economic support system and logistics. *The U.S. must continue to dominate in cyberspace technology* for offensive and defensive purposes.

3. **Tactics.** Muslim fighters and guerilla/terrorist tactics have had a measure of success in their own homelands. But, these tactics are problematic when projected beyond their borders. Projecting power would require missile and nuclear technology, a blue water navy and an air force. Remember, low tech pigs blood was weaponized by General Pershing and used effectively against Moslem guerillas one hundred years ago in the Philippines.

[10. "MUSLIM CRUSADES started four centuries before the Western Crusades" *FactReal* 12 February 2010 < http://tinyurl.com/q4wmqvs>]

11. Mark Durie, "Challenging Islam's License to Kill" 25 March 2015 *Wildolive.com* <http://www.meforum.org/5133/challenging-islam-license-to-kill> "What Does Islam Teach About Violence?" 14 Mar. 2016 *What Makes Islam So Different?* <http://www.thereligionofpeace.com/pages/quran/violence.aspx>]

4. **Divide and conquer.** Not all Muslim nations would choose war with the West. Furthermore, there is a built in fracture in the Muslim world between Sunni and Shia. That divide is ripe for exploitation in the event of a conflict.

Furthermore, a western army would not engage all Muslim armies simultaneously. No doubt, some Muslim countries would be our allies.

Question: Does the Qur'an, in effect, give Muslims a license to lie to and kill infidels? Remember Thermopylae!

[What follows is an academic discussion of the killing of civilians in wartime. In no way is this to be construed as the author condoning or endorsing the killing of civilians under any circumstances. Ed.]

13. FALLACIOUS ECONOMICUS: Human shields.

Yes, all civilians, civilian goods and resources have a direct or indirect military application. Women, children, the infirm and the aged are excluded. No obvious military role is possible for them.

Correct Reasoning: Unfortunately, women, children, the infirm, the aged, et. al., have a military application; one conjured up from the darkest of hearts. Even today, and against the rules of war, these folks are used as hostages and human shields. Weapons are stored in hospitals, houses of worship and schools. Thus, these seemingly benign folks and institutions have been weaponized and pressed into military duty.

14. FALLACIOUS ECONOMICUS:

No doubt, civilians have been killed in the recent U.S. wars in Iraq and Afghanistan. The U.S. knew (innocent) civilians would be killed during its invasions. They knew this and went on with the attacks anyway. These are crimes under international law.

Correct Reasoning: War Crimes? There are legal, moral, and economic issues with respect to civilian deaths in wartime. In law, the principle of proportionality must be applied to these cases to determine if American actions were, in fact, war crimes. Believe it or not, under certain conditions international law allows the killing of civilians in wartime. Read all about it:

> Under international humanitarian law and the Rome Statute, the death of civilians during an armed conflict, no matter how grave and regrettable, *does not in itself constitute a war crime*. International humanitarian law and the Rome Statute permit belligerents to carry out proportionate attacks against military objectives, *even when it is known that some civilian deaths or injuries will occur*. A crime occurs if there is an intentional attack directed against civilians (principle of distinction) (Article 8(2)(b)(i)) or an attack is launched on a military objective in the knowledge that the incidental civilian injuries would be clearly excessive in relation to the anticipated military advantage (principle of proportionality) (Article 8(2)(b)(iv)).

[12. Italics mine. Luis Moreno-Ocampo, Chief Prosecutor at the International Criminal Court commenting in 2006 and quoted in "Proportionality (law)" 1 October 2014 *Wikipedia* < http://en.wikipedia.org/wiki/Proportionality_(law)>]

[13. "Rome Statute of the International Criminal Court" 20 Oct. 2012 < http://tinyurl.com/l5w7y4m >]

Technically, legally, civilian deaths under the conditions outlined above do not constitute war crimes. [See box, the Enemy Sandwich on p. 205]

On the economic aspects of civilian deaths, one must recognize that in many instances there is a thin veil between enemy combatants and associated civilians. One day a farmer, the next day a soldier. One day a homemaker, the next day a bomb maker. One day a school kid, the next day a bomb carrier.

Remember: every resource and good possessed by the enemy has a direct or indirect military application. International law does not recognize this idea nor does it sanction the killing of civilians outside accepted norms discussed above.

On moral grounds, killing civilians in a just war remains a debatable issue. During World War II the Allies fired bombed Dresden, Germany, fire bombed Tokyo, nuked Hiroshima and Nagasaki at a considerable loss of noncombatant, civilian lives. However, the bombings spared a massive invasion of Japan, saving millions of lives on both sides.

World War Two era battle tank

"Heavenly shades of night are falling, it's twilight time ..."
- Buck Ram

Is it twilight time ... for America?

Has Globalism pulled the shadow of night over the United States?

Is the United States the test laboratory for world governance of diverse peoples, religions, belief systems, cultures and languages?

Chapter Twenty-Three
Oil and National Security Fallacies

The economy, powered by oil, is the mother ship of national security.

—Theo Dosius

Black gold, Texas tea, crude, shale oil, coal oil, lube, grease, petrol – you name it. Nations cry they need it to survive and develop. Others complain they cannot prosper without it.

Been There, Done That

1. FALLA<IOUS <<ONOMI<US: We should invade one of those OPEC countries, take over its oil fields, turn on the oil spigot and break up OPEC. The world would thank us for getting those bloodsuckers off their backs.

Correct Reasoning: Uh, excuse me, sir, but where have you been since 2003, when we invaded Iraq? After conquering them we had complete control of the country, including the oil. We had them by the "barrels," and could have turned on the oil spigot. We did not. Why not? Were we worried about push back from our business partner and chief exploiter, Saudi Arabia?

So, let's get this straight: we "liberated" Iraq, and left OPEC intact. Then the cartel reverted to restricting production and extorting its buyers by hiking prices above the free market level. So, in effect, we "freed" Iraq so it could "thank" the U.S. by overcharging it – and the world – for its oil! Duh? Big Oil (Exxon-Mobil, BP, et.al) and good pals the Saudis approved, no doubt, as profits grew. After all, a decline in the OPEC base price would no doubt have a ripple effect on oil prices worldwide, chipping into the profits of Big Oil, OPEC collaborators.

Question: Would a breakup of OPEC and drop in Middle Eastern oil prices be good or bad for American producers? Distinguish old line producers (Big Oil) from recent upstart "frackers and shalers."

A case can be made for a new Iraq invasion to deny oil to the ISIS fighters. Denial of the proceeds from the sale of that oil would diminish their ability to fight. Remember, an army cannot fight when hungry, naked and empty handed.

The Oil Curse: Do Smooth Seas Make Poor Sailors? Despite advances in alternative fuels and energy generation, oil remains the pre-eminent energy source and foundation of economic and military security. However, a nation endowed with oil (or other mineral deposits) may not be blessed. It may be cursed! Read all about it.

2. FALLACIOUS ECONOMICUS: Lucky is the nation that finds oil, natural gas or diamonds on its land. It puts the nation on the high road to economic development.

Fallacious Reasoning: It is only logical. The more resources you have to use and sell, the greater the productive (and income) potential of the nation. What good fortune to find such wealth right under your feet!

Correct Reasoning: Experience does not bear out this assertion. Yes, some nations use their non-renewable, natural resource deposits to vault onto the high road to economic development. However, more than a few resource rich nations suffer the "resource curse" and find themselves worse off due to mismanagement, misfortune and odd circumstance. Read about it in this scenario discussing Nigeria's "oil curse."

> The discovery of oil sets off a scramble among elites to secure shares of the profits, rather than investing to build roads, power plants and factories. Foreigners pump in money to buy the oil, which drives up the value of the currency, in turn making it difficult for local factories—what few exist—to export their goods. The oil windfall tends to destroy every local industry other than oil. That is the story of Nigeria.
>
> [1. Ruchir Sharma, "Nigeria Is a Case Study in the Curse of Oil," 2 April 2015 *WSJ.Com* <http://tinyurl.com/o6877mv>]

The "oil curse" is also known as the Dutch Disease and the Paradox of Plenty. This degeneration has occurred in a number of countries around the world. This includes   Venezuela (oil), Angola (diamonds, oil), the Democratic Republic of the Congo (diamonds), and various other nations.

So, the gift of a rich resource endowment is not necessarily a blessing. Indeed, it could wind up being a curse.

The Curse ... in Reverse

3. FALLACIOUS ECONOMICUS: A nation *lacking* in natural resources such as coal, oil, water, land, minerals and timber is doomed to long run poverty.

Fallacious Reasoning: Logic backs up this (fallacious) assertion. Natural resources, simply called Land by economists, are critical factors in producing all products. A nation lacking in such resources has to be at a tremendous disadvantage compared to the relatively better endowed nations. Some goods may be impossible to produce while others can only be produced in small amounts at a high cost. Poverty Road here we come.

Correct Reasoning: The logic of the fallacious reasoning is trumped by real world experience. Recall the story of the frog with one leg tied down, as told in Chapter Eleven. **Sometimes adversity makes you stronger by forcing you to marshal and focus your other resources to the task at hand.** Yes, some nations are torpedoed by a lack of natural resources. Other nations can overcome the lack. The fact is, experience does not support the fallacious assertion that natural resources are indispensable for economic development.

Actually, a generous in-country resource endowment is not needed for economic development ... if other factors are called into play and take up the "slack." Oil, the dominant resource of our times, need not be found at hand. It can be imported or, given the technology and desire, created synthetically.

Japan and Italy are but two of the most advanced nations economically. However, each nation is woefully short of natural resources, especially oil, today's critical resource. Yet, these two nations excel economically despite the lack of natural resources. How can that happen? Other factors promoting development must be brought to bear. Superior organization of the other resources must take up the slack of unavailable natural resources. Abundant human capital, especially technological and administrative know-how, must complement the physical capital stock.

Use export proceeds to import oil. In Japan, Switzerland, Taiwan, Belgium, Singapore, and Hong Kong a national development policy of **export-led growth** makes the world forget those nations are short on natural resources. Consider the case of Singapore, a high standard of living island nation:

> Singapore has achieved it all despite being absolutely zero in terms of resource possession. It is deprived to the extent that it has to even import drinking water from neighbouring country of Malaysia. Singapore is a tiny island but it stands among the leaders in terms of re-exports, economic growth figures as well as development policies of the government. It imports raw material, processes and refines it, manufactures products and exports those commodities which fetch high prices for this country.

[2. "Top 10 Most Resource Deprived Countries" 19 January 2014 *Before Its News* <http://tinyurl.com/ou6mh5y>]

Leaders of those nations would not let a little something like *lack of natural resources* stand in the way of their plans for development. Those leaders also avoided the cozy capitalist corruption endemic in some resource rich nations!

4. FALLACIOUS ECONOMICUS: Too bad we can't make oil from other substances. Then we wouldn't have to worry about any curses from oil or the lack of it. And we wouldn't have to worry about paying extortionist prices to the gangsters in white robes who run the OPEC cartel.

Correct Reasoning: Hey, fella, where have you been the last 100 years? Various methods for synthesizing oil have been around for at least that long. The technology is for sale or licensing on the world market. **Synthetic oil production (from coal)** originated in Germany in the 1920s. Lacking adequate domestic supplies, oil imports into Germany were severely restricted during World War II. Cut off by the war, cost was not a major consideration. Synthetic oil production was pushed by the NAZIS during World War II as a source of gasoline for military vehicles and planes.

In the 1950s South Africa built on acquired German technology to jump start their synthetic oil industry and avoid dependence on imported oil. South Africa, cut off from oil imports in the 20th Century, has replaced nearly all oil imports with domestically produced synthetic oil. Indeed, South Africa has become a leader in synthetic oil technology in part because the world community forced them to. So, it may be that austerity and being cut off from imports may stimulate domestic energies to develop substitutes for the prohibited import.

Struggle can strengthen you, if one chooses to engage in the effort. Lack of oil was not a blessing for South Africa but certainly it was not a curse for all time. (Again, recall the story of the frog's leg and the scientist from Chapter Twenty-Seven!) **The U.S. has nearly a thousand years worth of coal deposits!**

The U.S. has an abundance of coal should synthetic fuel production gear up here. The natural crude oil price would have to be around a minimum of $60 per barrel to make synthetics scale up and be price competitive.

[3. Brian Westenhaus, "It is Possible to Replace Crude Oil with Synthetic Oil," 12 December 2012 OilPrice.Com <http://tinyurl.com/o4lre2d>]

Sweet tooth for fuel. *Brazilian* sugar is not all destined for cups of coffee. Brazil has parlayed it abundant sugar cane capacity into the production of ethanol. Brazil gave up *cheaper at the moment* imported oil and sought substitutes to avoid subservience to the OPEC cartel and its cohorts. The ethanol industry was developed over many decades, despite the high cost during the developmental years. The aim was to free Brazil from dependence on high priced, imported oil.

Today, Brazil is an exporter of crude oil and ethanol from sugar cane. To top off their good fortune, in the early 21st century they discovered huge undersea oil deposits off their coast.

5. FALLACIOUS ECONOMICUS: The development of new oil reserves, oil substitutes and new methods of production promises to reduce or eliminate our reliance on imported oil. But, OPEC will fight back if we threaten to take market share away or become independent.

Correct Reasoning: OPEC does not welcome competition. In response, OPEC activates the "yo-yo" price policy. Basically, it would over-produce to drive the price down. Unable to compete and suffering losses at the lower prices, those upstart American competitors will "get out of Dodge." That is, they would shut down increasingly unprofitable operations. Then, free of the upstart competitors, OPEC production is cut back causing the price – and profits – to go back up. Case closed. (N.B. There are short run situations -- producing losses -- when the falling unit price still recovers all the variable cost and *some* fixed cost. In that loss case, the oil firm should stay open and lose less than if it shut down. (See **Chapter Seventeen, Accounting Fallacies**, #8).

Forgotten strategy. If this were the 1970s, a **boycott** – abstain from buying – of OPEC oil would be the most effective counter strategy. Get them fighting amongst themselves, destroying the trust needed to run a successful cartel. A boycott involves severe short term costs but significant long term benefits for the customers. Is a boycott impractical today? Probably.

Put a floor price for oil: Are you crazy? Yes, you read it correctly: a *floor* price. It would not be popular with the U.S. consumer but would be welcomed by U.S. producers. Here is the proposal: Have the U.S. government announce that it will use its economic power to establish and maintain a floor price for oil. Yes, a *minimum* price. The floor price will be high enough for domestic producers - yes, those inefficient producers – to stay in business. Hey, what is a little inefficiency when national sovereignty and security are at stake?

Example: The world price is $70 per barrel and the U.S. nascent producers can be competitive only as long as the world price remains above $50. If the world price threatens to go to $40 due to a supply glut, then the floor mechanism activates. *The U.S. government steps in and buys enough oil to* *drive the price back up and keep it above $50.* The oil is put in storage. (This begs the question: where will the money come from?)

This ought to inspire the domestic producers to maintain and possibly expand operations. Yes, there are problems and cost associated with this plan. Every activity involves a cost, remember TANSTAAFL? But, the payoff will be enormous. Hopefully, dependence on foreign energy suppliers will end. **National security depends on it!** (See later in the chapter for further discussion).

6. FALLACIOUS ECONOMICUS: When it comes, energy independence will free the U.S. from involvement in the Middle East and its problems. So, drill, drill, and drill ... here in the U.S.!

Fallacious Reasoning: If we do not need their oil, who cares what happens there? We can kiss goodbye that part of the world. Let them rot.

Correct Reasoning: Sorry to disappoint you, but the fallacious statement is very naïve. It betrays a superficial understanding of the way the real world works. Unfortunately, U.S. energy independence does *not* mean the U.S. can ignore problems in and withdraw from the Middle East.

The U.S. will be heavily involved as long as U.S. based, **Big Oil** does business there. **Big Oil is an OPEC partner, its fortunes rising and falling with contracting or expanding OPEC oil production.** It buys, refines and markets Middle Eastern oil *worldwide*. Big Oil "has the ear" of the U.S. government. Indeed, it will keep the U.S. involved in oil patches around the world. This is true even if the continental U.S. becomes self-sufficient in oil and other energy resources. Energy self-sufficiency is not a *get out of jail free* card.

Furthermore, there remains **a national defense rationale for staying involved in the Middle East.** Consider these points:

> ➤ The U.S. small and medium sized crude producers (from shale and fracking) remain interdependent with OPEC actions.
> ➤ Although the U.S. may no longer be in need of region's oil, we may want to deny access to it by other nations hostile to the U.S. and guarantee access to our allies. A threat to allied nations impacts U.S. national security.
> ➤ We want to shut down the channeling of oil monies to terrorist groups populating the region.
> ➤ We want to deny training areas to terrorist groups in the region.
> ➤ The U.S. will remain concerned about Israel's defense and survival.
> ➤ The Suez Canal still is an important transit point for international commerce and well-being and must be kept open.

Since the end of World War II the U.S. Navy has kept the sea lanes open for world commerce. It is not likely to abandon that responsibility.

Given these concerns, it would be naïve to conclude that oil/energy independence would cause the U.S. to yield its blue water naval super status and withdraw into its territorial waters.

Big oil. Incidentally, Big Oil is a term used to refer to the so-called super major oil companies. The super majors are the six largest *non-state* owned oil companies: Exxon Mobil, Total S.A., Royal Dutch Shell, BP, Chevron and ConocoPhillips. (Total S.A. is a French integrated multinational)

7. FALLA⟨IOUS ⟨⟨ONOMI⟨US: Do not lose any sleep over security related

U.S. companies selling themselves or their strategic technologies to foreigners. Fear not, for Uncle Sam is "on the job." Since the middle 1970s the watchdog government Committee on Foreign Investment in the United States (CFIUS) screens proposed sales and foreign investments in the U.S. for national security concerns. Of special focus are those U.S. businesses directly or indirectly supplying the U.S. Department of Defense. They will nix any deal threatening national security.

> **CFIUS.** The Committee on Foreign Investment in the United States (CFIUS, commonly pronounced "sifius") is an inter-agency committee of the United States Government that reviews the national security implications of foreign investments in U.S. companies or operations. Chaired by the United States Secretary of the Treasury, CFIUS includes representatives from 16 U.S. departments and agencies, including the Defense, **State** and Commerce departments, as well as (most recently) the Department of Homeland Security. **Secretary of State Hillary Clinton sat on the committee and voted yes on the uranium sale to Russia ...** thanks, Hill.   Sleep lightly, my friend!!!
>
> [4. "Committee on Foreign Investment in the United States" 17 July 2014 *Wikipedia* <http://tinyurl.com/gmox2 >]

Correct Reasoning: And the moon is made out of green cheese!   Sorry to say, do not put too much confidence in CFIUS actually protecting national security. In 2015, CFIUS **approved the Russian takeover** (full ownership) of Uranium One Corp., headquartered in Toronto, Canada. It controls at least 20% of the uranium in the U.S.! How can this **not** be a threat to our security?

[5. Jo Becker and Mike McIntire, "Cash Flowed to Clinton Foundation Amid Russian Uranium Deal" 23 April, 2015 *NY Times* <http://tinyurl.com/k3b6umz> See also, Amy Davidson, "Five Questions About the Clintons and a Uranium Company" 24 April 2015 *New Yorker* <http://tinyurl.com/kvu54h3>]

In the last thirty years the U.S. has experienced an onslaught of foreign suitors for U.S. assets of all kinds: tech companies, semiconductors, natural resource deposits, cyber systems, aerospace, robotics, banks, **toll roads** and others. Most of this interest has been expressed by Japan and (still Red) China, both armed with huge stocks of U.S. dollars earned from rigged trade surpluses.

[6. Note that Saudi Prince Alwaleed bin Talal recently sold the second-largest block of stock (7%) in News Corp., parent company of Fox News. He remains a major share holder in Citicorp < http://tinyurl.com/p9yjuba>]

One might argue that outsiders are using *our own money* to buy U.S. assets and control of the U.S. economy to use for their own advantage.

Panama Canal turned Red? Oddly, properties near U.S. military bases and related facilities have attracted interest. One example is the (still Red) Chinese control of ports on each end of the (formerly American) Panama Canal.

> When the United States gave Panama full control of the canal, critics raised concerns about foreign influence and control over the canal's operation—particularly during an international crisis. Prompting the concern was the potential strategic reach of the Chinese military through the financial interests of Hong Kong tycoon billionaire Li Ka-shing, whose fortune and power derive from his connections to the government of the People's Republic of China. Panama Ports Company, a subsidiary of Hutcheson Port Holdings of Hong Kong shipping firm Hutcheson-Whampoa, Ltd., began a 25-year lease (with an 25-year renewal option) to operate port facilities at Balboa (Pacific side of the canal) and Cristobal (Atlantic side of the canal).

[7. William W. Mendel "Under New Ownership – It's *Panama's* Canal" *Military Review*, July-August 2000 <http://tinyurl.com/nbo8tjn >]

A Damaged Economy Undermines National Security

National security, meaning the continuance of our way of life, rests atop a vibrant, healthy, thriving economy. Without a doubt, Globalism, meaning cheap imported labor, cheap imported goods, so-called free trade and off shored output has been bad for the American economy. Sadly, these measures signal a threat beyond the realm of economics and our falling *standard of living*.

They signal a threat to national security, our *way of life*.

Where does CFIUS draw the line between businesses involving national security and those not involving national security? Don't they recognize uranium as a strategic resource impacting national security? Duh?

The fallacy of a purely civilian or humanitarian resource has been exposed elsewhere in the volume. Does CFIUS appreciate that all resources, even those commonly designated civilian or humanitarian, have some direct or indirect military application? Does this idea figure in their decision making? For example, consider a technological improvement in fertilizer. This seemingly benign innovation, sold to (still Red) China or North Korea, could enable the release of manpower, land and capital to be re-deployed to the military.

Beware that CFIUS is advisory; the President makes the final decision. Another problem is the waiver of rules by Bill Clinton and other Presidents.

> ...dozens of American supercomputers, many with possible military applications, have been sold to Russia and China since 1996 *without* Federal licenses. These sales did not require Government approval because they were made under **greatly relaxed export controls for supercomputers issued by President Clinton in 1995.** [Unbelievably]Under those rules, the Government *transferred to companies* the responsibility for screening buyers to insure they were not diverting sensitive technology to military uses.
>
> [8. Bold and Italics mine. Jeff Gerth, "Clinton Administration Tightens Rules on Supercomputer Sales to 13 Foreign Groups" *New York Times Archives* 1 July 1997< http://tinyurl.com/oxhpkvk>]

Ostensibly, some of the computers were to be used to improve weather forecasting. But, any third grader knows that battles are fought "in weather." Weather forecasting is a military technology.... duh!

At Swords Points: The End of a Nation?

At any time, a nation is buffeted by two forces, winds that blow from opposite directions. One force is **commonality**, drawing people together. This is the common core of similar beliefs, values, language, food, history, heroes and symbols that initially drew people together. A common ancestry or ethnicity, religion and language strengthen the ties. These forces cause folks to see themselves as a distinct group, different from other peoples. This awareness and approval of commonality is a **binding force**. Thus, commonality is the CENTRIPETAL force, drawing people together to embrace their common core. However, simultaneously, a contrary, *splintering* force is working against the *binding* force.

These are the winds of diversity, a CENTRIFUGAL force that urges folks away from common core. Excess Diversity is a **splintering force**. It involves new music and art, the innovative, different values and lifestyles, foreign religions and languages. These forces are surging today as immigration expands as a percent of the population. Diversity worship abounds in public and private institutions, including the mass media. The legal system has defined deviancy down. Indeed, what behavior is considered deviant today?

It seems traditional American culture is about to blow away.

Over time, a healthy, living culture absorbs, adopts and adapts diverse elements until they become part of the core. The U.S. has always been receptive to diverse influences, slowly incorporating the worthy ones into the common core. **But, if the diverse factors are too many and too extreme, the nation fractures.**

Remember, the economy is the "mother ship" of national defense and national security. And oil is the fuel of the mother ship.

The U.S. is challenging Saudi Arabia for the number one spot among nations in crude oil production. Shale oil and fracking technology have resurrected the American oil patch. But, America is not out of the energy "woods" yet. The Saudis have co-conspirators in their pursuit of domination of the world crude oil market. *When the Saudis get their "gang" together their production outstrips U.S. output nearly three to one.* That gang is known as OPEC and it is still the heavyweight champion. OPEC uses its output muscle to bend world prices their way, despite the U.S. challenge. **When OPEC countries *act as one* they still dominate world prices**. Meanwhile, crude oil exports from the U.S., outlawed since the 1970s, are loosening up. Crude oil imports are permissible and respond to world prices. When OPEC flexes it muscles and *temporarily* **drops world prices by raising supply**, the following sequence of events is likely:

1) U.S. users switch to cheaper imports.

2) Higher cost domestic drillers are now left with uncompetitive, unprofitable wells.

3) After a time, domestic producers shut wells to cut losses. Price rebounds.

4) Defaults increase on bank loans to oil exploration and development companies.

5) OPEC applauds #3. It now cuts output to enforce a price rise.

6) American drillers are tempted to re-open closed wells. Some do, some don't.

Overall result: Given inelastic demand, OPEC's (and big oil's) profits soar. Competition has been rattled if not stifled. OPEC has won this engagement!

If OPEC disbanded and crude oil prices came down, there would be a good news-bad news outcome. Which of the following would occur:

1. Would U.S. higher cost upstart producers be hurt and some have to shut down?

2. Would the U.S. become *more dependent* on cheaper imported oil? If so, how would that impact U.S. national security? You had better watch what you wish for!

Economics in Ancient Egypt?

The ancient Egyptian Pharaoh ImSoHep knew how to deal with discontent in the populace: keep the people BUSY.

First, ImSoHep asserted ownership and dictatorial control over all the people, resources and land in Egypt. He asserted ownership over the Nile River, as well.

Then, half the people were ordered (at spear point and threat of the lash) to tear down a nearby mountain. Under orders, the rest of the people tended crops, stitched clothing and otherwise provided comfort for the workers.

After tearing down the mountain, ImSoHep ordered the workers to haul the pieces to another spot where the pieces were re-assembled. So, mountains were torn down and re-assembled, one after another. In this manner, all the people were kept busy, generation after generation, all the time, for thousands of years!

Yes, ImSoHep was a great leader, far ahead of his time!

Today, we call his program full employment.

Today, the re-assembled mountains are called pyramids.

Chapter Twenty-Four
Some Trade Fallacies

*International trade is the big leagues, with everything at stake,
including national survival.* —Theo Dosius

Some ideas are so stupid only intellectuals could believe them.

—George Orwell

"Trade has nothing to do with jobs." A laugher, from Dr. Art Laffer

HAS the big media fallen for the myth of riches from free international trade? Is free trade the road to riches ... or the road to poverty? It depends. Often ignored, trade policy ranks in importance right alongside monetary and fiscal policy. **The record shows that, over time, free trade impoverishes some nations and enriches others.**

Traditional economics favors international trade. In general, *voluntary* trade enhances both parties by lowering costs and widening consumer choice. **Trade can improve general welfare by enabling an economy to consume more – at the moment –**

than it could produce (and consume) in isolation. This sounds like a good thing, and it is ... up to a point. However, as with all things, an excess of a good thing turns good to bad. Read all about it: "Free" implies there are no obstacles such as tariffs, quotas or regulations imposed on a market. Over the past fifty years, the U.S. eliminated these on most imports.

Today, the U.S. is, basically, a free trade nation, an open economy. Advancing "free trade" means embracing the Globalist platform: multilateral, complex trade deals that a. infringe on sovereignty and b. *override* U.S. Federal and state law. The deals typically allow unhindered, unlimited mobility of labor (read: open borders). The deals surrender American sovereignty to foreign quasi-government agencies, transnational corporate committees and international non-governmental agencies. The end game of Globalism is a borderless world, one world government.

Economies of scale yield export led growth. Smith taught that larger markets permitted a greater the scale of operations. Larger markets enabled 1) narrower but more productive specializations for workers and 2) more specialized, dedicated capital equipment. Specialized workers with specialized tools boost worker productivity and help lower unit costs. Industrialization brought standardization and interchangeability of parts, a force multiplier.

A "Joke" Circulating on the Internet

John Smith started the day early having set his alarm clock (MADE IN JAPAN) for 6 am.

While his coffeepot (MADE IN CHINA) was perking, he shaved with his electric razor (MADE IN HONG KONG).

He put on a dress shirt (MADE IN SRI LANKA), designer jeans (MADE IN SINGAPORE) and tennis shoes (MADE IN KOREA).

After cooking his breakfast in his new electric skillet (MADE IN INDIA) he sat down with his calculator (MADE IN MEXICO) to see how much he could spend today.

After setting his watch (MADE IN TAIWAN) to the radio (MADE IN INDIA) he got in his car (MADE IN ITALY) filled it with GAS from Saudi Arabia and continued his search for a good paying AMERICAN JOB.

"12:14"

At the end of yet another discouraging and fruitless day checking his Computer (MADE IN MALAYSIA), John decided to relax for a while.

He put on his sandals (MADE IN BRAZIL), and played his guitar (MADE INDONESIA) while he poured himself a glass of wine (MADE IN FRANCE) and turned on his TV (MADE IN GERMANY), and then called his girlfriend on his cell phone (MADE IN NORWAY). He apologized for missing their date and promised her a big box of chocolate (MADE IN BELGIUM).

Then wondered why he can't find a good paying job in AMERICA.

Excess, anyone?

Standardization of parts takes a complex product, e.g. an automobile, and standardizes production of each component. Each unit of the same component is made to the same specifications. This allows for **interchangeability of parts,** shattering the requirement that specialists work in close proximity. This, in turn, permits the international division of labor – on the *same* unit of production, say, a car! The drop in production costs allows for price reductions which further expand the customer base, enabling even larger scale of operations.

Economies of scale can provide the main weapon – price reduction – for undercutting foreign producers and penetrating foreign markets. Such is the rational for seeking wider markets. But, beware overreach: overexpansion and mismanagement lead to **diseconomies of scale,** causing unit cost to rise.

Grand Total of Trade: A Bad Measure for the Nation

Proponents of free trade often cite the *grand total* of trade or job creation as a rationale for free trade. Reference is made to the *total amount of trade* being enlarged after a reduction in trade barriers, i.e., a total or partial freeing up of trade. More stuff produced, more for folks to enjoy, no?

Free trade critics charge that the total trade metric masks many important consequences of free trade and so-called "free trade" pacts. **But notice, in praising free trade, advocates rarely mention its impact on the American standard of living, current and future!** (See # 6 below) The **total trade** figure:

1) Ignores whether the gain in trade came from imports or exports.

2) The grand total of trade ignores the type of goods exported or imported (computer chips or potato chips?).

3) It ignores the long term effects of **dependence** on specific imports or export markets. For example, one could argue that devotion to near-sighted free trade ideology got the U.S. hooked on cheaper imported oil after the mid 1970s, with detrimental long term effects.

4) Ignored is the impact on economic and national security from expanded trade in particular goods, e.g., defense related goods. Recall: the economy is the mother ship of national security and must remain robust.

5) Job quality, occupational and job security are ignored by total trade.

6) The total amount of trade is not a good proxy for the **standard of living** (SOL) of the great majority. Total trade could expand while the SOL falls.

7) Ignored is the distribution of benefits and costs from the freeing of trade. Exports are goods lost to the nation but provide income to the exporters. Imports provide goods to the nation but lost are the out-bound payments. (See the Absorption story)

8) Exports and imports could have ripple effects throughout the economy. Whose ox is gored and whose field is plowed by free trade?

9) Ignored is the impracticality of activating the *compensation principle* whereby, in effect, gainers compensate losers and still come out ahead.

10) Free trade *within* a nation, should it result in monopoly, can be countered by anti-trust action. In contrast, *international* (free) trade can make a nation a victim of foreign monopolies, quasi-governmental international committees, cartels and trade schemes, e.g., OPEC, without an adequate peaceful remedy.

Barriers or obstacles to free trade include tariffs (taxes on imports) and nontariff barriers (import quotas, safety regulations, product specs, etc.) Since the mid 1960s the U.S. has reduced or eliminated barriers on most imports. In addition, nations might limit or forbid the export or transmission of strategic goods and technologies. Those advocates favoring barriers to imports are traditionally referred to as *protectionists.* Observe in Diagram #1 below the wide spectrum of possible trade policies:

Diagram #1: Overview of International Trade Policies

International Trade Policies

Isolation or autarky ——————————— Free trade

(NO trade, in or out)   (No government imposed
A rare policy   hindrances to trade, in or out)
                                   Unilateral
                                   Bi-Lateral
                                   Multi-Lateral

Managed Trade

Policies include:
Mercantilism
Neo Mercantilism
Protectionism
Trade agreements,
    bi-lateral and multi-lateral
Economic integration
    (unification of
    different countries)

Today, "free trade" is a euphemism for Globalism. Historically, China and Japan had long periods of voluntary autarky, isolation or no trade. Today, most nations trade. The *free trade* movement seeks to reduce and eventually eliminate all the artificial impediments to trade: quotas, tariffs and the like. Free traders assert **goods will be cheaper to all parties and economic welfare will be improved.** (Free movement of labor has been tacked on by the Globalists, as well, a feature ignored by orthodox free trade theory.) So, what is not to like about free trade? What is wrong with the free trade model? Consider Keynes' opinion:

> "Practical men who believe themselves to be quite exempt from any intellectual influence, are usually the slaves of some defunct economist. Madmen in authority, who hear voices in the air, are distilling their frenzy from some academic scribbler of a few years back." —John Maynard Keynes

1. FALLACIOUS ECONOMICUS:
Leaders of both political parties support free international trade as the nation's road to greatest prosperity. Most academic economists support free trade. The U.S. Chamber of Commerce supports free trade, along with Nobel economists. So, why the opposition?

Fallacious Reasoning: Can all these experts be wrong?

Correct Reasoning: Yes, experts can be wrong! **Look at history, not theory!**

The American System: Restricted trade This fallacy is a whopper, courtesy of British gurus Adam Smith (*The Wealth of Nations*, 1776) and David Ricardo (*On the Principles of Political Economy and Taxation,* 1821). **Correct reasoning puts economic theory aside and looks at the historical record.**

Remember: the U.S. economic colossus resulted not from free trade policies. It resulted, at least partially, from a nationalist policy favored by Hamilton, Friedrich List, Lincoln, Henry Carey and Henry Clay. That policy favored protectionism and tariffs. This was coupled with a strong domestic Industrial Policy. It became known as the American System, as opposed to the British free trade system. **Every President on Mount Rushmore was a proud, unapologetic American economic patriot.**

A Mantra for Free Trade

Do not make it yourself if you can buy it for less.

This would apply to individuals trading inside the nation (intra-national trade) and as a guideline for trade between nations (inter-national trade). The implication is this: if you buy it for less than your own cost, you wind saving on the price and having the good, as well. You come out ahead, as your budget goes further. Alternatively, if you buy it for *more* – when you could have made it yourself for *less*

> - then you have overpaid and end up with fewer goodies to enjoy.
>
> Sounds eminently logical but is short-sighted and can lock a nation into economic stagnation. **Beware: cheaper at the moment may be more costly in the long run.**

Hubristics

Economic Nationalism gave way to Globalism in the second half of the 20th century. Under Globalism, the U.S. made protectionist restrictions on imports an endangered species. (One way) free trade was adopted to help the free world economy recover from the devastation of World War II and deter nations from going Communist. The U.S., as Mother Importer, was to wet nurse the free world's economies back to economic health. The motive was not entirely altruistic. Once restored, the devastated nations could buy U.S. goods once again. **At least that was the plan. Unfortunately, it never fully materialized.**

No threat at first, trading partners' competitive imports were invited into the rich U.S. consumer market, and took full advantage of the opportunity! Access to foreign markets for American exporters was given secondary priority even into the 1960s, even though there was full recovery from the war. This was called free trade but, in reality, was mainly an *inbound* free trade system, apparently by U.S. design. U.S. producers jumped on the bandwagon, going off shore to benefit from this policy. At this point the U.S. is embarking on the same disastrous path tread by Great Britain a century earlier.

Flee Free Trade, An Alien Ideology?

Why did the high minded British free trade movement of the mid 1800s fail to enlist its major trading partners?

> The British statesmen believed they were helping to spread universal economic truths and a new moral order based on international peace and mutual prosperity. **Their European counterparts thought mainly of their own national producer interests and how to strengthen them, promote nation building, and increase military strength. [Echoes heard today!]**
>
> [2. "British Free Trade, 1850-1914: Economics and Policy" Autumn 1999 Refresh 29: Recent Findings of Research in Economic & Social History <http://tinyurl.com/pys9adj >]

Does this motivation sound familiar? Does the outcome sound familiar?
Hey, Uncle Sam, wake up, you've been duped!

Era of the Asian Trojan Horses: Ungrateful Babies Backstab Mama

Trading with the frenemy. The economic "wet nurse" - good old Uncle Sam - found another infant in need when, with bi-partisan support, trade opened up with (still Red) China. The Asian tigers -- more like a herd of Trojan horses -- of Japan, Taiwan, Singapore, South Korea and Hong Kong already were getting their teat time. Extension of the *wet nurse era* brought goods to the U.S., but industrial destruction, as well. One way free trade brought the weaponized Asian "Trojan horse" filled with cheap imports. An *excess* of autos, consumer electronics, textiles, shoes and a host of other cheaper imports swamped America, destroying whole industries, occupations, and livelihoods. Today, job, occupational, and income security continue to be imperiled as foreign producers return to pick up the "crumbs."

Command and control of the American economy is slipping away due to foreign acquisitions of U.S. strategic assets.

Final Stage: Globalization and Globalism

The off shoring boom and open borders have assured continuing U.S. relative economic decline. The U.S. current and future standard of living is imperiled, aggravated by the budget and foreign trade deficits. Critics would say the twin deficits - both maintained by U.S. IOU's - keep the economy running on what amounts to nothing but fumes. The **relative decline** of American economic dominance begins once (one way) free trade and Globalism are adopted in the mid 1970s. [Massive *trade* deficits of goods and services $500B in 2015 mean, in effect, the U.S. is living partially on borrowed goods and services.]

The tremendous economic gains of (still Red) China, Japan and the so-called Asian Tigers (Hong Kong, Singapore, South Korea, and Taiwan) are from export-led growth. They used exports to the willing and able U.S. as a springboard to economic development. Export-led growth is a form of Neo-mercantilism.

Free Trade No Road to Riches

History shows not one nation got rich through free trade! Free trade is an elegant academic construct but a poor guide to practical international trade policy. Both Great Britain and the United States adopted (inbound) free trade *after* they had become wealthy nations following other policies. Arguably, the adoption of free trade had the opposite effect than intended, contributing to the *relative* decline of both nations in different centuries.

[3. Fletcher, Ian. *Free Trade Doesn't Work: What Should Replace It and Why.* Edition [Paperback]. Wash, D.C.: U.S. Business and Industry Council, 2011.]

In the mid 1800s, the U.K. drops the Mercantilist version of *economic nationalism* and mistakenly embraced the free trade paradigm. The U.K. had gotten rich from the Mercantilist approach to economic nationalism. Then, in the mid 1800s, attempting to add to their vast riches, they tried to open restricted foreign markets by adopting free trade and promoting it among their trading partners. "Look," they said, "we'll drop import barriers if you do the same." The infamous **Corn Laws were repealed**, resulting in cheaper imported food. British farm workers were thrown off farms. Those workers streamed into the cities looking for – and finding – newly opened manufacturing jobs. Apparently unafraid of foreign competitors, Britain acted unilaterally, gave up Mercantilism and adopted free trade in manufactured goods. In doing so it opened up its economy to what would become increasingly competitive foreign imports.

But, the U.K. was not up to the challenge. Over the next fifty years cheaper (and, eventually, better) imported goods proved to be problematic for British industry. Seems the Brits switched to the wrong horse!

Free trade was called **the British System**. The government guided, private enterprise U.S. Industrial Policy – inspired by Hamilton, Freidrich List and Henry Clay – was called **the American System**. The American economist Henry Carey, advisor to Lincoln, was key to fashioning this policy. The Brits met with resistance to their free trade scheme. It came mainly from smaller economies outside the Empire and Commonwealth. Meanwhile, their free trade policy, welcoming to cheap competing imports, eventually backfired on British industry and the standard of living in the U.K. Instead of greater prosperity, a gradual but persistent decline set in. **America would suffer a similar fate one hundred years forward.**

The big mistake. How could U.S. policy makers fifty years ago make such a stupendous blunder in adopting free trade and Globalism? Didn't they know the British, adopting free trade in the 1850s made the same mistake of thinking their industrial core was impervious to foreign competition? Did **hubris** play a role? Didn't free trade help mortally wound British dominance of world manufacturing in the late 1800s, allowing the surging, protectionist U.S. to vault into first place?

By providing an export market for her trading partners Britain allowed them, especially the U.S., to achieve unbeatable **scale economies**. By 1900, America was the predominant world economy, out producing the U.K., France and Germany- combined! **The protectionist American system triumphed in the end over the British free trade system.**

Replay of U.K? Is the same scenario being replayed today with a new cast? Is the U.S. taking the U.K. role of free trader and export market, playing "wet nurse" for protégé, frenemy and still suckling (still Red) Chinese industry and export goods? It portends to be worse for the U.S. Thanks to **standardization of parts and** containerization, production facilities are sub dividable and moveable today, unlike in the 1850s.

In each case, the U.K. in the 1850s and U.S. in the 1950s, the adoption of inbound unilateral free trade, clearly a policy choice that could have been avoided, sowed the seeds of continuing *relative* economic decline. Will the struggle between (still Red) China and the U.S. mirror the outcome of the U.S./U.K. battle one hundred years ago, but this time with the U.S. as the loser?

Remember: the growth of the U.S. economic colossus did not result from free trade policies. The tariff, a child of **economic nationalism,** played the starring role in nurturing and protecting the nascent American manufacturing baby.

Beware: Globalization does *not* require the surrender of sovereignty and governance to international committees. It does not require the harmonization of laws and regulations, ending in global government. GLOBALISM DOES. Globalism has its end game the yielding of national sovereignty to anonymous unelected committees and functionaries outside the nation. Ultimately, embracing Globalism fully means ditching the Declaration of Independence and self-governance. Then, kiss goodbye America's control of its own destiny. Outsiders will rule America.

2. FALLACIOUS ECONOMICUS: Corporate *economic patriotism* will limit the amount of off shoring of industry and loss of jobs from the United States.

Corollary Fallacious Statement: Don't worry; government will monitor the sale and transfer of strategic technologies to foreign nations, especially "frenemies" like (still Red) China.

Correct Reasoning: The government itself displays very little economic patriotism! Globalthink has displaced Nationthink as the mindset of U.S. economic, trade officials and transnational corporations. Thanks to Bill Clinton, **maximization of shareholder value** (*uber alles*) has become the mantra of transnational corporations born and raised in America.

Profits earned overseas are not taxable! Duh? Firms have the OK to desert the U.S. for foreign production platforms. Is it a surprise there is very little economic patriotism among the Global minded captains of American transnational companies? GE, GM, IBM, APPLE, you name them and they are creating more jobs in their foreign facilities than here in America.

Thomas Jefferson on Economic Patriotism
"Merchants have no country. The mere spot they stand on does not constitute so strong an attachment as that from which they draw their gains."

Indeed, there is an ongoing American manufacturing and jobs Diaspora ... encouraged by a Globalism embracing Uncle Sam! Urged on by trade deals like the North American Trade Agreement (NAFTA) and U.S. involvement in the World Trade Organization (WTO), American industrial icons have behaved like rats leaving a sinking ship.

Even patriotic producers are forced to move production facilities off shore to stay alive and competitive! Government must remove the incentives to off-shore!

Major Question: Can the *lower wage/lower income* labor force left behind by off shoring production afford to buy the exports from foreign platforms? Not without expansion of consumer credit here in the U.S. Even then it is problematic. Nominal wages have fallen further than prices, signaling a drop in real wages. **Occupational degeneration compounds the problem** of limp purchasing power.

Suckling Pigs

Suckling pigs have a reputation for greediness as they compete with one another for their mother's milk. The U.S. has been suckling its piglet trading partners – by embracing their cheaper exports, lower wage workers and tolerating job theft – for the last fifty years! This has sapped the strength and accelerated the relative decline of the vaunted U.S. economy.

[4. Kenneth W. Michael Wills, "What Is a Suckling Pig?" 5 Sept. 2014 *eHow* <http://www.ehow.com/info_10020615_suckling-pig.html.>]

---

3. FALLACIOUS ECONOMICUS: Creating jobs *for Americans* in America is the highest priority for the U.S. government economic authorities.

Fallacious Reasoning: The landmark **Employment Act of 1946** mandated that the government maximize employment. Subsequent legislation reinforced that mandate. In addition, the Federal Reserve is committed, by law, to promote long run growth in employment as well as general price stability. With this entire official "huff and puff," how could the economic authorities put job growth for Americans on the "back burner"?

Correct Reasoning: Understand this: to the disgrace of American policy makers, **creating jobs in America is not the same as creating jobs for Americans.** The embrace of Globalism has embodied a particular antipathy toward U.S. native born workers' occupational and job security.

Shameful Treatment of Americans ... by Uncle Sam! Economic growth, immigration and trade policy are the underlying policies impacting long run quantity and quality of new job creation. Sadly, looking at the record of the last twenty years, one may conclude that immigration and trade policy have propelled the creation of jobs for (still Red) Chinese, Mexicans and other new entrants into the top priority slot.

[5. Consider the analysis by Edwin S. Rubenstein, "National Data | October Jobs: Unemployment Up, Immigrants Beating Out Americans...As They Have Throughout Obama Years" 3 November 2012 *Vdare.com* < http://tinyurl.com/perzg8t >]

[6. also see: Edwin S. Rubenstein, "Immigration Not Only Displaces American Workers— It Also Reduces Incomes" 5 Feb 2015 *Vdare.Com* <http://tinyurl.com/psudu92>]

Adding insult to injury, many of the newly arrived (legal and illegal) fall into affirmative action ethnic categories. This gives employers (in hiring) the legal right to bypass Native American and indigenous workers in favor of someone newly arrived. Duh?

U.S. in the world. Exports create jobs, but the government has failed to aggressively negotiate export growth, *relative to imports,* across a wide range of products. The U.S. is the import king, the world's biggest customer, to the extent that imports exceed exports by $750 billion as measured by the merchandise trade balance. Measured by merchandise AND services balance, the deficit "shrinks" to $500 billion.[Figures are for 2015] **The U.S. is the number two exporter in the world but the number one importer, i.e., the largest single importer of the world's goods.**

Beware the Trojan Horse

At first, in moderate amounts, cheaper goods and labor appear to be gifts. Recall, the Trojan horse of antiquity was first thought to be a gift. **However, like the Trojan horse of old, designed to aid conquest, the mission of cheaper imports is to conquer and destroy industries.** Taken to excess, cheap imports and cheap labor have destroyed American jobs, industries, incomes and depressed the standard of living.

Unfavorable Tax Policy

Unremitted foreign profits are free of U.S. income tax as long as they are left overseas! In that way the U.S. corporate tax system intentionally (or unintentionally) encourages the use of foreign production platforms, called off shoring, and leaving profits overseas for reinvestment in foreign lands. That means foreign jobs instead of U.S. jobs and lost tax revenue to the U.S. Treasury. The unremitted earnings amounted to around 2 trillion dollars in 2014 or around 10% of current GDP. Note: Any *foreign* taxes paid on that income are deducted from the U.S. tax liability.

[7. Michelle Hanlon, "The Lose-Lose Tax Policy Driving Away U.S. Business," 12 June 2014 *The Wall Street Journal* <http://tinyurl.com/op7hdh2>]

4. FALLACIOUS ECONOMICUS: There is no significant difference between intra-national trade and international trade, other than a possible currency transaction in international trade.

Fallacious Reasoning: Each type of trade involves at least two immediate parties who, if trading voluntarily, believe they are made better off by the trade. The location of the traders has no impact on overall costs and benefits to each party, except for transport costs, where significant. All benefits and costs are private and accrue *only to* the traders involved. Currency conversion fees may apply in international trade, as well as currency hedging costs.

Correct Reasoning: International traders can impact their respective nations. International trade involves trading partners in different nations. As always, traders seek to better themselves. The *nation as a whole* must be considered a passive third party, usually without a voice in making the deal. It may win or lose in international trade between private individuals. Indeed, the survival of the nation and the independence of the nation-State may be at stake in international trade between private individuals.

Example 1: If the traded good involves a sensitive military technology transfer, then the relative strength of the two nations may be altered.

Example 2: Open trade or smuggling of weapons of mass destruction can have an impact beyond the trading parties. Trade in destructive, addictive illegal drugs is included. Indeed, such trade can impact the nation's survival.

Example 3: Trade in industrial secrets can impact the both nations for generations. Michael Lind describes how Britain tried to prevent the export of industrial technology and machinery:

> Hindering the transfer of technology from Britain to America was another mercantilist technique. In 1719, Britain banned the emigration of skilled workers in industries including steel, iron, brass, watch-making, and wool. The law punished suborning, or recruitment, of skilled workers for employment abroad with fines or imprisonment. ...Britain followed its ban on the emigration of skilled workers with a ban on the export of wool and silk technology in 1750. In 1781 and 1785, the act was enlarged into a comprehensive ban on machinery of all kinds. The ban on skilled emigrants was repealed only in 1825, while the ban on technology exports lasted until 1842.
>
> [8. Michael Lind. *Land of Promise: An Economic History of the United States.* New York: Harper Collins, 2012, pp. 25, 39-41. <http://tinyurl.com/o5vwgys>]

Example 4. Consider the U.S. sale of supercomputers and missile guidance technology to China in the 1990s during the administration of Bill Clinton. Did that not enhance China's economic capacity, absolutely and relative to the U.S.? Does not continued trade with China continue to enhance its economic prowess?   Does not enhanced economic prowess actually or potentially enhance "frenemy" China's military capability?

Example 5: Both Bill Clinton and George W. Bush approved the sale of supercomputers to China. They were intended for civilian use, of course. (But, recall: there is no such thing as purely civilian resource or good).

[9. The working of CFIUS, The Committee on Foreign Investment in the United States (CFIUS, commonly pronounced *sifius)* was considered in an earlier chapter.]

Strategic assets must be closely held and their trade closely regulated!

Trade as a Substitute for Migration

Economists have long held that imports substitute for immigration. They have an equivalent impact on domestic wages and employment. American workers have been caught in this pincer movement between imports and cheap labor. Both excess cheap imports and/or excess immigration put downward pressure on domestic wages.

.

International Trade Can Be a Maker or Breaker of Nations

International trade is an ancient activity going back thousands of years. Over those years folks have traded to lower costs and enrich domestic consumption. International trade has costs as well as benefits, at any moment and over the years. That is, there are static (at the moment) and dynamic (over time) effects.

Contact with foreign cultures/new ideas can result in acquisition of improved technologies, sparking invention and innovation in production, transportation and finance in the homeland. International trade opens domestic producers to a wider range of competition than internal trade. Foreign competition can swamp some home industries but strengthen others. You don't run so fast as when someone is chasing you. Here are some effects of international trade: *Bilateral* international trade opens domestic producers to more foreign customers, boosting prosperity in that export sector. Yes, but:

> ➢ International trade can impact job creation and destruction, and domestic wages (recall: trade is a substitute for migration.)

> ➢ International trade policy can affect the birth, life and death of entire industries, at home and abroad!

> ➢ International trade policy can strengthen or weaken the entire economy *relative to its rivals, thereby impacting national security!*

The stakes are high, the lesson is clear: **international trade must be managed.** Ditch laissez-faire. Government's top priority must be the survival and *broadly shared* prosperity of the nation and support of its way of life.

Currency Issues. Foreign trade may have to be conducted in a foreign currency, a currency whose value is not fixed relative to the dollar. It may be that an American exporter agrees to accept Euros from a French importer. The Euros have to be converted into dollars so the exporter can pay his bills in the U.S. But, what if the Euros ultimately convert into fewer dollars than expected? Then the exporter has suffered a loss. The possibility of foreign exchange rates changing so as to harm a trader is called foreign exchange risk. **Foreign exchange risk deters trade.** No such risk exists in one-currency deals, as in intra-national trade conducted in U.S. dollars by Americans.

In response, traders and international bankers have developed sophisticated financial instruments to reduce such foreign exchange risk and encourage trade. Globalists believe having a single worldwide currency would eliminate foreign exchange risk, spur international trade and enhance profits of giant transnational corporations. Moreover, a new world currency, administered without U.S. dominance, would de-throne the U.S. dollar (and U.S. monetary authorities) as the centerpiece of the world economy.

Scenario for Dollar Crash?

"Dollargedden" crashes U.S. standard of living

Could the huge U.S. foreign trade and balance of payments **deficits** lead to a dollar crash, the rejection of the dollar for international transactions and as a reserve currency? Here follows some speculations about a dollar crash. A dollar crash means a drastic, catastrophic fall in the *external* nominal value of the dollar caused by massive dollar dumping by major holders, viz., (still Red) China, Japan and the oil exporters. Along the way **the dollar loses its reserve currency status, prompting additional dumping. With it goes much of its source of strength.** The U.S. goods will get much cheaper to foreign currency holders. We will give up *more* exports in exchange for *fewer* imports. Absorption and well-being will fall as the U.S. will be paying more for goods on the world market and getting fewer in return.

> ➤ An import dependent U.S. public would likely experience import "inflation," initially damaging the standard of living. Alternatively, the cheaper U.S. dollar would likely expand exports, benefiting factors of production in the export sector. However, the U.S. export earnings surge will be overwhelmed by the loss in real purchasing power of the dollar on world markets. The U.S. standard of living crashes!

➤ As the "pie" shrinks, the struggle at home between Guns and Butter factions will get more heated, with Butter likely coming out ahead.

➤ **The dollar loses its reserve currency status.** A new international currency favorite will emerge. Could it be the Yuan, the (still Red) Chinese currency? Perhaps this will be new worldwide money. Globalists believe a single worldwide currency would eliminate foreign exchange risk, spur international trade and enhance profits of giant transnational corporations exploiting scale advantages.

➤ A new world currency would dethrone the U.S. dollar as the centerpiece of the world economy. U.S. monetary authorities would be demoted from it prime role. De-throning the dollar would reduce external demand for it as a reserve currency and vehicle currency in third party transactions. Its *nominal* exchange value will fall as it becomes just another currency among many.

➤ **Consequently, unless foreign prices fall, the *real* external value of the dollar - its buying power on foreign shores - will drop.** This is described as the dollar weakening, falling or depreciating. In the extreme one would call this a collapse of the dollar as it degenerates into the status of an ordinary **currency.**

➤ The smart money would bet the overall impact of a dollar crash will be nearly disastrous for the American standard of living, economic and national security!

➤ As the crash proceeds, foreigners (and Americans, as well) will liquidate dollar denominated securities, i.e., stocks and bonds. A likely decline and possible crash in those asset values ensues. This will rattle the world financial and banking system.

From Bad to Worse. Foreigners will view the U.S. as posted with one big "For Sale" sign. Due to the collapse of the dollar, **command and control of the U.S. economy will gradually accrue to foreign interests through sales of assets (real and financial), political influence and big media. Can U.S. sovereignty survive?** The U.S. is threatened with becoming subservient to its creditors, a captive colony, ripe for exploitation. But, will the American people resist this surrender of sovereignty by their leaders ... and elect new leaders? Too late now. Thus, beware continuing massive trade deficits that grow U.S. foreign debt to "dollargeddon" levels! Sleep lightly, my friend!

Back to Trade Theory: The Compensation Principle

Orthodox trade theory admits there may be losers in international trade. Unable to compete, domestic producers and workers may be hurt by imports when trade opens up. But, trade theory says the gains to the gainers enable them to compensate the losers and still come out ahead. This is called the *compensation principle*, developed by British philosopher/economist David Hume.

Hume tried to make international trade more palatable by reasoning according to the following example. Suppose trade open us and some domestic workers are thrown out of work by cheaper imports. They lose $100 income. But, the gainers from increasing exports gain $150. So, the gainers from trade gain *more* ($150) than the losers *lose* ($100). Then, the gainers of $150 can transfer $100 to the losers and still come out ahead by $50. Everyone lives happily ever after. What a brilliant solution!

Actually, the **Trade Adjustment Assistance Act** provides for Federal transfers from taxpayers to losers. Job retraining is included. So, do the deal! Everyone can benefit! Why is this reasoning fallacious? It is fallacious because, for various reasons, rarely are such compensations adequate to the task! It is assumed government can a. know who the gainers and losers are, and b. how much is gained and lost. Free riders must be weeded out. Many legitimate losers never receive the compensation they are due. Enacted compensations have time limits.

Payments have not covered all losses for all losers all the time.

The compensation principle remains mainly an intriguing *principle*, an interesting theoretical construct. However, in reality it has fallen far short of its promise to promote a fair distribution of gains from trade.

[10. See "Trade Adjustment Assistance," *Wikipedia*, Sept, 2011
<http://en.wikipedia.org/wiki/Trade_Adjustment_Assistance>
See also, "What is Trade Adjustment Assistance?" 22 April 2015 *United States Department of Labor Employment and Training Division*
<http://www.doleta.gov/tradeact/factsheet.cfm.>]

5. **FALLACIOUS ECONOMICUS:** Static analysis, i.e., reasoning based on the perpetuation of the current situation, is good enough to set comparative advantage and specialization "for all time."

Correct Reasoning: In finding the nation's best area of specialization in a *dynamic* setting, laissez faire and free trade are not good guides. Comparative advantage at the moment may lock a nation's economy into specializing in dead-end industries. These are industries that are attractive at the moment but lack quality growth potential. Essentially, these dead-end industries are like infertile trees, with few branches and seeds. *They spawn very few off shoot and descendant industries and technologies.* There are few upstream (tool, equipment), cross stream (similar products, byproducts) and downstream (descendant products) spin-offs. They have little upscale potential. Agriculture, forestry and mining are examples. Hence the term, "dead end" industries.

Free trade theory is nearsighted, not looking beyond the current moment. In truth, its conclusions may not hold as time passes, under dynamic efficiency. The free trade model of Adam Smith and David Ricardo is too restrictive and simplistic. The nation' picks might turn out losers *over time.* It implies a world where technology, innovation, human and physical capital do not improve or degenerate.

Locked In! But, what if a nation gets locked into producing its current comparative advantage good, but that industry is a dead end street? By "dead end street" is meant an industry that is not a mother, brother or cousin to other industries. Few, if any, upstream or downstream spin-offs arise. There are no offspring, no spark of creation for other provider and supplier industries. No cluster of industries such as sprung up around the American automobile industry: steel, tires, batteries, gasoline, upholstery and so on.

Left Back at School?

Educational theory and practice does not subscribe to endless repetition of the same grade when a student is capable of advancement. A student completing the third grade excels at third grade work and would get better and better at it should he be left back to repeat the material. But, potential growth, change and development are ignored if he gets locked in to endless repetition of the same grade. It is a dead end street.

Why should economic theory ascribe endless specialization within a dead-end industry? But, this is the street you can go down if you follow Adam Smith's rule of economic efficiency: don't make it yourself if you can buy it for less at-the-moment.

National security should not be surrendered robotically, slavishly to such "free trade" ideology. (Nor should it be sold for a few bucks. Nor can an international agency such as the World Trade Organization be entrusted with power over our national survival!)

Limiting development to one's abilities at-the-moment *fails to allow for future improvements.* An assessment of the prospects for the United States after gaining independence would have put American comparative advantage in agricultural goods. England would have come up superior in higher valued added manufactured goods, the higher road to development and improved living standards. Acquiescing to these advantages of the moment would have relegated the U.S. to being content to specialize in agriculture, forestry, mining, ship building and shop keeping. In retrospect, those industries are mainly "dead end" industries relative to manufacturing and industrialization.

> Free trade creates winners and losers — and American workers have been among the losers. Free trade has been a major (but not the only) factor behind the erosion in wages and job security among American workers. It has created tremendous prosperity — *but mostly for those at the top*....Since the 1970s, economic orthodoxy has argued for low tariffs, free capital flows, elimination of industrial subsidies, deregulation of labor markets, balanced budgets and low inflation. ...The irony is that during the Industrial Revolution, today's rich countries — Britain, France and the United States — *pursued the very opposite policies*: high tariffs, government investment in industry, financial regulations and fixed values for currencies. Trade expanded, and capital flowed anyway.
>
> [11. Jeff Madrick, "Our Misplaced Faith in Free Trade," 3 October 2014 New York Times Online <http://tinyurl.com/poj4v2w>]

6. FALLACIOUS ECONOMICUS: Yes, free trade didn't do all it promised. I agree. And those dopey trade deals made things worse. Not to mention open borders. Trouble is, there is no good alternative trade policy. What, *economic nationalism?* That means tariffs and protectionism. They smell of fascism, Nazi Germany, Fascist Italy, militaristic Japan trade wars and the Great Depression.

Correct Reasoning: Those nations cited are examples of countries that distorted and twisted nationalism and racism into a Fascist ideology bent on conquest. As discussed earlier, a good idea or policy can be corrupted by carrying it to **excess**. Is the desire for national sovereignty, i.e., self rule, a radical idea? Does it imply the desire for conquest and subjugation of other peoples?   Indeed, **one may argue that the healthy nationalism of the Allied Powers gave them enough "backbone" to defeat the excessive and sick nationalism of the Axis Powers.**

Excess turns good to bad, sweet to sour. In the U.S., Globalism has been carried so far that the nation-State itself is threatened. Globalthink has replaced Nationthink for U.S. policymakers, setting the U.S. on a declining path. Any remedy will involve some hurt, here and abroad. Folks, you do not get something for nothing. "To make an omelet you must break some eggs."

TANSTAAFL! Well, you know the rest. To continue on the current course will involve even greater hurt!

Economic Nationalist Program Has These Features

Economic nationalism, viz., Americanism, is the antidote to Globalism. It is a plea for the **assertion of American Sovereignty**. Here is an IDEAL program:

1. Economic nationalism elevates the nation above narrow, special interests who would have policy serve their selfish ends. Nationalism emphasizes widespread prosperity and rejects the Globalism bible: a) imported **illegal cheap labor** through open borders b) artificially **cheap imports** and c) **offshoring** of manufacturing. Each has been **weaponized for destruction of the nation!** This unholy trinity **destroys industries and jobs,** threatening national security. **Nationalism rejects as unsustainable prosperity based on excessive debt manifested in the budget deficit, the trade deficit, and cheap imports.** Nationalists believe this kind of **artificially derived prosperity at the expense of nationhood is a fool's errand,** ultimately leading to loss of freedom and subservience to foreign power(s). Economic Nationalism aims to reverse the ravages of Globalism. It took hundreds of years for Rome to fall. How much time do we have left?

2. The economy is the mother ship of national security. Economic nationalists assign a primary role to the economy: support national survival. A decimated manufacturing sector cannot fulfill this obligation. Before all else, government must, where possible, restore manufacturing prowess in critical industries.

3. Adopt the long view. The economy must provide and perpetuate the means of national survival, i.e., Guns *and* Butter. All other national goals are secondary. Again, a vibrant manufacturing sector is essential.

4. Re-assert American sovereignty. Make **America First** again. The Prime Directive could be made an operating principle, impacting major decisions.

Beware: The prime directive requires that government policy and private behavior, by action or inaction, do no harm to U.S. national security i.e., the nation and the nation's way of life. Should a conflict arise between the nation and *special interests* in the economy, the nation reigns supreme, even if costs rise and/or profits are sacrificed. **Do no harm to the nation, through action or inaction.**(Thank you, Isaac Asimov). **Indeed, enhance the nation.** No more supercomputer or missile guidance tech sales to possible enemies, simply to make a few bucks, reward a political crony or score points with an overseas buddy. **No more sales of American uranium to Russia.**

5. Stop contributing to the buildup of monster rival nations, e.g., still Red China. Yes, even their civilian economy threatens in many ways! Remember, every good and resource has a direct or indirect military application. Resources are easily shifted from civilian to military use.

6. After national survival, the economy is charged with satisfying wants and encouraging long term, **widespread** prosperity. The emphasis is on *widespread*. Special interests conflicting with the nation must be suppressed, ignored or harnessed to the national good. Notice the hierarchy in the Vulcan motto: live long, *then* prosper. First, one must stay alive!

Beware: In today's political doublespeak, the expression "free trade" is code for furthering globalization, yielding sovereignty and achieving one world governance

7. FALLACIOUS ECONOMICUS: Every producer can get rich by off shoring

production to a low wage country like (still Red) China. Customers can raise their standards of living as cheaper goods come to our shores.

Fallacious Reasoning: Instead of making it here, make it there at a lower cost and sell back here for the same or a similar price. This is a flawless plan for raising profits and shareholder value.

Correct Reasoning: A small group of manufacturers may enrich themselves by firing U.S. workers, leaving the U.S. and relocating to China, India and Mexico, intending to use cheaper labor, then export the goods back to the U.S. (Unfortunate side effect: U.S. workers are forced by cheaper imports to accept lower wages.)

But, the result changes when firms leave *en masse*. Left behind workers are also impoverished customers! **At some point the fallacy of composition kicks in.** How long can high import levels be sustained if customer buying power is emaciated? (The U.S. is the largest importer in the world!) That point is fast approaching, if not here already. Rule one in macro: what goes around comes around. **If low wages (or *no* wages due to job losses) go around, then low spending comes around.** Incomes fall further than prices, cutting *real* incomes. Low wages or no wages suppress U.S. workers-turned-customers' incomes.. With suppressed incomes comes suppressed capacity to buy all goods, domestic and imported, although purchasing favors cheaper imports. Exports no longer "pay" for imports.

Business and consumer credit are called upon to fill the purchasing power gap, i.e., to replace lost income. Standards of living are not enhanced in the U.S. *despite* cheaper imported goods and expanded credit. Unashamed, firms hopscotch the world looking for lower cost production platforms, the infamous "race to the bottom." Vietnam now rivals China in offering cheap labor. So, **off-shoring can be a successful strategy for a few firms but will fail if tried in large numbers because of a customer purchasing power collapse.**

8. FALLA<IOUS <<ONOMI<US: Free trade ideology has "dug in" since the days of Adam Smith publishing the *Wealth of Nations* in 1776. Coming later was the British formal adoption of free trade in the 1850s. The U.S. adoption followed about 100 years later, with similar negative consequences setting in after a time. There is no academic literature preaching against it. And both nations have stuck with it, no? Condemning free trade is like condemning apple pie.

Correct Reasoning: Both nations had to yield their dominant positions mainly because of free trade policies. Historically, Alexander Hamilton and Friedrich List are the foremost spokesmen for U.S. economic nationalism. Both have written extensively in favor of economic nationalism. Currently, *there is a growing body of academic literature condemning free trade as stifling economic opportunity and growth.*

Mt. Rushmore for Globalists?

An ant hill ... with miniature impressions of H.W. Bush, Bill and Hillary Clinton, G.W. Bush, and Barack Obama.

Tariff Policy

9. FALLA<IOUS <<ONOMI<US: Selective re-imposition of import tariffs is a key element in any plan to restore economic nationalism to the U.S. But, new U.S. tariffs are likely to trigger retaliatory tariffs from our trading partners, as did the Smoot-Hawley tariff of 1930. Smoot-Hawley caused the stock market crash of 1929 and reinforced the Great Depression of the 1930's.

Correct Reasoning: First of all, Smoot – Hawley Tariff law passed in June, 1930, eight months *after* the market crash of October 1929. Therefore, it could not have caused the crash, as the law was enacted months later. Yes, other nations reacted and retaliated by raising their tariffs. They resented the massive trade *surplus* the U.S. had *before* enacting the tariff and felt the U.S. was worsening their deficits, "rubbing salt in the wound." But, **total U.S. trade represented less than one percent of U.S. GDP.** Any fall in U.S. exports could not have made a dent in aggregate demand and GDP big enough to perpetuate a great fall.

Revenue tariff. Unfortunately, today, a **protective tariff** is unlikely to be enacted, given the degree of U.S. commitment to Globalism and its subservience to the World Trade Organization (WTO) and NAFTA. But, consider: a tariff of around 10% might be more feasible. In 2015, U.S. **imports** of goods and services stood at around **$2.7 trillion, the largest of any nation!** Goods alone, $2.3T. Other things being equal, a tariff of 10% on just $1 trillion of those goods would bring in tax revenue of $100 billion. That could reduce the budget deficit (approximately $500 billion) by 20%. Would this trigger a trade war? It is doubtful our trade partner beneficiaries would want to mortally wound their benefactor and chief customer? (Another issue: would a revenue tariff trigger *inflation*? No. See Fallacy #13, Chapter Twenty-Nine)

10. FALLACIOUS ECONOMICUS: Restricting *imports* by imposition of a tariff actually backfires and reduces *exports!*

Fallacious Reasoning: On a **circular flow** basis, yes, restricting foreign imports (by quota or tariff) denies purchasing power to our trading partners. They have less money with which to buy our exports.

Correct Reasoning: Restricting imports is indeed an effective way to reduce the trade deficit *without* suffering retaliation from trading partners. Given our massive **trade deficit on manufactured goods of nearly $750 billion**, even a fifty percent cut in the deficit still puts hundreds of billions of dollars *each year* in foreign hands. (Their export earnings are not cut significantly.) In addition to this outflow of dollars there is a **stock of dollars in foreign hands,** available to buy U.S. goods. They are awash with nearly $3 trillion dollars and dollar financial assets.

Given all the years of a merchandise trade deficit, these partners have chosen not to expand their current buying of U.S goods. Instead, major trading partners, especially (still Red) China and the OPECs, have concentrated on using trade earned dollars to acquire **structural components** of the U.S. economy: already standing assets, mineral deposits, other resources, corporations, toll roads, high tech companies and financial institutions. The latter do not count as currently produced goods, exports. Restricting imports from these trading partners would seem to have little effect on their ability to buy our exports. What is lacking is their *willingness* to buy our exports.

Trade Rules Worsen the Massive U.S. Trade Deficit

While the United States has a corporate income tax, our trade rivals use a **value-added tax.** At each level of production, a tax is imposed on the value added to the product. *Under the rules of global trade, nations may rebate VAT levies on exports, and impose the equivalent of a VAT on imports.*

> Assume a VAT that adds up to 15 percent of the cost of a new car in Japan. If Toyota ships 1 million cars to the United States valued at $20,000 each, $20 billion worth of Toyotas, they can claim a rebate of the VAT of $3,000 on each car, or $3 billion - a powerful incentive to export. But each U.S. car arriving at the Yokohama docks will have 15 percent added to its sticker price to make up for Japan's VAT. This system amounts to a foreign subsidy on exports to the United States and a foreign tax on imports from America. Uncle Sam gets hit coming and going.
>
> [12] *Italics and bold mine.* Pat Buchanan, "How to Bring Manufacturing Back Home" 29 September 2006 *Patrick J. Buchanan, Official Website* <http://tinyurl.com/pvmxzpg>]

Not only is the Chinese currency **artificially undervalued**, but the Value Added Tax system also works against the U.S. trade balance. Read all about it:

Are the trade rules discussed in the box above emblematic of free trade? No, it is Globalism in action and the rules are stacked against the U.S. Consider these rules:

> *U.S. exports* are, in effect, slapped with a surcharge, the VAT of foreign made competitive goods, when they reach foreign shores. This jacks up the import price of U.S. goods. This makes U.S. exports more expensive than when they leave American shores. Demand for U.S. exports is reduced accordingly.

Meanwhile, consider *U.S. imports* from a country utilizing Value Added Tax (VAT).

> U.S. imports are *reduced* in price by the VAT (of the exporting country) as they leave foreign ports. This creates an unfair advantage to foreign exporter in a VAT country. This works well for the U.S. importer but bad for overall trade balance of U.S.

By this practice, American exports are more costly and foreign buyers are *discouraged.* The VAT policy widens the price gap between U.S. exports and U.S. imports. Imports from VAT countries appear cheaper and are *encouraged* by trade rules. Today, nations employing VAT taxes include (still Red) China, Japan, and the European Union countries. Should the U.S. adopt the VAT tax or find another way to eliminate this harmful practice?

Appendix One

Backdoor to eliminating immigration caps?

The Proposed TPP (Trans-Pacific Partnership)

The TPP (Trans-Pacific Partnership) which is an agreement to manage trade and investment on behalf of large corporations, will put downward pressure on wages of workers in the United States, and will likely lead to growing trade deficits and job displacement.

[13. Robert E. Scott, "TPP Agreement Will Be Bad For Workers in the U.S. and Other Member Countries" 5 October, 2015 *Economic Policy Institute* <http://tinyurl.com/onb9a8k>]

Beware: Critics have warned that the TPP deal opens a backdoor to massive immigration from the countries involved, avoiding legal maximums of U.S. law. Business visas (L-1) with no numerical caps would accompany in-shored businesses. Remember, treaties are the law of the land, the equivalent of constitutional provisions. [14. James Swoyer, 6 Nov. 2015 <http://www.breitbart.com/big-government//tpp-trade-deal-hits-u-s-immigration-law-massive-way>/]

Appendix Two

Works Critical of the U.S. Open Economy Policy

Ravi Batra. *The Myth of Free Trade: The Pooring of America.* New York: Touchstone Books, 1994.

Sherrod Brown, Congressman. *Myths of Free Trade: Why American Trade Policy Has Failed.* New York: The Free Press, 2006.

Pat Buchanan. *The Great Betrayal.* New York: Little, Brown 1st edition, 1998.

Ian Fletcher. *Free Trade Doesn't Work: What Should Replace It and Why.* [Paperback Edition]. Wash, D.C.: U.S. Business and Industry Council, 2011.

Ian Fletcher. (video) *Free Traded Doesn't Work.* 16 July, 2010. <http://www.c-spanvideo.org/program/294588-4>

John Fonte. *Sovereignty or Submission: Will Americans Rule Themselves or be Ruled By Others?* New York: Encounter Books, 2011.

Bill Gertz. *The China Threat: How the People's Republic Threatens America.* Wash., D.C.: Regnery Publishing, 2002.

Friedrich List. *The National System of Political Economy.* 2011< http://tinyurl.com/jghppno>

Paul Craig Roberts. "Off Shoring has Destroyed the Economy," 30 May 2011 *Vdare* <http://vdare.com/roberts/110530_globalism.htm>

Jane Sasseen. "Economists Rethink Free Trade," 30 January 2008 *Business Week* http://tinyurl.com/pawxb9z

---

Appendix Three

For those with advanced curiosity, a question:

Is it desirable and realistic to maximize *absorption* (IMPORTS minus EXPORTS)?

BUT, if your answer is YES, be certain absorption has these attributes:

a) is sustainable, long term (given U.S. balance of payments constraints),

b) is consistent with national security (strategic industries, occupations, technologies and resources cannot be degraded, discarded or destroyed)

c) is compatible with long term, robust economic growth.

Appendix Four

NAFTA, Agreement or Treaty?

U.S. trade agreements such as the North American Free Trade (NAFTA), World Trade Organization agreements, and bilateral free trade agreements (FTAs) have been approved by *majority* vote of each house rather than by two-thirds vote of the Senate—that is, they have been treated as *congressional-executive agreements* rather than as treaties. [So say government lawyers ... see footnote below]

[15. Jane M. Smith, Daniel T. Shedd and Brandon J. Murrill. "Why Certain Trade Agreements Are Approved as Congressional-Executive Agreements Rather Than Treaties" April 15, 2013 Congressional *Research Service* <https://www.fas.org/sgp/crs/misc/97-896.pdf>]

It is difficult to free fools from chains they revere .... -Voltaire

Appendix Five

Cuba, Cubism, Cubist, Cubes

Let's listen in on the pros and cons of normalizing relations with Cuba.

Pro: Lifting the embargo will renew trade between Cuba and the U.S. This will accelerate the demise of Communism.

Con: Trading with (still Red) China and Vietnam for more than thirty years has not caused them to shed the Communist system and way of life. Why should Cuba be different? *These Castros are not convertible!* Castro daughter Mariela has asserted, "The US is dreaming if they think Cuba will return to capitalism."

[15. Doug Giles, "US Is Dreaming If They Think Cuba Will Return to Capitalism" 9 December 2014 *ClashDaily* <http://clashdaily.com/2014/12/castros-daughter-us-dreaming-think-cuba-will-return-capitalism/>]

Pro: It's about time the U.S. normalized relations with Cuba. Normalization would aid family re-unification for Cuban Americans who left relatives behind after the revolution.

Con: Sure (*wink, wink*). The real reason is to encourage Cubans to add to the flood of cheap labor flowing into America, depressing already low wages. Relieving them of some surplus population will make it appear Communism is creating a higher standard of living in Cuba.

Pro: It has been fifty years since Cuba has been off limits to Americans. The two peoples ought to get to know each other once again.

Con: Why? To reward another repressive, hate American regime? Why, so some fat cat American can smoke a Cuban cigar and sip on a rum drink?

Pro: Maybe they will welcome some American industry to re-locate there, helping to cut costs.

Con: Why? So American companies will enjoy a bonanza? Cuba will be another off shore location American industries and jobs can flock to. Look for casinos and hotels to lead the way.

Score: Cuba 1, U.S. 0

Appendix Six

The Main Event: Saturday Night at the Garden!

Free Trade or No Free Trade?
Heavyweight Championship Bout

Adam Smith, Free Trader   versus   Alexander Hamilton, Opponent

Winner Determines Future of America!

Next week: David Ricardo takes on Friedrich List

Get your tickets now!

Chapter Twenty-Five
Globalism and Globalization Fallacies

Resistance is futile ... you will be absorbed.
—Borg Commander, *Star Trek, Next Generation*

G LOBALISM is the latest (and greatest?) incarnation of so-called "free trade" doctrine being force fed to Americans. It extends beyond goods, to free trade in services, harmonization of laws, delegation of sovereignty to corporate committees and international organizations. Add the unrestricted mobility of labor (read, open borders) and money capital. Globalism has **political goals** (worldwide centralized governance) that supersede Globalization (global dispersion and subdivision of economic activity). **The record shows the adoption of Globalism has coincided with the onset of American relative economic decline** since the mid 1970s.

Mum on Trade is the Word from Politicians!

Forget Social Security: international trade issues seem to be the real third rail of American politics. The Republicans and Democrats are using their propaganda machines to suppress all discussions of our trade policies. Their motto is: see no evil, hear no evil, speak no evil. They want to avoid such a discussion at all costs, because those with the money and power to fund their campaigns are profiting from selling out America. They fear a backlash from the American public if they figure out what is really going on. During the 2012 Republican candidates debate one candidate came on stage speaking Chinese! Donald Trump is the only candidate to consistently raise the trade issue in the 2016 campaign.

[1. Bold mine. J.R. Martin, *Selling U.S. Out,* Edina, MN: Beaver's Pond Press, 2012, p. 116]

---

1. FALLACIOUS ECONOMICUS: Open borders are no threat to U.S. national security.

Corollary Fallacious Statement: Open borders present no threat to U.S. living standards or national security. Only honest, hard working job seekers cross the border.

Correct reasoning on national security. Aside from the ongoing threat to the **standard of living,** open borders present an immediate threat to the **common cultural core and national security.** Few economists would disagree there is, in effect, a bottomless pit of folks who want to come to the U.S., attracted by jobs and assorted free social goodies. Other folks have announced they would like to come here to destroy the U.S. Here is a radical idea: why not believe them and take the most elementary precautions? Duh? Why jeopardize national security by leaving an open border for a cheaper nanny or day laborer? Yes, open borders present a serious threat to national security.

Dereliction of Duty by Federal Government: Welcome, All Comers!

The massive in-migration of illegals has proceeded with the tacit consent and sometimes overt approval of the Federal government. However, the U.S. Constitution *requires* the Federal government to undertake the defense of the nation. Without a defense, the independent nation may lose its sovereignty, i.e., the people lose control of their own destiny. Outsiders would rule the U.S.

Article IV, Section 4 of the U.S. Constitution reads, "The United States [the FEDERAL government] *shall guarantee* to every State in this Union a Republican Form of Government, *and shall protect each of them against invasion.*" [Italics mine].

[2. "The US constitution online" 2 Jan 2014.<www.usconstitution.net/const.html>]

MAJOR CONCEPT: Note the emphatic and declarative nature of the responsibility as spelled out in the Constitution! This is not an optional activity of the Federal government, to be pursued on weekends and after regular work hours ... it is a mandatory, every day, 24/7 obligation!

The argument for border control focuses on the *excessive* number of illegal entries, too many to be assimilated, even if we tried! If not a military invasion the influx of illegals, 10 to 20 million people, is an *economic and cultural* invasion. It is a form of *gain by conquest,* appropriating jobs and services formerly reserved mainly for legal residents and citizens. **Excess immigration *without* assimilation is colonization, threatening national destruction via fragmentation of the culture.**

Correct reasoning on living standard. Though battered and bruised over the last forty years, U.S. wages still *exceed* third world levels. That wage gap, along with free social goodies, remains a tremendous magnet for entry by outsiders. Coming in large numbers, year after year, the *excessive* immigrant cohorts help depress the wages of earlier immigrants, as well as native born workers.

2. FALLA<IOUS <<ONOMI<US: Open borders are a disaster. There are billions of folks in third world countries who want the advantages of living in the U.S. They will generate a *never-ending* stream of indigent, illegal entrants to the U.S.

Correct Reasoning: Don't worry, folks. There will be a large, but *not* a "never ending" stream of illegal entrants. Economic theory predicts it will end when the *relative* wage differential and social service advantages of coming to the U.S. have been destroyed. That is, the **inward flow will stop when U.S. wages have been driven down so low they nearly match (rising) third world wage levels**. Also contributing to the end of entry: when the *relative* advantage in social services (medical care, schooling, welfare, housing, retirement benefits, and other free goodies) has evaporated. These disastrous effects will be reached after a massive but not unlimited stream of legal and illegal entrants. Then, the U.S. winds up being somewhere between a first world country and a third world country. Should this script be acted out, we can kiss goodbye American prosperity as well as current and future living standards.

The Factor Price Equalization Model in Action

Assume barriers to migration between low and high wage countries are removed, as well as trade barriers. Opening the borders between a low and   high wage nation is like blowing up a dam. Workers gush over the border from the low wage nation and flood the high wage nation. Such are the predictions of the renowned Factor Price Equalization Model. **The original wage gap narrows and, *theoretically*, migration continues until the gap is eliminated and the wages equalize. For those in the high wage area, this usually means a lower wage.**

Workers' cross-migration tends to lower the wage in formerly high wage area (U.S.) and raise the wage in the formerly low wage area.

In addition, firms from the formerly high wage (U.S.) area gradually reallocate to the low wage area. This is a slower movement than the worker migration. This tends to raise the wage in the low wage area and lower it in the high wage area.

After integration of high wage and low wage areas:

Who are the net gainers from migration?

> ➤   Formerly low wage workers now living and earning in the high wage area.

> ➤   Firms in U.S. now accessing labor at lower wage rates.

> ➤   U.S firms relocated in the low wage area.

Who are the net losers from migration?

> ➤   Formerly high wage workers in U.S. now forced to share social benefits, surrender jobs and/or accept lower wages.

> ➤   Firms in formerly low wage area now forced to pay higher wages to retain workers. *But, beware: wages need not rise if there is a substantial cushion of unemployed job seekers to access.*

Real world examples: 1) Re-unification of Berlin and Germany after fall of communism, 2) U.S. entry into NAFTA and 3) Formation of European Union. All these events signaled the movement of workers from low to high wage areas. An invasion of cheaper goods puts the same downward pressure on higher goods prices and higher wages. **Sleep lightly, my friend!**

[3. Italics mine. "Factor Price Equalization" 18 June 2014 *About.Com Economics* < http://tinyurl.com/omm85f9 >]

Open borders are a core component of Globalism. But, open borders are bad news for:

> American workers (through lower wages and job losses).
> American taxpayers (through higher taxes for social services).
> Ordinary American citizens through increased competition for public services (schools, hospitals and law enforcement) and housing.

To the extent that open borders weaken the economy - the mother ship of a strong military - they also damage national defense and national security.

Question: Do open borders presage a fragmentation of the U.S. into a hodgepodge of immigrant enclaves?

Economic Nationalism is NOT Isolationism

Economic nationalism does not reject international trade nor does it require isolationism. International trade has been going on for thousands of years and brought benefits to countless people. Economic nationalism supports international trade. But, support for international trade has limits. **Trade and migration policy must support the nation and its way of life, not undermine it.** As with all things, an excess of a good thing is a bad thing. Economic nationalism rejects trade, trade deals and migrations that only serve special interests, infringe on U.S. sovereignty and threaten national security. **Economic nationalism applauds trade deals that raise the current and future standard of living on a wide front while strengthening the nation. As such, economic nationalism stands in stark contrast to Globalism.**

---

3. FALLACIOUS ECONOMICUS: Open borders -- eventually, no borders -- a key feature of Globalism, do not infringe on the sovereignty of a nation.

Correct Reasoning: Open borders and national sovereignty are a contradiction; they are **incompatible!** Open borders are a surrender of sovereignty to whom? The answer: to any outsider who decides to enter. The nation no longer rules itself. It is ruled, instead, by the whims, fancies and plots of other nations and peoples. No longer in the hands of the American people, the control of entry at the border shifts to outsiders. Self rule (national sovereignty) is surrendered and the nation's common core is put at risk of dilution from unscreened, unchecked illegal foreign entry.

In the "no borders" iteration, the nation's border is reduced to a mere line on a map, no longer signaling a genuine divide. Everyone would have the right to go everywhere. **What once was a nation of value rich, spiritually connected and spirited countrymen threatens to degenerate into a collection of immiserized workhouse hired hands and their masters.**

Things to Come (H.G. Wells): Wings Over the World

The new world (dis)order. The end game of Globalism is the abandonment of sovereign nation-States and the adoption of a **one world governing system, viewed as a panacea for the world's ills.** National sovereignty is being chipped away, trade deal by trade deal. As a policy, Globalism advocates the free movement of more than just goods. It seeks no government restrictions on the movement of labor and financial assets. **Everyone free to go everywhere.** Artificial impediments to international trade and movement of people are to be eliminated or reduced. Laws governing trade are to be "harmonized." Disagreements are to be settled by international tribunals of one sort or another. Quotas and tariffs on goods and immigration quotas and qualifications are to be gradually eliminated. American sovereignty is being delegated to quasi-governmental international committees by so-called *free trade* deals. The world is to be one gigantic integrated market for goods, people and money.

Ultimately, the nations of the world will come under some form of global governance. Resistance is futile! You will be absorbed! The sovereignty of nations is to be eliminated or severely restricted. Sovereignty is to be "pooled." By some wild chance, could "pooled" be a euphemism for *surrendered?*

In other words, Americans will no longer control their own destiny. **Home rule dies and the rule of outsiders begins.** Is this fear mongering and xenophobia? Is it too farfetched? Wake up, the rule of outsiders has already begun ... thanks to our open borders!

Globers promise this will bring greater prosperity to the world and the U.S.A. But, *talk is cheap.* **The record shows Globalism has inflicted severe if not mortal wounds on U.S. economic dominance, standard of living and national security.** Recall: a mighty military requires the support of a mighty economy, not one crippled by off shoring, open borders and free trade. In short, open borders are incompatible with prosperity, economic security, national defense and homeland security.

Globalization versus Globalism

4. FALLACIOUS ECONOMICUS: The terms Globalization and Globalism are interchangeable terms. They have the same meaning.

Correct Reasoning: No! Globalization and Globalism are related but *not* synonymous. Consider these points of difference:

➢ Globalism is an ideology, a modern intellectual construct.

➢ Globalization is a factual reality, evolved *spontaneously* over thousands of years.

➢ Globalism is a discretionary, *deliberate* policy choice for nation.

➢ A degree of Globalization is inevitable. As a choice, Globalism is not inevitable.

➢ Globalism abhors the system of nation-States. Globalists intend to end it.

➢ Globalism favors open or no borders, free trade, people movement and Global governance.

➢ **Islam's political goals include a worldwide Caliphate, i.e., worldwide Islamic rule ... Globalism!**

Globalization is the world economy as it is evolving. It is a fact of international *economic* life. **Globalism** deals with the world economy *and* world governance. Key aspects of Globalization can be reversed –especially illegal migration, off-shoring and lop-sided trade -- should Globalism lose favor..

Political and economic objectives. On the other hand, Globalism has political *and* economic objectives. It is an advocacy ideology aimed at advancing Globalization and, ultimately, creating a world government to service it. For the U.S., Globalism has been the policy of choice the past fifty years. Globalism wants the international economy under one worldwide governing apparatus.

If this goal is achieved, kiss goodbye American sovereignty.

Stoking the Fire

What came first, Globalism or Globalization, the chicken or the egg? No doubt Globalization emerged spontaneously without the help of Globalism. After all, international trade has gone on for thousands of years.

Today, Globalism supercharges the advance of Globalization.

Globalization is a fact of life, a reality of today and tomorrow's world. Globalization owes a debt to division of labor, economies of scale, and efficient, containerized shipping. A giant debt is owed to standardization of parts, arriving with the industrial revolution. Standardization enables goods to be made in "bits and pieces" all over the world, then brought together at various assembly points, also scattered around the world.   Like it or not, Globalization is here to stay. It was born before the 18th century and spread more or less spontaneously. It slowly nurtured in the 20th and is being brought to maturity in the 21st.   Technological and managerial advances allow the *subdivision* of finance, production, distribution and consumption on a global scale. It includes the world-wide investment in and financing of those activities.

Globalists promote free trade. Central to the advance of Globalization is the gradual reduction and removal of government barriers to the movement of goods, people and financial assets around the world. Bye, bye to tariffs, quotas, immigration limits and other barriers. International legal institutions and agreements like the World Trade Organization facilitate the settlement of disputes.

Free trade backfires. With the advance of Globalization, laissez-faire and free trade started working *against* U.S. economic dominance. It turned from best friend to worst enemy. One might say **laissez-faire has been carried to excess**: followed for **too long** and allowed to range **too far** as cost minimization, profit maximization, and the bottom line have become the new Gods of enterprise. Economic patriotism has become a forgotten relic of an earlier era.

Karl Marx and Free Trade, Redux

Karl Marx favored international free trade for *exactly* this reason: free trade would *widen* the income differential from high to low, within the trading nations and between the trading nations. This would inflame the proletariat, provoking revolution sooner rather than later. A consummation devoutly to be wished ... if your name is Karl Marx!

Political Conservatism versus Economic Nationalism

Do not assume *political conservatives* are *economic nationalists.* For economic nationalists, the top priority is economic nationalism: having the economy support the people's way of life (culture, including language), promote widespread prosperity, national security (including secure borders) and national sovereignty.

False Friend: The Wall Street Journal

Consider the Wall Street Journal (WSJ), paragon of conservatism and booster of market capitalism. It has long advocated open borders, embraced NAFTA and the World Trade Organization. It encouraged industry killing cheap imports, cheap labor and other globalist suicidal concoctions. It has done so despite the damage to the American standard of living wrought by these policies. It's all good for business, you see. Apparently, for the WSJ, the U.S. is just a giant workhouse. These conservative Globalists at the Wall Street Journal Editorial Board do not care about the damage to the nation's economy done by their policy endorsements. According to the WSJ, providing for national security and improving the American standard of living have to take a back seat to *maximizing shareholder value ... globally.*

Beware the enemy within ... Cicero

---

5. FALLA<IOU5 E<ONOMI<U5: Globalism and Globalization are not responsible for widening the unequal distribution of income *within and between* nations.

Related **FALLA<IOU5 E<ONOMI<U5:** Globalism and Globalization are not responsible for torpedoing the American, middle class standard of living.

Correct Reasoning: Yes, there may be other factors involved in American decline. But, Globalism and globalization have played the starring roles in this tragedy, and the final act has yet to be played. *Globalism has unleashed the dogs of capitalism by turning long time American friend laissez-faire into an enemy.* TANSTAAFL! Capitalism has degenerated into crapitalism and created the American manufacturing Diaspora! Off-shoring and a manic quest for cheap labor – the "race to the bottom" - have become the prime goals.

A shrinking middle class and middle class share of total income is a *symptom* of American decline, not the cause. Again, most of the blame can be assigned to the adoption of Globalism, enabling the gutting of economic opportunity for the native born, working middle class.

"All the kings horses and men," i.e., fiscal and monetary policies, cannot reverse the damage done by Globalist "free trade" and open borders!

6. FALLACIOUS ECONOMICUS: Since its inception in the 1960s, Globalism has brought prosperity and a higher standard of living to the U.S.
Correct Reasoning: Poppycock. Twaddle. Buffalo chips. Read the newspapers. Globalism has turned good friend laissez-faire into a heartless, disloyal destructive beast. An *excess* of freedom to range, unimpeded, world-wide has capitalists into crapitalists and bankers into banksters. Contrary to its vaunted promises, U.S. prosperity has taken a gigantic hit from Globalism, as gains were concentrated in the top income group while the middle class withered on the proverbial vine.

The standard of living, general prosperity, national security and American sovereignty have all degenerated during the Globalist era, begun in the 1960s. Off shoring has spearheaded an American manufacturing Diaspora, scattering production and jobs worldwide ... with the blessing of Uncle Sam! Moreover, given open borders, the suppression of wages will continue until the wage and benefit differential between native and immigrant is narrowed, meaning a significant *fall* in American wages. This narrowing gap between American and foreign wages foreshadows a continuing decline in the American standard of living. Amnesty, if enacted, will run up the white flag at the border. It will accelerate illegal entry into the U.S. With it comes further decline in the current and future American standard of living of the middle class.

Pincer Movement: Cheap Goods and Cheap Labor

Open borders for workers. The American standard of living has been caught in a pincer movement bent on eroding it. Open borders have enabled an **invasion of an economic worker army** along the Southern border of the U.S., not to mention the entry of all sorts of social parasites, criminals and disease carriers. The assault is relentless. Employers welcome this flow, but competing native workers see doom!

This invading economic army has used the open border, as well. This invading army has suppressed *already low wages in a host of low wage occupations* including agriculture, hospitality, meat packing and landscaping. As stated above, the suppression of wages will continue until the wage (and benefit) differential is narrowed, meaning lowered standard of living for competing American workers. BTW: Terrorists get a free pass, too.

Open borders for goods: the Trojan horse, a false friend. The other pincer gripping American welfare is the trickster called cheap goods, modeled after the ancient Trojan horse. **Artificially cheap imports of goods from off shored American factories in Asia suppress wages, destroy jobs and competing U.S. industries.** Real wages fell in the mid 1970s and have stagnated ever since. Cheap labor and cheap goods are the gifts ... that keep on taking!

These are the devil's details. Do not be fooled by statements that GDP is up and total trade is up. **Lower standards of living and increasing economic insecurity are the true legacy of forty years of Globalism. (Still Red) China, wet nursed by America is poised to displace the U.S. as the world's largest economy ... and dominant nation.**

➤ Ever rising income and wealth inequality in the U.S. is a reality.
➤ U.S. economic growth sputters and coughs while poverty increases.
➤ The struggle between adversaries Guns and Butter intensifies. Butter advocates dominate as politicians pander to illegals for votes.

An impoverished American family living in a shanty, 1936 ...redux in 2036?

Daddy, You Cut My Allowance

Daddy?

Yes, child.

Daddy, you cut my allowance.

I had to do that, my child.

Why, Daddy?

Because I lost my good job. Then I had trouble finding this new one. And it pays less.

Daddy, I can't afford to buy ice cream and candy like I used to. I am a kid, but I had a certain, what is it called? Yes, a certain standard of living ... and mine is falling!

Your standard of living is falling, my child, and so is mine.

But, why, Daddy?

The monster came and is gobbling it up!

What monster, Daddy?

An experiment gone horribly wrong, who escaped from the economics laboratory. Now, it is stomping around America, trashing the American economy, gobbling up your standard of living and mine...The "townspeople" don't know what hit them!

Globenstein? Why do such monsters exist, Daddy?

Globenstein was deliberately created by Uncle Sam. He cobbled together Globenstein from bits and pieces of defunct economic theories about free trade. Then he scavenged around in the graveyard of academia. There he found some pretentious Utopian babble about Globalism, world peace and world government. He mixed them in and... poof- out came Globenstein!

Daddy, just how evil is Globenstein?

Well, actually, my child, not to frighten you, but Globenstein is a *nation killer.*

A nation killer?

Yes, he has already bludgeoned the great American economy into an unrecognizable shadow of itself. He got suckered by cheap imports, spawning the American manufacturing Diaspora. He opened our borders, inflicting unfair competition on our workers. But, that is not enough for this insatiable monster.

You mean there is more, Daddy?

Yes. *He wants to eliminate the sovereign nation as a political unit.* Yes, he is a nation killer. Yes, if he gets his way, no more self-rule for America. Governance by invisible international committee.

When the nation-State is merged with others, out go our freedoms and way of life.

Now, you are scaring me, Daddy. I thought Uncle Sam was supposed to be watching out for us, seeing that we prosper?

Yes, child, I thought so, too.

Couldn't you stop him, Daddy?

No, my child, he is too big, too strong and had too many friends to fight, even for Daddy. Apparently, and sadly, he is also pretty stupid to buy into the trade practices that helped dethrone Britain as the world's dominant economic power.

How did the monster get so big and strong, Daddy?

Well, child, as I said, Uncle Sam created Globenstein. Then he was pampered, fed and cared for by the main stream media, the Ivy League and progressive "think tanks." So, the monster grew big and fat. He grows, even today, biting off pieces of our economy and spewing them over the world. Then he was babied by the politicians, progressive think tankers and "trannie" corporations and imposed gradually on the populace, over a fifty year period. Oh, and don't forget Hollywood and the big banks. Just about everybody except ordinary folks is in on this scam or has been fooled by it.

I don't think I like those people, Daddy. They made you cut my allowance and ruined my little kid standard of living.

Yes, child, and ruined my adult standard of living, too.

Group of Breaker boys in Pittston, Pennsylvania, 1911. Child labor was very common in U.S. and Europe in late 19th and early 20th century.

7. FALLACIOUS ECONOMICUS: Globalism and free trade brought cheaper goods and with them a higher standard of living to Americans.

Correct Reasoning: Such was the unfulfilled promise of Globalism. Globalism hurt ordinary folks more than it helped. Yes, at the moment, *some* of the goods were cheaper when compared head with head with their American counterparts. What benefit are cheap goods when one lost his job? Certain industries were targeted: steel, autos, textiles, shoes, consumer electronics being the most prominent. Trade rules and **currency manipulation** worked against American exporters and favored foreign imports. Demand shifted "big time" from domestic to imported goods.

The trade may have been *free* but was not *fair*. Goods from (still Red) China were artificially cheap due to **currency manipulation** and government **subsidies** to exporters. Extortionist oil import bills compounded the trade deficit and dollar outflow problem for 40 years. Huge trade deficits became routine for over thirty years, enabling the trading partners to accumulate a large stock of U.S. dollar reserves. Soon those reserves are bounced back to the U.S., gobbling up command and control of U.S. properties, businesses, and technologies. In addition, opinion leaders in government, academia and communications have been targeted for influence. Treasury bonds found a ready market in foreign buyers as some trade deficit dollars were recycled to the U.S. through the capital markets.

The Rest of the Price: U.S. road tolls(Indiana) and parking meter revenue (Chicago) being sold to foreign companies by revenue hungry localities: In retrospect, the *point of sale* price for cheap imports was a mere **down payment** for another "bill" to follow, specifying the rest of the price. Only this time the nation as a whole will pay the rest of the price. The **loss of command and control** of strategic private and public assets, companies and resources is the rest of the price for what were supposed to be cheaper imports. (Thanks to Michael Savage for this insight.) **Question: Were cheaper goods just a trick, a scam, a Trojan horse to later gain control of key parts of the American economy? Still think Globalism is a good idea, given the U.S. government and people can be so easily blinded, scammed and suckered?**

8. FALLACIOUS ECONOMICUS: It doesn't matter what goods are imported or exported. It is the total of exports and the total of imports that matters. Potato chips or computer chips; the goods involved are irrelevant.

Correct Reasoning: Computer chips are more essential to national defense than are potato chips, crude oil more important than olive oil and real cars more important than toy cars. Get the idea? The content of trade *does* matter.

Question: Is the U.S/world better off with Globalization?

Bastion of Conservatism Favors Globalism

The notorious "conservative" Wall Street Journal could not be more explicit about its advocacy for Globalism than the call for open borders, began thirty years ago! "If Washington still wants to 'do something' about immigration, we propose a five-word constitutional amendment: **There shall be open borders.**" Same stance today!

[4. Robert L. Bartley, Editorial "In Praise of Huddled Masses" 3 July 1984 *Wall Street Journal Editorial* < http://tinyurl.com/bgv52rh >]

---

9. FALLACIOUS ECONOMICUS: The spread of Globalization has enabled many developing nations, such as China and India, to narrow the gap between rich and poor.

Correct Reasoning: The data indicate otherwise. From a report released on January 29, 2014:

> The UNDP report said income *inequality increased* by 11 percent in developing countries over the two decades between 1990 and 2010. The majority of households in developing countries — **more than 75 percent of those nations' populations — are living today in societies where income is more unequally distributed than it was in the 1990s,** the report said....The *widening* income gap comes as some major developing countries - such as China and India - have seen strong economic growth and an overall increase in national wealth. But that wealth has not been evenly distributed, *which has contributed to greater inequality in those societies.* (Italics mine)

[5. Bold mine. Louis Charbonneau. "U.N. Sounds Alarm on Worsening Global Income" 29 June 2014 *Reuters* <http://www.reuters.com/article/global-economy-un-idUSL2N0L317K20140129>]

10. FALLACIOUS ECONOMICUS: For the U.S., there is no connection between the *trade* deficit and *budget* deficit.

Fallacious Reasoning: The trade deficit deals with international trade whereas the budget deficit involves a totally different, purely financial process. There is no connection.

Correct Reasoning: They are interconnected. *Trade* deficits give foreigners the dollars to buy bonds and finance our *budget* deficit. This is, in effect, a re-cycling of the dollars back to the U.S. If there were no trade deficit, (still Red) China, Japan and other nations would not earn the dollars needed to buy U.S. bonds. Nor would they have the enormous dollar holdings needed to acquire other dollar denominated financial and real assets.

Running on fumes. Trifecta of debt. Digging deeper reveals deeper problems! This does not mean we should continue to run trade deficits so we can finance our budget deficits! Both *continuing* deficits signal fundamental problems with our economy. The recurring Federal **budget deficit** tells us recurring incomes are not sufficient to generate the level of taxes needed for recurring government goods and social services spending. The **trade deficit** signals we have become addicted to *borrowing* artificially cheap foreign goods, as **our exports no longer earn enough to pay for all imports.** Payment to cover the deficit is with U.S. dollars. **Household debt** has soared.

Is the U.S.A. for Sale?

Cheerleaders for Globalism apologize, "Don't worry about the trade deficit ... we have the goods and they have the money, and it's the goods that are important." They tattle on as if there were no negative consequences from the accumulation of U.S. dollars in foreign hands. The implication is the U.S. can disavow, i.e., fail to honor, its IOU's when foreigners arrive to buy **command and control** of this company, that property ... or the country at large. But, bear in mind these foreign holders of U.S. dollars are no fools. Have they been "buying insurance" against this eventuality by using $ to curry favor with the powers that be in America, namely, the political, economic and cultural elite?

Others say all those dollars in foreign hands in foreign lands can buy influence among U.S. government officials. In that case, renouncing our IOU's would not be an option and America would be for sale. (See page 198 on absorption for other aspects of Globalism.)

Cain and Abel in Utopia

11. FALLACIOUS ECONOMICUS: The end object of the Globalist movement will be *one government, worldwide.* A world without borders is the Globalist goal. Once achieved, everyone will live under the same tent; nations will surrender their sovereignty to a worldwide unelected, governance body. **Glocialism** shall reign. Jobs, income, and wealth will be redistributed from haves to have-nots in an equitable manner. Wars will end once worldwide unified governance is achieved. We will be "over the rainbow."

Fallacious Reasoning: Under one governance people will learn to care about one another. They will be compelled to share more equally with one another. The economic motive for war will be eliminated. Then, war will be abolished and humanity will have peace at last. Everyone will live happily ever after.

Correct Reasoning: Sounds like a fairy tale ... and it is. The claim that one world government will bring world peace is an unproven assertion based on a distorted view of the real world. Everyone living under the same authority or even the same roof does not guarantee peace and tranquility. **Fact: there are**

not enough *haves* in the world to rescue all the *have-nots* from poverty. The lifeboat would sink! Unified nations have had their civil wars. Family members have killed each other. Cain killed Abel (how?)

Unsatisfied want will spark discontent. Discontent will fester and cause unrest. Rebellion against undemocratic, unified governance is likely. There are many types of peace: peace with surrender and subservience (Germans and Japanese after World War II), peace without freedom, dignity or joy (slavery), and peace with victory and freedom. Which type of peace is promised by Globalism?

Some Rotten Fruits of the Globalist Vine

U.S. *real* wages have barely increased since 1974, even as American worker productivity doubled. Cheap imported goods and cheap imported labor have the American worker in a deadly pincer movement. **In effect, lower median *nominal* wages due to occupational degeneration were not offset by cheaper imports.** This translates into a fall in *real* wages for a large swath of the U.S. labor force. No doubt the drop in real wages further translates into a decline in the current and future standard of living, SOL.

> ➤ **"Since Bush I [1988], we have run $12 trillion in trade deficits, $4 trillion with China. ... the U.S. has lost 50,000 factories and a third of its manufacturing jobs."[6]**

> ➤ **Low wage** American workers, including earlier immigrants, continue to be swamped by even **lower** wage immigrants, legal and illegal.

> ➤ Manufacturing workers, many unionized, displaced by trade and off shoring have taken significant pay cuts in more competitive labor markets.

> ➤ The **inequality** between rich and poor in America has expanded to levels not seen since the robber baron era. International inequality has expanded in the Globalist era, as well.[7]

> ➤ In the minds of many outsiders, migrating to the U.S. has evolved from an (optional) privilege into a God-given right.

> ➤ Banks have grown **"too big to fail,"** despite the "fix" of Dodd-Frank legislation. Failure of *one* big bank threatens world financial security! Duh?

> ➤ Dubious financial "investments" have been devised and unleashed on the world. De-regulated U.S. banksters and broksters spread these scams.

A trifecta of unsustainable debt (household, Federal budget and trade deficit debt) has been marshaled to stave off steeper, faster decline. Aside from the damage to the greatest economy in the world, the continuance of the United States as a sovereign nation has been put in jeopardy. **Failure of Uncle Sam to push assimilation of new arrivals threatens morphing immigration into colonization.** Multiculturalism has been a flack for de-nationalizing the U.S. Fragmentation of the nation would be welcomed by Globalists. **A *fragmented* nation becomes, in effect, many nations, no longer able to resist Globalist, one-world scheming.** Sleep lightly, my friends.

Such is the rotten fruit of the Globalist vine

References for **Some Rotten Fruits of the Globalist Vine**

[6. Patrick J. Buchanan, "Why Trump Is Routing the Free Traders" 30 June 2016 <http://buchanan.org/blog/trump-routing-free-traders-125393>]

[7. Ben Beachy, "Obama Laments Inequality, Calls for Another Inequality-Spurring Trade Deal" 4 Dec. 2014 *Public Citizen Trade Watch* <http://citizen.typepad.com/eyesontrade/>]

Future of Globalism and Globalization

Globalism must be stopped and reversed. As a discretionary economic policy taken to excess, it can be rolled back or even reversed. Indeed, it must be reversed before full American sovereignty is surrendered. National security *requires* a rollback, especially of open borders. This is a matter of political will, i.e., those who govern must ditch Globalism. Globalization, on the other hand, will go on, bounded by the pull back in Globalism. International trade and incremental Globalization provides net benefits and will likely continue.

Let us enjoy the fruits of Globalization ... without the rot of Globalism.

What's so Scary About Open Borders?

Many Americans, particularly **Hillary Clinton**, favor open borders. Taken literally, an open borders policy is committed to the unrestricted movement of people, goods, securities, factories, and money across national boundaries. Imagine the six borders of the U.S. without any restrictions!!! Who is coming in from where??? We could get an inflow from all directions! Consider:

    1. Southwestern border with Mexico.
    2. Northern border with Canada.
    3. Atlantic border, on Atlantic Ocean.
    4. Southern border, on Gulf of Mexico
    5. Pacific border, on Pacific Ocean, including Hawaii.
    6. Alaskan border, on Bering Sea (West) and Beaufort Sea (North).

Is this a realistic scenario, given open borders: **any people, in any number, at any time, can enter (or leave) through any border, without challenge from U.S. authorities?** What would it mean for the U.S. economy and the American standard of living, given the predictions of the Factor Price Equalization Model? Is our fate determined by outsiders? **What happens to America as a free standing, sovereign nation?**

WarEnomics

Dropping the Econ Bomb...
or
How to Win a War without Firing a Shot, Dropping a Bomb or Raising an Army

Do you recall a tactical nuclear weapon from the 1970s called the *neutron bomb*? It was an anti-personnel weapon, i.e., a people killer. Essentially, the radiation from the neutron bomb was intended to kill people but largely spare buildings, equipment, bridges and other structures from destruction. It was never used in actual battle. Most folks do not realize there is an economic equivalent of the neutron bomb, only it works in reverse.

Here is how an economic "neutron" bomb would work. It would destroy buildings, equipment, private and social overhead capital. But it would not kill people, at least not directly. Comparing the impact on people, the economic "neutron" bomb seems more humane than the actual neutron bomb.

Deploying the Bomb

The economic neutron bomb would not be dropped from a plane or delivered by ballistic missile. The econ "bomb" is deployed when a nation adopts economic policies that are self-destructive of the economy. These are policies that inhibit overall economic growth, degrade key industries, or warp the distribution of income. The econ bomb promotes decline by sparking social disharmony, mainly by flaming the rivalry between supporters of butter (civilian goods) versus supporters of guns (military goods). Globalism is the econBomb.

Recall, the rivalry between guns or butter, swords or plowshares, is a source of internal conflict in all countries. Guns versus butter supporters engage in a perpetual tug of war for the government budget dollar. In a democracy, stirring up that conflict will likely manifest in voters choosing butter over guns. This results in the failure to replace depleted, worn out and obsolete military equipment, diminishing the nation's military capabilities. Moreover, as incomes fall so does real saving. As real savings falls, so does real investment, across the spectrum of capital formation.

In effect, there would be the slow destruction of military equipment and capability but not the killing of people. This is the neutron bomb effect in reverse. A contraction of military "capital," other factors unchanged, will diminish the fighting ability of the nation's military, thereby threatening national security.

Deploying the Policy

Why would a nation adopt an economic policy that destroys its military capability and imperils national defense and national security? The answer is: by mistake, foolishness, trickery, or hubris, believing disaster could not possibly result. Globalism was sold by academics and do-gooders to U.S. politicians as a prosperity generating machine for the U.S. Another planned outcome was world governance, ultimately leading to world peace. These were appealing but unrealistic objectives.

Well, after forty years of globalist policies neither goal has been achieved. Instead, Globalism has been the destroyer of U.S. prosperity and decimator of its manufacturing base. It expanded poverty and reduced the ability of folks to maintain or improve their standard of living in the U.S.

Remember: Globalism- the *economic neutron bomb* -degrades the economy which, in turn, sparks internal conflict, degrades military capabilities and, ultimately, imperils national security.

A Part of Military Strategy

Get your adversaries to adopt Globalism, but, for God's sake, do not ever adopt it yourself! Of course, nothing is all bad. Globalism has produced some winners, supporters and defenders. But, they are outnumbered by the vast numbers of losers. On balance, adopting Globalism is the equivalent of dropping an economic "neutron" bomb on the economy. Experience proves it.

Appendix

Are cheap goods and cheap labor ... cheap tricks?

Neo-mercantilism and the United States trade deficit. The rest of the world has accumulated a large stock of U.S. dollars, over $3 trillion, and other financial assets, as well. This treasure trove has been accumulated by selling more goods to the U.S. than goods bought back from the U.S. It may be argued that the major trading partners of the U.S. (Still Red China, Japan and others) have been pursuing a modern version of Mercantilism. The U.S. trading partners seem intent – and content – to accumulate U.S. dollars and not use them to buying currently produced U.S. goods. Hence, the wide gap between U.S. imports and the smaller U.S. exports. From the U.S point of view this is a massive foreign trade imbalance, called a *trade deficit.*

Surprise! This foreign treasure trove of U.S. dollars – earned by selling us artificially cheap foreign goods and artificially expensive foreign oil – is being used to buy strategic economic and national security assets of the U.S.!

Foreign uses of U.S. dollars: Buying up the U.S.? Trading partners accept money (U.S. dollars) and trade payables (accounts and notes payable) in exchange for the U.S. excess of imports over exports. These instruments, money and IOU's are, in effect, claims on U.S. assets: real, financial and political. This includes current goods (but not now, or X would be larger), past goods such as real assets (plant, equipment, property, real estate) and financial assets (corporate stocks in high tech firms, manufacturing firms, and banks.) Farm and water assets are on the shopping list, as well. Also favored are government and corporate bonds. And, oh, yes, when the time comes, future goods are claimable, as well.

Darker side: Attack on U.S. nationalism. Critics charge dollars accepted for U.S. trade deficit may also be used to make illegal political donations: to U.S. political campaigns, media outlets and Universities for long term propaganda purposes.

The Ivy League so-called **feeder universities** are special targets for the establishment of propaganda machines euphemistically labeled "study" or "research" centers. The objective: propagandize; advocate replacing nationalism with Globalism and Glocialism. The students someday become teachers and professors of the next generation at lesser institutions. They pass the message along as gospel truth.

Chapter Twenty-Six
Fallacy of the Level Playing Field

IN a **level playing field** situation, no side has an unfair advantage — contrived or natural — as to the outcome of the conflict. It is argued, in public, at least, we should seek a level playing field in U.S. trade and diplomatic negotiations. The concept **level playing field** is not a fallacy ... but, preferring it in economic policy is a mistake. It is acclaimed by pseudo-intellectual journalists and academics as the Holy Grail of fairness, even in life and death situations. Is there any merit to this position?

1. FALLACIOUS ECONOMICUS: We should seek a *level playing field* in trade and foreign policy negotiations. After all, it's only fair and honorable. And fairness is an American core value. Honor is an American virtue.

Fallacious Reasoning: Gee wiz, it is only fair that there be a level playing field with no tilt toward one side or the other. Then we'll see who is better! We certainly do not want to be accused of being a bully or taking unfair advantage of other nations. So, let us "get small" to play fair with other nations.

Correct Reasoning: Are you kidding? Fair? Fair, *when national survival may be at stake,* we are worried about fairness? Who plays fair in international struggles? The Russians, the (Red) Chinese, maybe the North Koreans or Syrians play fair? Forget a level playing field. There is no objection to giving the *appearance* of a level playing field. However, every effort must be made to tilt the playing field in our favor. National survival may depend on it.

Somehow, level playing field has come to be understood as synonymous with fair play on the sports field or in the boxing ring. The level playing field, a "leveling out" of exogenous forces and then letting the teams battle it out, has worked its way into our collective psyche. It is considered by some as the only fair way a game can be played. Also, this mythical level playing field, trumpeted *ad nausea* by know nothing self appointed pundits, seems to have become part of the mindset of U.S. trade negotiators.

The concept of a level playing field has been thrown about in the trade debate about China. It is charged that China is not playing fairly, but rather creating an unfair advantage for itself with artificially cheap goods and an artificially cheap currency. So, in effect, China has "tilted" the playing field in its favor, making it an uphill struggle for the U.S. to compete. **And the U.S. complied!** Critics cry, like the buffoon cited above: "If only they would 'play' fair, on a level playing field, then no one would have an initial, unfair advantage and we would out compete them! Yes, just put us on a level playing field and we'll show them who is better."

Really? *What if you are wrong?* Want to wrestle with a gorilla? Who will make up for the damage? What if you "play fair" and get wiped out? Could it be that their massive army of cheap labor will overwhelm our advanced technology? Should our leaders gamble our futures on some strange rule of competition left over from the grammar school playground?

To the level playing field cheering section, here is some advice. One should stop treating the adoption of a level playing field as if it were one of the Ten Commandments. Get real! Put the bravado aside and realize that, yes, one may have a better chance of winning on a level playing field than when the field was tilted in the rivals' favor. But, make no mistake: **the U.S. still has a chance of losing a competition played on a level playing field.**

A Game of Canasta

There is no guarantee the U.S. will come out the winner on a level playing field. And this isn't tiddlywinks or canasta we're talking about. Everything is at risk in this game. National survival is at stake!

Remember: the economy is the mother ship of national security! Cripple the mother ship and jeopardize national security.

Major concept: A level playing field is for children's games, card games and sporting competitions, but not for international trade dealings where national survival is at stake. Indeed, one should want a playing field tilted in one's favor, no? Duh?

Consider that throughout history, when national survival is at risk, nations have sought to tilt the "playing field" to their own advantage. Hannibal used elephants against the Romans and the U.S. used cruise missiles in Iraq. And everyone knows it is harder to go uphill than advance on a level plane. It is the normal, rational way to engage in conflict: seek all the advantage you can get.

Major recommendation: forget fair play in national economic and military rivalry. Yes, read it again: **forget fair play.** What good is fair play if life and death are at stake and one loses the contest? Oh my God, the reader must be asking himself. That recommendation is so totally politically incorrect!

Yes, ditch political correctness and "get real." When survival is at stake, adhering to the politically correct "level playing field" could spell national doom.

Again: a level playing field is for children's games. In the real world, national survival demands you always seek the advantage.

If one loses a sporting event one does not risk loss of freedom and control over one's life. One does not risk loss of living standard, way of life and life itself. One does not risk enslavement for oneself and family. The cost of losing a schoolyard game is infinitesimal compared the cost of losing an economic and military struggle against a determined predatory adversary.

America's **external predators** have been tilting the playing field against us. (Still Red) China (artificially cheap labor and currency, lax environmental rules), OPEC (criminal conspiracy) and Mexico (cheap labor emigration, lax environmental rules) have been tilting the playing field against us. Tilting the playing field against us hasn't given these predators any sleepless nights.

Ask yourself this question: With so much at stake, do we want to play by **schoolyard rules?** Duh? Obviously, the stakes are much higher in international trade. Why seek merely a level playing field? On a level playing field one may lose one's standard of living or, indeed, one way of life, not to mention one's life itself. Worst case scenario, the nation ultimately is defeated and enslaved in military/economic conquest. At that point, who is going to be around to say, "It was a 'fair fight' and we lost. No hard feelings, we concede, we are beaten. We, the losers, therefore deserve to be slaves or live by some alien ideology."

Tilt in our favor. There are no do-overs in this game of national struggle. There are no referees or committees to appeal to. This may be a **one round fight.** If so, it is even more imperative the playing field ought to be tipped in our favor. **Recommendation: U.S. trade negotiators should approach trade talks as if joining in a bare knuckled, back alley brawl.**

2. FALLACIOUS ECONOMICUS: I am glad I live in the U.S., a democracy!

Correct Reasoning: The U.S. is not a democracy! At least, it is not a *direct* democracy. It could have been, but the Founding Fathers deliberately shunned the direct democracy model and chose to institute a Republic. In a Republic laws are made by elected representatives of the people, not the people themselves. Of course, the Republic form has strong democratic core features, mainly the popular election of the representatives. The U.S. political system is considered a **democratic republic** or a **republican representative democracy.**

> **Direct democracy** (also known as **pure democracy**) is a form of democracy in which people decide (e.g. vote on, form consensus on) policy initiatives directly, as opposed to a representative

democracy in which people vote for representatives who then decide policy initiatives.

[1. "Direct Democracy" 27 September 2014 *Wikipedia*
<http://en.wikipedia.org/wiki/Direct_democracy>]

The Founders hated democracy. They believed that democracy's main feature – majority rule – could degenerate into mob rule (**mobocracy**), in turn leading to the oppression of minorities. A kind of dictatorship of the majority would be created. Consider these statements: "A democracy is nothing more than mob rule," said Thomas Jefferson, "where 51 percent of the people may take away the rights of the other 49." James Madison agreed, "Democracy is the vilest form of government." Their Federalist rivals concurred. Benjamin Franklin intoned, "Democracy is two wolves and a lamb voting on what to have for lunch. Liberty is a well-armed lamb contesting the vote."

Democratic Republic. A Democratic Republic is a special kind of democracy, a *representative* democracy. People elect representatives to make decisions or laws on their behalf. Unelected people are subject to but do not enact laws, as they would in direct democracy. Nevertheless, at the State level some issues are put before voters for a direct vote, a referendum.

Use of supermajority. A supermajority of legislators may be the rule for important issues such as a constitutional amendment.

> A **supermajority** or a **qualified majority** is a requirement for a proposal to gain a specified greater level of support than a 50% simple majority. In some jurisdictions, for example, parliamentary procedure requires that any action that may alter the rights of a minority has a supermajority requirement (such as a two-thirds majority). Changes to constitutions, especially those with entrenched clauses, commonly require supermajority support in a legislature.

[2. "*Supermajority*" 22 May 2015 *Wikipedia*
<http://en.wikipedia.org/wiki/Supermajority>]

"By minority, the Founders meant almost anything. It could refer to the rich, the merchant, the small state, the immigrant, the unpopular religious sect or viewpoint, or a thousand other things."

[3. Steve Farrell, "The Electoral College: Part 2, Protecting Minority Rights," 14 November 2000 *Meridian Magazine* <http://tinyurl.com/nn69vol>]

On the other hand, a majority could be a homogeneous majority or a coalition of minorities.

Basically, the approach in the U.S. system boils down to this guideline: **dilute the power of the majority and enhance the power of the minority, but not to the extent that they are equal.** At the Federal and State levels this is done partially through the separation and division of powers. Without the Electoral College and with direct popular election, Presidents would be elected by the populations of the most populous states. Campaigns and government programs would be geared to those bulging population pockets. Small states and rural population would be ignored. As it stands today (in the election of President) the structure of the Electoral College is somewhat redistributive of elective voting power from the most populous cities/States to less populous, mainly rural States. Here are some instances where a **supermajority is required**: impeachment of a President, expulsion of a member of Congress, overriding a Presidential veto, ratifying a treaty, and amending the Constitution. Private organizations such as co-ops, business corporations, and clubs may require super majorities for major decisions.

[4. "The Supermajority Vote in US Government," 04 April, 2016 *Aboutnews*

<http://tinyurl.com/zzo9z7v>]

Question: We know **an excess of a good thing becomes a bad thing. In this connection, a question arises with respect to protections afforded minorities.** Given the tendency in popular culture to "define deviancy down" and worship diversity, has the U.S. become a *de facto* inverted democracy, where majority core values have become subservient to tiny, vocal minorities?

3. FALLACIOUS ECONOMICUS: The U.S. Constitution is firm and unwavering as to the rights granted to me, a citizen.

Fallacious Reasoning: Only amending the Constitution, a difficult process, could take away or embellish those rights.

Correct Reasoning: So Your Rights Are Inalienable, eh? Strap yourselves in, kiddies. Would you believe Constitutional Rights we take for granted could be jeopardized by our foreign treaties? Yes, in fact, foreign treaties -- passed by POTUS with two thirds Senate approval -- are *equal* to the Constitution in coverage, authority and enforceability. Treaties may override State and local laws and regulations, as well. No matter, **treaties are the supreme law of the land**.

In addition, treaty legalisms, minutia and technicalities may be a stealth means of diminishing U.S. sovereignty. Why? To promote the end favored by U.S. Globalist elites: **one world governance**. So, beware what appear to be benign and beneficial treaties that actually promote the Globalist agenda. Shun treaties that give away American sovereignty in economic and social policy to international committees, agencies, and foreign private parties.

Sleep lightly, my friend.

[5. See John Fonte, *Sovereignty or Submission.* New York: Encounter Books, 2011]

Chapter Twenty-Seven
National Debt Fallacies

*I don't write jokes. I just watch the Federal government
and report on what it does.*

— *Humorist, Will Rogers*

A billion here, a billion there, pretty soon, you're talking real money.
— Senator Everett Dirksen

FEDERAL or national debt or sovereign debt is what the Federal government owes in direct Treasury obligations, in United States dollars. (See Appendix for other usage of the term **Sovereign debt).** The money is owed because it had been borrowed at an earlier time and spent for government purposes. The debts are in the form of bonds, notes and bills, payable in U.S. dollars. Bonds, notes and bills also represent the order of longest to shortest term to maturity. It excludes agency debt and social security commitments.

Do not confuse the Federal **debt** with the related Federal **deficit.** The **Federal deficit** is the yearly excess of planned spending over anticipated tax collections. The deficit is the top layer on the debt "cake." Federal borrowing is engaged in to fill the annual shortfall of taxes below spending. **Federal debt** is composed of all unpaid deficits accumulated from prior years. So, each new annual deficit adds to the historic Federal Debt.

[1. <http://www.usdebtclock.org/>]

See Diagram #1 below for the full range of Federal Budget outcomes. As 2015 begins the Federal debt and GDP both amount to approximately $20 trillion, giving a debt to GDP ratio of about 1:1. This is an historic high for the U.S.

Diagram #1: Overview of Federal Budget Outcomes

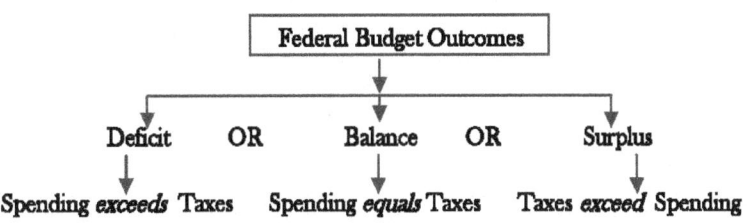

There are numerous fallacies associated with the Federal debt. Read all about it.

1. FALLA<IOUS €<ONOMI<US: Hey, the Feds should live within their means and spend only what they collect in taxes. NO BORROWING!

Correct Reasoning: There are situations when it is best for the Federal government to borrow and spend, rather than tax.   Let's look at a few examples:

1. Tax collections tend to spike around the quarterly tax due dates, especially April 15. But, expenditures may be more evenly spaced throughout the year. So, should the Federal government default on payments due or should they *borrow in anticipation* of a later tax collection? Borrowing is the appropriate strategy in this circumstance. Municipalities follow this strategy, as well.

2. The government may wish to undertake a very expensive and very **long life capital investment project** that will not pay off for years.   Long term capital projects include a nuclear power plant, a port facility, canal, bridge or water tunnel. Let us say a bridge costs $100 million and must be paid up front in year one. But, the life of the bridge is 100 years. It is best to borrow $100 million up front rather than raise taxes all in year one. Why do taxpayers of year one have to bear the entire burden of a project that will benefit all the taxpayers of the next 100 years? Repay the loan, bond by bond, year by year over the useful life of the project. This is a technique (serial bonds) for spreading the financial burden more equitably over current and future taxpayers.

The situations discussed above provide the rationale for Federal, State and local government borrowing. Beware that **nearly all the individual States have laws mandating a balanced (operating) budget.** This requirement does *not* apply to the Federal budget, giving the Federal government more flexibility.

[2. "State Balanced Budget Provisions" 2 Oct. 2015 *National Conference of State Legislators* < http://tinyurl.com/oeh8cty>]

The following situations, numbers 3 and 4 apply to the Federal government.

3. The Federal government is charged by law to promote maximum employment, maximum output and maximum purchasing power (minimize inflation). This was taken as a cue for the government *to borrow and spend,* adding demand if it found a demand short economy. **Managing aggregate demand** became the by-words of the Federal effort to fulfill the mandates of the **Employment Act of 1946.**

4. It important to keep up **civilian morale during a foreign war**. Heavy tax burdens are de-moralizing. The government has borrowed to finance expensive wars which, absent the borrowing, would have required crushing tax burdens on a civilian population. Buyers of "war" bonds believe they can cash in the bonds after the war's end. On the other hand, taxes paid are nonrefundable! Thus, a dollar of tax is considered consumption forgone forever whereas a dollar surrendered for bond purchase is considered consumption postponed, a much preferred alternative.

Politicians have to stand for re-election. This gives them a bias toward borrowing instead of taxing. Taxes impose an immediate and visible pain on taxpayers whereas borrowing masks and postpones the pain. Borrowing appears less painful to voters, in peace and war.

Unfortunately, deficit spending has become a way of life for the economy in the last half century. As a result, the Federal debt as a percent of GDP has bloated to historic proportions, about equal to a year's GDP. Could the borrowing "party" soon end?

2. FALLACIOUS ECONOMICUS: The U.S. had better stop issuing debt. After all, there IS a limit to how much debt a nation can issue.

Fallacious Reasoning: It is common sense not to over borrow.

Correct Reasoning: "Yes" and "no" as to the limit on government borrowing. Yes, there is a legal limit to the amount of debt the Treasury can issue. It is called the **legal debt limit (a.k.a. public debt ceiling)**. However, it is a limit in name only. Congress and the President have always been willing to raise the debt limit to keep cash coming in to pay the government's bills.

Thus far, the U.S. has maintained its solvency. Today, debt as a percent of annual Gross Domestic Product (GDP) is hovering at around 100%, nearing $20 trillion. There are solvent nations with higher and lower Debt to GDP ratios. Debt/GDP is only *one* marker for assessing debt burden.

The U.S. government would be bankrupt if a) all its debts were due on one day and b) it was unable to pay them. But a) is not true, so b. is irrelevant. Debts are spread out in time and not due on one day or one year. Moreover, maturing debts can be paid by *rolling them over*, i.e., borrowing new funds to pay off maturing debt.

3. FALLACIOUS ECONOMICUS: Who cares about the Federal debt? Alarmists have been screaming about the danger for thirty years.

Correct Reasoning: Would it still mean little to you if the Federal government started taxing your savings and seizing your retirement funds to repay its debt? Argentina has followed this path to help repay its debts. (But, to no avail as

Argentina has defaulted on its Federal debt in 2001 and 2014.) Or, what if the government made it mandatory to buy government bonds for retirement accounts?

Poland joined the "seizure" club and added a few new twists, as well.

Read all about it:

> Poland has pulled a destructive stunt worthy of Argentina. It is seizing half of the Polish people's private retirement funds. All government bonds in these pension-plan portfolios are being forcibly transferred to the government. Since the bonds are no longer held by investors, the government is declaring that the national debt has been reduced by the face value of those securities. Neat trick, including the spin on this Soviet-style seizure: The government is calling the nationalization a 'pension overhaul.' The ghosts of Stalin and Lenin must be smiling.
>
> [3. Steve Forbes, Forbes Staff, "Poland's Piggish Pols--They're Not Alone" 17 Sept. 2012 *Forbes* < http://tinyurl.com/qcc75ya>]

Could a similar path be followed in the U.S.? Remember POTUS (the President of the United States) has expressed a high regard for communal over private property.   Sleep lightly, my friend.

Are the following statements true?
Budget deficits are harmful and are to be avoided.
Budget surpluses are beneficial and are to be embraced.

Answer:

It depends on the context. Deficits could be good and surpluses bad, depending on the **state of the economy** and **level of Federal debt**.

- **Budget deficits** add to government spending. This is *good* when the economy needs stimulus. But, deficits also add to Federal debt, *bad* when in deep debt and have debt service obligations already.

- **(Unspent) budget surpluses** reduce government spending. This is *good* if it trims an over-sized aggregate demand. *Bad* if it reduces an already under-sized aggregate demand.

The good and bad effects must be weighed to determine a *net effect* of a surplus or deficit in a particular context.

Deficits Forever? The U.S. is NOT bankrupt!

4. FALLACIOUS ECONOMICUS: All debt issued by the Federal government has a maturity date, the date when the bond must be paid off. Therefore, there will come a time when the entire U.S. national debt has to be paid off. So, aren't we burdening future generations with re-paying current debt?

Fallacious Reasoning: When money is borrowed it is not being gifted to the Federal Government. The borrower commits itself to pay periodic interest and repay the principal (or par value) at a certain future date. Failure to meet either of these promises would constitute a breach of contract called a **default.** The same holds true for debt of a nation. So, someday all U.S. debt will come due and have to be paid off, no?

Correct Reasoning: Yes, all debt has a maturity date, but the government has an infinite life, like a corporation. **If managed properly the debt never has to be paid.** Just in case you missed it, here it is again: IF managed properly the debt never has to be paid. But, that is a mighty IF! What is the secret?

U.S. debt maturities. Most Federal debt is set to mature in 10 years or less. All the debt will come due and must be paid during that time frame to avoid default. That reasoning may apply to most national debt in the world but need not apply to U.S. national debt, today to around $20 trillion dollars.

Investors (or lenders) favor U.S. national debt because of its relatively certain interest and principal paying ability. In their view, U.S. debt reliably pays interest and, up to now, bears a very low risk of defaulting. **(A default occurs when a debt instrument fails to pay interest or the principal at maturity).**

> **Federal entitlements** (or mandatory) spending includes Social Security, Medicare, Medicaid, other welfare, pension commitments, and interest on debt. They have grown to nearly 70% of the Federal Budget as of 2016. Like the monster that devoured Cleveland, entitlement growth threatens to squeeze out discretionary spending and absorb nearly 100% of the Federal budget in ten years!

The U.S. Treasury and the Federal Reserve System cleverly avoid defaulting on maturing debt by "rolling it over." **Rolling over the debt (a.k.a. refinancing the debt)** involves issuing new debt, and then using the proceeds to pay off the old debt.

Total debt remains the same until the next deficit adds to it. Consider British consols, a British government issue close to being a perpetual bond with no mandatory pay back (maturity) date.

In effect, rolling over the debt avoids the necessity for paying off the debt!

A Ponzi Scheme?

Rolling over the debt sounds like a Ponzi Scheme, but is not. If new bond buyers are scarce, the Federal Reserve can create money to buy the new bonds. This is called monetization of the debt. Ponzi couldn't create new money.

Question: Is it advisable to pay off Federal debt by selling off government assets or having a ginormous (SIC) lottery!

Issue special Infrastructure Bonds to corporations for investing repatriated overseas profits!

5. FALLACIOUS ECONOMICUS: If government decides to finance rising expenditures with *tax* dollars instead of borrowed dollars, then tax *rates* must be raised, especially the income tax rate.

Fallacious Reasoning: A higher *percent* of a given absolute amount of income will yield more tax dollars.

Correct Reasoning: A common fallacy is that higher *income* tax rates *guarantee* to bring in more tax dollars. Experience proves higher rates generate more $ tax revenues only under a certain set of circumstances not always available. **It depends on where you start and how high you go.** This relationship is shown by the Laffer Curve, developed by economist Arthur Laffer. An example is reproduced below in following **Diagram #2:**

Diagram #2: The Laffer Curve

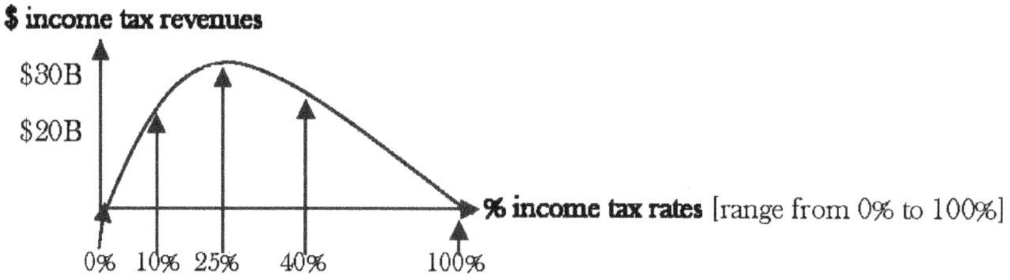

$ income tax revenues

$30B

$20B

% income tax rates [range from 0% to 100%]

0% 10% 25%   40%   100%

Consider these proposed changes:

Raising the tax rate

Raising rate from 10% to 25% *raises* tax dollars collected from $20B to $30B.

But, raising rate from 25% to 40% *lowers* tax dollars collected from $30B to $20B.

It is suggested that the higher rate discourages entrepreneurial activity.

Higher rates encourage avoidance and evasive behavior.

Lowering the tax rate

Lowering the rate from 40% to 25% provides *more* tax revenues, despite the lower rate. Imagine that! Lower rates bring in more tax dollars!

Analysts attribute this to greater entrepreneurial activity and less avoidance and evasive behavior by taxpayers.

But, lowering the rate from 25% to 10% may stimulate additional economic activity but also lowers tax dollars collected, aggravating a budget deficit.

In sum, lower rates are recommended if the existing rates are already too high. Arguably, this will discourage avoidance and evasive behavior, stimulate economic activity, and help narrow a budget deficit ... despite lower rates!

So, will raising rates raise revenue? Economists believe the answer depends on where the tax rates are *before* they are raised.

➤ If rates are generally low, raising rates will likely produce more revenue.

➤ If rates are already high, raising them further will likely trigger avoidance and evasion behavior, producing *less* revenue.

➤ Also, if rates are already high, then lowering them will likely *raise* revenue as avoidance and evasive strategies are called off. (See the Laffer Curve depicted above.)

[4. Arthur Laffer "The Laffer Curve" 2 July 2014 the *Laffer Center at the Pacific Institute* <http://tinyurl.com/or8rx6l>]

Is Sequestration National Self-Flagellation?

A bickering Congress, unable to reach budget agreement, created sequestration by the 2011 Budget Control Act. Congress couldn't agree on the best way to lower the deficit, so it used the sequester or automatic across the board cuts in spending. It seems the sequester has replaced the normal, discretionary budget process.

The sequester is a ten year plan to cut Federal spending by $1.2 trillion. It cuts $109.6 billion from each fiscal year's budget. *It cuts an equal dollar amount each year from defense and nondefense spending, regardless of world conditions!*

Sequestration is like the robot cutting machine at the barber shop. It takes the same amount off in the front and back, regardless of what the final look is. In the barber shop it might hurt to take more off the back than the front. In the budget sequestration process national defense may be hurt more than civilian programs. Yet, so it goes. **Shouldn't those be discretionary decisions, made year by year based on conditions specific to those years? Is national security at the mercy of sequestration?**

President Obama wants to repeal sequestration!

[5. "Budget sequestration in 2013," 9 March 2015 *Wikipedia* < http://tinyurl.com/nwyj5m3>]

6. FALLACIOUS ECONOMICUS: I've heard about this **monetization of the debt,** turning the debt into money. People won't use IOU's as money.

Correct Reasoning: Oh, boy, this is a whopper. First of all, paper money is, in effect, a government IOU to the holder. It is a promise to pay that does not require payment ... huh? Yes, that is how paper money evolved. First, there was the promise to repay 100% gold or silver for those who turned in the paper. That was **representative money.** Then, the promise fell below 100%, giving us fractional conversion. Coins met a similar fate as debasement of the coinage was practiced. Then, the redemption promise behind paper money was removed entirely. And so, **fiat money** was born.

Fiat money was used in the Revolutionary War. It continued to be used in remote areas or company towns where precious metals were unavailable or inappropriate. (Fiat is Latin for "let it be done").

Irredeemable, inconvertible, intrinsically worthless paper money, called fiat money, is our currency today! Guess what? IT WORKS, giving us money for everyday transactions.

Extended Discussion

Now, back to the question of how the money supply can grow. One path is through **monetization of the deficit or debt. This occurs when the Fed buys bonds directly or indirectly from the Treasury.** It starts with deficits in the Federal budget. Recall ... a budget is a plan for future cash inflows and cash outflows for some future period. The anticipated inflows and outflows should be time dated, i.e., forecasted not only in amount but in timing. All large spending units - household, businesses, governments - should generate budgets to aid financial planning. Governments, by law, must generate and make public their budgets. The annual budget of the United States, i.e., the Federal Budget, is a law enacted by Congress and the President.

the Federal Budget is: Government Spending (G) minus Taxes

= (Deficit) or Surplus.

Depicted below are two alternative budget projections. Exhibit #1 below displays a budget *deficit* on the left and a budget *surplus* on the right.

Exhibit #1: FISCAL YEAR 20XX
Alternative Budget Projections

BUDGET ALPHA	BUDGET BETA
Government Spending $100B	Govt. Spending $ 80B
MINUS Taxes —80B	MINUS Taxes —100B
—$20B DEFICIT	+$ 20B SURPLUS

The Federal Budget is in deficit if it calls for spending more, say $100 billion, than anticipated taxes, say $80 billion, to be collected. That is reflected in Budget Alpha: The government must borrow the $20 billion to make up the deficiency, i.e., finance the deficit. Simply put, it borrows from the banking system, the public or from the Federal Reserve System.

Seed Money: the monetary base. Now, there is some bookkeeping wizardry going on behind closed doors, but it is all legal and above board. Recall, the Fed means of payment: When the Treasury borrows from the Fed, directly or indirectly, **the Fed *creates* the means of payment needed to buy government bonds.** These payments constitute a loan to the government.

Now, here comes the important part: The Fed uses no gold, silver or currency to do its purchasing. It draws a check on itself, which most bond sellers deposit in their own private banks' checking accounts. Voilà! New demand deposit money appears! This may properly be called *seed money.* The creation of money as discussed above is called *monetization of the deficit* or debt. The Fed is **converting debt into money** by creating and circulating an amount of money equal to the debt. The amount the Fed pays for the bonds (government debt) is the initial amount of new **seed money** created. This power must be used judiciously!

[When conditions are right, bank lenders and borrowers willingly can combine to expand the money supply by a multiple of the original created amount. For example, $100 in new money can grow to $1,000. (Consult a good Money & Banking text for the details)]

Monetization of the Debt: Good or Bad? It Depends

The Fed's power to monetize debt is, in effect, unlimited. Note that, in and of itself, monetization of the debt is neither good nor bad. Depending on the state of the economy, it could be your best friend or worst enemy! Sometimes an economy needs more money to ease demand creation. Sometimes it needs less money to dampen an earlier over-expansion of demand. The Federal debt is made up of outstanding bonds representing the accumulated and unpaid deficits from prior years. Each successive year's budget deficit requires additional bonds to be issued and adds another layer to the "cake" of Federal debt, already near $20 trillion in 2016.

Borrowing From Foreign Countries

The past twenty years has seen a huge growth in the participation of Japan and (still Red) China in buying U.S. bonds. In fact, about 40% of the total debt is now owned by Japan and China. They acquired the needed U.S. dollars by running massive   trade surpluses with the U.S. Those surpluses were fueled by undervalued currencies and welcomed by the U.S. consumer looking for bargains.

Beware: Has the U.S. become overly dependent on foreign trade partners to finance our Federal debt? Does this give Communist China and Japan undue influence on our economic policies and political/foreign policy decisions? Sometimes they are derisively referred to as **"America's bankers"!** (Recall: too much of a good thing, in this case borrowing, may become a bad thing). Important questions are indicated:

> ➢ Could U.S. dependency on foreign bond purchasers impair our freedom of action in world affairs? For example: could dependence on China for bond buying bend U.S. policy on the South Korea/North Korea struggle?

> ➢ Could the freedom of action of Americans be impaired or influenced by the return those deficit dollars to the U.S.?

7. FALLACIOUS ECONOMICUS: Government spending financed with borrowed funds is free to the taxpayer.

Fallacious Reasoning: Well ... I didn't have to pay any tax and the government provided me with a service. I got those services for free, no?

Correct Reasoning: Remember, nothing is free! There are no free lunches!

Government money transfers aside, Federal *spending* absorbs goods and services. No matter how the government secured the money, taxes or borrowings, there is an opportunity cost to society. The opportunity cost to society is the net enjoyment attached to the *next best* alternative goods that could have been produced instead of the ones bought by the government.

Consider this example: instead of having the aircraft carrier purchased by government, society could have had a cruise ship or two. The cruise ship is the lost opportunity, the opportunity cost. The opportunity cost still exists, even if the carrier was purchased with borrowed money.

In addition, there is opportunity cost associated with interest payments on the debt.

8. FALLA<IOUS <<ONOMI<US: What passes for money these days is worthless garbage.

Fallacious Reasoning: True, today's money has no intrinsic value as a commodity. It is not backed by or convertible into a valuable commodity. Pull back the curtain and there is nothing there! It is all a joke. How could something intrinsically worthless have any value?

Correct Reasoning: Here we go again. True, today's currency and coin has practically no value in and of itself. *It derives value from acceptability as a means of payment for goods, services, and properties real and financial.* Should today's currency and coin no longer be acceptable in payment, paper your walls with the fiat currency.

Under normal circumstances money is in tremendous demand and has value in many usages. Consider the following scenarios.

> ➤ The U.S. dollar commands goods and services, around the world. In a sense, the dollar is backed by goods *in general*, not gold or silver. That is, it has value in exchange. Much of this value derives from the fact that currency and coin are legal tender, i.e., declared legally capable of discharging debts.

> ➤ Currency and coin are legal tender and legally discharge *debts*. Refusal to accept legal tender discharges the debt. (However, there is no law stating that legal tender must be accepted for other purposes, say, buying a loaf of bread when no prior debt exists).

> ➤ Currency and coin legally satisfy tax obligations.

> ➤ Currency and coin are legal tender for the repayment of government debt.

> ➤ Currency and coin are financial wealth. They can store purchasing power for later use.

The means of transfer of currency and coin range from checks on bank deposits to electronic transfers.

9. FALLA<IOUS <<ONOMI<US: Sound or valid money must be **gold** or some other valuable commodity.

Corollary Fallacy: this fallacy is furthered when one wrongly accepts the fiction that valid money must be *backed by* or convertible into gold or silver.

Correct Reasoning: Silver and gold have served as money going back to antiquity. But, should a nation with no gold or silver, or a people with no knowledge of gold or silver, be denied the benefits of having some other commodity serve as a medium of exchange? Money is too useful to be without. Throughout history, valid money has been ANYTHING generally accepted as a means of final payment. The list includes *useful commodities* such as: copper, tobacco, eagle feathers, salt, wampum, alcohol, cigarettes, and live farm animals such as cows and chickens. Large limestone rocks served as money on the island of Yap. **Today's money is called fiat money:** money by decree, money by law. Fiat money is intrinsically worthless, but legal tender, nevertheless. **Gold and silver play no day-to-day role in our monetary system.**

Background: There is a rationale for having a useful commodity as money. In those harsh, sometimes lawless times, money, when offered to the next trader, had to be a *useful commodity* to promote acceptance. Should the next trader reject this commodity money the holder could still put it to some productive use. So, the usefulness of the commodity provided protection to the holder should the next trader fail to accept it. Gold and silver were useful commodities for decoration and ornamentation, then and now.

Shine on Metal Moon

A metal is **monetized** when, in addition to its commodity use, it is used as money. **De-monetization** occurs when the metal is withdrawn from use as money.

Monetizing a metal, other factors constant, raises its value.
De-monetizing a metal, other factors constant, lowers its value.

Pay off Federal debt: sell off government assets and/or have a ginormous lottery.

10. FALLACIOUS ECONOMICUS: Since fiat money is working so well, I have no need to collect gold and silver coins.

Correct Reasoning: Yes, you have no need for them to conduct exchanges. However, precious metal coins may be held as a store of value (investment). The holder hopes they will appreciate in (or at least retain) value.

Disaster scenario. In addition, gold and silver coins may function as a "hedge against disaster." Suppose there is a nuclear war followed by pestilence and famine. The U.S. government and the Federal Reserve are but memories. *Fiat money is no longer acceptable.* Then gold and silver coins are used when the

U.S. government no longer exists and people are papering their walls with intrinsically worthless fiat currency. Emerging from our shelters, silver dimes and gold dollars will be acceptable because of their intrinsic values as commodities.

So, some folks derive satisfaction by holding precious metal coins an investment and/or a "hedge against disaster." But, beware: precious metal coins pay no interest or dividends. They must be stored and safeguarded.

11. FALLACIOUS ECONOMICUS: The government can dictate what is and what is not used as money. Its power is absolute.

Correct Reasoning: This is another tough one with an element of truth in it. Certainly the government has tremendous powers of persuasion when it chooses to use them.

Indeed, history is riddled with episodes of governments using various means of trying to force acceptance of the *favored* money onto the populace. Consider some of its powers:

1. Declare other moneys illegal.
2. Threaten arrest and punishment – even execution – for users of outlawed moneys.
3. Declared the favored money legal tender for private and public transactions.
4. Declare contracts null and void if they specified payment in outlawed money.
5. Declare the favored money the only one acceptable for paying taxes.
6. Monopolize the issuance of the favored money.

Despite these powers, government power is not absolute and unfailing in dictating what people use as money! History is riddled with episodes of ordinary people rejecting what government declared they should accept as money. Old mining towns and remote settlements frequently issued their own money. In reality, in the United States the Treasury issues coins and the Federal Reserve System (a government agency) issues the paper money, called Federal Reserve Notes. People are free to create their own brand of money. Then again, who would accept it?

12. FALLA<IOUS E<ONOMI<US: It makes no difference to the economy if commodity money or fiat money is in use. As long as it is generally acceptable, it will perform the monetary function.

Correct Reasoning: The fallacy sounds reasonable, but: The use of a valuable commodity merely to facilitate exchanges involves a significant **real opportunity cost** not present with fiat money. The gold and silver circulating as money, while in circulation, cannot be used to produce other goods to satisfy other wants. As such, using a precious commodity as money involves a *real opportunity cost* to society. The metal cannot be used for other valuable purposes such as: jewelry, dentistry and electronics. Recall, gold is decorative and the best conductor of electricity. So, if society insists on using precious metal money when fiat money is available, then there is unnecessary harm, namely, *additional unsatisfied wants* imposed on the economy.

13. FALLA<IOUS E<ONOMI<US: An item has to be **legal tender** to function as money. No legal tender status, no status as money.

Correct Reasoning: Checkable deposits, perhaps 80% of our money supply, are NOT legal tender. The checkable deposits, transferred by check, are money because they are **generally acceptable** ... but are not legal tender. It is not the check but the checkable deposit that is the money, as it is the final means of payment. **Coins and paper currency are legal tender in the U.S.**

> **Legal tender status does not guarantee acceptance of money.**
> **Absence of legal tender status does not guarantee rejection.**

In fact, most payments in the economy are made by check, drawn on checkable deposits at banks. Of course, the check itself is not money. It merely transfers an amount from the bank account of the check writer to another party, the payee of the check. In sum, it is the deposit in the bank – the **checkable deposit**, privately issued money – that is really the final means of payment. **It is preferred and generally accepted, but is not legal tender!**

14. FALLA<IOUS E<ONOMI<US: Yesterday I was approved for a credit card. I already had a debit card. Now I have more money to spend!

Fallacious Reasoning: Try this system: Charge some purchases but avoid paying off the total. Switch the balance to other credit card companies to gain lower introductory interest rates. There should be a circulating or floating balance I can postpone paying for many years, no?

Correct Reasoning: The overuse of credit cards is epidemic in the United States. The program outlined in fallacious reasoning is not a realistic, long term practice. Interest rates can be murderous on the unpaid balances even when switching card companies. Sorry, folks, but **debit and credit cards are not money**. Debit and credit cards are convenient as they give you **point of purchase ability to buy**. Useful as these cards are, they are not money because they are *not* the final means of payment.

A debit card has no buying power unless backed up by a checkable deposit ("money" in the bank) at the moment of purchase. Purchases made by credit card can have enormous double-digit interest charges, even when rotated from one card to another: the debt remains. **Beware:** do not assume you have greater purchasing power simply because you have been issued a consumer credit card. Minimum monthly payments on credit card purchases may be ridiculously low and meant to lure you into paying in installments.

[6. See some useful credit card strategies at: Gerri Detweiler, "Six Smart Credit Card Strategies," 08 August 2013 *Credit.Com* < http://tinyurl.com/o9pc2u3>]

Liquidity can refer to a specific asset, as discussed in the box below. Cash is pure liquidity, ready to spend as is. Or, the terms *liquid* or *solvent* can refer to the firm's ability to pay its debts *as they come due,* dynamic solvency. **Firms want to be liquid or solvent to stave off bankruptcy and survive.**

A Liquid Asset

A liquid asset has two characteristics.

A liquid asset can be 1) *quickly* converted into spendable money (cash, checkable deposits) and 2) done so *without substantial loss of value.* Liquidity exists on a continuum from pure liquidity (money, itself) to gradually more illiquid (junk bonds), to totally illiquid (condemned, contaminated land). In general, **financial assets,** i.e., claims to money such as loans, accounts and mortgage receivables, bonds and stocks, are more liquid than **real assets.** Real assets include business inventory, business equipment, antiques, furniture, buildings, real estate and land.

When bills are due, the most liquid assets, cash and checkable deposits, are called to duty. I'll drink to that!

Question: Is the Liquor Store's unsold case of wine a liquid or illiquid asset? (wink)

---

15. FALLACIOUS ECONOMICUS: My bank is so big and financially strong it could never fail. It could easily withstand a **run**.

(A **bank run** occurs when depositors rush *en mass* to their banks seeking to withdraw cash from their accounts.)

Correct Reasoning: The most profitable, well managed, asset rich, low risk bank may simply not have enough cash on hand to withstand a "run." Its assets may be adequate but in illiquid form such as loans and mortgages receivable.

These assets are not so quickly liquidated (converted into cash) when needed. A "run" is a sudden massive surge in actual or potential depositor *cash* withdrawals. A **bank run** is usually precipitated by depositors' fears of a total bank failure and loss of one's entire deposit. Very often depositors are seen racing through the streets to beat out one another to line up for withdrawals.

This fear of bank default must be combated to stop the run. When word gets out that the bank is safely stocked with cash, then the urgency for withdrawal dissolves. A bank can stop a run by giving cash borrowed from other banks.

In our modern banking system, banks in need can borrow from cash rich correspondent banks, other banks or the Federal Reserve. If a run strikes the whole banking system, banks can borrow from **lender of last resort**, the Federal Reserve System. The run stops when depositors are convinced the bank is *solvent*, i.e., fully capable of meeting subsequent withdrawals.

16. FALLACIOUS ECONOMICUS: I am not afraid of bank failure. My bank is a member of the Federal Deposit Insurance Corporation. That means the government will pay me if my bank fails.

Correct Reasoning: Each depositor insured to at least $250,000 per insured bank. Technically, deposits beyond this level do not carry insurance. The F.D.I.C. has insufficient funds to pay off all the insurance at the same time.

However, the F.D.I.C. tries to cover insured *and* uninsured deposits by arranging the merger of a failing bank with a healthy bank. The healthy bank then assumes responsibility for all deposits of the failing bank, *even deposits in excess of the $250,000 limit.* When all these standard rescues are inadequate, the U.S. Treasury and Federal Reserve Bank stand ready to back up the F.D.I.C., as they did during the **financial crisis of 2008**.

[7. See: "Deposit Insurance" 19 November 2014 *FDIC* <https://www.fdic.gov/deposit/>]

Social security, unemployment and Medicare ENTITLEMENT BENEFITS eat up nearly **two-thirds** of the Federal Budget and are expanding. In comparison, military spending is a paltry 16% of the budget ... and 3.5% of the GDP. In World War II defense spending peaked at about 40% of GDP.

[8. "Federal Spending: Where Does the Money Go," June 2016 *National Priorities* <https://www.nationalpriorities.org/budget-basics/federal-budget-101/spending/>]

For earlier generations, those folks living into their senior years, "social" security was provided by the extended family, the church and private charity.

So Shall Security Issue

On the average, Social Security benefits provide about two thirds of retiree income. Consequently, a *total failure* of Social Security would have a catastrophic impact on their standard of living. Let's back up, take quick tour and see how the system works. Read all about it:

1. Employers match employee Social Security paycheck deductions and send the monies to Washington on behalf of their employees.

2. For many years, all those monies were not needed to meet immediate payouts. The "contributions" exceeded the benefits paid.

3. The excess contributions were invested in interest bearing government bonds, thereby creating the Social Security Trust Fund. Notice the absence of cash in the fund! (The Medicare Trust Fund operates in a similar manner.) There is no cash in these trust funds, but only interest bearing I. O. U.'s from the U.S. Treasury.

4. The fund grows as long as cash inflows (revenues plus bond interest) exceed payouts. This is the current tenuous situation.

5. Should payouts exceed contributions plus earnings the extra cash would be obtained by cashing in Trust Fund bonds with the Treasury. This is projected to begin in 2021. So, as of 2021 the Trust Fund will begin to shrink.

As of now Social Security is meeting all its obligations but trouble lurks ahead.

17. FALLA<IOUS <<ONOMI<US:

17. FALLA<IOUS <<ONOMI<US: In retirement my monthly benefit check does not cover my monthly bills. I am caught short every month and have to improvise the payment of my bills. I cannot "make ends meet." I feel betrayed by my government.

Correct Reasoning: You have not been betrayed. You simply expect more from the system than it ever promised. Social Security retirement payments or benefits were never intended to be your *sole* source of income in retirement. Benefits were intended to be your bare bones, safety-net level of financial support, *not your total support*. During your working years you should have planned to a) curtail your spending in retirement and b) supplement retirement benefits with personal savings, job pensions and other asset accumulation.

Redistributive effect. If you paid in twice as much as your lower income neighbor you do not receive twice as much in benefits. The benefits held back from you are used to boost your neighbor's benefits. Thus, Social Security is a vehicle for belated redistribution of income from upper to lower income strata.

18. FALLACIOUS ECONOMICUS: Social security is one big Ponzi scheme. There is no difference. When I retire in thirty years the trust funds will be exhausted and there will be no money left for me.

Correct Reasoning I: Corrected timeline. As of now, Social Security income (tax revenues plus interest on Trust Fund bonds) exceed payouts and the trust fund is intact. But, unless changes are made, around the year 2021 that net cash inflow will become a net cash outflow. Read all about it:

> Historically, Social Security has collected more than it paid out. The extra money built up a Trust Fund that collects interest. But due to demographic and economic changes ... it's expected that insurance payments will begin to exceed income in 2021. Around 2033, the fund will run out. *But even then, the revenue Social Security collects each year would still be enough to pay out about three-quarters of scheduled benefits as far as the eye can see.*[9]

Even after all the trust fund securities are cashed in, the tax revenues will cover about **three-quarters** of the benefit commitments. *This is not ideal but it is not a total failure of the system.*

[9. Ilan Moscovitz "5 Huge Myths About Social Security" 15 October 2012 *The Motley Fool* <http://tinyurl.com/ol63nuu>]

Correct Reasoning II: The other one quarter. Should the government run out of Social Security trust "money," the politicians will have to decide if they want to finance benefits in some other manner. Thus, ultimately, the solution is political. The U.S. government can issue bonds to the Federal Reserve, directly or indirectly, thereby *monetizing that debt* and creating new money. **This could be inflationary if the economy is at full employment.** The new money can be used to meet impending obligations under Social Security not covered by tax revenues. Essentially, this is the government "printing" new money. *This can be used to make up the other one quarter of benefits not covered by tax revenues.* Ponzi did not have the capability of printing U.S. dollars ... no private citizen does.

A plan should enacted today that raises the Social Security tax rate, income base, scales back future benefits and delays retirement dates.

[10. See for an extended discussion. Office of the Chief Actuary, "A Summary Of The 2013 Annual Reports" 14 July 2014 *Official Social Security Website* <http://tinyurl.com/mdy9qzv>]

> ### The Ponzi Scheme
> Ponzi paid off cash-ins from earlier investors with inflows from later investors. His scheme depended on a constant stream of new investors or subscribers. He was exposed once that stream dried up and the music stopped. He had only the reserves he chose to maintain to make good any shortfall. He had no money creating "machine" to back him up. The Federal Government has the money creating "muscle" when new inflows into Social Security fall short of outflows. For this reason, Social Security benefits are much more certain than the promises of Charles Ponzi. **Social Security is *not* a Ponzi scheme**.

19. FALLA<IOUS <<ONOMI<US: If social security fails totally, then folks in old age will have no source of financial support.

Correct Reasoning: A total failure is unlikely unless the total economy collapses. It will not be pretty in the absence of social security benefits, but there are some sources of support. There will be extreme hardship, especially if Medicare and Medicaid go down. Folks will have to go back to the practices they followed before Social Security benefits were paid. Private charity was a significant but still inadequate player before Social Security. The *private safety net* consisted of family, church, and private charity. These practices included reliance on the extended family, especially in agricultural households.

20. FALLA<IOUS <<ONOMI<US: It is a good thing my social security retirement benefits are not taxable. I will need every dollar of that distribution.

Correct Reasoning: OK. Sit down and get the digitalis. If your other income in retirement exceeds a certain level, then you will have to return some (but never all) of your social security benefits. *You will not lose more in benefits than you earn in income. In effect, the tax rate is less than 100%,* Therefore, work will always have some positive net monetary reward. Sleep lightly, my friend.

[11. Kevin McCormally, "Do You Have to Pay Taxes on Social Security Benefits?" 26 January 2015 *Kiplinger* <http://tinyurl.com/qzg7x9q>]

> **21. FALLA<IOUS <<ONOMI<US:** Make illegals legal, give them jobs and let them pay into the social security fund. This will pay for their own benefits and the benefits of Americans in general. Social Security will remain solvent, meeting its payouts.
>
> **Correct Reasoning:** The fallacy lies in the convenient failure to consider the U.S. policy of *chain migration,* i.e., allowing one legal immigrant to bring along a host of relatives. So, the multiple *indigent relatives* of legals and illegals get here and for benefits plug into Social Security (for the retired) and SSI (for the low earners). **More money will be sucked out of the Treasury than pumped in as the new withdrawals swamp any new taxes paid in.** The deficiency will be paid for by – guess who? – already overburdened U.S. taxpayers!

COULD THIS HAPPEN HERE?

Dear Citizens, from your President:

As you have heard, due to mismanagement by the opposition political party, our ballooning national debt has reached crisis levels. Insolvency looms. The planned government spending equal to the current Federal budget deficit is threatened by an inability to borrow the money needed to close the gap. In addition to floating the current new debt, the Treasury must arrange for the rolling over of existing debt, around $17 trillion. The debt must be rolled over because there is no way the entire debt can be paid off in one shot. Rolling over means that as older bonds mature, new bonds are issued and those funds are then used to pay off those maturing bonds. In reality, the Fed could create new money to both roll over the prior debt and finance the current deficit, appearing to solve the problem. However, it is reluctant to do so, lest monetary growth spur hyper-inflation.

What about taxes? Taxes have been raised as high as we can prudently raise them. To raise tax rates any further would bring unnecessary hardship on all earners, reaching beyond those greedy one percenters at the top end of the income distribution.

But, let us focus on the current deficit. An inability to borrow and then spend the deficit money will deal a serious blow to the American economy. Cutting the budget deficit from the year earlier level cuts Federal spending by the amount of the cut. People will lose the incomes that would have been created by the spending associated with the deficit. This will lead to more unemployment and hardship for the American people. When that happens, there will be a need for more Federal benefits- food stamps, unemployment and welfare payments and the like- to alleviate the pain, <u>just when we cannot afford to provide those benefits.</u>

My fellow citizens, a new course of action is required, not dependent on borrowing, raising tax rates or printing money.

Americans should re-think the concepts of "private" property and "community" property. The latest thinking on this is that your so-called "private" earnings and wealth were derived from a community effort and, therefore, part of community property. No one succeeds, earns or produces in isolation, i.e., without the help of the community. Yes, my fellow citizens, the success of the one stands on the shoulders of the many. Any financial success achieved by an individual is due to community involvement helping, nurturing and reinforcing that private success. Remember, you didn't build that business all by yourself. All fruits of that effort ultimately belong rightfully to the community. The main point I am trying to make here is this: your name may be on the bank account, <u>but the money really was earned by and, therefore, belongs to, the community at large.</u>

And now your community needs you to give back that money.

At this time, many so-called "private" enterprises and individuals are flush with cash, cash that could be used to plug up the deficit and avoid an economic meltdown. Unleash these cash hoards and the deficit can be eased and economic activity stimulated.

For all these reasons, given the current cash emergency in the Federal government and given the social origins of so-called "private" property and social benefits of government spending, I hereby declare that the cash balances held by private individuals, corporations, and other business entities be <u>subject to surrender to the Federal government</u>, up to 100% of the amounts involved. Pension fund cash is not exempt. If you prefer, call it a mandatory loan. Non marketable government bonds will be put in place of the money removed. Argentina, Poland and Cypress have similar programs.

One final note. This is not a voluntary program. All involved parties must comply. Do your duty to your country in this time of emergency. I have directed the Secretary of the Treasury, the Comptroller of the Currency and Federal Reserve Board Chairman to implement this policy immediately.

Respectfully,

Your President,

[This letter was found in trash basket behind the White House]

Chapter Twenty-Eight
Money Fallacies

The story is told that young George Washington once tossed a dollar coin across the Potomac River. The story is also told he was the last person to accomplish that feat. Many researchers have analyzed the feat and have a common conclusion. They have concluded a dollar simply doesn't go that far these days.

M oney is at it again. Money is wrapped up in more fallacies and myths than any other economic concept. Here is an overview of the many values of a nation's money. (First, re-read page 124)

Economists look at the value of money from four perspectives. See Diagram #1 below for the different perspectives on the value of money.

Diagram #1: The Many Values of Money

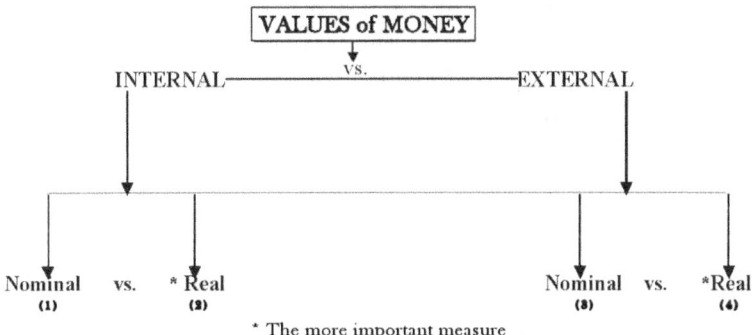

Ordinary people, in their everyday activities, consider *the* value of money as what a dollar buys at the store. This is the value of money in exchange, the *real* value. Where and when prices rise the real value of money falls. But, this immediate purchasing power of the dollar is only one of its many values. Most nations have their own basic monetary units and its subdivisions. In the U.S. we have the dollar and its subdivisions down to a penny. The British adopted this 100 penny:pound (decimalization) system about 40 years ago.

Specifically, **money has two values INTERNAL to the nation and two values EXTERNAL to the nation.** Note: all values are variable except number 1, the Internal NOMINAL value. **Internal Values**, the values of money *inside* its home territory:

1. Internal NOMINAL value is the face value stamped on the coin or paper money. Nominal value is FIXED, unaffected by inflation or deflation. A dollar is a dollar is a dollar. A dollar put in your pocket this year will still say ONE DOLLAR when you pull it out next year. One dollar exchanges for four quarters or ten dimes. **Beware:** *Nominal value* does not address the question of the amount of goods a unit of currency will buy, i.e., the purchasing power of the monetary unit.

*2. **Internal REAL value** is the purchasing power of money. What amount of *goods* will a unit of money buy, inside the home nation? How much can be bought at the local mall? **Inflation** lowers the *real* value of a unit of currency whereas deflation raises it. (However, the *nominal* value remains constant.)

It's the **real value, internal or external,** that matters to the holder of money!

External Values, the value of the home currency *outside* the home territory:

3. **External NOMINAL value** is the *foreign exchange rate*, the number of units of a *foreign currency* which may be exchanged (at the bank) for the home currency. For example, $1 buys 12 pesos. This exchange ratio may be fixed or variable. For example, the U.S. dollar is variable against most currencies but fixed at an *artificially low* price against the Red Chinese YUAN. This makes cheap (still Red) Chinese goods even cheaper (and U.S. exports more expensive).

*4. **External REAL value** of $1 is what goods can be bought with the foreign currency units bought by $1, in the foreign nation (or imported).

So, $1 buys 12 Mexican Pesos (External nominal value of $).

Then, what do those 12 pesos [= one dollar] buy *in Mexico?* This is equivalent to what one U.S. dollar buys of Mexican goods. Beware:

1. **A fall in the external real value,** ($ weakens, buys fewer units of foreign currency). This a. spurs lower cost exports b. imports cost more c) the general SOL in the U.S. is <u>hurt.</u>

2. **A rise in the external real value** ($ strengthens, buys more units of foreign currency) This a. makes imports cheaper b. exports cost more c. the general SOL in the U.S. is <u>helped.</u>

1. FALLA<IOUS <<ONOMI<US: Winning the lottery cured my poverty and gave me a luxurious lifestyle. That's it! More money for everybody will cure everyone's poverty! Let everyone win the lottery ... every week!

Correct Reasoning: Not so! Certainly, money smoothes the way to the acquisition of goods and services. More money can end an individual's poverty. So, why can't it end everyone's poverty? Answer?

The fallacy of composition "kicks in."

People often err in taking an individual experience and generalizing it, assuming the same outcome will apply if the event happened to everyone at the same time. People covet money as a means to the acquisition of goods and getting ahead.

Suppose these people now project their personal experience to the economy as a whole. Might they now conclude that the solution to general poverty is getting more money into the hands of all people? Moreover what if, at any moment, money falls from the sky (say, foreign aid) or is won in lotteries or is simply printed by the government? They are now flirting with the fallacy of composition. A projection from personal experience will not be valid.

What goes wrong when everyone gets more money? Read all about it:

Micro (narrow) perspective. As individuals, people learn that more money to them means more purchasing power and the ability to buy more stuff at the store. A child gets an allowance; a young person gets a first job. They now have more money and can get more goods and feel better off. Their poverty has been cured. No fallacy so far. Most folks learn at an early age that **money gives the holder potential command and control over goods and resources.**

Macro (broad) perspective. Now, change the scene to the whole economy. The macro economy follows a different set of rules from the individual or small group, the micro economy. These different rules are not intuitively obvious to an individual generalizing from his/her personal experience.

More Money Without More Goods to Buy Is a Fool's Errand

An economy overloaded with money but without traditional resources would improve economic welfare. Land, labor, real capital and entrepreneurship are needed to produce goods, along with know-how. Overwhelming a resource-poor nation with more paper money would not enhance the productive potential and standard of living of all the residents. All the ensuing spending would spark inflation and most folks will be back to square one in terms of real goods. Although folks would have more monetary units, e.g., dollars, each unit has much less purchasing power due to the inflation.

But, the failure of more money to improve at once the lot of *all people* in a nation does not apply when more money comes to only a few individuals. On the contrary, endowing a few people with lots of additional money could, in fact, enable them to enjoy a higher real standard of living! Their added spending draws goods away from other spenders without causing a general rise in prices, i.e., inflation.

Fallacy of composition redux. Suppose a small group of people win a big lottery prize. They are likely to go on a shopping spree and succeed in buying more goods. Their enhanced command of goods is real and valid. However, their added spending, *by itself*, could not cause inflation. Their added buying power and purchases are small *relative* to **total spending and purchases.**

EXCESS monetary growth. However, suppose ALL people come into more money and all of them go on shopping binges. Given a fixed amount of goods, the added spending will likely drive up prices, ultimately causing inflation. Reasoning in a macro context: what *goes around* – the greater spending – *comes around* as greater income. So, everything will cost more – **but incomes rise in tandem** – due to the inflation. Notice that **the inflation does not correct itself.** Higher prices do not choke off spending, due to the enhanced income.

At full employment, total output cannot expand. The inflation price hikes cancel out the benefits of having more money to spend. The folks spend more and more but do not increase their take-home of goods.

So, the gift of more money can benefit a few people ... but not the whole group! This is a re-visit to the fallacy of composition: the group could not do what was done by an individual.

To get ahead, an individual needs to have *income* grow *faster* than prices. Also, one needs to invest in *assets* – real estate, anyone? – that increase in price faster than the general price level.

Is **Money the Root of All Evil ... or ... the Root of All Good?**

2. FALLACIOUS ECONOMICUS: Money is the root of all evil. Get rid of it!

Fallacious Reasoning: Many evil acts have been committed in pursuit of money. Wars, murders, robberies all owe their genesis to the pursuit of gold, silver and even paper money. Get rid of it!

Correct Reasoning: Actually, the quote above, "Money is the root of all evil," is a misquote. The correct biblical quote is, "The *love* of money is the root of all evil." Malcolm Forbes asserts, "Money is the root of all good." What is going on here? In truth, money is simply an inanimate object, harmless until wielded in some effort. It has no consciousness and does not know right from wrong, evil from good. Yes, evil has been perpetrated in the name of money, but it was people who perpetrated the evil act, not the money.

Moreover, the availability of money as a **medium of exchange** supercharges the productivity of resources. Indeed, people invented money so they could be free of the *coincidence of wants* requirement for barter exchange. With that freedom, specialists could make more sales and more purchases using money, enhancing their standards of living.

In fact, money has aided economic development and done much more good than harm over its long history. Anthropologists have found evidence of monetary use in diverse cultures, worldwide, reaching back thousands of years. *Money unleashes the division of labor and, as such, is indispensable in helping an economy become prosperous.* The specialization or division of labor, enabled by monetary exchange, is a **force multiplier**. It is indispensable in maintaining and expanding productive potential. A modern economy – and society – would collapse without money!

Money has a number of **functions**, foremost of which is serving as a medium of exchange. It also serves as an (imperfect) store of real value, and a standard of nominal value (internal and external.)

The medium of exchange

> **Money is like a magic wand: wave it at a bunch of resources and they become exponentially more productive.** –Theo Dosius

Money unleashes the division of labor. Money serves a medium of exchange, making it easier for specialists to dispose of their surplus output. The farmer overproduces grain, more than his family needs. The surplus is sold for money. The farmer then takes the money and buys whatever he wants from another overproducing specialist, say, the shoemaker. This avoids the use of the specialization and output killer called **barter**.

Barter means swapping goods for goods. Barter requires a simultaneous **coincidence of wants** between the traders. So, the shoemaker and the farmer must spontaneously and simultaneously decide they want to trade with each other! Fat chance! So, many a proposed trade falls through. Traders get disgusted. They become "do it yourselfers," trying to make everything for themselves. But, the farmer is not a good shoemaker and the shoemaker is not a good farmer. As a do-it-your-selfer, each one would waste time and effort trying to do the other's job. Try as they may, they cannot out produce veteran specialists. The result is a fall in total output and rise in unsatisfied want.

Barter is the enemy of specialization and economic development. Leisure is decimated as time and energy are consumed in the acts of bartering. **Money eliminates the *coincidence of wants* requirement for a trade, setting the stage for more sales and more purchases using money as the medium of exchange.** A *monetized economy* will, with specialization, 1) yield more goods, at 2) lower costs, and 3) goods in greater variety than a barter economy. In this sense money is the root of all good! Money is a production and trade helper, increasing want satisfaction. A growing economy needs more and more money to enable additional exchanges.

Optimum Amount of Money

The optimum amount of money draws forth the economy's full productive potential while minimizing inflation. An economy with the *optimum amount of money* can enrich as many folks as possible, given the productive potential at that moment. It does this by encouraging enriching activities: the division of labor, specialization of production, and trade. With money encouraging specialization, lots of benefits appear: 1) goods cost less 2) goods appear in greater variety ... relative to a barter system of exchange and 3)) goods are as abundant as possible.

---

3. FALLACIOUS ECONOMICUS: Since money has this important role of easing exchanges among specialists, it must be a very valuable resource.

Correct Reasoning: Actually, **modern money is not a resource**, as economists define resource. Technically, *a resource is anything useful in making a good.* Today's money is sterile in terms of goods production. So, money is *not* a resource in the literal sense of the word resource. Paper money, as a commodity, is intrinsically worthless. (Okay, you could burn it in a campfire or make a little hat out of $100 bills.) Coins contain very little valuable metal, mainly zinc, manganese and some copper. They are referred to as token coins, merely representing value, but not having that value as a commodity.

Money is *so useful* as a medium of exchange that:
Money, in some form, preceded governments.
Money, in some form, will outlive governments.

–Theo Dosius

Money supercharges resources. Money is more than a resource helper. It is a **resource supercharger, a force multiplier.** With money comes specialization, division of labor, greater output and greater trade from the same resources!

Remember, it is the big four *real* resources and know-how – not money – that do the work of producing goods. Money "goes along for the ride" acting as an enabler, as a catalyst would in a chemical transaction. **Money eases the transfer of goods; it is the lubricant of trade.** It is common for an economics professor to correctly and emphatically to warn: a nation – already specialized, but poor but in real resources – cannot be enriched in real resources (and goods) and know-how purely by the addition of massive amounts of new money. If more money would do the trick, the elimination of world poverty would be at hand!

Remember: money is like the straw that *stirs* the drink, the magic wand that improves the taste of the drink or magnifies the productivity of resources, compared to a barter system.

Money as a time machine: a store of real value. Money can be active (used as a medium of exchange) or passive (used as a store of value). Most folks want to spread out their buying over time. Money can help them do that. Money can **be a repository of value, buying power,** for later use, much as a car running in neutral is storing acceleration for eventual driving. In its passive state, stored money enables the holder to pass up current purchases in exchange for future goods. In this way, idle money serves as a repository of purchasing power that can be drawn on to make purchases in future years. **But, beware: Money is not a *perfect* store of real value, i.e., buying power. In an inflationary period, each dollar loses real value. Inflation erodes the purchasing power stored in each monetary unit.** As a result, folks seek other ways to store value. Indeed, any valuable asset e.g., bonds, antique collectibles, real estate, could compete with money as a store of value. But beware: each alternative store of value has advantages and disadvantages of its own. (Take a course in Money and Banking!)

4. FALLA<IOUS <<ONOMI<US: Since money has such a beneficial presence, the economy can never have enough money.

Fallacious Reasoning: Well, you can never get too much of a good thing, right?

Correct Reasoning: Remember, excess causes good to turn to bad. An excess of a good thing backfires and becomes a bad thing. Too little money can ruin an economy. Insufficient money in circulation could force people to give up specialization and revert to barter, a disastrous outcome. Too much money can ruin an economy, as well. Too much money in circulation could lead to hyperinflation, rejection of money and economic collapse.

Recall the wisdom of the ancients: too little or too much of a good thing is a bad thing. **Moderation in all things** is the key.

In sum, money has critical functions to perform for individuals (micro level) and for the economy as a whole (macro level).

1. On a **micro** level, money is cited as satisfying the wants for a medium of exchange, store of value and standard of value.

2. On a **macro** level, excessive or deficient growth in the total money supply plays havoc with aggregate demand. The macro goals of full employment consistent with price level stability are jeopardized if money is mismanaged.

Macroeconomic Case Study

Follow the money as it expands economy wide and see its impact on an economy operating *below* its productive potential. What happens as more and more money is injected into the economy as a whole during a period of *involuntary* unemployment? Read all about it:

Approaching Full Employment (Full Capacity)

Eventually, continuing to add extra money to all buyers brings all employable resources into production and the economy reaches full employment **unless velocity, i.e., the rate of spending, falls. See Detour Ahead below.**

Warning, Detour Ahead: *Despite the expansion of money and credit,* if velocity crashes, the economy falls into a liquidity trap and will not reach full employment. The Liquidity Trap is discussed in the next chapter!

Assume monetary policy has worked, the liquidity trap has been avoided, and the economy has reached full employment. Now what?

At full employment no additional *real* output is possible as all employable resources are being used. At this point someone might reason: look at all the good more money has brought! "It's the money that created the prosperity," they cry! Well, not exactly. More money fueled *aggregate demand.* The additional spending activated idle resources and brought us from unemployment production levels to full employment production levels! But, a money delusion may persist.

Warning: Beware the **Liquidity Trap** discussed in greater detail in the next chapter! If velocity crashes the economy falls into a liquidity trap and will not reach full employment, despite the added money.

Beyond Full Employment – Where No Economy Has Gone Before!

Suppose the liquidity trap is avoided and full employment is reached. What if, at full employment, more money continues to pour into the economy? At this juncture folks might commit the fallacy: if a little of something is good, then more must be better! Wrong! If still more money is "injected" and spreads to all people they wind up trying to outbid one another in a tug of war for the limited amount of goods. Producers react by hiking prices. Prices are driven up, but there are no idle resources to put to work producing more goods. This is **demand-pull inflation**. Folks subsisting on fixed incomes (pensioners, labor contract workers, retirees and others) find their buying power unfairly diminished for no economic justification.

If the money spigot is opened all the way, then the economy is on the road to **hyperinflation** and ... ka-boom goes the *real* economy. Witness the Germany of 1923, gutted by skyrocketing inflation.

Expectations Can Create Havoc: The Asset Bubble

Expectations in micro world: the asset bubble. Normally, excess monetary growth is not needed for a *single* price to rise or for the formation of an asset bubble. There is a bubble when price rises *in excess* of standard norms for that asset. Witness the subprime mortgage housing bubble of the early 2000s.

Scenario. Suppose buyers and sellers expect an asset, for example, a house to rise in price. Buyer AND seller **expectations of a rising price** spark additional, even irrational, buying of the asset (a stock, a house or a collectible work of art). The price can rise in a micro context if, say, bank credit is overextended for the purchase of the asset. At government urging, shamefully excessive credit was extended to home buyers who drove housing prices up. This occurs even when folks consider the asset would be overvalued in normal, buy and hold circumstances. Normal gauges of value are thrown aside, swelling the bubble. Many buyers are looking to buy and re-sell quickly at a gain, not hold the asset for retirement.

Eventually, there are not enough frenzied buyers to feed the higher and higher price. Buyers, sellers, and lenders come to their senses and realize the price rise cannot go on forever! So, beware: bubbles are hyper sensitive and likely to break easily!

*The people who cast the votes decide nothing. **The people who count the votes decide everything.*** Joseph Stalin

Chapter Twenty-Nine
Money, Inflation and Deflation Fallacies

Money is the root of all good. — Steve Forbes

Inflation and deflation are what economists call monetary phenomena. That is, they originate in an economy wide excess or deficiency of money and in its speed of circulation, called *velocity.*

1. FALLACIOUS ECONOMICUS: I wish I could issue my own money, with my picture on it. But, the government will not allow it.

Correct Reasoning: Hey, fella, go for it. For many years money in America was privately issued, no government imprimatur (or approval) needed. Government is a relative latecomer to issuing paper money (except for the War of Independence and the Civil War).

By the way, ordinary folks can still issue their own money. **There is no law prohibiting you from issuing your own currency and coin.** Of course, it cannot be a copy of official money. That would be counterfeiting and is illegal. But, you are free to bring out money with a different design. Ithaca Hours was privately issued money that found a degree of success in its locality. [1]

[1. "Ithaca Hours" 7 May 2014 *Wikipedia* <http://en.wikipedia.org/wiki/Ithaca_Dollars>]

The major problem with issuing your own money is **acceptability.** How are you going to get people to accept it if the "money" is not backed up by or convertible into something of real value? Gold or silver coins were valuable in themselves. Gold certificates were convertible into gold coin. Perhaps each unit of currency issued could be backed up by one hour of housekeeping services or one hour of lawn maintenance? This convertibility feature would backup any exchange value garnered by the currency. Essentially, the currency would be an IOU that has value because its issuer is considered trustworthy and will "make good" on his promise.

Background. From the onset, many problems afflicted the American banking system and the issuance of money. Gold and silver legal tender coins were minted, as provided in the Constitution. Copper coins were minted, as well. Spanish dollar coins circulated as legal tender until 1857. Fixed ratio **bimetallism (gold to silver, 1:15)** was problematic, and ultimately abandoned in 1873. Also, starting in the 1860s, national (private, commercial) banks were chartered and issued paper currency. Previously, private state chartered banks had been issuing their own currency.

Lust for money is the root of all evil. — New Testament

But, problems remained without a cohesive, integrated money/banking system. Some problems eased with the creation in 1913 of the Federal Reserve Banking System. The "Fed" was to function as a bank to the national government and to the private banking system. **Gold coins** were confiscated by the government and withdrawn from circulation in 1933 to fight deflation and depression of the time. The minting of **silver coins** gradually came to a close in the mid 1960s as free market silver prices persistently exceeded the Treasury's 'pegged' value.

All coins today are tokens. Today, the U.S. dollar is **defined** in terms of gold, i.e., it has an official gold content for bookkeeping purposes. Since 1973, one troy ounce of gold is valued at $42.22 "in the books." Today, the *book* value of the

Twenty Dollar Gold Coins

U.S. gold stock approaches $12 billion whereas the *market* value is nearly $300 billion (values as of January, 2016.)

So, though **defined** in terms of gold, dollars are not **backed** by or **convertible** into gold or silver. The money supply and the government's gold supply are independent. These are *nonmonetary* gold ingots, stored at the United States Bullion Depository at Fort Knox, an army base in Kentucky.

Today, neither gold nor silver coins *for circulation* are issued by the Treasury. (The Mint produces bullion coins and limited edition coins sold to collectors). Today's coins are an alloy of zinc, manganese and some copper. (In 1974, an aluminum alloyed penny was minted, found deficient and never issued.) The face value of each circulating U.S. coin exceeds the market value of its metal content. For example, there is less than five cents worth of resource in a nickel.

[2. "Value of Coins" 12 Dec. 2012 Political Connection <http://tinyurl.com/ha347hb> also: Status Report of U.S. Government Gold Reserve , 31 Jan. 2016 <http://tinyurl.com/zzecos3>]

Capital Lexicon

In the business world, the word *capital* has different meanings in different contexts. To understand business, one must understand these differences. It is imperative to comprehend these variations in meaning. Read all about it:

Capital in the accounting class: In accounting, capital appears in the fundamental equation, actually an identity: ASSETS = LIABILITIES + CAPITAL. Say, $30 = $20 + $10. The assets are considered property of the creditors and the owners, exclusively. Capital is the book value of the owners (or stockholders) share (legal stake) in the assets of the business. Should the assets be liquidated – turned into cash – owners would receive what is left over *after* creditors – represented by Liabilities – have been paid. In this context, Capital is synonymous with Net Worth or Owners' Equity.

Capital in the finance class: In the finance class, *capital* usually refers to *money* capital or money. Cash on hand and cash in the checking accounts. *Raising capital* means raising money. *Capital budgeting* means allocating that money to long-term projects.

Capital in the economics class, I: real capital. Capital most often refers to tools, equipment, software or things we make that help us to make other things. In this sense, it is often referred to as *real* or physical capital. **Real capital** is not considered a consumer good, an end in itself. It satisfies no wants *directly.*

Rather, real capital is a means to an end, a stepping stone to the production of other goods. As with the division of labor, real capital is a **force multiplier**, providing tools to workers, thereby expanding their bar hand capabilities. But, real capital does not come free, TANSTAAFL. Real capital wears out physically or technologically and has to be renewed, at a cost. Real capital requires resources drawn from consumer goods production, putting a crimp in the current satisfaction of consumer wants.

Capital in the economics class, II: human capital is the stock of 1) acquired and 2) useful abilities embodied in a person. These are abilities beyond natural talents. For example, people are not born with ability to write software or design bridges. They must acquire that capacity. Human capital must be acquired through schooling, formal or informal. Also, as with real capital, human capital makes a worker more productive. However, as with physical capital, a sacrifice of consumer goods and enjoyment is required to absorb human capital. Moreover, skills and abilities must be updated as needed.

Note: In international *trade,* capital equipment is imported and exported. However, in **international *finance*,** reference to "capital flows" between countries usually refers to money, not physical or human capital.

2. FALLACIOUS ECONOMICUS: Inflation means all prices are rising.

Correct Reasoning: Yes, inflation is an economy wide concept. But, no, all *prices need not rise at the same time or at the same rate.* Some prices could rise faster than others. Some prices could actually decline in the face of a general price rise. **Inflation requires that only the *average* of all prices must be rising persistently, over a multi-year period.** The average can rise even if some prices are falling or constant because rising prices dominate.

So, inflation is a persistent rise in the economy's average price level.

A Tidbit

Around 1500 Spain issued a silver dollar coin that could be divided into 8 pieces, or bits. It came with perforated marks for ease of separation, as a round pizza comes with pre-cut slices. Pieces or bits of the coin could be broken off and used for small payments. There were 8 bits to the dollar. Each bit was worth 12 and ½ cents. Two bits represented 25 cents or a quarter dollar. It is still slang today. "Two-bits" is synonymous with a quarter. It is also slang to demean something as cheap or someone as unprofessional, such as a "two-bit" politician or a "two-bit" lawyer.

The Spanish dollar was legal tender in the United States until 1857!

---

3. FALLACIOUS ECONOMICUS: Inflation has been described as a persistent rise in the *average* price level. Therefore, a rise in the price of one good cannot create economy wide inflation.

Correct Reasoning: It depends on the significance of the good. Apples? No. Shoes? No. A rise in the price of a widely consumed or sourced raw material, say, gasoline, can have a domino effect on a host of other prices causing the average to rise. This one price increase is like a contagious disease that spreads throughout the economy.

Example: Crude oil has a multitude of uses, beyond gasoline and electric power generation. After all, production, distribution, heating and lighting all depend on energy, much of it derived from oil. A jump in OPEC dominated crude oil prices in the 1970s spread to many other goods. However, **it is debatable whether a *onetime* rise in the price of energy – enabled by a *onetime* episode of *excess* monetary growth – could spark a *multiyear* inflation.**

4. FALLACIOUS ECONOMICUS: Duck! Everyone is hurt by inflation!

Correct Reasoning: Not true. Actually, some folks are helped by inflation! Recognize that people play many roles in the economy: wage earner, saver, homeowner, lender (creditor) or borrower (debtor and mortgage debtor). Some are helped in one capacity and hurt in another. Also, one must consider whether the inflation is expected or unexpected. (A complete exposition of this topic is beyond the scope of this book).

An analysis requires a breakdown of the different roles people may play in the economy. To illustrate: consider the case of *unexpected* inflation.

Debtors, those who owe a fixed nominal amount of money, benefit from an unexpected inflation. Debtors benefit by paying back in dollars with lower purchasing power than the borrowed dollars.

One thousand dollars bought more before the inflation than after one.

Example: Assume a $1000 loan was made from Judy to Sam before the inflation. After the inflation Sam and repays his debt. Judy can buy less than before because the $1000 she got back buys less than the $1000 loaned. In terms of goods, Sam returned fewer goods than he was loaned. This amounts to a transfer of purchasing power from Judy to Sam, from creditors to debtors. Creditors include banks and other lending institutions. Creditors, e.g. banks and mortgage lenders, are hurt by receiving dollars with lower purchasing power than loaned. In sum, **debtors gain and creditors lose from inflation.**

Unexpected inflation inflicts punishment on some people, mainly, those on fixed incomes (salaries, pensions, bank and bond interest.) Social security is adjusted upward with a one year lag.   Inflation reduces the purchasing power, the real value, of those on the receiving side of fixed incomes, pensions, debt payments and bank balances. Inflation may reward those on flexible incomes such as business profits and owners of inflation protective assets. **These rewards and punishments are handed down without any underlying justification!**

5. FALLACIOUS ECONOMICUS: I am just a working stiff. There is no way I can shield myself from inflation eating up the purchasing power of my income and savings.

Correct Reasoning: Ask your employer for a Cost of Living Adjustment (a pay raise), known as a COLA. Social security beneficiaries have a built in COLA. They get a yearly benefit adjustment for inflation. Securities known as *real return* or *inflation indexed* securities (such Treasury Inflation Protected Securities or TIPS) attempt to boost the return on a security as inflation accelerates. You might **invest in assets expected to rise in value along with inflation.** Private homes, co-ops and condos have fill that role since the 1950s.

VELOCITY IS THE MISSING LINK!

6. FALLACIOUS ECONOMICUS: Inflation and deflation are *purely* monetary phenomena. Excess money growth *relative* to available goods *guarantees* inflation whereas deficient money growth guarantees deflation.

Correct Reasoning: Suppose at full employment the productive potential now grows. Then, assuming stable velocity, more money and credit are needed to provide the purchasing power to boost demand and call forth the additional

goods. But, money growth should not be excessive relative to growth potential for goods.

But, even when excessive, *excess* monetary growth does not always spike inflation and deficient monetary growth does not always signal deflation. There are no guarantees in either direction. Two facts emerge from the postwar U.S. experience:

1. Rarely does the money supply decline.
2. The policy choices available to the Federal Reserve are usually between a faster and a slower growth path for money.

Inflation threatens, *but is not certain,* when there is *excess* money growth relative to goods available for sale. The absence of a guarantee lies in the fact that the money has to enter the spending stream and circulate through the economy to certify higher prices. If it doesn't, then the higher prices do not stick.

The frequency of turnover of money or rapidity of circulation is called the velocity of money. And *velocity can drop, offsetting a spurt in money growth that would otherwise be inflationary!* This has been the situation since 2009. Note that (Money Supply) times (Velocity) = Total Spending or GDP.

Similarly, deflation threatens, *but is not certain,* when there is a decline in money or money growth. Velocity can accelerate or spike. This would offset the decline in money and prevent what would otherwise be a deflationary movement. So, an increase in M can be offset by a decrease in V.

The bad news is velocity cannot be controlled by the monetary authorities. It has been called the *missing link* in monetary policy. [See Fallacy # 8]

The good news is velocity normally cannot vary significantly, especially in the upward direction. In fact, velocity has been on a steady decline since 2008.

[3. Michael Snyder, "The Velocity Of Money In The U.S. Falls To An All-Time Record Low" 1 June 2014 *The Economic Collapse* < http://tinyurl.com/qght9dr>]

Despite the lack of perfect correspondence, bet on inflation if there is persistent, excessive monetary growth, as in the German hyperinflation of the early 1920s!

7. FALLA<IOUS <<ONOMI<US: Don't worry about inflation. **Inflation is self-correcting.** Inflations are bound to extinguish themselves as higher and

higher prices spread throughout the economy. Buyers will not be able to pay the higher prices and they will drop.

Fallacious Reasoning: A lone greedy seller will lose some or all of his customers if his price is jacked up excessively. Then he has to change his strategy and drop his price in hopes of retaining and re-capturing his customers. What happens to one seller will happen to the whole bunch, i.e., all customers will "bail." It will be the same result if all sellers tried the same road to higher profit. Then, prices will fall back.

Correct Reasoning: Use macro reasoning. Inflation will *not* self-destruct if:

1. Excess money is continually injected into the economy *and*

2. People continue to spend it at the same or rising rate. (Velocity of money does not fall). A note on the velocity of money:

> The (income) *velocity of money* is the frequency at which one unit of currency is used to purchase domestically produced goods and services within a given time period. In other words, it is the number of times one dollar is spent to buy goods and services per unit of time.
>
> [4. Federal Reserve Bank of St. Louis
> "Velocity of M2 Money Stock" 23 Dec 2014 *FRED - St. Louis Fed*
> < http://tinyurl.com/26sb2xq />]

Higher prices, *bolstered by money expansion*, will generate higher incomes. Higher incomes enable buying, even at the higher prices. **In the macro world** *what goes around comes around:* **higher prices come back as higher incomes. Thus, the inflation need not self-destruct; the higher prices can stick.**

Yes, of course, a fire will burn out unless more fuel is added. It is the same process with inflation or hyperinflation. More and more money creation is like adding fuel to the fire of inflation so it cannot burn out. Without #1 and #2 higher prices could not persist and would fall back.

Thus, higher and higher prices, fueled by excess monetary growth and steady rate of utilization, do not self-extinguish! **Inflation does not cure itself.**

Monetary Policy and the Liquidity Trap: Collapse of Velocity

8. FALLACIOUS ECONOMICUS: More money and lower interest rates are *guaranteed* to end a recession.

Correct Reasoning: Speeding up the flow of money into the system may be called an expansive monetary policy, quantitative easing or easy monetary policy. Either way, the growth of the money supply is accelerating. The objection in the fallacious statement is to the *guarantee*. In life, guarantees are few; in economics, even fewer. Sometimes interest rates are lowered and sometimes a recession is ended. But, again, there is no guarantee. Let's see:

Scenario one: slack in the economy. Here is a positive outcome, no fallacy. As more money spreads throughout the economy much of it is spent, assuming no liquidity trap. At first, this may bring the economy to full capacity, where further increases in output are no longer possible. This is a success story for this use of monetary policy.

Scenario two: full employment. Continuing monetary growth *beyond* the full employment level, coupled with constant velocity, will cause buying intentions to spike. This creates an *excess* of aggregate demand across the economy. When there is *excess aggregate* (or grand total) *demand* buyers are trying to buy more goods than sellers are offering. Shortages emerge in many markets across the economy. Some buyers get left out but are undeterred. These left out buyers, fueled by the growing money supply and easing credit availability, are agreeable to higher prices. **A "feeding frenzy" emerges for the full capacity quantity of goods.** Sellers exploit the situation by raising prices. In sum, the excess money added to a fully employed economy is like throwing gasoline on a fire. Demand-pull inflation -- without added output -- is the result. **Over-expansion of money and credit is a failure of monetary policy!**

Impact of Inflation

Unexpected inflation imposes injustices on certain segments of the economy such as creditors and those living on fixed incomes. Debtors gain by paying back with dollars with less purchasing power than dollars borrowed.

Scenario three: stagnation instead of stimulation. Sometimes more money fails to stimulate if "gloom and doom" dominate the outlook. In these cases, velocity drops, offsetting the increase in money. The old saying is, "You can lead a horse to water, but you cannot make him drink," applies to this case. In this case, the Federal Reserve Bank can add seed money to the banking system. But, the banks and a cooperating public are needed to make the seeds sprout into more and more spending.

Here is how it works: The powers of the Federal Reserve are limited in this area. The Federal Reserve Bank can **add seed money but cannot make it grow.** Gloom and doom kick in. To start, banks hold that seed money. The banks are unwilling to lend and/or the public seeks fewer loans. Or the banks must buy bonds with that seed money. If the public and the banks (holders of the seed) hold back in that fashion, then the "seeds" never sprout into monetary growth. (The "seed" money is called the **monetary base**.)

Fall in velocity. This failure to sprout is reflected in a fall in the velocity of money. The *(income) velocity of money* refers to the speed of money circulation or turnover from spender to spender in buying new goods. It cannot be dictated by the government. Velocity is normally a stable variable, changing very little. However, *sometimes the velocity drops drastically, reflecting the failure of the seeds to sprout.*

The collapse in velocity as the monetary base is expanding signals a failure of monetary policy to stimulate a sagging economy. The excess money drives down interest rates but *does not inspire added demand for goods.* This may occur before full employment is reached. Indeed, it could occur with significant unemployment! Famed British economist John Maynard Keynes called this situation a *Liquidity Trap*. See a chart detailing the drastic drop in velocity during the recovery from the 2009 recession.

[5. "Research," 2 Oct. 2015 *St. Louis Fed* < http://tinyurl.com/nfvy2fz >]

So, out goes the absolute guarantee of excess money creating inflation or bringing about full employment.

9. FALLACIOUS ECONOMICUS: Lenin was wrong when he said, "Destroy a nation's money and you destroy the nation." Pure poppycock! The dangers from hyperinflation have been greatly exaggerated.

Correct Reasoning: Listen to Lenin. If *excess* money growth persists – while *velocity of money* holds steady or rises – a nation risks creating a hyperinflation. Hyperinflation kicks in when inflation reaches and then surpasses approximately 100% per year. The *real* value of each unit of money falls drastically. As prices soar one dollar buys fewer and fewer goods. More and more money is needed to assemble the same purchasing power as before the inflation. Money ceases to be a good store of value, real goods replacing it.

Hyperinflation. In hyperinflation (sometimes called *runaway or galloping inflation*), prices rise so unpredictably fast, so far and wide that, at some point, people lose confidence in the money and refuse to accept it. There is a story told of a German man in 1923. He left a wheelbarrow full of money outside a store as he shopped inside for a loaf of bread. When he returned, the money was still there – but the wheelbarrow was gone! People store value in *real goods* instead of fiat, intrinsically worthless money. Folks become reluctant to give up goods (or work) for money the next person will not accept!

Goodbye money, hello barter. So, folks do not accept money any longer. This causes people to work less and revert to time consuming, cumbersome barter to make their exchanges. But, barter is the arch enemy of specialization, division of labor and surplus production. Reverting to barter causes an exodus from worker specialization and a return to self-sufficiency. Production and incomes collapse! In the extreme, everyone tries to do everything! Now, the downward spiral begins. These backward steps lead to general economic collapse. (Read about the destructive power of a collapsing monetary system in the case study of the Roman Empire).

True, debtors (borrowers and governments) *gain* and creditors (banks, ordinary people) *lose* from unexpected hyperinflation. Inflated wages and salaries more easily pay off old, "uninflated" fixed debts.

But, hyperinflation can destroy a whole economy and social structure. The rule of law is threatened, anarchy looms. The destructive impact of hyperinflation can be observed in the German economy of the early 1920s.

> German currency had become completely worthless. Purchasing power of salaries and wages was reduced to zero. The life savings of the middle classes and working classes were wiped out...All [the people] knew was that a large bank account could not buy a straggly bunch of carrots, and half peck of potatoes, and few ounces of sugar, a pound of flour. They knew that as individuals they were bankrupt. And they knew hunger when it gnawed at them, as it did daily. In their misery and hopelessness, they made the Republic the scapegoat for all that had happened. Such times were heaven-sent for Adolf Hitler.
>
> [6. William L. Shirer. *The Rise and Fall of the Third Reich*, New York: Simon & Schuster, 1960. pp. 61-62]

General impact of hyperinflation: the money ceases to be accepted, specialization declines, and barter returns. As a result, production and the economy collapse. The rule of law is threatened, anarchy looms.

Counterfeiting

Successful counterfeit currency may also destroy the acceptability of all currency. It can have the same effect as a hyperinflation: destroy a nation's money. According to Lenin, this can destroy the economic and social fabric of a nation. Recognizing the power of money, the Nazis had a failed plan to inundate Britain with counterfeit currency during World War II.

Remember: The economy is the mother ship of national security, the source of Guns and Butter. An attack on money - its acceptability, its real value - is an attack on the economy's capacity to produce Guns and Butter. Thus, a persistent, successful attack on money - by over (or under) expansion, counterfeiting, or cyber attack – leads producers to drop division of labor and traders to revert to barter. Should that occur, the production of Guns and Butter would collapse. Misery and deprivation would abound. In effect, national security would be "nuked"! So, mortally wound the modern economy and you mortally wound national security!

10. FALLACIOUS ECONOMICUS: Excess monetary growth guarantees there will be no **deflation**.

Correct Reasoning: There is no guarantee! *Velocity could collapse, offsetting the rise in money supply.* That is, the circulation of money could crash.

Experience shows that buyers may not immediately spend every ounce of purchasing power they have access to. Cash may be set aside for a future purchase, a possible emergency, a rainy day or as reserve for unknown contingencies. A new line of credit or lower borrowing costs may not spark more borrowing and spending. Expectation of a worsening economy might explain the reluctance to spend. If most buyers are of that mind, then spending will not increase and may actually fall, indicating a drop in prices in spite of a bump in the money supply. After the fact, economists will attribute the spending drop to a drop in the income velocity of money.

In sum, excessive money growth cannot guarantee the absence of a deflation. Deflation can occur in an environment of excessive growth in the money supply. The drop in velocity *more than offsets* the rise in money supply.

[The above analysis relies on the relationship in the *equation of exchange*, **(M x V ≡ P x Q)**, developed – discovered? – over 100 years ago by the American economist, Irving Fisher. Where:

M equals the money supply, V equals the velocity of money.

P equals the average price level and Q equals real output. (PxQ) = $ GDP]

Take a course in Money and Banking to get a full explanation of how economists work with the equation of exchange!

[7. "Equation of Exchange (MV=PQ) / Quantity Theory of Money" 27 January 2015 *Econmentor* < http://tinyurl.com/nlg6hxm >]

Zero Inflation?

11. FALLACIOUS ECONOMICUS: It is best to reduce inflation to zero.

Fallacious Reasoning: Since inflation causes so much pain throughout the economy why not eliminate it, or at least try to eliminate it?

Correct Reasoning: Easier said than done! But, eliminating inflation may not be desirable. Of course, there would be benefits to zero inflation. But, again, beware excess! But, there would be costs, as well. To bring inflation down to zero is to flirt with another even more harmful process: deflation. Zero inflation is like sitting on a fence with inflation on one side and deflation on the other. Neither side is desirable, but deflation is the bigger threat. Indeed, zero inflation has never been a public policy goal in the United States. So, inflation is to be minimized ... perhaps to the low single digits, but not brought down to zero. At zero it would come too close to deflation, the larger evil!

General Wage and Price Controls for Inflation (GWPC)

12. FALLACIOUS ECONOMICUS: Legal wage and price controls on a *macro* level are an effective means of dealing with inflation.

Correct Reasoning: These nation-wide, across-the-board regulations either *freeze* wages and prices or drastically limit their *rate of increase.* Generally, one rate of increase applies to all covered goods and services. (Import prices and selected markets are not covered, i.e., exempt). A price freeze helps by dampening inflationary expectations.

GWPC have been tried for millennia in a variety of circumstances. They have many built in weaknesses and are, at best, a temporary measure. 1) They should be the remedy of "last resort" in a free society. 2) GWPC can easily be defeated by ingenious people. 3) In general, the longer they are in place, the less effective they are. 4) GWPC suppress changes in *relative* prices, causing malfunctions in the allocation of resources. 5) An army of enforcers and a cooperative public are needed to make GWPC be a success. World War Two witnessed a relatively successful application of GWPC. The more effective remedy is to **restrain monetary growth and the velocity of money.** For that resolution you have to see the folks at the Federal Reserve Bank.

The Lid on the Pot

In effect, imposing price and wage controls to suppress an emerging inflation is like pushing down on the lid of a pot about to boil over. In each case the "remedy" deals with the symptom, not the cause. The cause of the pot wanting to boil over is the persistent excessive heat, the high flame. The cause of an emerging inflation usually is persistent excessive monetary growth. So, again, *excess* is the culprit. So, turn down the flame under the pot and restrict monetary growth in the economy.

General wage and price controls are favorite anti-inflation tools during full mobilization in wartime. The controls impose ceilings throughout the economy. They help discourage the demand for civilian goods, thereby releasing resources (real saving) to flow into military goods.

General wage and price controls, side by side with selective price controls, dominate Fascist and Communist economies. In those systems the elite rulers believe they must control everyone, and most of their activities. This includes all production, distribution and prices ... and school curriculums.

Tariffs and Inflation

13. FALLACIOUS ECONOMICUS: A onetime 10 % tariff hike (sales tax on imports) will create inflation of 10%.

Fallacious Reasoning: Ten percent is added to the in-country selling price. This way the importer can recover the 10% sales tax (tariff) he paid.

Correct Reasoning: Consider raising a tariff – or any sales tax, one time – from 5% to 10% with no further increases. This onetime 10% across the board tariff may prompt prices to rise for one year or so to a new plateau. But, **inflation requires the prices rise persistently for a number of years.** A one year rise is not enough. If a tariff is raised *every year,* say from 10% to 15% and so on, then inflation can result – if accompanied by excess monetary growth (or ratcheting up of velocity.) The onetime import tariff is paid *once* at the port of entry. As an imported intermediary good or component works its way through the U.S. production/distribution chain, the *relative* impact of the tariff is diluted at each stage of value added. The rise in price of the end product is less than 10%.

Yes, the more basic the "tariffed" import, the more widespread the *short run* inflationary pressure. For example, imported oil and feed grains have wide impact. **In the long run**: new in-country industries may be stimulated by a **protective tariff. An import tariff may stimulate domestic production which, once achieving scale economies, ultimately allows undercutting of import prices.** So, initial, short run higher prices may spark new entry of domestic firms in the long run. In the long run these new firms may ultimately bring down prices. Anti-trust laws can be applied to domestic competitive firms raising prices behind tariff wall.

Redux: A onetime tariff (or increase in any sales tax) is neither necessary nor sufficient to create a (persistent) inflation. It was demonstrated elsewhere that excess monetary growth and/or a speed up in the velocity of money are necessary for inflation.

[8. For an in depth discussion, see Ravi Batra, "Are Tariffs Inflationary?" 17 Feb. 2003 *Review of International Economics* < http://tinyurl.com/ntpp9j7>

Appendix One

Short Primer on Economic Policy for War

Re-allocation of resources from civilian to military purposes. During wars government is trying to marshal resources to support the war effort. Tanks, gasoline, uniforms and barracks are needed instead of sports cars, fancy suits and vacation resorts. Consumption of Butter must be cut back so resources can flow into military uses, i.e., the production of Guns. A command economy (communist or Fascist) can simply seize resources by issuing orders to resource holders to release them. Market economies function differently.

In a private property, free enterprise system there can be a degree of resource seizure via raising of taxes. Consumers are forced to cut back consumption spending, and so resources are released.   This is called **forced saving**. However, there is a limit to how much a civilian population can be ordered to sacrifice before their morale is destroyed. Enter government bonds. Government bonds are issued to encourage the civilian populace to, in effect, *voluntarily* surrender purchasing power, releasing even more resources (real saving) for the war effort. Celebrities are asked to make appeals at bond selling rallies. The more bonds sold, the more real saving, the less the urgency to raise taxes.

To civilians, bonds are more appealing and acceptable than taxes. Money lent by buying bonds can be retrieved after the war by cashing in the bonds. Taxpayers can kiss goodbye taxes paid as tax money is not refunded by the government.

Appendix Two

Did Bad Money Management Mortally Wound the Roman Empire?

What contributed more to the fall of the Roman Empire: barbarian invasions or bad money management within the Empire?

The **early** Roman Republic and, later the early Empire, had been based on the expansive conquest of new lands. At first, conquered lands were plundered, then integrated into an empire wide free trade area. New taxable provinces were added. Roman roads promoted trade. Division of labor, specialization and the long distance exchange of surpluses appeared. Scale economies were gained. Costs and prices fell for many commodities. But, these prosperous days ended as conquests ended and other revenues had to be acquired via **debasement of the coinage**. Read all about it:

Commodities, e.g., gold or silver, became money because they had intrinsic value as a useful economy. If this "money" would not be acceptable to the next person, one could always put it to use as a commodity. Gold and silver were useful for jewelry and decorative purposes.

Roman rulers conquered, plundered and taxed to raise revenue for lavish lifestyles, finance engineering projects and pay soldiers (like the one pictured below, at the left). They were reluctant to use borrowed funds to finance government activities. But, taxation was overused at the margin, leading to *debasement of the coinage* as a sort of back door approach to financing government expenditures. Noted authorities have given major attribution for the decline and conquest of the Roman Empire to a deliberate **abuse** of the commodity money supply.

The Debasement of the Coinage

The generalized debasement model. It started with the recall of outstanding coins. The (silver) coins were then melted down and a baser (cheaper) metal, say, copper was added to the melt. Then, new coins – silver coated with a copper core – were minted in greater quantity than were turned in. The re-minted coins had a lower intrinsic, metal value but kept the same original face value. This resulted in more coins coming out of the mint than had gone in for re-minting. Brand new debased coins may also be issued. The original number of coins were returned to the public, but t**he monarch retained the additional coins.** Those added coins got into general circulation when spent for public projects, armies or lavish lifestyles of the emperors. Each debasement expanded the money supply. Inflation was a common result as economic capacity did not expand in tandem. **In modern or ancient times: Inflation results when the monetary growth is *excessive* with respect to available goods, given a constant rate of circulation.**

Forced Real Saving from Debasement

In general, an expansion of the money supply is not inflationary if the available goods expand accordingly. Rapid expansion of available goods was a difficult prospect in ancient times. Agricultural produce, the dominant output, was subject to the constraints of a growing season. Specialized industrial methods involving standardization of parts had yet to be invented. This meant that **growth in available goods rarely could keep pace with monetary growth.**

Remember, **each debasement expanded the money supply.** In our typical debasement model, the ordinary folks are left with coins of the same face value as before the monetary expansion. The rulers have additional coins they did not have earlier. Inflation surges when they spend these additional coins in a fully employed ancient economy. Higher prices resulted, forcing spending cutbacks (and real saving) in the private sector. The private sector was armed only with the same money supply it had before the debasement. However, the government, flush with the additional coins, did not have to cut back its spending. **So, the government or rulers got a bigger slice of the pie while the private sector got a smaller slice.**

The effect was similar to modern day monetization of the debt - without the debt! The rulers then spent the resulting revenues. If prices rose due to the additional spending, the government, with its enlarged stock of money, could out-compete the private sector in bidding for resources and goods. Instead of ploughshares, the blacksmiths got higher prices from fashioning weapons. Hence, resource and goods were shifted from the private sector to the public sector and for public purposes. Modern economists call this process **forced real saving through inflation**.

Inflation encourages spending while deflation discourages it. Money held idle in a period of inflation means losing purchasing opportunities. So, people tend to quicken their spending (thereby raising the **velocity** of money). So, not only is there more money in the economy, the money circulates at a greater speed, giving added impetus to the inflation.

More pain from debasement So, as inflation accelerates, money deteriorates as a **store of real value** and becomes less desirable for savings, relative to other available assets. Taxes ballooned to supplement seized debased coins!

Price ceilings. Use of the debasement technique too often accelerated inflation. Price ceilings were imposed with the usual results: greater demand for foodstuffs and less grown (and sold) by increasingly impoverished farmers. Farmers rushed to the cities to enjoy free goodies.

Arch Enemies: Barter and Specialization

Barter (swapping goods for goods) and specialization cannot live together amicably. Rarely can they co-exist. Specialization is just too darn much trouble if one has to barter all the extra output. Without money to facilitate exchanges among specialists, people barter, specialize less and try to become self-sufficient, a "jack of all trades." So, barter discourages specialized production, collapsing the economy.

Despite town markets and trading posts for producers to meet and conduct trades, bartering remained a difficult and time consuming method of trading. Why specialize and create a surplus if one cannot easily trade it away? Barter requires a *coincidence of wants* between traders at the exact moment of exchange, a difficult standard to meet. Exchanges often failed because the *coincidence of wants* is the exception, not the rule.

The Final Phase: the Later Empire

The pie shrinks as barter creates *do-it-yourself-ers*. Understandably, producers were eager to minimize the harmful aspects of barter. One way to do this was to produce fewer goods for sale while struggling to produce a greater variety of goods for home consumption. So, the shoemaker only spent part of his day making shoes, his specialty. The remainder of the day he fumbled at baking, farming, and bartering away any surplus shoes. Most of the specialists had a similar problem: struggling at tasks they had no talent for.

"Do-it-yourself" becomes the new mantra among working people; but is a difficult blueprint to follow. Who excels at all tasks? After all, do city folk make good farmers? Are farmers good at city occupations? Even the handyman has strengths and weaknesses.

Consequently, the "pie" shrinks. Unsuited for small scale production, specialized tools and equipment go idle. **The result of the reversion to self-sufficiency is disastrous**: despite the same resources and technological availability, the abundance of output associated with division of labor and specialization begins to disappear.

Again, the economy of the **later Roman Empire** differs significantly from the Roman Republic and the early Empire. Folks had to adjust to inflation, debased money, invasions, **a crushing tax burden** and government controls. Insecure travel and transport discouraged cross empire trade. Pirates became troublesome. A "do-it-yourself" model emerged. But, the later, embattled Rome could not match the productive capabilities of the early republic and empire.

Headline from the *Roman Times*:

"Empire Fragments!"

"Rejection of Money Cripples Trade, Economic and Military Power" Subheading:
"Return to Barter And Self-Sufficiency Sinks Prosperity...Hardship Increases."

Debasement enriches the monarch but impoverishes the people by stealing their purchasing power. All kinds of problems issued from debasement. But, the excess monetary growth from debasement fueled inflation and spurred failed attempts to suppress inflation using price ceilings. Valuable coins had been a convenient, low cost method of making a long distance payment. But, **rejection of debased money** made long distance trades and payments problematic. Long distance trade declined as personal, local and regional security costs rose and safety declined.

Unable to sell goods Empire wide, producers **reduced the scale of production.** As a result of reduced scale, costs and prices rose. Focus returned to small scale production for local markets. Self sufficiency and barter re-emerged as markets and population centers fragmented. Aggregate output fell along with **the standard of living and quality of life declined. Remember, the economy is the mother ship of national defense and national security. Roman military might nosedived, imperiling empire wide commerce and travel.**

The vast military commitments associated with Empire contracted due to a revenue shortage and mismanagement. The legions could no longer safeguard the roads and other paths of commerce. The Empire started to fragment into self-sufficient, suburban estates. (These localized suburban estates were the forerunners of the medieval manors to come *after* the fall of the empire.)

Aqueducts, roads, and bridges were not maintained or defended, stifling trade. Empire wide markets began to fragment. Big cities lost population whereas they gained population in the earlier stage of decline. Even a region wide specialized economy was problematic. Local farms and localized farm markets returned. The exalted Roman standard of living collapsed. Many Romans even welcomed the "barbarians" to avoid increasing oppression from Roman tax collectors and price regulations.

In sum, the Empire fragmented. Scale economies were lost as markets shrunk, causing costs and prices to rise as production fell. De-urbanization emerged and the standard of living declined. Everyday life got more chaotic, insecure and uncertain.

The debasement of the money played a significant role in weakening the economic base that had supported empire security. Predictably, the retreat from empire wide (or even region wide division of labor and specialization) into communal pockets of "do-it-your-selfers" shrunk the Empire's overall productive capability. That is, **the size of the economic "pie" shrunk in terms of butter and guns.** It also de-moralized the populace and made them lose confidence in the Empire's ability to protect them and govern in their interest. The "do-it-yourself" mode of production, inspired by the demise of money and the difficulty of barter, could not maintain the security of the empire. So, as money collapsed, so did the economy – and Empire security. As the economy deteriorated, so did the empire's military prowess and its ability to provide personal security to its people. **Fragmentation and collapse was inevitable.**

Destroy a nation's money (through over or under expansion)

and you destroy the nation! (Lenin)

Pollice Verso (*Thumbs Down*) by Jean-Léon Gérôme, 1872

Here I am in an earlier life vanquishing another fallacy to the roar of the crowd in the Roman Coliseum.

Chapter Thirty
Inflation and Deflation: Evil Twins?

WHICH is the worst enemy, inflation or deflation? Each has its destructive capabilities. And, yes, each has cheerleaders, too. Each has its share of myths and fallacies.

1. FALLA<IOLIS <<ONOMI<LIS: Choosing between a **trace** of inflation (less than 2%) and even a **hint** of deflation (less than 1%), the deflation is preferable because a dollar will buy more!

Corollary Fallacious Statement 1: Deflations are beneficial because everything is cheaper and folks can buy more goods.

Corollary Fallacious Statement 2: Deflation should be encouraged because it raises the purchasing power of each dollar, enabling each paycheck to buy more goods.

Corollary Fallacious Statement 3: A deflation can promote an economic expansion and general prosperity.

(See Fallacy # 2)

Correct Reasoning: The correct choice is a **trace** of inflation. A *mild* inflation of 2% or less is not considered threatening. Actually, it might be bullish for business activity.

First of all, let us define our terms. **Deflation is a persistent drop in the average price level, economy wide. As with its evil twin, hyperinflation, deflation is an economic wrecking ball which must be feared and avoided.**

This is another case of committing the fallacy of composition. Yes, you get the extra buying power when one or two prices fall in a micro context. Your income is still unaffected. You make the same take-home pay, and a few prices at the store are coming down ... great! Your paycheck goes further. But, there is a different result if prices come down economy wide, i.e. if there is a deflation. Don't confuse this small scale event with an *economy wide* fall in prices. The causes and effects are very different. When all prices fall – as in (general) deflation – all incomes do NOT remain intact. **All incomes must fall along with all the prices. Buying power does NOT expand.** It falls in tandem with the drop in incomes. (See the discussion below). So, a general deflation is disastrous for a whole economy even though a single price decline may mean boom for a shoe store or computer outlet.

Deflation is actually a family of D's, and a **D**ysfunctional one, at that!

D1 = DISCOURAGE PRODUCTION, especially long term projects such as building construction and heavy manufacturing.

Falling prices might help firms in *buying* materials and inputs.

However, firms fear *selling* below cost as their *selling* prices fall.

This fear grows as the delay between production and sale gets longer, threatening to impose losses on the producers. Firms cancel production (and hiring) to avoid those loses.

D2 = DELAY = delayed customer buying.

Despite falling replacement prices for durables such as cars and refrigerators, customers stretch the use of durables. They delay replacing them in hopes of buying later at *even lower prices*. These delays and postponements can put a significant dent in current aggregate demand. **The fall in aggregate demand causes production (and incomes) to fall.**

Question: Why don't the falling prices stimulate greater sales, as is predicted in *microe*conomic theory?

Answer: Recall, what works for an individual may not work for the group when they try it (the fallacy of composition). When one or a few firms drop prices in **a micro context** - and cut payment to factors of production -- this does not significantly reduce the real incomes of *all* their customers. Only their workers and suppliers, a small fraction of the total income earners, suffer a decline. So, their customers, *their income largely intact,* react by expanding purchases of the lower priced item. But this result is predicted only on a small scale, a few prices falling here and there.

Whereas dropping a price may mean a boom in sales for a handful of firms, if *all* firms tried the same remedy it would not work!

Lower prices all around would mean lower incomes all around. They would fail as lower prices do not produce a sales boom because they are offset lower as incomes manifest somewhere else in the economy.

As a result, production, prices (the deflation) and incomes and all fall further. A continuing, self-reinforcing downward spiral may emerge.

Adverse effects on *financial sector* compound the problems of deflation:

D3 = DEFAULT = financial collapse?

Consumer nominal and real incomes fall due to cut wages and /or rising unemployment. But, cash hoards in mattresses and safes *rise* in purchasing power. Business nominal and real incomes fall due to selling goods at declining prices.

As employment and incomes drop, firms and individuals find it harder to service (pay off) **fixed** costs and **fixed** debts: fixed amount debts equal bank debts, bond interest and principal payments. Big debtors such as public utilities, airlines, home owners with mortgages and farmers are especially hard hit. Other rigid costs such as fixed union, minimum wages, and property taxes, rentals don't go away when incomes of those debt payers fall. Bankruptcies rise. And the damage rolls on. In order to service fixed payment debts, investors will likely liquidate securities. This may drive down securities prices.

Depositors, fearful of bank default due to uncollectible loans, run to withdraw their deposits and get cash whose real value per unit is *rising*.

Cash holders, reasoning they can get even better bargains *after* the crash, withhold purchases of goods! A full blown banking crisis *may* ensue!

But, once again: why don't the economy wide falling prices stimulate greater sales, as is predicted in *micro*economics for single markets? The *micro* effect of cutting a price leading to greater sales does not work in a *macro* context.

The *macro* perspective says: when *all* prices fall, *all* incomes must fall as a result. "What goes around comes around."

In short, Deflation spells Disaster ... for nearly everyone!

2. FALLACIOUS ECONOMICUS: A deflation can cure a recession.

Fallacious Reasoning: If cutting price can stimulate additional sales for the furniture store, then all firms should cut prices and all sales will be stimulated. Then the recession will be over.

Correct Reasoning: Deflation implies the big, macro economy, not just one business. From that perspective, total spending equals total income. Deflation means *lower* spending and *lower* income, economy wide. Lower income means lower purchasing power, despite lower prices. This does not cure depression or recession!

But, this fallacy ruled policy makers until the early 1930s! Despite the widespread pain, a deflation was seen as a kind of magic elixir, a cure-all for everything but in-grown toenails. Many economists believed it could "cure" economic depression or recession in a) a closed (no trading) or b) an open (trading) economy.

In a) **a closed economy, no trade: Fallacy–** lower prices (assuming the *same* nominal wages) would raise *real* incomes and re-boot sales. **Correct–** lower prices *necessarily* lower nominal incomes ... canceling the stimulation from lower prices! There is no boost to real income, no incentive to raise spending. Result: no boost to sales from the deflation.

In b) **an open economy, with trade: Fallacy–** lower prices would cheapen exports. An export boom would result and spread throughout. Money would flow in. This sparks aggregate demand, ends the deflation, and ends the depression. **Correct–** In the early 1930s demand for U.S. exports was a tiny fraction of aggregate demand. Any deflation-induced bump in export demand was too small to offset the huge fall in domestic demand. The deflation and the depression persisted.

These positions and policies pre-date the "invention" of macroeconomics by Keynes. This is another example of committing the *fallacy of composition.* What works on a small scale, viz., a lower price leading to greater sales, will not work on a large scale due to the deflation crashing customer incomes.

The Circular Flow of Income in Macro World: deflation cuts incomes and purchasing power. What *goes* around (prices **paid**) is what *comes* around (incomes received). **Cutting *all* prices cuts *all* incomes.** If less is "going around" then less is "coming around." When *all* firms cut prices and spending falls, they are cutting their *customer* incomes, preventing buyers from going on a buying spree and ending the recession.

In sum, a deflation cannot cure a recession.

3. FALLACIOUS ECONOMICUS: During a deflation the Real Wealth Effect

will boost purchasing power and trigger more buying. This may help end the recession.

Fallacious Reasoning: The *real wealth* effect (Pigou effect): falling prices would raise the real value of money *savings* and cash *stocks*, yielding a rise in purchasing power. Pumped up with additional purchasing power, consumers go on a spending binge that lifts the economy out of its slump.

Correct Reasoning: The Pigou effect has failed on a number of counts. If prices are expected to continue to fall, then the effect may be postponed as buyers await even lower prices. When activated, the effect on demand has proven inadequate to the task.

Question: Could excessive deficit spending be offset by "crowding out" – a reduction in – private spending?

The Island of Yap

Throughout the centuries, useful commodities did double duty and served as money as well as in their commodity role. Tobacco, arrowheads, farm animals, gold and silver are examples. For many years, dwellers of the Pacific island of Yap used large stones as money. Some stones were so large as to be unmovable. In what way was this commodity useful and valuable to the islanders? (They were not used in construction or consumed in any way.) Why did the Yap islanders value these large stones?

A very entertaining, elegant and surprising answer is found in the swashbuckling 1950s pirate movie, **His Majesty O'Keefe**, based on a true story.

Notice the donut shaped stones – Yap money – lying in front of a house.

Lovers and Haters

➢ Debtors love an *unexpected* inflation and hate an *unexpected* deflation ... why?
➢ Creditors hate an *unexpected* inflation and love an *unexpected* deflation ... why?

Chapter Thirty-One
Fallacies Concerning Character

Our character is what we do when we think no one is looking.
—H. Jackson Browne

Character determines behavior and behavior betrays character.
—Theo Dosius

When the law no longer protects you from the corrupt, but protects the corrupt from you — you know your nation is doomed. – Ayn Rand.

fter the survival instinct, character is the prime determinant of human behavior.

Character is '... the sum of qualities that defines a person.' These qualities include a man's intellect, thoughts, ideas, motives, intentions, temperament, judgment, behavior, imagination, perception, emotions, loves, and hates.

[1. Brett and Kate McKay "What Is Character? Its 3 True Qualities and How to Develop It" 25 June 2013 *Art of Manliness* <http://tinyurl.com/lo5xl45>]

One's character derives from multiple forces: upbringing (parental influence), religion, experiences, personal relationships and, perhaps, an innate sense of right and wrong. It has been said that one's true character is revealed by how one behaves **when no one is watching**. That is the litmus test for character: man alone, no one watching ... where does he steer the ship? What character traits emerge?

1. FALLACIOUS ECONOMICUS: Wealth, beauty, power and intellect are indicators of virtue and high moral character.

Correct Reasoning: Neither beauty nor intellect is an error free marker of high moral character. There is no guarantee beauty and virtue or intellect and high moral character go together. A person must *cultivate* virtue, including morality. Religion may be a source of morality training, but one religion condones the murder and violation of innocents. Family is another source of morality. But, in the real world the correlation is very loose.

Is there a causal relationship between virtue and beauty? Does real life follow the movies, where good people are also good looking and the bad characters are ugly? Those are fairy tales. Perhaps our pop culture comic book heroes are both virtuous *and* handsome (or beautiful), as are legendary figures in mythology. Mythology is just that..Are wealth, beauty, power and intellect God's rewards for virtue? It is doubtful, considering the evil folks possessing those traits. No doubt, some of the most evil people in history have been very smart, e.g., Hitler, Stalin and Mao. How could they have come to power if they were not intelligent? Yet, each murdered millions of innocent people.

The lesson is this: Do not assume wealthy, beautiful or smart people are virtuous and of high moral character. Beautiful but evil people always surprise.

Shamefully, in America today, good character is not essential for election to public office.

Indeed, people of any moral inclination – good or evil, kind or cruel – may be endowed with beauty and intellect.

2. FALLACIOUS ECONOMICUS: Intellect is a higher human attribute than character.

Fallacious Reasoning: It is better to be smart than to be good. "Smarts" keep you alive. What does being good do for you? Being a good person does not put bread on the table. Being a smart person does.

Correct Reasoning: The cynicism expressed in the fallacious reasoning above is very common in America today. This fallacy is committed when one *wrongly assumes* that the development of the intellect is more important than the development of a high moral character. Honesty, integrity, trustworthiness, courage and a sense of justice are but a few markers of high moral character. High intellect does not guarantee a person will also be of high moral character, i.e., knowing right from wrong, good from evil. Witness the evil genius cliché character from the movies. **High intellect does not guarantee a person will act virtuously.**

Character is the prime ruler of a person's conduct. Character goes where laws may not apply. A nation with most people of strong, virtuous character needs few overseers and few laws. **Aptitude without morals is a prescription for disaster**: personal, local and global. Plato explored the virtues of a high moral character in many of his dialogues. Aristotle spent much intellectual effort defining and elaborating on character and virtue, especially for civic leaders.

Beware: Recent educational practice has emphasized academic performance and vocational capability, at the expense of character development. But, expert witnesses overwhelmingly approve of high moral character and disapprove of the trend away from character and civics education. Read all about it:

"The glory of a nation rests upon the character of her men."

—President Herbert Hoover

"I have a dream that my four little children will one day live in a nation where they will not be judged by the color of their skin but by the content of their character."

—Dr. Martin Luther King, Jr.

"Character is higher than intellect."

—Ralph Waldo Emerson

Finally, a strong warning from President Theodore Roosevelt (photo on the right):

"Character, in the long run, is the decisive factor in the life of an individual and of nations alike."

President Theodore Roosevelt

3. FALLACIOUS ECONOMICUS: Everyone considers character to be an important determinant of success, no?

Fallacious Reasoning: Surely no one would dismiss character as unimportant. "No man is an island" and must interact with others, eventually revealing a bad character. High moral standards and a good character are prerequisites for success. How could one advance in life and achieve success if one has a flawed character?

Correct Reasoning: It is possible to conceal one's flaws, one's bad character and succeed *in spite of it.* Indeed, it is possible to attain the highest office in the land in spite of serious character flaws. Looking at today's world, it seems that low moral standards are required for success, especially in politics. Consider the opinions of experts:

"Character doesn't matter." [Who said that? ... Surprise]!!!

—President Bill Clinton

T.R. gets the final word: **"To educate a person in mind and not in morals is to educate a menace to society."**   —President Theodore Roosevelt

Roosevelt would be saddened to learn of today's practices in schools. Read all about it:

Our schools have retreated from the idea of moral education, except for some attempts at what is called 'values clarification,' which is generally a cloak for *moral relativism* verging on nihilism of the sort that asserts that whatever feels good is good. Even more vigorously have the schools fled from the idea of encouraging patriotism. In the intellectual climate of our time, the very suggestion brings contemptuous sneers or outrage, depending on the listener's mood.

[2. Donald Kagan, "Democracy Requires a Patriotic Education" 26 September 2014 *Wall Street Journal Online* < http://tinyurl.com/kc2vxfa>]

Shock and sadness is compounded by fear for the future of the nation.

4. FALLACIOUS ECONOMICUS: Once in office, politicians try to do whatever they want. They perpetrate schemes to line their own pockets and turn the screws on the public. But, laws, regulations, and watchdogs will keep them honest. Really!

Related **FALLACIOUS ECONOMICUS:** "Character doesn't matter," says Bill Clinton, former President of the United States, in influencing behavior.

Correct Reasoning: Dishonest and immoral politicians will behave immorally despite laws, regulations and codes of ethics. Moral politicians (an oxymoron?) do not need restraints and regulations to keep their behavior in check. You do not have to regulate and watch someone with high moral character. They have their own *internal* sense of right and wrong. They steer toward what is right and away from wrong. They regulate themselves, even when no one is looking.

Your true character is betrayed by your behavior when you know you are not being watched. Then you are free to be yourself, no? But, people of high moral character, in any path of life, have "governors." Governors are *built in* restraints on their behavior derived from proper guidance in their upbringing. Religious convictions matter to them. Having had good role models in the home and in the public arena is an advantage. Being surrounded by *prostititians* [a prostitician is crossbred between a politician and a prostitute] grinds on those with good character. Bad character is rarely restrained by rules and regulations, just as weeds in the garden are rarely eliminated by pesticides. Sorry, Bill. Character *does* matter, especially when the public trust is involved.

**Beware: Legality does not guarantee morality.
Legal but immoral, you pick:
war, abortion, drug testing on animals and the death penalty.**

5. FALLA<IOUS <<ONOMI<US: No one would doubt that bravery (in battle) and generosity (for indigence) are virtuous acts of someone with high moral character. So, brave folks should always "go full steam" and generous folks (or nations) should donate every penny.

Correct Reasoning: Recall, an excess of a good thing backfires and becomes a bad thing. Aristotle said, "moderation is the key." Not too little, not too much. Seek the golden mean. All out, *mindless* bravery on the battlefield becomes recklessness. Think Pickett's Charge at Battle of Gettysburg. It ruined the outcome of an engagement which tempered bravery might have won for the South. Excessive generosity impoverishes the giver – a person or a nation – impairing the ability to give consistently in later years.

The Beauty of Quotation

"**Watch** your thoughts, for they become words. Watch your words, for they become actions. Watch your actions, for they become habits. Watch your habits, for they become character. Watch your character, for it becomes your destiny."

Tom Krause

... every good tree bringeth forth good fruit; but a corrupt tree bringeth forth evil fruit. A good tree cannot bring forth evil fruit, neither can a corrupt tree bring forth good fruit ....**Wherefore by their fruits ye shall know them**. (Matthew 7:1)

Bribery is a two-way street often traveled in the conduct of business and politics, especially in third world countries. What is bribery? A common definition of *bribery* states:

> The offering, giving, receiving, or soliciting of something of value for
> the purpose of influencing the action of an official in the discharge
> of his or her public or legal duties. Thus, some bending of rules,
> laws or practices is gotten as a reward for the bribe.
>
> [3. http://legal-dictionary.thefreedictionary.com/bribery]

"Few men have virtue to withstand the highest bidder."
—George Washington

Bribery Fallacies

6. FALLA<IOUS <<ONOMI<US: Everybody knows what a bribe is. One guy gives an envelope full of money to another guy in exchange for some special favor or treatment. Its nighttime, raining and both are wearing raincoats.

Fallacious Reasoning: This is how they did it in the old movies. Cash is fungible and envelopes can be bought at the local stationery store. Easy!

Correct Reasoning: The bribery payment as a plain brown envelope stuffed with money is a leftover cliché from old black and white crime movies. Strictly *film noir.* As far as money is concerned, the definition of bribery does not specify money. It mentions the transfer of a nonspecific something of value. Implied is the notion that the something of value may be money but is not limited to it. Of course, bribes could be paid in the form of money.

But, today, bribery can be more subtle and sophisticated. The form and manner of payment is rich in diversity and creativity. A better conception of something of value might be this: the form of payment could be *anything of value that enhances the actual or potential well-being of the recipient, now or in the future.* Moreover, the "recipient" could someone or some entity close to the party expected to be influenced.

Diagram #1: Bribery Forms and Channels

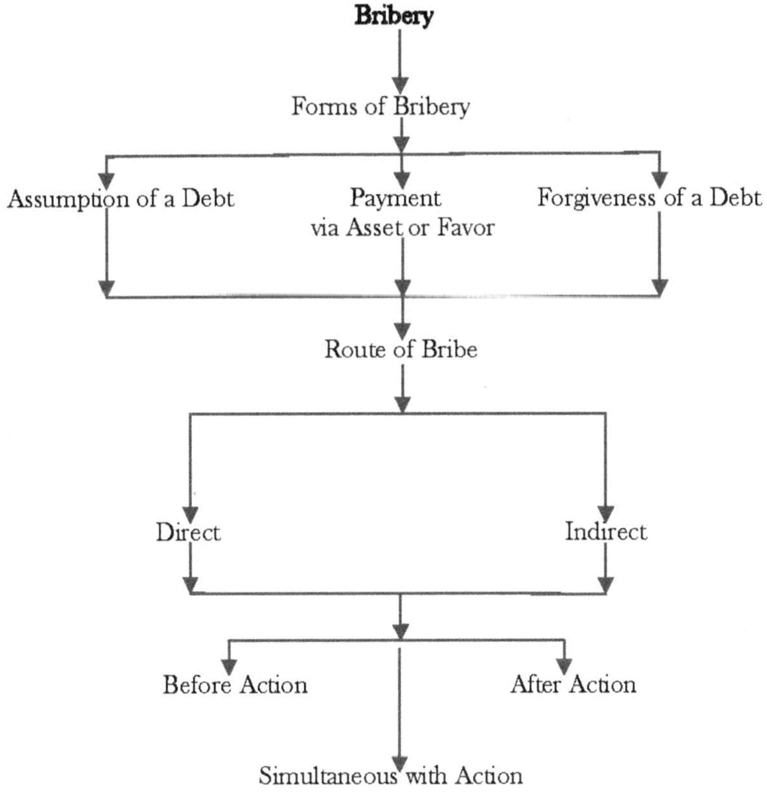

Bribery

↓

Forms of Bribery

Assumption of a Debt   Payment via Asset or Favor   Forgiveness of a Debt

↓

Route of Bribe

↓

Direct   Indirect

Before Action   Simultaneous with Action   After Action

Form of Bribe

> ➤ A bribe can take the form of an *actual or promised* real or financial asset. It could also be an actual or promised relief from a liability.

> ➤ A bribe could be in the form of *intangible* thing of value such as military, political or financial power.

> ➤ A bribe could have *psychological* value. Could one accept an intangible gift than enhances one's self-esteem, such as an honorary degree from a prestigious university?

Bribery is an ancient practice that has evolved over the millennia to take on various byzantine forms. An outline of some forms is depicted in Diagram #1 that follows.

In fact, the bribe can be delivered before, after or at the moment the favor is granted.

Example 1: **Pre-paid bribe?** Election campaign contributions have often been cast as attempts to buy favors once the candidate takes office. Are political contributions bribes? If, after taking office, a favor is granted to a contributor as a response to the contribution, certainly it is unethical. But, was the favor in response to the contribution and, if so, is it an illegal bribe?

A judge and court would have the ultimate opinion, but there is some wiggle room here for the defendant. A likely defense by the official is to declare the favor sought to have merit and would have been granted without the donation!

Example 2: **Delayed bribe?** It is common for former government officials take jobs in industries they used to regulate or otherwise interface with, e.g., former Treasury official taking a job with Goldman Sachs. Knowing one might secure a private sector position after leaving government, would one's official behavior be slanted in favor of that industry? In other words, is the slanted industry position taken in anticipation of delayed bribe, namely, a job, once one leaves government?

A defense? A likely defense by the official is to declare the favors granted on their own merits, not in anticipation of an industry position.

Cracks in the Clinton Foundation

Some folks confuse the Clintons with the Clantons, cattle rustlers from the old west. With no Wyatt Earp in sight, today's Clintons are much more unrestrained in their "pursuits." The Clinton Foundation has been accepting donations from unsavory foreign countries Hillary Clinton will deal with should she become President. Saudi Arabia, U.A.E. and Oman are among the donors. Will these donations influence her conduct as President? What of the speaker's fees from foreign governments paid to Mr. and Mrs. Clinton?

Critics charge high moral character is not the Clintons strong suit.

[4. Peter Nicholas and Rebecca Ballhaus, "Clinton Foundation Defends Acceptance of Foreign Donations," 18 February 2015 *Wall Street Journal Online* < http://tinyurl.com/pllorkv>

See also, Peter Schweizer. *Clinton Cash*. New York, Harper/Collins, 2015]

---

8. FALLACIOUS ECONOMICUS: A bribe is a direct payment between the principal parties. Yes, the payment goes from original source of the bribe directly to the one performing the favor. There is no need for intermediaries between the original source and the ultimate receiver.

Correct Reasoning: The fallacious statement is naïve. In reality, third parties may be used on either side of the transaction to mask the transfer! This method exhibits a higher level of sophistication concocted to avoid detection.

Again, the definition does not require a bribe be paid directly to the person granting the favor. Nor does the definition require the bribe come from the recipient of the favor.

The Art of Laundering Money: No Starch Please

Here is how it works. Initially, the bribe may be paid to someone distinct from but connected to the grantor of the favor, say a relative, friend or business associate. The bribe could come from someone called a "bagman" who is connected to the payer, who is making payment in expectation of a favor to be granted. This "bagman" could include briber's family, friends, or a front group such as a charity or foundation. Consider: The judge's cousin accepts money from the criminal's mother-in-law. Later, the cousin transfers the money to the judge and the criminal repays his mother-in-law. No money passed *directly* between the judge and the criminal.

In the above example there was no direct contact between the criminal, the giver of the bribe and the judge, the recipient.

Beware, as well: Dare one ask: could a charity, foundation or presidential library be part of a "money laundering" operation? One may question how thorough are government audits of such institutions, especially if they are of similar political persuasion to the party in power.

Question: Are Presidential libraries/foundations ever independently audited?

The Good Bribe?

Bribery, by definition, is illegal. But, is every illegal activity or action harmful to the economy? **Can an (illegal) bribe actually be *beneficial* to the economy?** In other words, is there such a thing as a good bribe or a beneficial bribe where benefits accrue to folks other than the bribe taker?

Some observers assert that there are such things as good bribes, i.e., bribes that do have good consequences. For example, consider a bribe to relax government **over regulation** that was creating inefficiencies or inequities. Overly strict zoning regulations can strangle development. Recall, **an excess of a good thing is bad thing!** A bribe can divert official oversight and allow for constructive development.

---

9. FALLACIOUS ECONOMICUS: Only the candidate spending big money wins an election for public office.

Corollary: Candidates cannot win an election without spending big money.

Correct Reasoning: Contrary to popular belief, spending big money in a political campaign helps but does not guarantee victory. Individual circumstances matter much in many political races. Perhaps money matters most in a campaign between two "nobodies" or two equally favored candidates. But, many candidates have spent and many have lost.

What do Lew Lehrman, Linda McMahon, Tom Golisano, Meg Whitman, Carly Fiorina, and Jeb Bush have in common? They have spent large amounts of personal funds in losing political campaigns. We are talking millions of dollars. McMahon's two losing campaigns for Connecticut Senator cost her over $50 million. Golisano outspent her ($93 million) in his two losing New York gubernatorial contests. Most of the candidates named above outspent their opponents. Yet, they came away as losers. Apparently,

> ➤ Elections can be won *without* spending big money.
> ➤ Big money spending does not guarantee victory.

[5. Robert Frank, "Why Rich Candidates Failed" 3 November 2011 *Wall Street Journal* < http://tinyurl.com/nbs94jb />]

The next presidential election may be an exception! In the 2016 Republican primary race, Donald Trump spent very little money. Ultimately, he won enough primaries to win the nomination.

Question: Could it be that popularity determines donations and it's the popularity that wins the election, not the donations? In other words, are donations a proxy, a stand-in variable, for the real power variable, *popularity?* If one follows that line of reasoning an interesting question arises. *Could a case be made that big money spending is neither a necessary nor a sufficient condition for winning an election?* The record shows a minority of candidates win elections without spending big money. Popularity and approval can carry an election. That rules out big money spending as a necessary condition.

So, big spending is not a necessary condition for victory. But, is it sufficient? No, as we see cases where big money is deployed it does not lock in an election victory. In other words, big money is not sufficient as it, alone, cannot guarantee the result, victory in an election.

In sum, spending big money on an election campaign does not always and only guarantee victory. There are exceptions where money does not rule.

> Even during the most competitive cycles, when control of Congress is up for grabs, at the end of the day the candidates who spend the most usually win eight of 10 Senate contests and nine of 10 House races.
> [6. Bob Biersack "The Big Spender Always Wins?" 11 January 2012 *OpenSecrets.Org* < http://tinyurl.com/okamx9k />]

Fallacy of Forecasting Result from Intention

10. FALLACIOUS ECONOMICUS: Intentions matter. Trust the one with good intentions and shun the one with bad intentions.

Correct Reasoning: Sometimes good intentions backfire and give a bad result. Stalin, Mao and Hitler had what they considered "good intentions" but each murdered millions. So:

> Good intentions are not enough to guarantee a good result.

"Well, he means well." Remember, **the road to hell** is paved with good intentions," goes the old saying. In sum, don't judge the intention. Talk is cheap. Judge the likely result.

The Best President: Bill Clinton?

11. FALLACIOUS ECONOMICUS: Bill Clinton was the best President of the last thirty years.

Fallacious Reasoning: He ran a budget surplus, reformed welfare and presided over the creation of more than ten million jobs.

Correct Reasoning: This one is a dousey!

> **The quality of new jobs created did not measure up to the quality of jobs shipped out during his tenure.** On his watch **America's job profile degenerated.**

> The Clinton "prosperity" owed a huge debt to the taxes generated by the dot com bubble of the late 1990s. The bubble fueled higher incomes and tax collections.

> The budget surpluses of the late 1990s came with Republican urging. They reduced aggregate spending and set up the recession of the early 2000s.

> His welfare reforms were inspired by Republicans and gutted by later administrations.

Bill Clinton brought to "full flower" the destructive ideology of Globalism. Many folks praise Bill Clinton and long for a return to the good old days of his Presidency. Is this admiration justified? Aside from his renowned moral depravity, consider the case *against* Bill Clinton.

A Very Particular Bill

1) He supported and signed the so-called **Motor Voter Law (1993)** that allowed voter registration at State motor vehicle offices. In practice, have proper ID standards been applied or have many unqualified people been certified to vote?

2) He signed (1993) the **North American Free Trade Agreement (NAFTA),** ultimately establishing a free trade zone between the U.S., Canada and Mexico. Almost immediately, Mexico devalued the peso, thereby lowering the price of Mexican goods in the U.S. and raising the price of U.S. goods sold to Mexico.

Why wasn't this devaluation anticipated by U.S. watchdog Robert Rubin? This sparked a surge of Americans buying Mexican goods but selling fewer goods to Mexico. Very quickly a pre-NAFTA trade *surplus* with Mexico became a *trade deficit* that has persisted ever since. Also, NAFTA triggered an outflow of American companies (and jobs) to low wage area Mexico as goods could now be brought back duty free. **Adding insult to injury, millions of Mexican farm workers, thrown off increasingly uncompetitive family farms by NAFTA, entered the U.S. legally and illegally.**

3) He sponsored the creation (1995) of the **World Trade Organization (WTO),** ceding to it partial control of U.S. trade and sovereignty.

4) He brought (still Red) China into the WTO (2001), dropping most barriers to Chinese exports, even though China kept its currency – and goods – artificially cheap. Chinese exports to the U.S. grew to *four times* the U.S.

exports to China. The U.S. trade deficit also grew with the rest of the world. This was a gift to American ex-patriot companies relocated to (still Red) China.

5) The American **manufacturing Diaspora** to Mexico and China grew unopposed. In addition to NAFTA, laws and administrative policies promoted the export of companies, industries and jobs – and incomes – from the U.S. **Better jobs were shipped out of the U.S. than were created in the 90's.**

6) As G.W. Bush would do after him, Clinton approved the **sale of supercomputers** to China. Remember, every resource has a direct or indirect military application. Moreover, in the middle 90's he allowed the Loral Corp. to sell sensitive missile guidance technology to China. Why? Critics suggest "donations" were involved. But, serious questions remain:
a) How much did China save in research and development costs? b) How many years were cut from the Chinese missile development research?
c) **How much must the U.S. spend to overcome this Chinese relative advance?**

7) During the middle 1990's Bill and running mate Al Gore were accused of accepting illegal re-election campaign donations from ... guess who? ... (still Red) China! Thanks, Bill! But, wait, there is more.

8) On his last day in office, he pardoned tax deadbeat **Marc Rich**, costing the Treasury $1 billion in penalties and interest. In an unrelated (wink, wink) development, Denise Rich (wife of Marc) earlier had donated $450,000 to the Clinton Library. Duh?

[7. Jackie Judd and David Ruppe, "Denise Rich Gave $450,000 to Clinton Library," 9 February 2002 ABC News < http://tinyurl.com/pe2sbpx>]

9) Late in his second administration he supported and oversaw the repeal of the 1933 **Glass-Steagall Act (1999), allowing mergers of commercial banks, investment backs and insurance companies.** Too Big to Fail **(TBTF)** and Moral Hazard entered the public vocabulary. In the Commodity Futures Modernization Act **(2000)** he approved the removal of government oversight of the **derivatives market. His deregulation efforts were supported by Republican heavyweights Larry Summers and Alan Greenspan.** Coincidentally, after leaving office Bill enjoyed a series of paid speeches at big banks. (Even then he knew!)

Opening Pandora 's Box could not have released more maladies on the world! The cowboy, mad-dog crapitalists, banksters and brokesters of Wall Street – of which there are some -- were uncaged. Unleashed on the world, they instigated the sub-prime mortgage financial collapse of 2008-2009 and trillion dollar U.S. bail-out.

10) In 1993, Bill Clinton's effort to **limit traditional executive pay** - section 162(m) of the Internal Revenue Code) - led to compensation supplemented by stock options. This provoked almost manic efforts to juice up the stock price and options value by off-shoring.

[8. Keith Epstein and Eamon Javers, "How Bill Clinton Helped Boost CEO Pay," 26 November 2006 *BloombergBusiness Magazine*, <http://tinyurl.com/njuqdax>]

11) Bill Clinton trivialized terrorism after the **1993 attack** on the World Trade Center. He (and his administration lawyers) bent over backwards to label it a civilian **crime,** not an attack on the United States as a nation and worthy of military response.

The bombing was degraded to the level of a purse snatching or mugging, to be investigated by civilian authorities under civilian criminal law rules. Suspects got Miranda and 5th amendment rights. [They still do, on the battlefields of Afghanistan and Iraq ... Duh?] This allowed Al Qaeda to fester until it struck again on 9/11/2001. **Could Clinton have taken Bin Laden then?**

Did Clinton undermine national security, directly or indirectly? The economy is the mother ship of national security and survival. Clinton brought the mother ship under attack by urging on the American Manufacturing Diaspora (decimating our middle class), embracing the Trojan horse of cheap imports **So, thanks, Bill for accelerating America's economic and moral decline.**

The Clinton foundation needs to be audited by at least two independent firms and the audit report made public. Do any of the following quotes have relevance to the Clinton story?

The creatures outside looked from pig to man, and from man to pig, and from pig to man again, but already it was impossible to say which was which.

George Orwell, Animal Farm

Every great cause begins as a movement, degenerates into a business

and

ends up a racket   ...   Eric Hoffer

Beware the enemy within ...Cicero

Here is a conversation recently overheard behind some Federal buildings in Washington, D.C.

Why did you put your peddler's stand here? You are in the back of these buildings.

Yes, that is what I wanted, the back of the buildings.

Why?

Because that is where they come out when they leave government.

When who leaves government?

You know, the government officials, legislators, regulators. Oh, yes, the President and Vice President will come out of those back doors some day, too.

No kidding?

Yes, their terms are up and they come flying out of those doors...and they shoot right over to me. Many of them trip over themselves in a race to get to me. It is funny to watch!

Hey, good for you. But, what makes you such an attraction?

Yes, I have what they want. They cannot wait to get my product and slap it on their backs. They tell me they make tons of money once they put this on. The money just rolls in.

Are you selling sun-tan lotion, or something?

No, only Southern politicians would need that.

Can I buy one of your products? I certainly could use a lot of money.

Sorry, you could buy one but you do not have the qualifications needed to make money with it.

Oh, I see. Say, just what is it that you sell like "hotcakes" to these ex-government officials that they take and turn into gold?

I sell these little tee-shirts. I've even sold a couple to ex-Presidents and Vice Presidents.

I don't understand. What is so specialized about an ordinary tee-shirt?

Well, you see, it is not the shirt itself. It is the inscription on back of the shirt that makes it valuable.

And, just what is written on back of these tee-shirts bought by former government officials?

It says:

PROSTITITIAN HERE
INFLUENCE FOR SALE
GET IT CHEAP
NO "REASONABLE OFFER" REFUSED

Prostitician - 1) a politician who takes money and does anything you want.
          2) the second oldest profession.
          3) favorite habitat: Washington , D.C.

Chapter Thirty-Two
A Few Statistical Fallacies

Economic statistics are like bikinis. What they reveal is important,
but what they conceal is maddening! —Anonymous

Figures don't lie, but liars can figure...

STATISTICS, as an academic discipline, is a highly specialized, complex, and advanced branch of mathematics. Practicing statisticians usually have advanced degrees. Statisticians do valuable work in government, private enterprise and in non-profit institutions. They are trained not only to conduct statistical studies but also to understand, interpret and communicate the results and limitations of such studies.

We are constantly bombarded with the results of this or that statistical study. They are presented are scientific. (**But, beware:** *scientific* does not guarantee *accurate.*) Thus, some understanding of statistical methods and language seems essential for the public. Technically speaking, **a *statistic* is a measurement derived from a sample, the sample derived from a larger parent population.** For example, the statistic may be *average income*, an **arithmetic mean** in statistics lingo.

Hopefully, the sample arithmetic mean mirrors the (unknown) arithmetic mean in the (statistical) population. The latter value is called a **population parameter**. Population parameters are unknowns approximated by sample statistics. (BTW: Merely *describing* the sample result is the job of *descriptive statistics*. The use of sample statistics to approximate population parameters is called *statistical inference*.)

Statistics are critically important in private and public decision making! For example, government derived statistics are relied on in formulating government macroeconomic policies, foreign trade policy, and monies earmarked for social programs.

Ninety-nine point nine percent (99.9%) of government published data are statistics based on scientific samples. These include the unemployment rate, the inflation rate and even GDP data.

Beware: Despite their scientific methodology, statistical techniques are not infallible and statistical studies are subject to error. Policies based on faulty statistics can damage part or all of the economy ... and hurt national security!

1. FALLACIOUS ECONOMICUS: Want to avoid mistakes associated with sampling? Then, examine every item in the statistical "population." This will eliminate the possibility of error. In short, do a complete census and you cannot go wrong.

Fallacious Reasoning: Ideally, a complete census of the entire population is taken and values are recorded, processed and reported without error or bias. An accurate picture of the population is the result.

Correct Reasoning: In reality, these ideals are nearly impossible to live up to, especially when dealing with a human population and human processors of data! Yes, a complete census of a population sidesteps problems related to sampling. Nevertheless, the census rarely is without error. Mistakes are likely in collecting, recording, transcribing and tabulating data. Moreover, a complete census rarely captures all elements of the population. Missing observations compound the other errors.

2. FALLACIOUS ECONOMICUS: Again, why rely on a sample to learn about a whole population? Why not simply examine all the units in the population?

Correct Reasoning: Samples are a short cut taken when examining the total population is impractical, too costly, too destructive, too time consuming, or, at the extreme, impossible!

Example: Quality control in the factory. Periodically, part of a production run must be tested to determine if the units produced are living up to pre-determined standards. Here is a case where it might be possible to examine the entire population. However, each unit would be destroyed in the testing process. Suppose light bulbs have to be tested for hours of operation. If every bulb off the assembly line is tested till it burned out, then every unit would be destroyed and not available for sale. What if the baker took a bite of every donut?

In short, sampling is used when 1) the target population is accessible, but examining sample elements is too destructive or too expensive 2) the total population is beyond the grasp of the researcher.

Two Points

1. Believe it or not, a sample study that has been well designed, executed and processed may yield a more accurate picture of a population than a sloppily conducted complete census! Sampling methods are considered below.

2. Nonsampling (after-sampling) errors: processing errors may appear *after* the sample elements have been selected. The errors that may occur in measurement, recording, tabulating and transcribing the sampled elements are

called **non-sampling errors.** A response may be misunderstood. Some responses may be lost. A column of numbers may be added incorrectly. These mistakes are not related to the method of sampling. Changing the method of sampling has no impact on the potential for non-sampling error.

Sampling frame (or frame). The **sampling frame** is the collection of population elements from which sample elements are *actually selected.* Ideally, the **sampling frame** is identical to the **target population**, the one under study. However, in reality it may differ and be a source of error. Conceptually, the **target population** is the *total* of elements under study, for example, all residents of the U.S. Frequently, the sampling frame differs from the target population. For example, "people who have registered to vote" is a smaller group than "all residents." Even the U.S. Census misses folks. See the example below:

Example: A professor seeks to compute the average age of students in her class. This is the equivalent of a complete census of her class. The "sample" is the entire target population. What could possibly go wrong if the plan calls for all elements of a population to be included in a "sample"? Read all about it:

1. Possible sampling error: the *sampling frame* is smaller than population.

> a) Some students are outside the room or absent when the teacher conducts her "census." Other students, not registered in the class, may be visiting their friends. Thus, the sampling frame – those available to be sampled, those in the room – differs from the target population. This magnifies the probability of error by chance.

2. Possible nonsampling error: result from processing the sample responses.

> b) Some students in the room may give an incorrect response, deliberately or by accident.
>
> c) Responses may be recorded incorrectly, e.g., a 4 year old as entered as an 8 year old.
>
> d) Some responses may be mistakenly entered twice or not entered.
>
> e) A mistake could be made in processing, i.e., tabulating and manipulating the recorded observations.

Beware: Researchers might wrongly assert their conclusions apply to the target population. Technically, the conclusions are valid only for the sampling frame.

Problems Using Samples

1. Sampling errors occur during sampling process.

Sampling error I: Chance or "luck of the draw." Even without non-sampling error, a sample selected in the most studious and diligent manner *may be unrepresentative ... due to chance.* **Chance** is the catch phrase for all the unnamable, unknowable and numerous micro events that determine the outcome of an event such as a coin toss. Even the highly touted random sampling approach is subject to **error due to chance.** Oddball or **outlier observations** may be over represented in the sample and distort an average or some other measure.

Sampling error II: Bias (or Favoritism). Sampling bias is a design flaw in the sampling plan that deliberately favors some elements of the population over others. Bias may be intentional or unintentional. With **bias,** some members of the target population are favored over others for the sample. Taller students may be overrepresented in the class sample to measure average height. Presumably, **random sampling** eliminates possible errors due to bias. Every member of frame has same chance of being picked for sample. Bias reduces the possibility of drawing a representative sample.

Question: Why would a researcher deliberately bias the selection of sample elements?

2. Nonsampling errors occur *after* sample is selected

The measurement, recording, tabulating and transcribing errors that may occur constitute **nonsampling error.** These are errors that are not related to the method of sampling or census taking. These errors occur during the processing phase, *after* the sample units have been selected.

Major Warning

Studies on global warming use sampled data subject to sampling and non-sampling error. The consistency, comparability, longevity and reliability of such studies is questionable. These sampled temperatures are subject to sampling and nonsampling error. Many scientists believe more research must be conducted before U.S. sovereignty is surrendered to international committees of bureaucrats and functionaries. **The jury is still out on climate change.**

[Statistical error = sampling plus nonsampling error.] It causes the sample result to go "off track," i.e., to differ from the unknown true population value sought in the study.
(See Diagram #1 below).

Diagram #1: The Types of Statistical Error

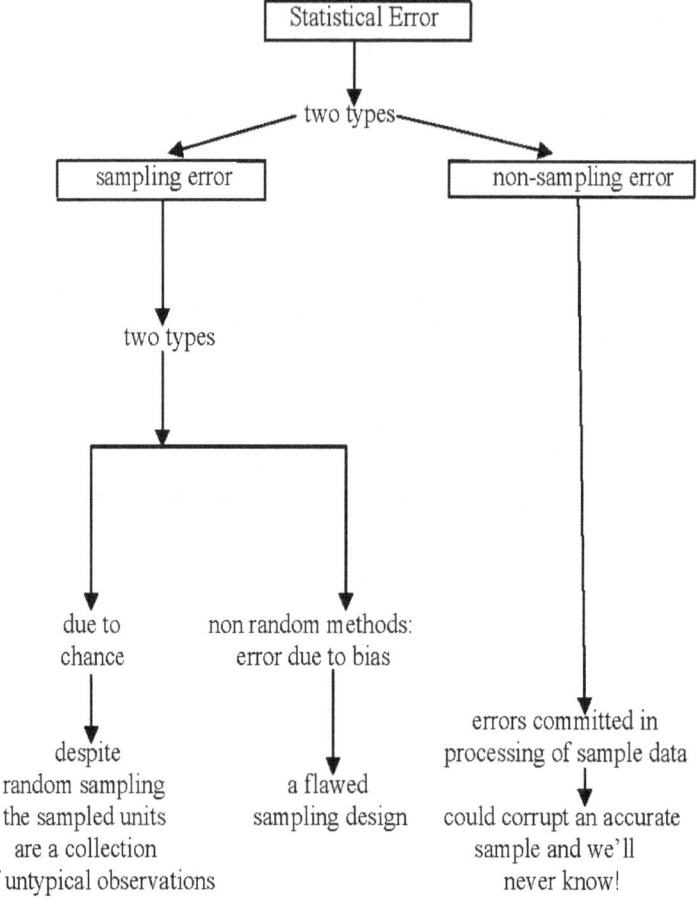

Modern statistical techniques are not infallible. Statistical error can creep into any study. It seems problems crop up everywhere! The statistician has to ward off potential errors from chance, bias and sloppy processing. Quite a job! (The reader is advised to enroll in a college level applied statistics course).

The One Study Fallacy

3. FALLACIOUS ECONOMICUS: I saw on the news a study had been done, proving A and disproving B. Funny thing is, yesterday they reported on a study that said just the opposite! Which do I believe?

Correct Reasoning: By sheer luck and some cunning, one study may, in fact, reveal a truth. It may hit the mother lode ... but how would we know? To what do we compare the study results to validate them? If we knew the truth before the study, it is likely we would not be conducting the study! This is especially true in pioneering studies where previous, comparable research is scant or nonexistent. The problem is **we cannot trust one study to establish fact or reveal a truth.** Once again, one well-fashioned and conducted study may, unknown to the researcher, reveal a truth. But, short of repeated, successful replication, we cannot proclaim it as such. (See Diagram #1 on previous page for possible errors).

Remember, all studies are at risk for sampling and nonsampling error. Read all about it: sometimes honest and diligent researchers unknowingly work with unrepresentative samples, replicate bad studies or corrupt them in processing. Biased researchers will corrupt or make up sample data! Even legitimate samples can be mishandled.

The Failure of One

➤ *One word* from a sentence cannot give you the full meaning.

➤ *One page* from a novel cannot tell you the whole story.

➤ *One piece* from a jigsaw puzzle cannot give you the total picture.

➤ *One note* cannot convey the beauty of the whole song.

Similarly, one economic number or study *cannot be relied on* to provide an accurate view of a stock, a firm, a market or a whole economy.

To gain credibility for the findings, the study must be replicated (duplicated) with the same results. A serious study must include an explanation of its methodology to enable replication or duplication.

> Replication is a term referring to the repetition of a research study, generally with different situations and different subjects, to determine if the basic findings of the original study can be generalized to other participants and circumstances.

> [1. Kendra Cherry, "What is Replication?" 9 September 2014 *About Education* <http://tinyurl.com/phu2hrj>]

BEWARE: Significant risk is involved if a life decision or a government policy is based on the results of *one* unverified study.

Enhancing Credibility

One study does not make a fact, but the breadth and depth of a study can impact a study's general credibility. In general,

> ➤ *Lengthen* the time period and the *enlarge* the sample size to, enhance the credibility of the result.
> ➤ Use control groups, where appropriate.

But, beware: long run, widespread error. For thousands of years (many periods) millions of people (the greater the sample size) observed the night skies and would swear the Earth was the center of the universe. No doubt this would be considered a study with many subjects and much longevity! But, given today's perspective, the conclusion deserves no credibility. Traveling further down *the wrong road* does not increase the chances of arriving at the correct destination. **Do not hesitate to change "roads" when going in the wrong direction.** Remember, sunk costs – even research costs – are irrelevant!

Beware, also: Misspecification error or **an explanatory variable *behind* the explanatory variable.** Very often one variable serves as a deliberate or accidental stand in (proxy) for another more influential variable omitted from the study. For example, for many years stagnant water was considered the prime explanatory variable attributed as the cause of malaria. Then, a variable associated with that variable (the stagnant water) was uncovered, mosquitoes. Then, looking deeper into the issue, researchers found another variable masked by the mosquito: a parasite carried by the mosquito.

Beware, also: Compound variables that mask more subtle connections. For example, consider the variable *consumer spending* as an explanatory variable. Instead, one may disaggregate it and use consumer *durable* goods spending as one explanatory variable and consumer *nondurable* goods spending as another explanatory variable. So, be careful in selecting the correct version of each variable for your study! (See also Chap. 32 for more on the *one study fallacy*.)

[2. Kyle Hill, "What is a Good Study?: Guidelines for Evaluating Scientific Studies" 15 September 2015 *Science Based Life* < http://tinyurl.com/otwwagq />]

Beware: A special approach is useful in planning studies of interventions on humans. For example, in medical effectiveness studies researchers set up control group(s) to help refine conclusions drawn from the study.

4. FALLACIOUS ECONOMICUS: Our most carefully selected sample *guarantees* the sample statistic, an average, is representative of the average in the population.

Correct Reasoning: No! To what value would we compare our pinpoint (single value) sample value to judge its veracity? We might have a general idea or expectation. An old population study, a production target or pilot sample result might be referenced. But, still we do not know the "jewel in the crown," the true population value, say, the average of all population values (the arithmetic mean, to be precise). Ignorance of the population is why we conducted the study.

Interval estimate. The chances of our *pinpoint* estimate "hitting the nail on the head," i.e., being exactly correct, are astronomical. Our procedure is adjusted.
1) To enhance the probability of an accurate sample, the pinpoint value is extended into an **interval.** An interval is, say, 44 through 50, inclusive. The center value, the pinpoint sample mean, is 47. **The estimated value is expressed as 47 (plus and minus) 3 or the interval {44<47>50} inclusive.** The true and still unknown population value is deemed to lie somewhere inside the interval. The width of the interval is called the **margin of error**, implying **precision.**
2) Moreover, a pre-determined likelihood or probability, say, 95%, of landing in the interval is set by the width of the interval. **For a given sample size, accuracy and precision are inversely related.** Widening the interval to increase accuracy reduces precision. In general, the less precise the estimate, the muddier it is and the less useful it becomes. TANSTAAFL!

5. FALLACIOUS ECONOMICUS: Random sampling is the only reliable and practical sampling method to secure a representative sample.

Correct Reasoning: Be aware, there is no "sure thing" sampling approach. Reliable it may be, sometimes random sampling may not be practical or even desirable to employ. **Random sampling is not error proof. Random sampling is subject to error by chance.** Consider these alternative methods of sampling, all subject to sampling bias: convenience, judgment and self-selective. Despite the risk of sampling bias, one of those *nonrandom* methods may be preferred in certain situations. Consider the following situation:

Pierre arrives from France and is eager to develop a personality profile of Americans. He goes to a party at the French embassy, with many Americans in attendance. His statistical population is all the folks at the party. He cannot meet all of them, so he must, in effect, select a sample, a subset, from the group. Here are some methods for compiling a *nonrandom* sample.

1) Pierre, at the bar, speaks only to people around him ... this is a *convenience* sample made up of the most easily accessible members of the population.

2) People come up and introduce themselves to Pierre ... this is a *self-selective* sample, a group of volunteers.

3) Pierre seeks out only tall blonde ladies under thirty ... this is a *judgment* sample, based on the personal preference of the researcher.

All of the above samples are at risk for sampling error due to bias. In each approach only certain types are selected and others are excluded. Remember, the sample will not be representative if these biases manifest themselves.

Alternatively, consider this approach: Pierre blindly picks twenty names from a box containing all the party invitations. Each attendee has the same chance of being selected on each pick. This comes closest to being a random sample, thereby eliminating the risk of sampling error due to bias (liking only tall blondes or being at the bar). But, there is still a risk of sampling error due to chance or sheer bad luck. Of course, nonsampling error is always present.

And Now, The News of the Day

"Scientists report the world will end tonight at 8pm. Details on the 11 o'clock report!" The stories on the evening news are a news editor's *judgment sample* selected from all of what is happening in the world. Special emphasis is on what changed, what *diverged* from the norm (say, folks swimming at a New York beach in January.) The persistent, on-going norm (say, the gradual decline in the standard of living or the erosion of American sovereignty through trade deals) is typically ignored.

---

6. FALLACIOUS ECONOMICUS: Thank God for random sampling! Then, for sure the sample will be representative of the population.

Correct Reasoning: here we go again. Sorry, there is no "sure thing" method of extracting a representative sample. Even random sampling methods do not *guarantee* a sample will be representative of the population. Random sampling eliminates *sampling errors* due to bias but cannot eliminate the risk of sampling errors due to chance (bad luck) and, afterward, nonsampling errors. Oddball or outlier observations could be included in the sample and distort an average or some other measure. Therefore, samples selected by random methods are free if bias but still do not *guarantee* to be representative of the population.

Beware: In some circumstances random sampling can be time consuming, expensive and technical overkill. Other methods (convenience, judgment and self-selective) may be used when: the researcher is close to the process, the population is relatively small and scientific inferences are not going to be made. **However, despite their shortcomings, sophisticated statistical *inferences* are based only on studies using random methods.**

7. FALLACIOUS ECONOMICUS: If data from sampling can be subject to so many errors, then why use the technique at all?

Correct Reasoning: Frequently, the whole population cannot be surveyed. But, here are a few tips for improving sampling reliability or accuracy:

> ➢ enlarge the sample size

> ➢ improve the sample design to be more representative, e.g., the sampling frame may be stratified (subdivided) and each strata sampled.

> ➢ In some situations, more frequent or repetitive sampling can be employed. Average the sample results.

> ➢ improve the processing of sample results.

But, all these improvement come at a cost! TANSTAAFL! Make sure the improved results justify the added costs!

The Expert Fallacy

8. FALLACIOUS ECONOMICUS: Well, an expert said *this* or testified to *that*. Then this or that must be true.

Correct Reasoning: Be aware, experts are like guns for hire in the old west. Experts such as Nobel Prize winners often will testify on opposite sides of court cases and issues before Congress!

They can manipulate and slant data any way their "bosses" prefer and claim legitimacy. Remember, they are the experts and know how to do those things. Unfortunately, these charlatans taint the studies from honest and competent sources. **Figures don't lie, but liars can tamper with the figures.**

An Application: The Political Poll

9. FALLACIOUS ECONOMICUS: I heard a poll stating 65% of the voting public favored repealing the Affordable Care Act. So, let's do it.

Correct reasoning: One poll is equivalent to one study in the laboratory. It is to be approached with skepticism as to its validity. [See the One Study Fallacy earlier in this chapter.]

In political polling or product preference assessment, questioners are often interested in the *percentage (or proportion)* of respondents favoring a political candidate, political position or product. Sometimes respondents are selected in such a way that the results can be considered a sample suitable for statistical inferences about the entire population. (Note that informal straw polls or surveys based on convenience or judgment samples cannot be properly, scientifically applied to a whole population.)

Suppose a survey is taken in a manner suitable for further statistical analysis, i.e., statistical inference or drawing a conclusion about the target population.

The question might be: Do you favor Mickey Mouse or Daffy Duck as the next President of the United States? The results are reported in this manner:

Sample results: "Based on the scientific sample study of Presidential preference, we estimate 70% of the people prefer Daffy Duck. There is a level of confidence of 95%, with a margin of error of plus or minus 3%."

What does that statement mean in ordinary language? It means this:

Interval estimation and margin of error. The true population figure lies somewhere between 70% plus 3% ... and ... 70% minus 3%. That is, the study is asserting the unknown true population figure lies somewhere within the interval range of {67%<70%>73%}. **In reality, the study produces an INTERVAL ESTIMATE, a range estimate, not a pinpoint estimate.** So, the true population proportion could be any of these figures: 67% or 68% or 69% or 70% or 71% or 72% or 73%. Seventy percent "anchors" the interval. All of the figures are equally possible as the true but still unknown population value! The researcher is, in a sense, "hedging his bets" by not picking a single value.

This *interval estimate* is particularly important in close races where intervals might overlap and no clear preference emerges. For example, suppose Daffy Duck gets 49% preference and Mickey Mouse gets 51%, *each* with a 3% plus or minus margin of error. Then, their intervals overlap and no clear preference emerges. Hold on, it gets worse!

Level of confidence (LOC), the chances of success. Not only is the researcher unwilling to pick a single percentage, she issues a warning about the entire study, namely, that it was conducted with a "degree of confidence of 95%." What does that little piece of statistical jargon mean?

Suppose this study were repeated many hundreds, thousands of times, each time with a different scientifically selected, random sample. And each time an interval estimate would be calculated! We would have thousands of interval estimates. **The 95% confidence qualification tells us that 95% of such intervals would encompass the true (but still unknown) population proportion.** Five percent of such intervals would not enclose the true value. Of course, we are only going to make *one* interval estimate. The one study actually conducted is interpreted to come from one of thousands of studies which could have been conducted. So, did we get lucky? Did we pull one "out of the hat," and get one of the correct intervals? We may act on the assumption we have captured a true population value. But, in truth, who knows?

Point of view *before* constructing interval estimate: the LOC. All we can say *beforehand* is the *proposed* interval estimate has a 95% chance of being correct. There is a small chance (5%) that the interval we will construct will not contain the true population value! The process is similar to assigning a probability to which team wins the championship.

Point of view after constructing interval estimate: right or wrong

Probabilities are assigned to outcomes of *future* events. There are no probabilities associated with *past* events. Before a toss, the coin has a 50% chance of turning up head or tail. A tossed coin either winds up a head or a tail, period. The event already occurred. Similarly, before the estimation we had a 95% chance of constructing an accurate interval estimate. **Once constructed, the interval estimate is a past event,** a done deal, just like the tossed coin. The interval estimate is either correct or it isn't. It either contains the true population value or does not.

[3. Another way of expressing the result is that it is *statistically significant* at the 5% level. That is, there is a 5% chance (1.0 minus LOC) of our estimate being incorrect and *not* capturing the true population proportion. In other words, there is a 5% chance the true population proportion lies outside the interval estimated from the study. - Editor's note]

Random Sampling Not Welcome Here

Random sampling is not welcome in the creative arts. Would a composer, poet, or painter choose creative elements at random? It is not likely, not in traditional art and music. A composer uses artistic, personal judgment in the selection of musical elements to write a song. The composition is *not* a random sample mechanically selected from a universe of tones, tempos, rhythms and styles.

The musical composition is a judgment sample drawn from all the elements in the musical universe the writer has command of. "*What* note goes best *where*?" pondered Gershwin, Beethoven and Puccini. They drew on an innate musical aesthetic, not a random number table. Similarly, the poet does not use words chosen at random. The painter uses personal judgment, not randomness, to select colors from her palette.

Art and music lovers thank the Gods that randomness
is *persona non grata* in the search for artistic beauty!

---

10. FALLA<IOUS E<ONOMI<US: Why not expand the interval estimate, i.e., cast a "bigger net," so we are sure to capture the true value, that is, we are sure to improve the *accuracy* of our estimate. Why not widen it so much we cannot miss capturing the true value, 100% accuracy?

Correct Reasoning: Accuracy is an important feature of the estimate. **Accuracy** relates to the probability an estimate will be correct or fall within the interval calculated. And, yes, widening the interval improves accuracy, the chance of capturing the true population value. But, how useful does the figure become as it becomes less precise, taking on more and more values in a wider interval? Improved **accuracy** is not free ... it comes at a cost in **precision**, the narrowness of the estimate. Consider the usefulness of the following interval estimates:

1) Tomorrow's *high* temperature will lie between 40 and 90 degrees.

2) Take this diet formula, then lose between 5 and 50 pounds next year.

3) This investment will yield a return between 2% and 22%.

Are these "accurate" predictions so wide as to be useless?

Beware: Given the sample size, <u>accuracy</u> and <u>precision</u> are inversely related.

Enter precision: This raises the question of **precision**, the narrowness or tightness of the interval. Precision may be thought of as the difference between the highest and lowest estimates in the interval.

➤ As that difference *shrinks,* the estimate becomes *more* precise.

➤ As that difference *expands*, the estimate becomes *less* precise.

Increased precision aids the usefulness of an estimate. But, increased precision comes at a cost, a lower chance of accuracy.

An Average Family

Arithmetic mean. The average is a common calculation in descriptive statistics. An average is one number that aspires to represent *central tendency* or *cluster* within a group of numbers. An **average** family resides in every statistics book. The family has more members than most people realize. Most folks think of an average this way:

{average = (sum of a group of numbers) divided by (the number of numbers)}

They calculate it this way: if the numbers are arrayed as 5, 5, 10, 15, and 65, then {5+5+10+15+ 65} = {100 ÷ 5} = 20, the average. Calculated this way, the average is, technically speaking, **the arithmetic mean, the head of the family. It is the head of the family and its workhorse.** But, it gives a distorted view when pulled by outliers – that 100 – the far out, most untypical observations. How representative of the data is 20? Most of the data lie below it.

Median. To avoid this shortcoming of outlier distortion, other measures of centrality are used. One such measure is "kid brother" **median, close rival for head of family status.** The median is the halfway point in a lowest to highest ordering of numbers, called an **array.** The median of the array cited above is 10, with two numbers above and two numbers below it. It is also known as the 50th percentile.

The median is a useful **measure of centrality** when **outliers** distort the mean as a typical value. The median is a common measure used for income and wages.

Mode. The "cousin" **mode** is the most frequent value. In this array the mode is 5.

Weighted average. A weighted average is sometimes required to get a clearer idea of the data. In such an average, temperatures in the more populous states of New York, Florida and California would carry more weight than temperatures in Montana, North Dakota and Nebraska. The **national *weighted* mean**, using population as weight, would be more descriptive of the "people impact" of any climate change than a national *unweighted* arithmetic mean where each state's temperature counts equally.

Chapter Thirty-Three
Junk Science or Legitimate Study?

There are lies, damn lies, and then there are statistics. – Mark Twain

Facts do not "speak for themselves." They speak for or against competing theories.
Facts divorced from theory or visions are mere isolated curiosities. – Thomas Sowell

Through the centuries curious minds learned from personal experience, careful observation, pure cogitation, without experimentation. But, casual observation, common sense and pure cogitation are subject to error, as indicated in Chapter One. Formal, scientific studies, **also subject to error**, go beyond common sense and casual observation, thereby inspiring more confidence. But, there are potholes on the scientific "road" to truth, as well.

FALLACIOUS ECONOMICUS: Formal, scientific studies are guaranteed to be free of error.

Correct Reasoning: Formal studies are still subject to error, i.e., there is no guarantee of accuracy despite meticulous and proper execution. (In certain types of studies statisticians can pre-specify the likelihood of getting an accurate outcome once the study is executed.)

Remember and beware: There are too many ways error could creep into a study to trust one study to be the Holy Grail of investigations.

So, hope an independent researcher will do the study over, then observe the result. Due to the uncontrollable nature of many variables under study, repeated or replicated follow-up formal studies can give varying results, i.e., they may confirm or conflict with the original study.

Whether follow-up results match or not, further studies may still need to be done. The number of studies depends, to an extent, on the degree of reliability one seeks. When human life and health are at risk, independent researchers and multiple studies are required. Will the plane fly or not? Will the foundation hold up the building or not? Will the medicine work or not? For example, the U.S. Food and Drug Administration (FDA) will not allow the sale of a new drug unless it has been proven safe AND effective by years of studies. Note that nearly all preliminary and advanced drug testing is done on groups of sick *volunteers*, not patients selected at random from the wide range of afflicted. [1. See FDA protocols at <http://tinyurl.com/povf8v3>]

Recall the one study fallacy discussed in the previous chapter. Multiple studies can provide clarification. Or, they may add to the confusion.

What is going on here, when so-called reliable studies by credentialed researchers have contradictory outcomes? Perhaps one must appreciate the *potential for error – deliberate or innocent – in the design and execution of a study.* Consider the complex nature of a formal, study as outlined below.

[*Galileo showed the Doge of Venice how to use the telescope.* Fresco by Bertini]

Here is a general procedure for the conduct of a study.

1. Identify the purpose of the study. For example, this is an investigation into what determined consumer behavior in early 2000s.

2. Define objectives for study outcomes. For example, how did consumers behave the year *after* 9/11 compared to the year before? If you have an expectation, state it as a hypothesis.

3. In **social science** (economics, sociology, psychology, anthropology, et.al.) in most instances researchers *observe* and record an outcome and seek its causes or associations. The researcher may refer to earlier studies for clues and direction. In **physical sciences** and medical testing, very often one starts with the suspected causative and associative factors, conducts an experiment and *observes* and records the outcome. (Non-sampling Statistical Error may occur when observing, recording and tabulating results).

The many variables study. Some phenomena or behaviors have complex explanations, beyond the power of one explanatory factor. Consumer behavior is such an area. For example, economists may question why consumer spending dropped last year. The *outcome* is the drop in consumer spending. It is referred to as the **explained or dependent variable.** The researcher then hypothesizes, i.e., makes an educated guess, or looks at past studies, as to the causative and associative *factors* that go with that outcome. The researcher may select these explanatory factors: higher unemployment, depressed home values and a falling stock market. These factors are referred to as **explanatory variables or independent variables.** The study is called a **multi-variate** study.

The numbers are crunched with a statistical program and a result is obtained. See Junk Study tricks below!

Types of Data

1. Time series. Some data, such as employment, is available monthly, a data point for each month in each year. These points constitute **a time series data set**. Median income per month for consecutive 48 months constitutes a set of time series data. The study over multiple time periods is called a time-series study. The object of the study is to determine the *relative* importance of the each stand-alone explanatory variable (e.g. government spending) to the behavior of the *explained* variable, employment. Also sought is the explanatory power of the independent variables *as a group.*

2. Cross sectional. Alternatively, a cross sectional study looks at different data sources *at the same time* reference. For example, median income from county to county for the *same* month of the year would constitute a set of cross sectional data. (Seasonal adjustment is not needed.)

Be Skeptical of Anecdotal Evidence

> #### Did You Hear About Uncle Fred ... ?
>
> Anecdotal (accidental) evidence is sometimes offered in place of scientific evidence or study. Sheer luck has anecdotal evidence, without scientific backup, revealing a truth. But, how would we know it is a truth? In general, be skeptical of conclusions drawn from *anecdotal evidence,* i.e., isolated personal observations, incidents or unique experiences. Chapter One warned of "truths" based on common sense. The fact that Uncle Fred smoked cigars until he passed away at age 92 is not concrete proof that cigar smoking is harmless. It could be an oddball, *atypical* observation. Without cigars, he may have lived ten more years! In short, **anecdotal evidence lacks the rigor of a scientific study** employing wider sampling procedures, double blind control groups, and replicability. In spite of its faults, anecdotal evidence may have this redeeming quality: it may inspire a genuine scientific study!

Beware: sophisticated software actually crunches the numbers, i.e., conducts the study. Remember, errors are possible at each step in conducting a study. Varying the treatment of the data will likely alter the outcome and conclusions drawn from the study. Independent researchers using the same data but different research methods may reach different conclusions.

Every study, even carefully crafted follow-ups, is at risk for error.

Junk (or Vodoo) Science

Legitimate science is not perfect and can be in error. Presumably, error is not deliberately built into a legitimate process. But, *junk science* is *imitation science* with built-in faults and biases designed to slant the outcome. It is usually perpetrated or financially underwritten by someone with an ax to grind, some special interest to promote. It could be a pharmaceutical company seeking approval for a new drug, a politician seeking votes on an environmental issue or a research professor seeking promotion or approval.

> Wrong science becomes junk science only when it's obvious or easily-determined flaws are ignored and it is then used to advance some special interest.
>
> [2. Steven Milloy, "What is junk science?" 24 April, 2015, *JunkScience.Com.* <http://tinyurl.com/okudcrb/>]

Remember, experts can be like "guns for hire" in the Old West. They could slant the study design to find the conclusion you pay them to find, even when it violates the true outcome. **Here are only a few junk science tricks:**

Design the study to produce a pre-determined outcome!

➢ Biased researchers may "cherry pick" sample elements to study.

➢ Biased researchers may "cherry pick" prior studies to replicate.

➢ Researchers may ask survey questions in a manner designed to elicit a biased response. Remember, "When did you stop beating your wife?"

➢ Researchers have been known to fake – create – their own data.

➢ Researchers may design and execute a study in a manner rendering it impossible to **replicate.**

➢ Bias the design of a study so its outcome will *confirm* earlier studies. For example, follow-up climate change studies may be designed to show ... climate change!

➢ Omit the use of control groups where they are, in fact, required.

➢ Failure to submit studies to reputable, refereed academic journals.

The straw poll. An *unscientific*, informal *sample* survey of opinion. A naïve straw poll is quick and inexpensive, based on a relatively small judgment sample.

A tracking poll. May be more scientific than the straw poll. The tracking poll follows and surveys the same group of people each time an opinion is sought.

Question: How can a researcher create bias in a straw poll?

Answer: Over sample the favored cohort; **under sample** the unfavored cohort.

Remember: One Study Does Not Establish a Fact or Reveal a Truth. Basing a decision or policy on *one* study is a perilous undertaking.

There are two kinds of statistics, the kind you look up and the kind you make up. - Rex Stout

Temporary resolution: If one is unsure and the outcome of a study was intended to lead to some action, there is another path: **reserve judgment.** It is not an acceptance nor is it a rejection. It is a middle, neutral path, a no decision, no judgment until more information becomes available.

Publish or Perish: Move Forward or Stagnate?

The practice of publish or perish can lead to the homogeneity of research outcomes as junior faculty "copycat" senior faculty. Junior faculty in many Universities across the country feel the pressure to publish. If not, they lose their university appointments, fail to gain tenure, or are rejected for promotion. This is the so-called **publish or perish policy.** Moreover, less well-known is the pressure to publish articles *in agreement with* or *reinforcing* the research from senior department members who sit on promotion and tenure committees. Articles departing from the prevailing departmental positions will be viewed with disdain or even malice. *This encourages homogeneity of academic opinion within departments.*

Replicability can help. Indeed, studies seeking respectability ought to enable replicability. A study which cannot be replicated becomes suspicious and "leaks" credibility. Inability to replicate can expose junk science, as earlier results cannot be verified. Alternatively, similar results by similar methods give credibility to earlier studies.

> To a scientist, replication is like breathing. Successful replications strengthen findings. Failed replications root out false claims and help refine imprecise ones. Testing and re-testing make science what it is.
> [3. Jay Van Bavel, "Why Do So Many Studies Fail to Replicate?"
> 27 May 2016 *New York Times Sunday Review* ‹http://tinyurl.com/hrw4dnf›]

The Placebo Effect

The greatest cure-all of all time! Mind curing body? Could it be? Yes, the placebo! No prescription or insurance required! The **placebo effect** occurs when an improvement is based on one's **strong personal belief** that an intervention, e.g., medicine, is actually working. It could occur with false or real intervention.

A placebo effect may be ferreted out by the judicious use of control groups.

Replicability: Second Thoughts

Replicability is not the ultimate standard of good design for a study. Control groups may be required. Studies involving **interventions** (for example: drugs, counseling, therapy, or advertising) are complex. Control of extraneous explanatory variables (excluded, but perhaps impacting variables) is critical. One method of control is to neutralize their impact by random sampling. Hopefully, random selection will result in **equal allocation** of the extraneous factors to the treatment group and a control group.

When Replicability Fails: Who is in Control Here?

Let us assume a treatment (massage, medicine, physical therapy, etc.) is administered to a group of patients and, after a time, an improvement is observed. **Beware:** do not jump to the conclusion that the treatment created the improvement. In fact, we can assign the improvement to a) the treatment, b) a placebo effect, or c) other unobserved forces at work during the same time frame. Conceptually, there could have been improvement *without* the treatment. The problem could have resolved itself with the help of unobserved forces. How can we know?

Replicability does not necessarily answer the question of what caused the improvement. Suppose **the study could be replicated with the same result.** That would not unravel the mystery of discovering the cause of the improvement. Successful replicability confirms associations. **There remains the same nagging question as to cause:** a, b or c?

Get control of the study! We can try answering the question by designing the study to involve one or more **control groups** who do *not* get the real treatment.

Randomized, controlled studies are used in many fields, especially in drug testing, marketing and product design. Researchers consider this to be the most objective and scientific approach. There are numerous configurations of controlled studies. The simplest version, employing one control group, works like this:

1. Subjects are assigned at random, "blindly," either to a test group or a control group. Hopefully, extraneous forces are present with equal strength in both groups, in effect cancelling out each other and having no impact.

2. A new treatment or intervention is applied to the **treatment group** and a **placebo** (an inactive substitute or the standard treatment) to the **control group**. Each group was constituted by random selection. Neither the subjects nor the administers know *who* is getting *what.* That is, those applying the treatment do not know if they are applying the real treatment or the placebo. Those receiving the treatment are similarly "in the dark" as to the nature of the treatment they are receiving. This is called a **"double-blind" study** and is common in drug testing.

3. If the treatment group improves but the **placebo group** does not, one is tempted to attribute the improvement to the drug.

4. **What if both the treatment and the control groups show improvement? Some approaches:** Additional control groups could be set up to refine the study.

Chapter Thirty-Four
Correlation and Causation

STATISTICAL techniques are used in an attempt to sort out the complexities of association, co-variation and causation when working with two or more variables. Numerous statistical approaches are available to investigate this issue, ranging from simple line graphs to complex mathematical equations.

1. FALLA<IOUS <<ONOMI<US: When *A* and *B* occur together, one of the pair must be a *cause* and the other an *effect.*

Correct Reasoning: This is another tricky one if you are not careful. When two or more events occur at the same time statisticians call this **correlation** or **co-variation.** But, they are quick to point out the possible reasons for correlation, only one of which is causation.

> One of the most common errors we find in the press is the confusion between *correlation* and *causation* in scientific and health-related studies. In theory, these are easy to distinguish — an action or occurrence can *cause* another (such as smoking causes lung cancer), or it can *correlate* with another (such as smoking is correlated with alcoholism). If one action causes another, then they are most certainly correlated. *But just because two things occur together does not mean that one caused the other, even if it seems to make sense.*

[1. "Causation vs. Correlation," 25 October 2014 *George Mason University* < http://tinyurl.com/preqg3q>]

Follow these guidelines before attributing causation:

1. A causative link, an explanation, a "connection of the dots," must be offered in order to attribute causation to correlation. Which is cause and which is effect? Perhaps they both issued from the same cause! Or, are they unrelated? The step-by-step mechanism by which *A* causes *B* must be spelled out. Beware these traps:

> ➤ **Simultaneous events.** Two events occurring *simultaneously* are not enough to attribute causation. There are too many accidental and nonsense correlations in the universe. This is the classic **cum hoc, ergo propter hoc** ("with this, therefore because of this") fallacy. Sales of beds and hiking equipment both declined last year. Cause and effect is doubtful!

> **Sequential events.** One event *following* another is not enough to attribute causation. This is the classic **post hoc ergo propter hoc** (Latin: "after this, therefore because of this") fallacy. Consider:
> a) The rooster crowed *(A)* and the sun came up *(B)*. Cause and effect? There is correlation but no causation from *A* to *B*.
> b) Taking medicine and feeling better. The improvement may be due to medicine, other operative factors or the placebo effect.
> **Causation may *not* be inferred in the *absence* of correlation.** Correlation is a prerequisite for causation – but does not guarantee it. To attribute causation, a **causative mechanism** must be revealed by explaining how A causes B, the underlying connection.

Types of Co-Variation: Positive Correlation vs. Negative Correlation

Direct variation (positive correlation): when variables change in the **same** direction, examples:

> Miles driven and gasoline used.

> Excess money growth and inflation.

> The amount of risk and the *potential* for return on an investment.

Inverse variation (negative correlation): when variables change in the **opposite** direction. Examples:

> Bond prices and market interest rates

> Accuracy and precision in statistical estimation.

> **Nationalism and Globalism are inversely related policies.**

Third party effect. You find that *A* and *B* are highly correlated. But, an investigation for causation reveals no causation exists between *A* and *B*. Instead, they are both are caused by a third agent, *C*. So, both *A* (umbrella sales) and *B* (rain boot sales) are caused by *C* (rainfall).

Multiple causative agents and multiple effects. Consider that multiple factors, say *C, D* and *E*, have multiple effects *H, J* and *M*. The researcher may choose to study only the relationship between *C* and *J* and *M*, deliberately or by mistake ignoring the more complete family relationship among the variables.

Nonsense correlations. There is another possibility: *A* and *B* are associated by sheer coincidence, i.e., by accident, without any causative link. These are nonsense correlations. Avoid mistaking an associative relationship for a causative relationship, where no causative relationship should be inferred:

> The number of accounting majors and the total inches of snow both rose last year. Did the snow inspire careers in accounting?

> ➤ A rise in the number of dentists in Cleveland has been associated with a fall in crime rates. Did criminals suddenly go straight and start pulling teeth?

> ➤ Just as Maria stepped outside her dorm, it started to rain. Did Maria provoke the rain?

2. FALLACIOUS ECONOMICUS: There are statistical techniques that can sort out the correlations that are coincidences from the correlations that involve causation.

Correct Reasoning: Not true. Statistical techniques such as correlation and regression analysis **cannot prove or disprove causation.** At best, they measure the degree of association, or co-variation, if any, between one variable and one or more other variables. Causation is attributed by an examination and analysis of the interconnections, if any, in the underlying process at work. [Want to know more? See coefficient of determination and coefficient of correlation in a statistics book.]

Economic Forecasting : The Deductive Approach

Follow these steps in analyzing *sales forecasting*.   Start with the economy.

1. Where is the *economy* going? Identify current phase of the business cycle, then forecast the next phase change.

2. Where is my *industry* going within the economy? The industry may be pro-cyclical, contra-cyclical or a-cyclical.

3. Where is my *company* going within the industry? Focus on market share, sales and profits.

4. Where are different *product lines* going within the company?

5. Where are different *products* going within the *product lines?*

6. Where are different *products* going within the *product lines within different geographic areas?*

7. How does #6 break down year to year, quarter to quarter, month to month?

Economic Forecasting: Extrapolation

Economic forecasting is an attempt to know ... the unknown *future.* Expert judgment and experience coupled with a firm command of the available data and advanced math are necessary for sophisticated forecasting methods. In their absence, we can use mechanical, easy to learn techniques such as extrapolation. **Extrapolation is one of the most popular forecasting methods.**

3. FALLACIOUS ECONOMICUS: All extrapolations are wrong, as they are but simply extensions of current trends.

Correct Reasoning: There is an element of truth in this fallacy. True, an extrapolation is based on historical data, it is relatively simple to execute and is very popular. Extrapolation is second in popularity only to judgmental forecasting. The simplest form of extrapolation **starts with drawing a straight line** between two data points, say, five years apart.

Extrapolation involves mechanically *extending* the **straight line** forward or backward into unknown "territory." In extrapolation the future is only **an extension of the past.** So, forecast (the future) by *extending* the past trend, the historical record. It is going from the known to the unknown by continuing down the same road. [In diagram #1 at the right, the straight line has been **extended** northeast from (x,y), creating forecasted values of y_1 on vertical axis, given x_1 on the horizontal axis.]

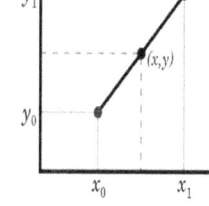

Extending the straight line enables the forecaster to sidestep the advanced, mathematically intimidating forecasting techniques associated with extrapolation. Extrapolation may also be expressed by an exponential function. More sophisticated extrapolation methods include moving averages, exponential smoothing and regression. These are beyond the scope of this discussion.

How Can Extrapolation Go Wrong, Go Wrong?

Assumption of historic continuity. Extrapolation is a risky forecasting technique. The future is only an extension of the past if the *complex of conditions* that existed in the past extends into the future. This is called the assumption of *constancy* or *historic continuity.* But, *this underlying condition becomes more unlikely as the time horizon is extended.* The further the time horizon is extended, the more likely the complex of conditions will change. **Significant changes in conditions are more likely the longer the time horizon. This diminishes extrapolation as a reliable, long term forecasting technique.**

Not all is lost, however. Extrapolation may have some usefulness for near term forecasts, where historical continuity holds. The **further forward (or backward) you extrapolate, the more opportunities there are for a historical continuity to be broken.** The reliability of the extrapolation technique continues to drop as the forecast horizon is extended further into the future.

Improper Extrapolation: Example: Stock A has grown 3% in value the last 5 years. By *extrapolation,* it will continue to grow at that pace for the next five, fifteen or fifty years! Historic continuity will not hold for fifteen or fifty years!

Useful Applications

Given all these pitfalls of extrapolation, it may be useful in some contexts. For example:

1) Many securities traders look for the *momentum* of a stock, expecting it to last for an indeterminate period. A stock with momentum persists in rising or falling for a spell. But, when does that phase end? Extrapolation by building on a *moving average* is one technique. Moving average users are trying to uncover underlying momentum or capture subtle changes in momentum of a stock. **Accurately forecasting the reversal point is the holy grail of stock price forecasting! When will momentum cease and reverse?**

2) Business cycle forecasting relies on the idea that, once underway, an expansion will last for four or five years. The best time to use extrapolation is *early* in the expansion phase.

3) Demographers have used extrapolation to heroically project long run population growth while epidemiologists speculate as to the spread of disease.

But, bear in mind, the longer the forecast horizon, the greater the risk of historic continuity collapsing. Beware of major policy changes today based on extrapolations extending fifty or one hundred years into the future.

"Predicting" the past? Backwards extrapolation. Backwards extrapolation is an attempt to "predict" or reconstruct unknown *past values*, based on recent trend. An *extrapolation path*, curve or equation based on current values is used to project backwards in time to re-create an historical value. For example, based on current values and recent trend, what was the stock of real capital in 1700 or the earth's population in 1000 B.C.? Based on the current rate of disease spread, how many patients were infected in 2000?

The extrapolation may be done **algebraically or by pencil and ruler,** i.e., by the extension of a line into earlier years.

But, beware: Backwards extrapolation suffers from the same weaknesses as forward extrapolation. **The further the forecast extends into the distant future – or, the distant past – the more likely *historic continuity* will not hold and the forecast be inaccurate.**

Independent Events, Games of Chance and Correlation

4. FALLACIOUS ECONOMICUS: I've tossed this quarter 10 times in a row and it turned up heads each time. This makes its more likely the *next* toss will be a tail, or at least there will more tails in the next ten tosses.

Correct Reasoning: As logical as this fallacy sounds, it violates the correct idea that each flip of the (balanced) coin is independent. That is, each flip is an *independent event,* unaffected by all the prior outcomes of all prior flips.

This conclusion derives from the nature of the experiment, i.e., the toss of a  fair, well-balanced coin. On each coin toss there are **two equally likely but mutually exclusive outcomes:** a head or a tail. (Each outcome is determined by *chance,* an innumerable and unquantifiable collection of forces). On each flip the probability (or likelihood) of a tail is ½ or fifty percent. Similarly, the probability (or likelihood) of a head is ½ or fifty percent.

The number of flips does *not* alter these one trial probabilities! No matter if the coin is tossed 100 times or a million times and each time the outcome is a head. The probability of a tail on the next toss *does not increase.* It is still 50%. So, a tail could occur on the next toss – but is no more likely than it was in toss #24 or toss #870.

However, over the very long run, say, hundreds of thousands of tosses, the Law of (Long run) Averages dictates outcomes will tend to even out at 50% heads and 50% tails. But, again, the probability on any *single* toss is unaffected by all prior outcomes!

Examples:

1) Each outcome from the throw of fair dice is **independent** of the outcomes of prior throws. The odds do not change as the number of outcomes and throws increases. Be careful in asserting a certain outcome is "due" because it has not occurred recently.

2) Each outcome on the fair roulette wheel is independent of all prior outcomes. If black has not come up on fifty spins of a roulette wheel, then some gamblers will say black is "due" to come out soon. But, technically, that does not increase the chances of black coming up on the *next* spin. Each spin is the world anew!

Good luck at the casino!

End Thoughts

Adventures of the mind are wonderful and exhilarating and, at times, maddening. The tools for such adventures are at hand today. The internet, search engines and word processing software, ease the embarkation costs of these intellectual journeys. These tools also provide a ticket to never-ending labor, should one not know when to exit the ride. At some point, every author must stop and allow the world to view the "fruit" of his labors, including the lemons!

This work has attempted to introduce a body of information designed to help the reader avoid mistakes in private and public decision-making. **Overcoming scarcity is the central theme of economics**. Moderation in that pursuit - the avoidance of *excess* - has been the theme of this book.

Another concern is America's self-inflicted loss of prominence and continuing relative economic decline. Blame for the decline can be assigned to the adoption of Globalism by the economic policymakers and the elites. Globalism has forced the U.S. to resort to the Trifecta of debt (private, public and national) to stave off a faster, steeper decline.

However, all is not lost. Decline can be halted and reversed if the Globalist mindset and policies are rolled back and abandoned. Sustainable economic development must be based on sound fundamentals, not the **Trifecta of debt** (household debt, national debt and the trade deficit).

American Nationalism must be restored and re-invigorated.

So long and good luck.

One man's truth is another man's fallacy ....

—Theo Dosius

About the Author

For more than thirty years Theodore Muzio dedicated himself to teaching graduate and undergraduate economics, accounting, finance, and business statistics classes at New York City colleges and universities. These include St. John's University, undergraduate and graduate business colleges. He also taught at Pace University, Marymount Manhattan College, Long Island University, Graduate School and LIM (Laboratory Institute for Merchandising).

He has an M.B.A. in Financial Management from Pace University and an M.A. in Economics from the Fordham University Graduate School of Arts and Sciences. While at Fordham, he also pursued the Ph.D. in Economics. Professor Muzio studied education at the Graduate Center of the City University of New York.

Ted has been a member of the American Economic Association and the American Association of University Professors. As a graduate student at Pace University, he was an invited member of Delta Mu Delta, a national honor society for excellence in business studies. As a graduate student at Fordham, he was invited to join Omicron Delta Epsilon, the International Honor Society in Economic studies.

Early in his teaching career at St. John's University, students voted him *Professor of the Year*. In addition, the University awarded him the Outstanding Faculty Achievement Medal.

INDEX